1979

The Fairness Doctrine and the Media

STEVEN J. SIMMONS

The
Fairness Doctrine
and the
Media

University of California Press

Berkeley • Los Angeles • London

University of California Press
Berkeley and Los Angeles, California
University of California Press, Ltd.
London, England
Copyright © 1978 by
The Regents of the University of California
ISBN O-520-03585-2
Library of Congress Catalog Card Number: 77-085740
Printed in the United States of America

1 2 3 4 5 6 7 8 9

This book is dedicated to my mother and father

CONTENTS

FOREWORD

Once upon a time, we lived in a world where the major forms of public communication were speeches and debates on soapboxes in public parks, hand-printed leaflets, and hand-set newspapers. In an emergency, one tried to get a friend to ride by horseback and shout the message to the rooftops. With roughly equal decibels and tongues, people competed for attention and approval using their own wit, persistence, and eloquence. The most powerful potential for abridging free speech and a free press came from the threat of government censorship or suppression.

It was in such a world that the drafters of the First Amendment sought to ensure freedom of speech and a free press for the fledgling United States. But what legal language could protect this freedom as individuals learned to amplify their voices to outshout each other? What constitutional guarantees could preserve freedom of expression once some people acquired microphones and the power to exclude others from the speaker's platform?

This was the dilemma introduced when radio and television became the major forms of communication in our nation. Freedom of speech could no longer be preserved by simply preventing governmental restriction. The right to be heard—and the right to hear—sought protection through other guarantees during the electronic era. A decade ago, the Supreme Court upheld the Federal Communication Commission's fairness doctrine against constitutional attack in its famous *Red Lion* decision. The Supreme Court said, in *Red Lion*:

> But the people as a whole retain their interest in free speech by radio and their collective right to have the medium function consistently with the ends and purposes of the First Amendment. It is the right of the viewers and listeners, not the right of the broadcasters, which is paramount.

The fairness doctrine is a policy developed by the Federal Communications Commission to address this problem. Reinforced by Congress in 1959, the doctrine requires that television and radio stations devote adequate time to important and controversial public issues. At the same time, it demands that broadcasters allow reasonable opportunity for opposing viewpoints to be expressed on the air.

Many people today, especially broadcasters, believe that the fairness doctrine is unfair. They regard it as unfair to journalistic freedom, unfair to our basic traditions of free speech and a free press, and unfair to the American radio listener and television viewer. Advocates of the doctrine, on the other hand, regard it as essential to a free press, a necessary outgrowth of our constitutional traditions, and a vital instrument for ensuring an informed electorate.

Certainly, the doctrine has developed incrementally over time, resulting in ragged edges and logical inconsistencies. Initial efforts were often clumsy. Terminology and thinking had to be borrowed from entirely different industries and technologies. Senator Clarence Dill, principal sponsor of the Communications Act, once told me that he had borrowed the language for the FCC standard of "public interest, convenience, and necessity" from the provisions of public utility laws; yet the Communications Act states explicitly that broadcasting is not a public utility.

The standards for fairness evolved on a case-by-case basis as issues arose in political coverage, as consumer and health groups criticized advertising, and as muckraking documentaries raised the ire of their subjects. The FCC has ruled that the broadcaster's duty to present contrasting views on controversial issues of public importance does not apply to brief, peripheral references to such issues. It has also decided that the absence of financial payment or sponsorship cannot interfere with the public's right to hear contrasting views on important issues. Not all interested parties must be granted the right to speak on the air; yet stations are not permitted to prevent a particular viewpoint from being broadcast simply by avoiding coverage on the entire topic. The doctrine has been found to apply to documentaries but not to situation dramas or reenactments of news crises. Fred Friendly aptly described it as a "crazy quilt pattern of refining" of the original statement.

Beyond the inconsistencies, there are serious dangers inherent in a regulatory effort such as the fairness doctrine. Federal bureaucrats must never be allowed to enter the radio and television newsrooms of the United States and substitute the government's judgment for the news professionals' experience.

Certain groups can and have harassed stations by convincing scores of individuals who have been criticized on the air to request reply time under the fairness doctrine. Inevitably, stations react by trying to avoid such critical programs. Walter Cronkite has testified that, "It is only natural that station management should become timid, and newsmen should sidestep controversial subjects rather than face the annoyance of such harassment."

Such unfortunate consequences led Judge David Bazelon to comment, "If we are to go after gnats with a sledgehammer like the Fairness Doctrine, we ought to at least look at what else is smashed beneath our blow." The most serious danger is that, while acting as overseer in the name of free speech, the government may act as censor and suppressor, the very role forbidden by the authors of the Bill of Rights.

Emotions run high in debates over the fairness doctrine. The stakes are as high as the value of our constitutional heritage and our commitment to freedom. The task is tortuous, and demands wisdom and restraint, both qualities in short supply in the emerging national debate.

On this vital and difficult subject, Professor Simmons has filled a long unanswered demand for careful, reasoned, and analytic discussion of the fairness doctrine. First, he provides a useful narrative history of the complicated development of the doctrine, placing its irregular contours in the appropriate context. He reminds us that just as the quality of broadcasting is tied to the standards observed by individual broadcasters, the quality of regulation is related to the standards observed by government regulators. By exposing shortcomings of past regulatory practices, this book points out important areas for reform. Professor Simmons also offers a thoughtful proposal that reexamines the original rationale for the fairness doctrine and recommends expanded airwave access in order to minimize the need for regulation.

Above all, this balanced work satisfies the toughest test of the fairness doctrine by its carefully reasoned presentation of a controversial issue of public importance. I believe the Simmons book will become a basic text for serious students of communications law. It illuminates hard questions and offers some sensible answers. Hopefully, it will force broadcasters, scholars, regulators, and critics to reexamine some of their long-held assumptions. I commend it to all sides of the fairness debate as a model for scholarly contributions that will deepen our understanding of a tough public issue.   NEWTON MINOW

PREFACE

It is my hope that this book will be valuable to a variety of audiences. For students in journalism, mass communications, and other areas that focus on government regulation of the media, it provides a thorough review of one of the most important aspects of this regulation—the fairness doctrine. Law students concentrating on communications, administrative, and constitutional law should find information here that is relevant to their studies. The book should aid practicing attorneys who deal with fairness doctrine matters; thorough case and subject indexes are provided to help these readers quickly find a point of immediate concern. Broadcasters, who must live under fairness doctrine regulation, may gain a greater understanding of what that regulation requires in varying situations. Individuals who may be contemplating filing a fairness complaint against a television or radio station may, I hope, learn from the discussion. And members of the general public who are interested in such issues as mass media regulation, freedom of speech and press, and television and radio may benefit from the pages that follow.

I would like to express my sincere appreciation to those who have helped make this book possible. The John and Mary Markle Foundation of New York City, which has done so much to encourage study of the media in this country, provided invaluable funding aid. Special thanks go to Kandace M. Laass for her interest and support. Ernest Callenbach, my editor at the University of California Press, has contributed insights and encouragement and has been a pleasure to work with. The Boalt Hall Law School and its library staff provided courteous hospitality for over five months of solid research and writing when I participated in the school's "Visiting Scholars Program." The UCLA law library staff also provided cordial assistance during many months of research and writing. The staffs of COLUMBIA LAW REVIEW, PENNSYLVANIA LAW

REVIEW, CALIFORNIA LAW REVIEW, COMM/ENT, and the FEDERAL COMMUNICATIONS BAR JOURNAL offered many invaluable suggestions. Much appreciation goes to Carol Wyatt and Elizabeth Duke, who devoted long hours to typing the manuscript.

During the more than two years that this book has been in preparation, I have discussed its contents with many individuals and interviewed a number of people, some for hours. Of course, the book's conclusions and analyses, unless otherwise indicated, are solely mine, and I accept full responsibility. My sincere thanks go to the following (the positions indicated are those as of the date of the interview): FCC Chairman: Richard E. Wiley. FCC Commissioners: Glen O. Robinson, Benjamin Hooks, Charlotte Reid, James H. Quello, Robert E. Lee. Other FCC personnel: Larry Secrest, Administrative Assistant to Chairman Wiley; Martin I. Levy, Chief, Broadcast Facilities Division; Richard J. Shiben, Chief, Renewal and Transfer Division; James J. Brown, Assistant Chief, Renewal and Transfer Division; James A. Hudgens, Barry D. Umansky, Cable Television Bureau; Florence Kiser, broadcast analyst, Fairness/Political Branch. Special thanks go to Milton Gross, Chief, Fairness/Political Branch, Complaints and Compliance Division, for his courteous assistance. Other federal government personnel: John Eger, Acting Director, Office of Telecommunications Policy; the late Torbert Macdonald, Chairman, House Subcommittee on Communications; Chip Shooshan, Counsel, House Subcommittee on Communications; James E. Graf, Staff Counsel, Senate Subcommittee on Communications; Nicholas Zapple, former Counsel, Senate Subcommittee on Communications; Carl Eifert, Press Secretary (and legislative aide on media regulation bill) to Senator William Proxmire. Media reform spokesmen: Frank Lloyd, Charles Firestone, Citizens Communications Center; Harvey Schulman, Media Access Project; Nicholas Johnson (former FCC Commissioner), National Citizens Committee for Broadcasting. Broadcasters or broadcast spokesmen: John Summers, General Counsel and Executive Vice President, National Association of Broadcasters; Richard A. Salant, President, CBS News; Ben Raub, Vice-President and Assistant General Attorney, Marshall Wellborn, Assistant General Attorney, Russell Tornabene, Public Relations, National Broadcasting Company; Bill Monroe, NBC News; Richard N. Hughes, Senior Vice-President,

WPIX, and President, National Broadcasting Editorial Association; Varner Paulsen, Vice-President and General Manager, WNEW-AM; John Goldhammer, Program Director, WTOP-TV.

I am also indebted to many other media reform spokesmen, broadcast spokesmen, government officials, and communications scholars whose views I obtained from their writings and discussions.

Finally, the manuscript for this book was first submitted to the publisher before I took a job in Washington, and it represents about two years' prior research and writing. Neither the book nor any part thereof represents official administration policy.

Abbreviations of Journals, Reports, and Services

Abbreviations	*Journals, Reports, Services*
AIR L. REV.	Air Law Review
App. D.C.	Appeals Cases, District of Columbia
ARIZ. L. REV.	Arizona Law Review
B.C. IND. & COM. L. REV.	Boston College Industrial and Commercial Law Review
BUFFALO L. REV.	Buffalo Law Review
CALIF. L. REV.	California Law Review
C.F.R.	Code of Federal Regulations
COLUM. JOURNALISM REV.	Columbia Journalism Review
COLUM. L. REV.	Columbia Law Review
COMM/ENT	COMM/ENT, Journal of Communication and Entertainment Law (Hastings Law School)
CONG. REC.	Congressional Record
CORNELL L. REV.	Cornell Law Review
DUKE L.J.	Duke Law Journal
F.; F.2d	Federal Reporter; Federal Reporter, Second Series
F.C.C.; F.C.C.2d	Federal Communications Commission Reports; Federal Communications Commission Reports, Second Series
FED. B.J.	Federal Bar Journal
FED. COM. B.J.	Federal Communications Bar Journal
Fed. Reg.	Federal Register
FORDHAM L. REV.	Fordham Law Review
F.R.C.	Federal Radio Commission Reports
F. Supp.	Federal Supplement
F.T.C.	Federal Trade Commission Decisions
GA. L. REV.	Georgia Law Review
GEO. L.J.	Georgetown Law Journal
GEO. WASH. L. REV.	George Washington Law Review
HARV. CIV. LIB.-CIV. RIGHTS L. REV.	Harvard Civil Liberties-Civil Rights Law Review

HARV. J. LEGIS.	Harvard Journal on Legislation
HARV. L. REV.	Harvard Law Review
HOFSTRA L. REV.	Hofstra Law Review
H. Doc.	House Document
H.R.	House Bill
H.R.J. Res.	House Joint Resolution
H.R. Rep.	House Committee Report
H.R. Res.	House Resolution
IND. L.J.	Indiana Law Journal
J. BROADCASTING	Journal of Broadcasting
MINN. L. REV.	Minnesota Law Review
Nw. U.L. REV.	Northwestern University Law Review
NOTRE DAME LAW.	Notre Dame Lawyer
OP. ATTY. GEN.	Opinions of the United States Attorney General
P&F RADIO REG.; P&F RADIO REG. 2d	Pike and Fischer Radio Regulation Reporter; Pike and Fischer Radio Regulation Reporter, Second Series
S.	Senate Bill
S.D.L. REV.	South Dakota Law Review
So. CAL. L. REV.	Southern California Law Review
S. Rep.	Senate Committee Report
Stat.	Statutes at Large
SYRACUSE L. REV.	Syracuse Law Review
TEXAS L. REV.	Texas Law Review
TRADE REG. REP.	Trade Regulation Reporter (Commerce Clearing House)
U. CIN. L. REV.	University of Cincinnati Law Review
U. PA. L. REV.	University of Pennsylvania Law Review
U.S.	United States Reports
U. SAN FRANCISCO L. REV.	University of San Francisco Law Review
U.S.C.	United States Code
Wall St. J.	Wall Street Journal
WM. & MARY L. REV.	William and Mary Law Review
YALE L.J.	Yale Law Journal

1

Introduction

American television and radio constitute the most extensive mass communications system in history. Recent studies indicate that 97 percent of United States homes have television sets[1] and that a set is running over six hours per day in the average household.[2] It is not unusual for more than 40 million people to be watching the same show on the same evening. A 1974 survey of 490 prominent educators, labor leaders, bankers, businesspeople, members of Congress, government officials, and clergy rated television the most powerful institution in the country. The White House was second. The Supreme Court was third.[3]

Television and radio play a particularly important role in transmitting information about news and public issues. For example, a national poll released in 1975 asked respondents where they usually got most of their news about "what's going on in the world today—from the newspapers or radio or television or magazines or talking to people or where?" A substantial 65 percent checked television, 47 percent newspapers, and 21 percent radio.[4] In another recent poll 75 percent of adults surveyed stated that television was their prime source of information on the energy shortage, 68 percent received most of their information on environmental issues from television, and 64 percent listed television as their prime source of consumer protection information.[5]

The vast power of the broadcast media has fundamental implications for American democracy. An underlying theme of the democratic process is that the people will control the course of government through their elected representatives and thereby affect their own welfare. The key to the effective functioning of that system is transfer of information from and to people about the issues that affect their lives. Without this information transfer, citizens cannot know what or how particular problems, policies, and actions will influence their future, and population segments cannot convey their opinions and data on public issues to others. It

I

is through information transfer that ideas may clash and be presented for acceptance or rejection in the public interest.

The broadcast media can make a tremendous contribution to intelligent debate about issues of the day. In their living rooms people can actually see and hear advocates of positions on everything from women's rights to crime control to nuclear disarmament. Daily events that affect important issues can be conveyed instantaneously or described to a broadcast audience. People can be continually informed about and interested in important issues by this powerful and pervasive medium.

But just as the broadcast media have great potential to educate and inform the American people about issues important to the health of the Republic, many suggest that they also possess tremendous potential to abuse their informational role. Viewpoints on only one side of an issue may be aired, leaving an audience of millions uninformed about contrasting arguments. Documentaries may be biased, misinforming people about an issue. Television and radio stations may give scant—or no—attention to public issue programming, forsaking their potential contribution to democracy in order to air entertainment shows and reap high profits.

In light of the meaningful contribution the broadcast media can make in informing the American people about public issues, the potential of broadcasters to use their powerful, exclusive, and scarce airwave resource to bias informational programming, and the access opportunity the media present for various parties to convey their views to others, the Federal Communications Commission (FCC) imposed the "fairness doctrine" on all broadcast licensees. That doctrine requires broadcasters to devote a reasonable percentage of their programming to controversial issues of public importance and to cover contrasting sides of those issues fairly.

At first glance, the doctrine sounds appealing. Broadcasters are lucky enough to be given the privilege, by government fiat, to use a scarce airwave frequency to the exclusion of others. Why should they not devote programming time to informing the people in the public interest, and fairly, without bias? The fairness doctrine sounds eminently reasonable.

On closer inspection, however, the doctrine raises a number of difficult problems. Just who is going to determine whether a broadcaster is being fair? What controversial issues of public importance must a broadcaster cover in its programming? What is a reasonable balance between contrasting views on issues? How are groups to be guaranteed an opportunity to speak their views over the airwaves? Is there any workable formula applicable to all issues and programming? If the government is to answer questions such as these, is this an appropriate role for government to play? In a country that values a free press, do not broadcast journalists have some First Amendment rights to determine the content of their public issue programming? Does not government intervention to balance public issue programming inhibit broadcasters from doing such programming? Does not government intervention itself create the potential information distortion it is supposed to prevent? Are not the people better off, then, in a system that minimizes government intervention in the broadcast media?

Questions such as these have been at the center of debate about the fairness doctrine in recent years. Many broadcasters steadfastly insist that the fairness doctrine unjustly interferes with their freedom, and they demand abolition of the doctrine. A variety of public interest groups just as vehemently urge that the doctrine not only be retained but also be enforced more effectively and dramatically. The majority of Congress and the FCC support the present doctrine, but even here minorities urge alteration or elimination.

An intense debate has been carried out in the scholarly literature.[6] But the charges and countercharges about the doctrine's worth are not confined to legal journals. In recent days even the popular press has been filled with articles about the doctrine. Publications such as THE NATION,[7] the New York Times,[8] and CIVIL LIBERTIES[9] have had articles arguing the doctrine's merits.

The labels "conservative" and "liberal" seem to have no meaning with respect to this debate about the fairness doctrine. Thus, Senator William Proxmire, a liberal Democrat, joined with former Senator Roman Hruska, a conservative Republican, in supporting bills to abolish the doctrine completely.[10] Ironically, Senator Proxmire was the person who made the fairness doctrine an explicit part of federal law by offering an amendment to the Communications Act in 1959. Proxmire and Hruska are not alone in their opposition to the doctrine. Parties as diverse as the Board Chairmen overseeing the CBS[11] and NBC[12] television networks, a recent Chairman of the Federal Trade Commission,[13] former Supreme Court Justice William Douglas,[14] and former FCC Commissioner Glen Robinson[15] vigorously urge its abolition. A majority of the scholars, industry representatives, and others attending the 1973 Annual Chief Justice Earl Warren Conference on the First Amendment and the Media voted that abolition was the wisest course.[16] Yet renowned First Amendment media scholars such as Yale's Thomas Emerson,[17] George Washington's Jerome Barron,[18] and Hastings' Roscoe Barrow[19] urge retention of the doctrine. They are joined by, strangely enough, the ABC television network,[20] Richard Hughes, a past president of the National Broadcasting Editorial Association,[21] most members of Congress and the FCC,[22] and numerous consumer, environmental, media, and other public interest groups.[23]

I hope this book will contribute to this debate and shed some light on its subject. In my view, there are tremendous problems with the fairness doctrine as it presently is administered. In an effort to explain this complicated doctrine and its origins, I have provided an early history and a detailed discussion of how it is currently applied. But I have gone a step beyond and also severely critiqued the doctrine's contemporary administration. I then suggest a new policy with respect to public issue programming. I do not claim that the proposal is perfect or without problems of its own. Nor do I assert that other major policy changes might not be in the public interest. I do suggest that the proposed structure would at least be a significant improvement over the present fairness doctrine.

At many points throughout this volume, I discuss the constitutional problems arising from the fairness doctrine. Since recent Supreme Court decisions have declared the fairness doctrine constitutional, I have simply assumed that the doctrine is constitutional and, with the delicate balancing of constitutional interests in mind, have focused on administrative practice under the doctrine. This is not to say that the constitutional dilemma and the working out of a new constitutional rationale are not important. They are critically important. Numerous authors have already addressed themselves to these very problems.[24] But to explore fully the constitutional problems of and solutions to regulation of the broadcast media by the federal government would require another full book. It is work for another day.

Chapter Two focuses on the doctrine in its present-day form. It briefly describes how the FCC and the courts currently interpret the doctrine and the procedures through which it is enforced.

Chapters Three through Seven originally appeared in law journals but have been revised for publication in this book. Chapter Three, reprinted from the FEDERAL COMMUNICATIONS BAR JOURNAL,[25] extensively examines how the fairness doctrine developed before 1960. After a look at the problems faced by radio and the National Radio Conferences in the 1920s, relevant case law and legislative history are discussed. Unlike many authors, I conclude that, even before 1949, the purposes and broadly worded obligations of the fairness doctrine had been set forth.

Chapter Four examines important subcategories of the fairness doctrine, the personal attack and political editorial rules. These rules require that when a party is attacked over the air during discussion of a controversial issue of public importance, or a licensee endorses or opposes a political candidate, the attacked party or disfavored candidate(s) must be notified and provided a chance to reply. After a look at the early history of these rules and an analysis of current practices, the rules are critiqued. A new policy is suggested. The chapter appeared as an article in the UNIVERSITY OF PENNSYLVANIA LAW REVIEW.[26]

Chapter Five, which was first printed in the COLUMBIA LAW REVIEW,[27] takes a detailed look at the fairness doctrine's relationship to advertising. It begins with a brief discussion of the importance of commercial advertising to the structure of broadcasting in the United States, and then it analyzes and critiques FCC application of the fairness doctrine to such advertising before 1974. The FCC's important 1974 *Fairness Report*,[28] which represented a major policy change in this area, is explained. A variety of reasons are offered in support of the FCC's new policy.

Chapter Six first appeared in the CALIFORNIA LAW REVIEW.[29] It extensively explains and critiques the FCC's resolution of two key questions: what issue is raised in a broadcast that may require fairness balancing, and whether that issue is a controversial issue of public importance. The double standard recently developed by the FCC in enforcing the first part of the fairness doctrine, which requires licensees to cover controversial issues of public importance, is also analyzed. The chapter concludes with a suggested new policy to eliminate many of the problems of issue generated by the present application of the doctrine.

Chapter Seven was first published in the maiden issue of Hastings Law School's new communications–entertainment law journal, COMM/ENT.[30] This piece focuses on how the FCC has handled the problem of balancing diverse viewpoints under the fairness doctrine. The role of factors such as time devoted to various sides, frequency of broadcasts, formats, and audience size are explored. Fairness doctrine complaint and enforcement procedures and statistics are examined. A look at the great potential for abuse of the doctrine is followed by a discussion of how the doctrine as presently applied results in unfairness to the public, broadcasters, media access groups, and the FCC itself. The proposal for change introduced in Chapter Six is discussed further. I suggest that the proposed system would eliminate many of the present fairness doctrine problems yet more effectively ensure that television and radio meet the doctrine's basic objectives.

The volume concludes with several elements useful for both in-depth fairness doctrine work and simple, quick inquiries. The bibliography lists all articles and books cited in the volume. The case and document index directs the reader to discussions of particular FCC or court cases and various reports and other documents. The subject index can be used to find sections of the volume where various fairness doctrine subjects are addressed. In the front of the book I have included a list of the full names of law journals and reports that are abbreviated in the footnotes.

Notes

1. 1976 BROADCASTING YEARBOOK C-300. This amounted to a total of 69.6 million U.S. homes. Alaska and Hawaii are excluded from the figures. An estimated 71.4 million U.S. homes (98.6 percent) contain radio sets. *Id.*

2. According to figures from the A. C. Nielsen Company, the daily tuning average for U.S. households was 6 hours and 18 minutes in 1976. BROADCASTING, Jan. 17, 1977, at 5.

3. *Who Runs America? A National Survey.* U.S. NEWS & WORLD REP. Apr. 22, 1974, at 30.

4. ROPER ORGANIZATION, TRENDS IN PUBLIC ATTITUDES TOWARD TELEVISION AND OTHER MASS MEDIA. 1959-1974 (1975). Multiple answers were accepted. When multiple answers to the question were analyzed, 36 percent checked TV only, 19 percent newspapers only, 23 percent both newspapers and TV, and 4 percent newspapers and other media but

not TV. The survey also indicated that 51 percent found television the most credible media source, 20 percent newspapers, 8 percent radio, and 8 percent magazines.

5. *TV Ranks Highest as News Source on Fuel Problems*, BROADCASTING, Mar. 4, 1974, at 50.

6. Among the many noteworthy articles written in recent years are Michel Rosenfeld, *The Jurisprudence of Fairness: Freedom Through Regulation in the Marketplace of Ideas*, 44 FORDHAM L. REV. 877 (1976); Comment, *The Regulation of Competing First Amendment Rights: A New Fairness Doctrine Balance After CBS?* 122 U. PA. L. REV. 1283 (1974); P. M. Schnekkan, *Power in the Marketplace of Ideas: The Fairness Doctrine and the First Amendment*, 52 TEXAS L. REV. 727 (1974); Comment, *The FCC's Fairness Doctrine in Operation*, 20 BUFFALO L. REV. 663 (1971); Howard M. Weinman, *The F.C.C. Fairness Doctrine and Informed Social Choice*, 8 HARV. J. LEGIS. 333 (1971); Jerome A. Barron, *The Federal Communication Commission's Fairness Doctrine: An Evaluation*, 30 GEO. WASH. L. REV. 1 (1969); Roscoe L. Barrow, *The Equal Opportunities and Fairness Doctrines in Broadcasting: Pillars in the Forum of Democracy*, 37 U. CIN. L. REV. 447 (1968). Almost all the legal literature has focused on the balancing requirement in the second half (part two) of the doctrine. The one noteworthy exception is Richard A. Kurnit, Comment, *Enforcing the Obligation to Present Controversial Issues: The Forgotten Half of the Fairness Doctrine*, 10 HARV. CIV. LIB.-CIV. RIGHTS L. REV. 137 (1975).

7. Wayne Phillips, *Jamming the Fairness Doctrine*, 220 THE NATION 533 (1975).

8. John J. O'Connor, *The Fairness Doctrine and the Virtues of Diversity*, N.Y. Times, July 13, 1975, sec. D, at 21; Fred W. Friendly, *What's Fair on the Air*, N.Y. Times, Mar. 30, 1075, sec. G. (Magazine), at 11.

9. Nat Hentoff, *How Fair: The Fairness Doctrine*, CIVIL LIBERTIES, May 1973, at 4. See also Phil Jacklin, *A New Fairness Doctrine, Access to the Media*, THE CENTER MAGAZINE, May/June 1975, at 46; *The Right of Reply, Fairness in the News*, THE NEW REPUBLIC, Mar. 23, 1974, at 11; *The Press, Who Decides Fairness?* TIME, Feb. 4, 1974, at 59.

10. Bills that would have abolished the fairness doctrine were introduced in the 94th Congress by Senators Proxmire (S. 2) and Hruska (S. 1178) in the Senate and Representatives Drinan (D—Mass.) (H.R. 2189) and Thone (R—Neb.) (H.R. 4928) in the House. None of the proposed bills emerged from committee. *See* the dialogue between Senators Proxmire (D—Wis.) and Pastore (D—R.I.), 94th Cong., 2d Sess., 120 CONG. REC. 32181-33185 (1974); remarks of Senator Hruska (D—Neb.), *Fairness Doctrine Spawned Sleazy and Seamy Activities*, 121 CONG. REC. 5351 (1975). In January 1977, at the beginning of the 95th Congress, Senator Proxmire introduced a bill to abolish the fairness doctrine and other content controls over radio and television. Titled the "First Amendment Clarification Act," it is numbered S. 22 and cosponsored by Senators Spark Matsunga (D—Hawaii) and Lee Metcalf (D—Mont.). The companion bill, H.R. 837, was introduced in the House by Robert Drinan. BROADCASTING, Jan. 17, 1977, at 25.

11. William S. Paley (Chairman, CBS, Inc.), *Broadcast Journalism: At the Crossroads of Freedom, Dedication of Newhouse* [Communications Center—II, Syracuse University], May 31, 1974 (mimeograph).

12. Statement of Julian Goodman, Chairman, National Broadcasting Co., Inc., *Fairness Doctrine Hearings on S. 2, S. 608, S. 1178 before the Subcomm. on Communications of the Senate Comm. on Commerce*, 94th Cong., 1st Sess. 80, 81 (1975) [hereinafter cited as *1975 Fairness Doctrine Hearings*].

13. *FTC Chief Raps "Fairness Doctrine,"* L.A. Times, Oct. 30, 1975, pt. III (Business and Finance), at 17, col. 3.

14. *See* Columbia Broadcasting Sys., Inc. v. Democratic Nat'l Comm. 412 U.S. 94, 154 (1973) (Douglas, J., concurring in the judgment).

15. Separate Statement of Commissioner Glen O. Robinson, *1975 Fairness Doctrine Hearings, supra* note 12, at 54.

16. THE FIRST AMENDMENT AND THE NEWS MEDIA, Final Report, Annual Chief Justice Earl Warren Conference on Advocacy in the United States 21-32 (1973) (sponsored by the Roscoe Pound-American Trial Lawyers Foundation). Actually, by simple majority vote the

conference urged removal of FCC power to regulate all program content over television. An "overwhelming majority" urged such deregulation over radio stations and on an "experimental basis" for television in "limited geographical market areas." *Id.* at 21, 22.

17. Professor Thomas Emerson, *Dissent From Specific Recommendations on Broadcast Journalism, id.* at 30.

18. Dean Jerome A. Barron, *Dissent from Recommendation on Broadcast Journalism, id.* at 31.

19. Roscoe L. Barrow, *The Equal Opportunities and Fairness Doctrines in Broadcasting: Pillars in the Forum of Democracy,* 37 U. CIN. L. REV. 447 (1968).

20. Statement of Elton H. Rule, President, American Broadcasting Companies, Inc.; Accompanied by William Sheehan, President, ABC News, *1975 Fairness Doctrine Hearings, supra* note 12, at 70, 71. One possible reason for ABC's position may be the fears expressed by Sheehan that, "were the fairness doctrine taken off the book," it might be "replaced with a new and more onerous obligation," the license renewal process might become more complex, or there might be "renewed credence" in "a system of mandatory broadcast access." *Id.* at 72, 73. *See also* William Sheehan & Julian Goodman, *Guest Debate, The Fairness Doctrine—Fair or Foul?* DEADLINER (New York City Chapter of the Society of Professional Journalists, Sigma Delta Chi), July 1975, at 6.

21. Interview with Richard N. Hughes, President, National Broadcasting Editorial Association, by Steven J. Simmons, Aug. 27, 1975.

22. Interview with Torbert H. Macdonald, Chairman, House Subcommittee on Communications, by Steven J. Simmons, Sept. 19, 1975.

23. These groups are far too numerous to list; they appear as complainants in a variety of fairness doctrine cases. Among the many media reform groups that actively support the fairness doctrine and often aid citizens with complaints are the National Citizens Committee for Broadcasting, Citizens Communication Center, Media Access Project, and Accuracy in Media, Inc., of Washington, D.C., and the United Church of Christ Office of Communications in New York City.

24. One recent piece of particular merit is by Chief Judge David Bazelon of the District of Columbia Circuit Court of Appeals. *See F.C.C. Regulation of the Telecommunications Press,* 1975 DUKE L.J. 213. *See also* Schnekkan, *supra* note 6.

25. Steven J. Simmons, *Fairness Doctrine: The Early History,* 29 FED. COM. B.J. 207 (1976).

26. Steven J. Simmons, *The FCC's Personal Attack and Political Editorial Rules Recommended,* U. PA. L. REV. 990 (1977).

27. Steven J. Simmons, *Commercial Advertising and the Fairness Doctrine: The New FCC Policy in Perspective,* 75 COLUM. L. REV. 1083 (1975).

28. FCC, *Fairness Doctrine and Public Interest Standards, Fairness Report regarding Handling of Public Issues,* 39 FED. REG. 26372 (1974).

29. Steven J. Simmons, *The Problem of "Issue" in the Administration of the Fairness Doctrine,* 65 CALIF. L. REV. 546 (1977).

30. Steven J. Simmons, *The "Unfairness Doctrine"—Balance and Response over the Airwaves,* 1 COMM/ENT 1 (1977).

Fairness Doctrine: Contemporary Definition and Enforcement

I. DEFINITION

In its contemporary form, the fairness doctrine is the name given to two requirements applied by the Federal Communications Commission to radio and television broadcasters throughout the United States.[1] The first, called the part one requirement, demands that broadcast licensees devote a reasonable amount of their programming to controversial issues of public importance. The second, called part two, requires that when such issues are presented, contrasting views on them be aired. In the words of the FCC, the doctrine "involves a two-fold duty: (1) The broadcaster must devote a reasonable percentage of . . . broadcast time to the coverage of public issues, and (2) his coverage of these issues must be fair in the sense that it provides an opportunity for the presentation of contrasting points of view."[2] As put by the United States Supreme Court, the doctrine requires that "discussion of public issues be presented on broadcast stations, and that each side of those issues . . . be given fair coverage."[3]

Declining to issue specific rules with respect to these two general requirements, the FCC has not told licensees precisely how to determine what issue is raised in a broadcast, whether an issue is controversial or of public importance, what constitutes a reasonable opportunity to respond to viewpoints already aired, or what is a reasonable amount of programming on important, controversial issues. Rather, any guidelines that exist must be gleaned from FCC and court decisions and occasional Commission policy statements.[4]

Critical to understanding how the fairness doctrine is applied is the Commission's standard for judging licensees' actions under the doctrine: any fairness decision by a licensee will be

9

upheld if it is reasonable and made in good faith. Both the Commission and the courts "have stressed the wide degree of discretion available under the fairness doctrine" and have stated "ad infinitum ad nauseam, that the key to the doctrine is no mystical formula but rather the exercise of reasonable standards by the licensee."[5] The doctrine "cannot be applied with scientific and mathematical certainty."[6]

The Commission has stated that a licensee need not present contrasting views on any individual show if its total broadcast output presents differing viewpoints.[7] A licensee must seek out and air these viewpoints,[8] however, even if the opposing speakers cannot pay for broadcast time.[9] The broadcaster may choose the opposing speakers and arrange the format in which they appear.[10] And, although they are confused frequently, the fairness doctrine requirements are very different from the equal time rule requirements.[11] Among the many distinctions, one is that contrasting viewpoints need not be given precisely equal time under the fairness doctrine, only a reasonable division of time.[12]

Part two, the balancing part of the fairness doctrine, is by far the better known of the doctrine's two requirements, and the vast majority of Commission cases have focused on part two complaints. But in recent years the Commission has developed a separate standard with respect to part one of the doctrine that is even more deferential to licensee discretion than in part two situations. An issue that would require balancing under part two as a controversial issue of public importance if it were aired might reasonably escape coverage altogether under part one if it does not reach a sufficient level of importance.[13]

The personal attack and political editorial rules[14] are subcategories of the fairness doctrine in which the commission has attempted to set forth more specific standards for licensee compliance. These rules are applicable in a limited number of situations. They require licensees to take enumerated steps to ensure a reply by individuals personally attacked during discussion of a controversial issue of public importance, or by a nonfavored candidate(s) if a licensee opposes or endorses a political candidate.

Although the fairness doctrine has been severely criticized,[15] the FCC has stated that it does not take its requirements lightly. The Commission regards "strict adherence to the fairness doctrine as the single most important requirement of operation in the public interest—the 'sine qua non' for grant of a renewal of license."[16] The importance the Commission attaches to the fairness doctrine is a function of the doctrine's major purpose: keeping the American people informed on vital issues essential to a healthy democracy. As the Commission declared in its 1949 *Report on Editorializing,* it is the "right of the public to be informed . . . which is the foundation stone of the American system of broadcasting."[17] Inextricably linked with the goal of informing the public are the objectives of preventing powerful broadcasters from using a scarce resource—the airwaves—to control the data received by the public and of providing general access for airing the views of various groups and individuals.[18]

II. ENFORCEMENT

Over the last decade there has been an explosion of litigation and administrative activity involving the fairness doctrine. With the doctrine specifically approved by Congress for the first time in 1959,[19] the increasing reach of television, and the rise in public interest group activism, the number of fairness complaints and rulings has soared in comparison with previous years.[20]

The FCC is responsible for enforcing the fairness doctrine.[21] Rather than screen radio and television broadcasting itself to assure compliance, the Commission relies on complaints from the public about a particular licensee's broadcasts.[22] If a person believes that a licensee has presented only one side of a controversial issue of public importance, or has not presented any programming on a critical public issue, he or she should first complain to the local licensee.[23] In this way the broadcaster is provided an opportunity to "rectify the situation, comply with [the complainant's] request, or explain its position."[24] If the complainant either receives no reply from the licensee or is dissatisfied with the reply received, he or she may file a complaint with the Commission. It should contain the following specific information:

> (1) The name of the station or network involved; (2) the controversial issue of public importance on which a view was presented; (3) the date and time of its broadcast; (4) the basis for your claim that the issue is controversial and of public importance; (5) an accurate summary of the view or views broadcast; (6) the basis for your claim that the station or network has not broadcast contrasting views on the issue or

issues in its overall programming; and (7) whether the station or network has afforded, or has expressed the intention to afford, a reasonable opportunity for the presentation of contrasting viewpoints on that issue.[25]

When a fairness complaint is received at the Commission, it is logged and forwarded to a broadcast analyst at the Fairness/Political Branch, Complaints and Compliance Division, of the Broadcast Bureau. The analyst reviews all complaints, returning to the complainants those that need additional information and passing on to lawyers on the branch staff those that contain the necessary information.[26] No enforcement distinction is made between radio and television, and each complaint is evaluated on its own merits.[27]

The legal staff may also send the complaint back to a complainant for additional information. But if it decides that a prima facie fairness case has been made, it will request a response to the complaint from the licensee. At this level, both complainant and licensee have one more round to reply to each other's statements.

If the Commission staff finally decides against a licensee, a wide range of actions may be taken. A letter may be written to the licensee asking how it intends to comply with the doctrine or admonishing it for its behavior. These letters will be entered in the licensee's file, potentially playing a part in license renewal decisions.[28] A license may be revoked during its term,[29] only a short-term renewal may be granted,[30] or nonrenewal may be chosen,[31] all of which involve costly hearings. Theoretically, forfeitures may also be imposed.[32] The staff's decision and sanction may be appealed to the full Commission,[33] and the Commission's judgment may be appealed to the courts.[34]

This is the fairness doctrine in its contemporary form—what it means and how it is enforced. The doctrine's definition and procedure were a long time in the making. A look at its early history will provide a better perspective on how it developed its present-day contours.

Notes

1. The doctrine (and its rules on personal attacks and political editorials, described in detail in Chapter Four) is also applicable to cable television system operators who originate programming under their exclusive control. 47 C.F.R. secs. 76.205, 76.209. As stated by

James Hudgens of the FCC's Cable Television Bureau, "If a cable operator acts like a broadcaster, he's regulated like a broadcaster. If he originates programming that is under his direction and control, then the fairness doctrine applies." Interview with James A. Hudgens and Barry D. Umansky by Steven J. Simmons, Sept. 11, 1975. Fairness doctrine complaints against cable system operators have numbered less than a dozen. *Id. See* Steven J. Simmons, *The Fairness Doctrine and Cable TV*, 11 HARV. J. LEGIS. 629 (1974), for more on the doctrine as it relates to cable television. It should be noted that the FCC's Cable Television Bureau drafted a "notice of proposed rule making that would permit cable systems to substitute use of their access facility for compliance with equal-time and fairness requirements." BROADCASTING, Sept. 27, 1976, at 7. But after considering the proposed rule the FCC "abandoned" the "notion, at least for time being." BROADCASTING, Oct. 4, 1976, at 5. For simplification, throughout this book the doctrine will be spoken of as applying to broadcast licensees.

2. FCC, *Fairness Doctrine and Public Interest Standards, Fairness Report Regarding Handling of Public Issues*, 39 FED. REG. 26372, 26374 par. 15 (1974) [hereinafter cited as *Fairness Report*].

3. Red Lion Broadcasting Co. v. FCC, 395 U.S. 367, 369 (1969).

4. The Commission's five key fairness doctrine policy statements are: FCC, *Fairness Doctrine and Public Interest Standards, Reconsideration of the Fairness Report Regarding Handling of Public Issues*, 58 F.C.C.2d 691 (1976) [hereinafter cited as *Reconsideration Fairness Report*]; *Fairness Report, supra* note 2; FCC, *Broadcast Procedure Manual*, 39 FED. REG. 32288, 32290 pars. 12–14 (rev. ed. 1974) [hereinafter cited as *Broadcast Procedure Manual*]; FCC, *Applicability of the Fairness Doctrine in the Handling of Controversial Issues of Public Importance*, 29 FED. REG. 10415 (1964) [hereinafter cited as *Fairness Primer*]; FCC, *Report on Editorializing by Broadcast Licensees*, 13 F.C.C. 1246 (1949) [hereinafter cited as *Report on Editorializing*].

5. Democratic Nat'l Comm. v. FCC, 460 F.2d 891, 903 (D.C. Cir. 1971), *cert. denied*, 409 U.S. 843 (1972).

6. *Id.* at 900.

7. *Fairness Report, supra* note 2, at 26377; *Report on Editorializing, supra* note 4, at 1250 par. 8, 1255 par. 18.

8. *Fairness Report, supra* note 2, at 26376 par. 35.

9. Cullman Broadcasting Co., 40 F.C.C. 576 (1963).

10. *Fairness Report, supra* note 2, at 26374 par. 18.

11. The equal time rule mandates that, if a licensee allows a legally qualified candidate to broadcast over the licensee's facilities, it must offer equal time to all other such candidates for the same office. 47 U.S.C. sec. 315 (1970); 47 C.F.R. secs. 73.120 (1973) (standard broadcast stations), 73.290 (FM broadcast stations), 73.590 (noncommercial educational FM broadcast stations), 73.657 (television broadcast stations), 76.205 (cable television services).

12. *Fairness Report, supra* note 2, at 26378 par. 43. Other distinguishing characteristics should be noted. At the most fundamental level, the fairness doctrine is issue oriented and not triggered by personality appearance. It affects all programming involving controversial public issues, not just programs presenting legally qualified candidates. Unlike equal time, fairness does not necessarily require a broadcaster to offer time to a specific outside spokesman, and it is applicable at all times, not just during an election period. The fairness doctrine requires affirmative broadcaster action to air contrasting views, unlike the equal time rule, under which the broadcaster can remain passive until a competing candidate requests equal time. The fairness doctrine is applicable to bona fide newscasts, news interviews, and other news coverage, *see* 47 U.S.C. sec. 315(a), whereas the equal time rule is not. The good faith reasonableness standard for judging fairness compliance has less relevance in the equal time context, where precise compliance steps are spelled out. The political editorial rules obviously have a closer relationship with the equal time rule than does the general fairness doctrine. See Chapter Four for further discussion of this.

13. *Fairness Report, supra* note 2, at 26375 par. 25; Representative Patsy Mink, 59 F.C.C.2d 987, 997 par. 29 (1976). See Chapter Six, pp. 166-173, for a complete discussion of the alternative standard for part one cases.

14. 47 C.F.R. secs. 73.123 (AM radio), 73.300 (FM radio), 73.598 (noncommercial educational FM radio), 73.679 (TV broadcast stations), 76.209 (origination cablecasting over cable TV systems). See Chapter Four for a complete discussion of these rules.

15. *See* citations in notes 6–14 of Chapter One.

16. Committee for Fair Broadcasting of Controversial Issues, 25 F.C.C.2d 283, 292 (1970).

17. *Report on Editorializing, supra* note 4, at 1249. The Commission added: "It is axiomatic that one of the most vital questions of mass communication in a democracy is the development of an informed public opinion through the public dissemination of news and ideas concerning the vital public issues of the day." *Id.* More recently the Commission has declared: "Full information is the theoretical underpinning of the broadcaster's two [fairness doctrine] duties." *Reconsideration Fairness Report, supra* note 4, at 693.

18. *See* Red Lion Broadcasting Co. v. FCC, 395 U.S. 367, 390 (1969); Robert H. Scott, 11 F.C.C. 372, 376 (1946): *Report on Editorializing. supra* note 4, at 1248–50; Note, *The Mayflower Doctrine Scuttled,* 59 YALE L.J. 758 (1950). No particular individual, however, is entitled to access. Choice of spokesmen is made by the licensee.

19. 47 U.S.C. sec. 315(a) (4) (1970). Before 1959, FCC fairness doctrine enforcement was based on the broad "public convenience, interest, or necessity" language of the 1927 Radio Act and 1934 Communications Act. 47 U.S.C. sec. 303 (1970).

20. Until the early 1960s, there were few fairness complaints, and even fewer fairness rulings. It was only in 1963 that the Commission first decided to rule on complaints when they were received instead of holding them for review every three years at license renewal time. Letter to Oren Harris, 40 F.C.C. 582 (1963). *See* Chapter Seven, pp. 210–14, for statistics on fairness complaints and FCC rulings in recent years.

21. For a discussion of problems with FCC enforcement procedures and resulting difficulties faced by fairness complainants, *see* Chapter Six.

22. *See Broadcast Procedure Manual, supra* note 4.

23. *Broadcast Procedure Manual, supra* note 4, at 32290 par. 13. In "unusual circumstances" complaints may be made directly to the Commission. *Id.*

24. *Id.*

25 *Id.,* par. 14. In Interpretive Rulings—Commission Procedure, *Fairness Primer, supra* note 4, at 10415, the Commission provided a checklist of only five items for a complaint: "Where complaint is made to the Commission, the Commission expects a complainant to submit specific information indicating (1) the particular station involved; (2) the particular issue of a controversial nature discussed over the air; (3) the date and time when the program was carried; (4) the basis for the claim that the station has presented only one side of the question; and (5) whether the station had afforded, or has plans to afford, an opportunity for the presentation of contrasting viewpoints." It should be noted that the 1974 *Fairness Report, supra* note 2, at 26379 par. 50, cites these 1964 *Primer* requirements in explaining what is required in complaints. The *Fairness Report* thus ignores the requirements mentioned in the 1972 *Broadcast Procedure Manual,* 37 FED. REG. 20510, 20512 par. 14 (1972), that the complaint state the basis for the claim that an issue is controversial and of public importance and that it provide an accurate summary of the view or views broadcast; the *Fairness Report* also ignores other wording in the manual referring to "network," "public importance," "overall programming" and a "reasonable" opportunity. This additional information was included in both the 1972 *Broadcast Procedure Manual* which predates the 1974 *Fairness Report,* and the 1974 revised edition of the *Broadcast Procedure Manual, supra* note 4, which postdates the 1974 *Report* by less than two months. The *Broadcast Procedure Manual's* seven-point requirement may thus be considered authoritative. The FCC's citing of the 1964 *Primer's* five-point complaint requirements and failure to mention the *Broadcast Procedure Manual's* seven points in the 1974 *Fairness Report* must be seen as oversights by the Commission, which only add confusion to an already difficult area.

26. In 1975 there were five lawyers, one broadcast analyst, and two secretaries working in the Fairness/Political Branch, which also handles section 315 equal time complaints and inquiries. Approximately 60 to 70 percent of personnel time was spent on fairness doctrine work, and a "ballpark figure" for the annual cost to the Branch of administering the

doctrine, in terms of salaries and other expenses, was $200,000. Others directly involved in fairness doctrine administration include the Chief and Assistant Chief of the Complaints and Compliance Division, the General Counsel's Office, and, of course, the commissioners and their staffs. Generally, the Commission considered at least one fairness matter per week, and "there may be a hundred to a hundred and fifty fairness decisions" made each year. Interviews with Milton Gross, chief, Fairness/Political Branch, Complaints and Compliance Division, Broadcast Bureau, by Steven J. Simmons, Sept. 3, 9, 1975, Dec. 8, 17, 1976 [hereinafter cited as Interviews with Milton Gross].

27. *Id.*

28. *Id.* However, unless a fairness doctrine violation is alleged in a petition to deny renewal or in an informal objection filed against a renewal application, if the violation has been partially remedied by a licensee it is not likely to play a role at renewal time. In fact, "There are no questions on the new renewal forms which seek information concerning a station's policy with respect to the fairness doctrine. The Commission has found that such questions have rarely yielded useful information." Letter from Martin I. Levy, Chief, Broadcast Facilities Division, FCC Broadcast Bureau, to Steven J. Simmons, Dec. 8, 1976 (letter material relating to renewal process prepared under supervision of Richard J. Shiben, Chief, Renewal and Transfer Division).

29. 47 U.S.C. sec. 312(a) (1970). An outright license revocation for fairness doctrine violations has never occurred.

30. 47 U.S.C. sec. 307(d) (1970). *See* Springfield Television Broadcasting Corp., 28 F.C.C.2d 339 (1971); Butte Broadcasting Co., 22 F.C.C.2d 7 (1970). A comparative hearing also may be ordered. 47 U.S.C. sec. 309(e).

31. 47 U.S.C. sec. 307 (1970). The only instance of nonrenewal of a license based in part on fairness doctrine violations is Brandywine-Main Line Radio, Inc., 24 F.C.C.2d 18 (1970), *petition for reconsideration denied,* 27 F.C.C.2d 565 (1971), *aff'd,* 473 F.2d 16 (D.C. Cir. 1972), *cert. denied,* 412 U.S. 922 (1973).

32. This possibility is opened by considering the fairness doctrine part of the Communications Act, a codification suggested, albeit unevenly, in Red Lion Broadcasting Co. v. FCC, 395 U.S. 367, 380–83, 385 (1969), and more clearly in Straus Communications v. FCC, 530 F.2d 1001, 1007 n.11 (D.C. Cir. 1976). *See* the discussion of this question in Chapter Three. Under 47 U.S.C. sec. 503(b), violators of the act are subject to a $1,000 fine per violation day, up to a maximum of $10,000. The FCC has to date refused to impose forfeitures for general fairness doctrine violations, emphasizing in its 1974 *Fairness Report* that "[t]he danger of an unwise Commission decision in this area is considerably reduced by the fact that no sanction is imposed on the broadcaster for isolated fairness violations during the course of the license term. The licensee is simply asked to make an additional provision for the opposing point of view, and this is certainly not too much to ask of a licensee who has been found to be negligent in meeting his fairness obligations." *Fairness Report, supra* note 2, at 26378 par. 45. It intends to continue this policy in the future. *Id.*: interview with Larry Secrest, Administrative Assistant to Chairman Richard Wiley, by Steven J. Simmons, Sept. 4, 1975. According to Milton Gross, in a fairness doctrine case, "the ordinary sanction would be either setting them [licensees] for hearing on their renewal application or order to show cause or letters of admonition." But "[i]t's quite possible that the licensee could be issued a forfeiture upon that part of the fairness doctrine contained in Section 315. However, to date, no appropriate case has come before us. . . . It's quite feasible or possible that a case will arise where the Commission will find it appropriate to issue a forfeiture based upon a violation of the fairness doctrine. . . ." Interviews with Milton Gross, *supra* note 26. If considered part of the act, cease and desist orders should also be available to remedy general fairness doctrine violations. 47 U.S.C. sec. 312(b) (1970). The FCC considers monetary forfeitures and cease and desist orders available for violations of the personal attack–political editorial obligations, since these have been made specific rules, *see* note 12, *supra,* unlike the general fairness doctrine responsibility, 47 U.S.C. sec. 503(b).

33. 47 C.F.R. sec. 1.115.

34. 47 U.S.C. sec. 402(a) & (b).

CHAPTER 3

The Early History

Despite the plethora of academic and popular articles on the fairness doctrine and the current debate about its validity, there has been an almost total lack of publication on the fairness doctrine's early history. The typical law review article pays passing reference in a page or two to the doctrine's origins, and then goes on to discuss the doctrine as it is presently applied.[1] The only book entirely on the doctrine ever to be published, a very interesting volume written by a former broadcaster and oriented more to a lay audience than the specialized legal audience, devotes fewer than 15 out of 236 pages to the doctrine's early history, inevitably missing important early developments.[2]

The following pages discuss the history of the fairness doctrine through 1959 in detail. I hope that this effort will not only plug a gaping hole in the fairness doctrine literature but also provide some background for those debating the doctrine's existence when they look back over their shoulders and ask how it all began.

I. RADIO: SETTING THE STAGE FOR REGULATION

Throughout most of the "roaring twenties" radio communication in the air seemed as disorganized and frenetic as the bumping and charging Charleston dance antics taking place on the ground. Seemingly unable to plan for or anticipate the economic problems generated by the wild spending of the decade, the country soon showed more concern for control of its new means of electromagnetic communication: the radio.

In 1920, there were but 3 radio stations in the country broadcasting regularly.[3] By late 1925, the number of broadcasting stations had risen to 578.[4] As one author put it, radio stations had "sprung up like mushrooms across the land";[5] as grandly proclaimed by another, "there had never been a scientific development in the history of the world that was so quickly translated into popular use as was radio broadcasting."[6] By 1927, there were two national networks with a total of 64 affiliated stations providing regular network service from coast to coast.[7]

The Wireless Ship Act of 1910,[8] the nation's first radio legislation, had been concerned exclusively with the use of radio aboard ships at sea and provided no basis for regulating the explosive radio growth of the 1920s. The 1910 law was strengthened when Congress passed the Radio Act of 1912.[9] That Act, in addition to authorizing the famous Morse Code SOS as the international emergency signal and setting down other distress signal procedures, required that all radio stations receive licenses from the Secretary of Commerce and Labor. The Act compelled radio station operators to be licensed by the Secretary, and it specified wavelengths for various types of stations. A key purpose in regulating private and commercial stations was "preventing or minimizing interference with communication between stations."[10] There was nothing in the Act that gave the Secretary discretionary power to regulate stations in the public interest, much less to affect radio program content via balanced public affairs presentation.

Whatever regulatory authority Secretary Herbert Hoover had under the 1912 statute was dissipated in 1923 when the District of Columbia Circuit Court of Appeals held that the Secretary had no discretion to refuse a license to a radio applicant within the designated classifications.[11] Secretary Hoover's power to affect the course of radio development was all but eliminated in 1926 when a District Court in Illinois ruled he could not penalize the Zenith Radio Corporation for broadcasting on an unauthorized frequency.[12] The final blow to the Secretary's regulatory powers came in response to his request of the Attorney General for an advisory opinion on his authority. Within five weeks, Acting Attorney General Donavan declared that under the 1912 Act the Secretary had no "general authority" to assign wavelengths to broadcasting stations,[13] fix times for broadcast station operation,[14] or limit amounts of station wattage.[15] The Attorney General concluded that "the legislation is inadequate to cover the art of broadcasting, which has been almost entirely developed since the passage of the 1912 Act."[16]

While Secretary Hoover was fruitlessly attempting to regulate radio development based on the 1912 Act, the broadcasting situation was becoming intolerable. There were listener complaints about fraudulent get-rich-quick schemes and claims on behalf of "medical" cures broadcast over the airwaves,[17] dissatisfaction with offensive advertising,[18] and intense criticism of radio industry monopoly and refusal of some stations to carry political broadcasts.[19] But by far the single most disturbing feature about radio during most of the 1920s was the interference by one radio station's signals with those of another station. Listeners' ears were grated by the ensuing static, often making programs unintelligible. "The listener, tuning his none-too-sensitive receiver, found himself receiving not one station, but two or even three stations at the same time."[20] One typical example of the kind of interference occurring involved broadcasts from two churches in Washington, D.C. For three Sundays in a row in 1922 two stations broadcast religious services from these churches at the same time and on the same frequency. As stated by the late Professor Walter Emery, "What poured from the receivers was a pain-provoking jumble of noise that was more conducive to neuroses than quiet religious worship."[21]

People from all sections of the country complained to Secretary Hoover about the radio interference. "Every one of the ninety channels in the broadcasting band was occupied by at least two stations, many by three or more." In the congested urban areas competitors had been "compelled" to set up "complicated time sharing arrangements."[22] Radios from ships at sea, competing with land based radio stations for airspace, also contributed to the interference.[23] According to one author's history of the period, "chaos rode the airwaves, pandemonium filled every loud-speaker and the twentieth century Tower of Babel was made in the image of the antenna towers of some thousand broadcasters who, like the Kilkenny cats, were about to eat each other up."[24]

After issuance of the Attorney General's Opinion, Secretary Hoover, vitally concerned with making radio communication successful, ended his own efforts to minimize airwave interference and asked the radio industry to attempt self-regulation.[25] The Secretary's pleas were for the most part disregarded. "In short order 200 new stations crowded on the air. Broadcast reception was jumbled and sporadic."[26] The new stations went on the air using any frequency they desired, regardless of the interference thereby caused, and previously established stations jumped from wavelength to wavelength, changing their wattage and operating hours at will.[27]

The problem, in simple terms, was that there was not enough airspace for all the various broadcasting stations to operate at will. Unlike their print media brethren, who could distribute dozens of different types of newspapers and magazines on any one city newsstand, there could be only a single radio operator broadcasting successfully on the same wavelength at the same time and in the same area. The United States Supreme Court summed up the situation as follows: "It quickly became apparent that broadcast frequencies constituted a scarce resource whose use could be regulated and rationalized only by the Government. Without government control, the medium would be of little use because of the cacophony of competing voices, none of which could be clearly and predictably heard."[28]

The growing chaos and the apparent inadequacy of existing legislation to cope with the situation led President Harding in February 1922 to ask Secretary Hoover to call a meeting of government and civilian experts to discuss the problems of radio.[29] The ensuing conference was the first of four national radio conferences held annually between 1922 and 1925, which eventually led to the adoption of the 1927 Radio Act. With competing factions in attendance, "Conditions at the opening of the first radio conference were anything but cordial. About the only thing agreed upon was the need to reduce the radio interference."[30] At the opening session, Hoover stressed two themes that were to play a key role in justifying future regulation of the broadcast media, especially fairness doctrine regulation. He spoke of the necessity of eliminating radio interference in terms of protecting a natural resource.[31] And he said some government control was necessary to establish a "public right over the ether roads" so that "there may be no national regret that we have parted with a great national asset into uncontrolled hands."[32] So, first, the airwaves were to be considered a public resource, not private property. And, second, their use should not be exploited by "uncontrolled" entities—whether large numbers of small stations or powerful monopolies attempting to push their private viewpoints over the air.

Unfortunately, the Conference's technical recommendations to decrease interference were not accepted by the Department of Commerce.[33] Congressman Wallace White of Maine did introduce a bill in the House based on the Conference recommendations, claiming, "It is as difficult for two stations in the same locality to simultaneously transmit on the same wavelength as it is for two trains to pass each other upon the same track."[34] The bill was passed in the House but died in the Senate.[35]

The Second National Radio Conference, held in 1923, made a series of recommendations including urging reassignment of frequencies for various radio stations, supporting discretion in the granting of licenses "due to the limited number of channels available for broadcasting," and calling for public support of local radio stations.[36] Although the frequency recommendations were this time adopted by the Department of Commerce and the interference problem was somewhat alleviated,[37] a second radio bill based on the conference and introduced by Congressman White was never reported from House committee.[38]

At the Third Radio Conference, held in 1924, President Coolidge addressed the participants, and, as Secretary Hoover had done two years before, he stressed the danger of a few private interests gaining control of the airwaves. He said, ". . . one of the benefits of increased governmental regulation was that it would permit the Department of Commerce to better insure against the danger of a few organizations gaining the control of the airwaves."[39] The potential of station interconnection via radio networks was of particular concern to the President, and he stressed, "It would be unfortunate indeed, if such an important function as the distribution of information should ever fall into the hands of the Government. It would be still more unfortunate if its control should come under the arbitrary power of any person or group of persons. It is inconceivable that such a situation could be allowed to exist."[40] In addition to technical recommendations, the Conference recommendations included a strong stance against private monopolistic practices in the industry and against government censorship of radio program content.[41] No congressional bill was introduced based on the recommendations.

Secretary Hoover addressed the Fourth National Radio Conference in November 1925 and emphasized the now familiar scarcity basis for government regulation: "We can no longer deal on the basis that there is room for everybody on the radio highways. There are more vehicles on the roads than can get by, and if they continue to jam in, all will be stopped."[42] He also stressed a key concept that was to be used later by both the FCC and the Supreme Court in

ess doctrine: "We hear a great deal about free-
there are *two* parties to freedom of the air, and
for that matter. Certainly in radio I believe in
ner. . . . Freedom cannot mean a license to
ration who wishes to broadcast his name or his
opolize the listener's set."[43] Thus within the
the first outlines of the significant "clear and
or free speech were taking shape,[44] the idea of
dment right in broadcasting between broad-
s being suggested by the Secretary of Labor.
The two concepts have more in common than a chronological birth-
place. In both the emphasis is on the First Amendment rights of a
speaker justifiably being regulated to balance a greater public good.

Secretary Hoover also reiterated the public interest in the
airwaves: "the ether is a public medium, and its use must be for
public benefit." The main "consideration in the radio field is, and
always will be, the great body of the listening public, millions in
number, countrywide in distribution. There is no proper line of
conflict between the broadcaster and the listener . . . their interests
are mutual. . . ."[45]

The Conference recommended an extensive program of
legislation to amend the existing federal law, which it considered
inadequate. In addition to technical recommendations and increased regulatory authority for the Secretary of Commerce, the
Conference again opposed any government censorship as well as
private monopoly, supported "licenses being awarded based on the
'public interest,'" and concluded that broadcasting should not be
considered a public utility.[46] The recommendations of the Fourth
National Radio Conference were utilized by Representative White
in drafting H.R. 5589,[47] the bill that started the legislative process
leading to passage of the Radio Act of 1927.[48]

The National Radio Conferences and other developments
during the 1920s had highlighted some of the concerns that would
lead to implementation of the fairness doctrine. Critical among
these were scarcity of the airwave resource, the fear of powerful
private entities utilizing their frequencies to further their own
partisan and/or materialistic ends, the interests of the public in
receiving information, and the need to treat the ether as a public
resource. In calling for no government censorship of broadcasting,

the Third and Fourth Radio Conferences were also reflecting the perpetual fairness doctrine dilemma: how to reconcile the First Amendment rights of broadcasters with the public interest in some degree of control over the "public medium."

II. THE RADIO ACT OF 1927:
THE LEGISLATIVE HISTORY

The Radio Act of 1927 repealed the 1912 radio law, and created a five-person Federal Radio Commission (FRC) with full powers to grant and revoke licenses, assign frequencies, and determine station power and location.[49] Although the statute had deficiencies, at least Congress had recognized and acted upon the need to provide a federal "traffic cop" for the scarce airwave resource and minimize radio interference. The airwaves were established as a public resource that broadcasters could be licensed to use but not own.[50] Aside from this important acknowledgment, of particular significance for fairness doctrine purposes was the act's declaration that the FRC could exercise its enumerated powers "as public convenience, interest, or necessity requires,"[51] the declaration that licenses were to be granted if the "public convenience, interest, or necessity" would be served thereby,[52] the prohibition against FRC "censorship" or interference "with the right of free speech by means of radio communications,"[53] and the "equal opportunities"[54] provisions for legal qualified candidates. Most of the key provisions of the 1927 law were substantially reenacted in the 1934 Communications Act. Consequently the Radio Act of 1927 may "be regarded as the basis of current broadcast regulation,"[55] and the legislative history of the 1927 bill is relevant in interpreting the 1934 statute.

The legislative history of the 1927 act reveals a clear discussion of essentially what is today considered part two of the fairness doctrine, the requirement to afford contrasting viewpoints on controversial public issues.

. The concerns underlying fairness doctrine regulation that were voiced throughout the 1920s were also set forth in the congressional debate. Senator Dill, sponsor and chief author of the radio bill in the Senate, preceded the Senate discussion of the legislation with a description of "conditions regarding radio broadcasting that should be kept in mind as a background in the consideration of the legislation to be enacted."[56] He stressed that the number of broadcast channels is "limited, and Congress must legislate in accordance with that condition at the present time."[57] The Senator then posed the fairness doctrine issue still being debated fifty years later. Radio broadcasters were free from government restraint, he said, and "it is our desire and purpose to keep them free so far as it is possible to do so in conformity with the general public interest and the social welfare of the great masses of our people. It is this combination and purpose that complicates the problem of legislation on this subject. . . . We must steer the legislative ship between the Scylla of too much regulation and the Charybdis of the grasping selfishness of private monopoly."[58]

Senator Heflin spoke of the danger of only wealthy persons controlling radio for their own purposes,[59] and Senator Watson thought the agency regulating radio could have a tremendous influence on public opinion and thought.[60] The most ardent spokesman regarding these concerns, and the voice most fervently in favor of fairness doctrine type legislation, was Senator Howell of Nebraska, a member of the Senate subcommittee that reported the Radio Act.[61] After noting the scarcity of channels, Howell stated, "to perpetuate in the hands of comparatively few interests the opportunity of reaching the public by radio and allowing them alone to determine what the public shall and shall not hear is a tremendously dangerous course for Congress to pursue. . . . If any public question is to be discussed over the radio, if the affirmative is to be offered the negative should be allowed upon request also, or neither the affirmative nor the negative should be presented."[62] In broad strokes, he was urging the adoption of the fairness doctrine, part two.[63]

Despite Senator Howell's pleas, Congress did not enact a specific provision requiring balanced treatment of public issues. In the House, Congressman White, sponsor and key author of H.R. 9971, had emphasized the scarcity of frequencies[64] and the need to have the public's rights predominate over private rights in the ether.[65] Other members had mentioned the dangers of monopoly interests presenting only one point of view to the public.[66] But the Radio Act emerged from committee without any provision for balanced coverage of political candidates or political issues, despite a

minority opinion opposing this omission.[67] Representative White
stated in floor debate that the bill gave "no power at all" to the
Secretary of Commerce to interfere with "freedom of speech in any
degree."[68] He declared that broadcast personal attacks of one individual against another as well as political attacks were not dealt
with in the bill, and that he personally felt the common law of the
states should deal with such attacks.[69]

An amendment to provide "equal facilities and rates,
without discrimination accorded to all political parties and all candidates for office, and to *both the proponents and opponents of all
political questions or issues,*"[70] was offered on the floor by Congressman Johnson of Texas.[71] Reflecting the fears of many, he
stated that broadcasting could "mold and crystallize sentiment as
no agency in the past has been able to do. If the strong arm of the
law does not prevent monopoly ownership and make discrimination
by such stations illegal, American thought and politics will be largely at the mercy of those who operate these stations."[72] The Johnson
amendment's concern with balancing opposing spokesmen on political issues is analagous to the substance of the modern-day fairness
doctrine, but the amendment differs in its focus on equal facilities
and rates, and only "political" questions. The amendment was considered not germane, and ruled out of order.[73]

The Senate Committee on Interstate Commerce, to which
H.R. 9971 had been referred after passage by the House, added a
provision to the bill calling for equal opportunities for candidates
and discussion of public issues. The substitute stated that "if" a
broadcaster were to permit his facilities to be used by a candidate,
"or *for the discussion of any question affecting the public,* he shall
make no discrimination as to the use of such broadcasting station"
and would be, for these purposes, a "common carrier."[74] The provision did not address the affirmative part of today's doctrine, for it
spoke of a broadcaster obligation only "if" he chose to broadcast
public issues. As in the nongermane House amendment, the Senate
substitute did attempt to secure fair play for public issues over the
airwaves and as such resembles part two of today's fairness doctrine. However, the meaning of the amendment is extremely
unclear. How does a broadcaster make "no discrimination"? What
does it mean for a licensee to be a "common carrier" for these

issues? And does not every question under the sun affect "the public"?

Senator Howell, a member of the Committee, described the Committee's intent: "It must be recognized that, so far as principles and policies are concerned, they are major in political life; candidates are merely subsidiary. We recognized that fact when this bill was formulated, and provided that if a radio station allowed the discussion of a public question it must afford, if requested, an opportunity to present the other sides. I think it was the view of the committee that if any subject was to be presented to the public by any of the limited number of stations, the other side should have the right to use the same forum; and if such privilege were not to be granted, then there should be no such forum whatever."[75]

The substitute was amended on the floor by Senator Dill, and although equal opportunities for candidates were kept in the amendment, the public question provision was dropped.[76] Senator Dill stated that the public question and equal opportunity provisions had "caused more objection to the bill than probably all the other provisions combined," and that after the Committee had reported it out it had realized that "the 'common carrier' phrase was an unwise phrase, to say the least, at this time."[77] Senator Dill indicated that the "common carrier" language was the really "objectionable feature"[78] of the provision.

In responding to Senator Howell's objection[79] to dropping the public question part of the substitute, Senator Dill said he sympathized with Howell's viewpoints on the issue. But he indicated that there was danger in using the broad wording of public questions. "[T]here is probably no question of any interest whatsoever that could be discussed but that the other side of it could demand time."[80] A radio station, the senator felt, would either have to give all its air time for discussion of the issues raised or forbid any such discussion.[81] "In the minds of many" there was strong opposition to the public question language, and he thought it was not wise to include the provision "in the bill at this time, but to *await development, and get this organization to functioning* and the bill can be amended in the future."[82] The amended bill, without the prohibition against discriminating among sides on "any question affecting the public," was passed by the Senate, and went to a

House–Senate conference. Section 18 of the Radio Act that emerged from the conference contained an equal opportunities provision for a "legally qualified candidate," and the conference report did not include any additional explanation of the section.[83]

III. ANALYSIS OF THE LEGISLATIVE HISTORY

This legislative history does reflect a congressional sensitivity to the problems of airwave scarcity, the need to present balanced public affairs information to the American people, and the danger of private partisan interests propagandizing their own views through the ether. There is firm recognition that the airwaves are a public resource, not subject to private property claims, and that broadcasters can use that resource only as the "public convenience, interest, or necessity" requires. The latter terms are left undefined.

Congress gave no consideration to requiring broadcasters affirmatively to present public affairs programming. However, it did consider requiring fair treatment of public issues once a radio licensee had decided to present such issues. In the House a minority committee report protested the lack of this requirement in the bill, an amendment proposing it was ruled not germane and was not reconsidered, and the House sponsor of the Radio Act said that the bill did not contain such a provision and that the FRC could not interfere at all with broadcasters' free speech. In the Senate a bill emerged from committee calling for nondiscriminatory treatment of public questions. After debate and opposition, it was amended and the provision was dropped. The fairness concept remained in the bill with respect to legally qualified candidates, but not for public issues. It is clear that Congress in 1927 did not want to legislate an explicit provision requiring fair treatment of public issues. A key concern in the Senate seemed to be the unforeseen consequences of a public issues requirement for broadcasters, and the Senate wished to await future developments.

As a 1968 House staff study concluded, "These legislative events would appear to cast serious doubt on the proposition that the Fairness Doctrine, at least in substance, is a necessary corollary of the 'public interest' standard contained in the Radio Act."[84] But this does not mean, as the staff study further suggests, that the doctrine cannot be based on the public interest standard and that debate over the public issue requirements was mere surplusage.[85] Just because the requirements are not a "necessary corollary" of the public interest standard does not mean they are not authorized under that standard. Senator Dill expressed a desire to await future developments. Letting the FRC begin to function and develop more expertise in this area under a broad public interest mandate, as opposed to strapping broadcasters with a specific legislative requirement, may have been his intent. Senator Dill's comments during hearings before the Senate Committee on Interstate Commerce in 1930 support this view. At the hearings, Commissioner Robinson[86] of the FRC expressed the opinion that the law as it existed required the same equal opportunity for public questions as for candidates. Senator Dill did not disagree, and asked the Commissioner whether the FRC had considered making regulations requiring stations to provide equal opportunities for public questions. When the Commissioner responded no, the Senator declared, "It would be within the power of the commission, I think, to make regulations on that subject."[87]

In 1932, a bill to amend the Radio Act, including a fairness type provision, was in fact passed by Congress. The bill stated that, "it shall be deemed in the public interest for a licensee, so far as possible, to permit equal opportunity for the presentation of both sides of public questions."[88] In the House floor debate it was clear that the House members considered the bill to be only a clarification of existing law, not a grant of new authority to the FRC. Thus, Congressman Davis, managing the bill's passage on the floor, declared, "I will state that none of the provisions . . . change substantive law relating to radio."[89] And the bill "in its entirety" had the "unqualified endorsement of the Federal Radio Commission and their counsel."[90] After passage by both Senate and House, the bill was pocket vetoed by President Hoover. This legislative episode, following closely the 1927 enactment, supports the theory that Congress considered an FRC requirement of reasonably fair treatment of public issues to be within the Commission's public interest authority. The bill was meant to make the broadcaster obligation explicit, not to change the "substantive law." Thus it may be concluded that the FRC was authorized to impose a requirement of fair treatment of public issues under the public interest standard, although Congress had not specifically mandated such a requirement in the 1927 act.

IV. THE COMMUNICATIONS ACT OF 1934:
THE LEGISLATIVE HISTORY

Passage of the 1934 Communications Act was spurred mainly by the need to centralize regulation of the telephone, telegraph,
and broadcast media. Its key feature is creation of a seven-person
Federal Communications Commission with expanded regulatory
powers. A fairness doctrine type provision also played a role in
enactment of the 1934 communications law. The Senate passed a
bill that, in addition to calling for equal opportunities for legally
qualified candidates and their supporters, required "equal opportunities . . . in the presentation of views on a public question to be
voted upon at an election." An "equal opportunity" was to be given
to "an equal number of other persons" for presentation of opposite
views on these election questions. The provision differs from the
modern-day fairness doctrine in its focus on election issues only, its
apparent call for equal time, and its specification of an equal
number of spokesmen (as opposed to a reasonable time and a
reasonable opposing format at the licensee's discretion). The bill
additionally stated that it was "in the public interest for a licensee,
so far as possible, to permit equal opportunity for the presentation
of both sides of the public question,"[91] a provision analogous to the
one voted for in 1932.

The House Committee on Interstate and Foreign Commerce
omitted these provisions in a substitute bill.[92] In conference, the
Senate provisions were eliminated,[93] and section 18 of the 1927
Radio Act was carried forward in the 1934 Act verbatim.

The reasons for dropping the Senate fairness provisions are
not entirely clear. The change in section 18 was not discussed in the
congressional debates of either house. One strong possibility was a
reluctance to tamper with the provisions of the Radio Act via
statute and rather, as Senator Dill had implied in the 1927 debates,
a desire to let the regulatory agency develop policy. Congressman
Rayburn, the House manager of the bill in conference, stated on the
floor, "we did not think we should go into a revision of the radio
law, and I think personally it *is much better to go ahead and formu-
late this commission and let them study all these questions and
make their recommendations in light of their study.*"[94] Professor
Roscoe Barrow, a noted authority on the fairness doctrine, interprets Rayburn's words to mean "that abandonment of the changes

proposed by the Senate in Section 18 was prompted by the impracticality of including numerous changes in a comprehensive statute such as the Communications Act of 1934."[95] This indeed appears to be the most likely possibility, although the legislative history does not offer a precise answer. The 1968 House staff's observation that the enactment "provided another instance wherein language similar to the present Fairness Doctrine was unsuccessfully proposed for incorporation into the law," is certainly correct.[96]

V. THE LEGISLATIVE HISTORIES:
SOME ADDITIONAL THOUGHTS

What are the implications of this early legislative history with respect to the fairness doctrine? First, one must look at legislative histories in perspective. Given the variety of views in the legislature on what any bill means, legislative histories are often not the most accurate reflection of legislative intent, and different sides of the same issue can frequently find support in the same legislative history. Beyond this, committee reports, the considered written judgments of a number of congressmen who have studied the legislative subject matter, are more accurate indicators of intent than floor debate. Yet there is almost no language in the reports that sheds light on exactly what is meant by the "public interest, convenience, and necessity," and why a fairness doctrine provision is not explicitly included in the statutes.

Admittedly, floor debates have some relevance, especially here where the quoted congressmen are key authors and sponsors of the legislation or members of the committee that reported the statute. Based on this debate, and on the additions and deletions that were made to the statutes as they went through the legislative process, it is clear that Congress was not requiring broadcasters affirmatively to program public issues or to treat them fairly when programmed. The former alternative was not considered by Congress, and, when fairness treatment was proposed and discussed, it was only in terms of "if" the broadcaster chose to air public issues. The latter alternative was indeed proposed, debated, and even passed, but always was rejected in the end.

Just as clearly, Congress did not prohibit the FRC or the FCC from requiring balanced public affairs presentation under the very broad "public interest, convenience, and necessity" standard.

No such restriction appears in the statutes, and none were specifically discussed in debate.[97] In fact, there are statements by congressmen demonstrating deference to the Commission in developing regulations as it began to function.

Of critical importance in this regard are the problems Congress was concerned about when it passed the radio legislation. As I have mentioned, issues of frequency scarcity, the potential for informing the public on important public issues, and partisan control of the marketplace of ideas were key concerns during this period. By creating the FRC and FCC to see that the airwave resource was used as a public trust, as opposed to private property, Congress intended to deal with these problems. Those who were privileged to use the scarce airwave resource would have to do so in accord with the public interest. The fairness doctrine and the idea of providing balanced public affairs presentation have been developed to meet the problems of airwave scarcity and partisan broadcaster control and the need to inform the American public. There were indeed unsuccessful legislative attempts to tack on explicit fairness language to the radio acts. But in light of the broad "public interest, convenience, and necessity" standard, the deference in the debates to the development of regulations by the FRC and FCC, the 1932 bill including a fairness mandate that most congressmen agreed did not change the substantive law, and the problems the radio legislation addressed, there is support for the Supreme Court's opinion of the late 1960s that the FCC could impose the fairness doctrine based on the "statutory authority" of the public interest standard in the 1934 Act.[98]

VI. DEBATING THE DOCTRINE'S BIRTHDATE:
EARLY FRC AND FCC ACTIVITY

Despite the lack of specific statutory mandate, the FRC and FCC proceeded to fashion the fairness doctrine based on the "public interest, convenience, and necessity" standard. There is substantial disagreement over precisely when the fairness doctrine was set forth by the commissions. The United States Supreme Court maintains that the doctrine's twofold duty was imposed by the Federal Radio Commission "on broadcasters since the outset,"[99] an opinion also held by the Federal Communications Commission.[100] Authoritative commentators reinforce the conclusion that the doctrine had an early start. Former FCC Commissioner Houser has written that "almost immediately" after the FRC was established "it became apparent that inherent in the public interest standard was a requirement that the successful applicant provide fairness in the treatment of matters selected for broadcast,"[101] and Professor Barrow maintains that there was a "substantial history of the fairness doctrine" even before 1941.[102]

Other sources see a less substantial early development, claiming, as Professor Kahn does, that pre-1949 cases provide only the "glimmerings of 'fairness'"[103] or that they developed the "underlying rationale for the Doctrine" that was "enunciated" in 1949.[104] Still other commentators see little or no connection between early FRC and FCC cases and the fairness doctrine. Attorney Jonathan Blake's opinion in the FEDERAL COMMUNICATIONS BAR JOURNAL that "the early Federal Radio Commission and FCC cases did not stand for a fairness principle, or justify broad commission regulation,"[105] is echoed by former FCC Commissioner Robinson's view that to interpret early FRC opinions as handing down a fairness doctrine is to put "a gloss on its early decisions."[106] Even Professor Barron, a defender of the doctrine, has written that it was not until 1941 "that the fairness doctrine received its first tentative formulation by the Commission."[107] My own review of FCC, FRC, and court materials leads me to conclude that the affirmative part of the fairness doctrine, part one, did not surface until the 1940s. However, part two, calling for program balance, does have roots in pre-1940 actions of the FRC and FCC.

VII. GREAT LAKES BROADCASTING

Emphasis on a concept essential to the fairness doctrine is found in the FRC's SECOND ANNUAL REPORT, in which the Commission declared that the number of persons wishing to broadcast was far greater than the number of channels available. In deciding who should be allocated a channel, the Commission stressed that, "The emphasis must be first and foremost on the interest, the convenience, and the necessity of the listening public and not on the interest, convenience, or necessity of the individual broadcaster or the advertiser."[108] And on its questionnaire sent to all applicants for high-frequency broadcasting licenses, the Commission demanded "convincing reasons why such station will be in the interest and of value to the public," and a description of the "nature of programs" to be broadcast.[109]

But it is in its THIRD ANNUAL REPORT, in the case of *Great Lakes Broadcasting,*[110] that the FRC outlined the elements of and basis for part two of the fairness doctrine. In *Great Lakes* the FRC discussed the items the Commission would consider in deciding which radio applicant to license. Among the key considerations set forth by the FRC were the following:

> The emphasis is on the listening public. . . . In so far as a program consists of discussion of public questions, *public interest requires ample play for the free and fair competition of opposing views,* and the commission believes that the principle applies not only to addresses by political candidates but to all discussion of issues of importance to the public. . . .
>
> There is no room for the operation of broadcasting stations exclusively by or in the private interests of individuals or groups so far as the nature of the programs is concerned. There is not room in the broadcast band for every school of thought, religious, political, social, and economic, each to have its separate broadcasting station, its mouthpiece in the ether. If franchises are extended to some it gives them an unfair advantage over others, and results in a corresponding cutting down of general public service stations. It favors the interests and desires of a portion of the listening public at the expense of the rest. Propaganda stations . . . are not consistent with the most beneficial sort of discussion of public questions. As a general rule, postulated on the laws of nature *as well as on the standard of public interest, convenience, or necessity,* particular doctrines, creeds, and beliefs must find their way into the market of ideas by the existing public-service stations, and if they are of sufficient importance to the listening public, the microphone will undoubtedly be available. *If it is not, a well founded complaint will receive the careful consideration of the commission in its future action with reference to the station complained of.*[111]

The FRC in *Great Lakes* is clearly telling broadcasters that "In so far as" they air public issues, the Commission expects them to provide "fair competition" for contrasting views. Their performance in this regard would be reviewed at license renewal time under the "public interest" standard.[112] For radio stations, whose very existence depends on licensing, declarations of licensing standards have critical significance. Although the declaration differs from the present doctrine in not suggesting Commission action on complaints during the term of the license, and in the precise wording of "ample opportunity" and "issues of importance to the public," the requirement of balanced presentation of such issues is in essence what later became part two of the fairness doctrine.[113] In fact, one interpretation of the demand that "particular doctrines, creeds, and beliefs must find their way into the market of ideas" is that broadcasters must affirmatively broadcast diverse public issues. The latter interpretation is certainly not as clear as the former, but it does foreshadow part one of the fairness doctrine.

VIII. *TRINITY, KFKB, AND CHICAGO*

Three early cases in which the concept of fairness played a part are *Trinity Methodist Church,*[114] *KFKB Broadcasting,*[115] and *Chicago Federation of Labor.*[116] In *Trinity,* a Los Angeles station, KGEF, owned by the Reverend Dr. Shuler, had been denied renewal of its license by the FRC. The basis for nonrenewal was the content of KGEF's programming. After extensive FRC examination and hearings, it was revealed that the station had attacked judges and tried to influence the outcome of various trials, made unsubstantiated charges against a labor organization and the Board of Health, discussed prostitution, and made disparaging remarks about Catholics and Jews. When called upon to justify some of these matters, Shuler's only response was that "the statements expressed his own sentiments."[117] The Court of Appeals ruled that, in carrying out its statutory "public interest" obligations, the FRC had a "duty" to take notice of an applicant's previous use of his license and that its decision in KGEF's case was neither arbitrary nor capricious under public interest standards.[118] The court rejected the station's claim that its First Amendment rights were violated, declaring that, although prior restraint was prohibited under First Amendment guarantees, subsequent punishment, such as radio license denial, was not.[119]

The *KFKB* case involved another individual with a medical prefix to his name, Dr. J. R. Brinkley. Dr. Brinkley had been part owner of and the guiding hand behind a radio station in Kansas.

The FRC denied Brinkley a new license at renewal time, based on two major considerations. First, Dr. Brinkley had been diagnosing and prescribing treatment for listeners over the air based solely on letters they mailed in.[120] This practice was inimical to the public health and safety, and not in the "public interest."[121] Second, mainly because of a pharmaceutical association that sold drugs prescribed over the air by Brinkley, and Brinkley's constant pushing of his own medical views for profit, the station operation was "conducted only in the personal interests of Dr. John R. Brinkley." The Commission declared that the interest of "the listening public is paramount, and may not be subordinated to the interests of the station licensee."[122] The Court of Appeals held that the FRC's action was within its authority under the "public interest, convenience, or necessity" standard of the act. It further stressed that the number of available frequencies is limited and that "there is not room in the broadcast band for every business or school of thought."[123] Radio stations were consequently "impressed with a public interest," and the Commission had to consider the character and quality of the radio service being rendered. To KFKB's cries of censorship, the Court answered that the FRC had not censored prior to broadcast but had only exercised its undoubted right to review past conduct.

In *Chicago Federation,* a station applied for a modification of its broadcasting license to increase its power and hours of operation, on the ground that it broadcast programs of interest to organized labor. The Chicago Federation insisted that there was a large enough membership in its national labor organization to warrant the allocation by the FRC "of a frequency to be used for the exclusive benefit of organized labor."[124] The Commission disagreed. It declared that, if organized labor received a special frequency, many other groups could rightfully demand a similar privilege, yet there were not enough frequencies available for the various groups. The FRC concluded that, since only limited frequencies were available, "there is no place for a station catering to any group . . . all stations should cater to the general public and serve public interest as against group or class interest."[125] The Court of Appeals affirmed.[126]

These three cases were all extreme situations.[127] A minister was broadcasting defamatory and vicious accusations, a doctor was pushing his questionable diagnoses and drugs on citizens for profit, and a labor organization wanted to use a station to broadcast its own propaganda. But these cases do represent a firm FRC statement that the limited air space is to be used to benefit all segments of the public, not a private interest. Beyond this, there are the seeds of a fairness concept in *Trinity* and *Chicago*. The minister was not being fair in his one-sided presentations, and the Federation of Labor would not be fair in its exclusion of other viewpoints. The cases also illustrate that the FRC was willing to deny license renewal or modification based on one-sided, selfish program content, and this action would be affirmed by the courts.

Great Lakes is the earliest FRC case that discussed with some degree of clarity the requirements of presenting contrasting sides of public issues that a broadcaster chooses to air. *Trinity, KFKB,* and *Chicago* do not address this fairness concept directly, but taken together with *Great Lakes,* the early FRC cases reflect an FRC declaration that broadcasters are to use their licenses to benefit the public. They also indicate the FRC's view that, if public issues are discussed, the public interest statutory provision requires that balanced views be presented. No fairness procedures were specified nor was affirmative public affairs presentation required. At this point in time, only the crude fairness concept enunciated in *Great Lakes* was in existence. Although no licensee was refused renewal based specifically on a failure to broadcast contrasting views, the potential was there, at least in extreme cases.

That the FRC regarded balanced public issue presentation as a requirement is further substantiated by its unqualified backing of the 1932 congressional amendment that included a fairness provision. As discussed *supra,* all agreed that the amendment provided no change in substantive radio law. In light of the *Great Lakes* statement and the FRC failure to renew licenses in extreme situations, the congressional reenactment of the 1927 public interest, equal opportunity, and censorship provisions into the 1934 Communications Act takes on added significance. This congressional action, which left the previous administrative policy untouched, reinforces the interpretation that the 1934 Act authorized fairness doctrine activity.

IX. SOLIDIFYING PART TWO AND
BEGINNING PART ONE

The Federal Communications Commission continued development of the rudimentary fairness concept developed by the Federal Radio Commission under the "public interest, convenience, and necessity" standard. In 1938, in *Young People's Ass'n*[128] the FCC faced an applicant who proposed to use its station primarily to preach the fundamentalist interpretation of the Bible. Although some nonpartisan programming on civic and charitable topics would be broadcast, the applicant stated that religious broadcasts would be allowed only in accord with its own tenets and beliefs. Citing *Chicago Federation,* and quoting language from *Great Lakes* and *KFKB,* the FCC refused to grant the license. It stated that, if a station is to be devoted primarily to one purpose and is to serve as a mouthpiece for one organization, "it cannot be said to be serving the general public."[129] The FCC declared that in light of airwave scarcity, it "has accordingly considered that the interests of the listening public are paramount to the interests of the individual applicant in determining whether public interest would best be served by granting an application."[130] A one-sided presentation of viewpoint was simply unacceptable.[131]

In 1940 the FCC made the most direct statement to date of broadcasters' responsibilities under the fairness concept. In that year's ANNUAL REPORT, the Commission stressed that "broadcast stations have the duty of serving public interest, convenience, and necessity. The discretion left to the broadcasters in the selection of who may use the facilities and the conditions with respect to such use is subject to this legal requirement. In carrying out the obligation to render a public service, *stations are required to furnish well-rounded rather than one-sided discussions of public questions. The duty of serving the public interest* does not, however, imply any requirement that the use of broadcast facilities shall be afforded to the particular individual or group."[132] Appearing under a section titled *No Censorship,* the positioning of the statement clearly indicates that the FCC did not consider imposition of the fairness duty as censorship or a First Amendment infringement of broadcasters' rights.

The year after this ANNUAL REPORT statement, the FCC

resoundingly affirmed a licensee's obligation to broadcast balanced coverage of public issues in the *Mayflower* case.[133] At issue was Mayflower Broadcasting Corporation's construction permit application for a radio station using a frequency already allocated to WAAB, a licensee of the Yankee Network, Inc. Yankee Network was simultaneously applying for a renewal of its license, and the Commission consequently reviewed the requests together. After hearings, proposed findings, argument, and reargument,[134] the Commission denied Mayflower's application due to lack of adequate financial backing for the corporation and misrepresentation to the Commission of current solvency in Mayflower's application. Yankee Network's license was renewed, but not automatically. The reasons for the Commission's hesitance are the focal point of its fairness declaration.

The record showed that in 1937 and 1938 the editor-in-chief of WAAB's news service had broadcast editorials in favor of various political candidates and "supporting one side or another of various questions in public controversy . . . [N]o pretense was made at objective, impartial reporting."[135] WAAB's actions, said the FCC, "revealed a serious misconception of its *duties and functions under the law.*"[136] In light of airwave scarcity, a broadcast facility could not be dedicated to partisan ends. "A truly free radio cannot be used to advocate the causes of the licensee. It cannot be used to support the candidacies of his friends. It cannot be devoted to the support of principles he happens to regard most favorably. In brief, the broadcaster cannot be an advocate."[137]

WAAB had violated the Commission's nonadvocacy requirements. At a more fundamental level, it had failed to present the public with differing sides of public issues.

> Radio can serve as an instrument of democracy only when devoted to communication of information and the exchange of ideas fairly and objectively presented. . . . Freedom of speech on the radio must be broad enough to provide full and equal opportunity for the presentation to the public of all sides of public issues. Indeed, *as one licensed to operate in a public domain the licensee has assumed the obligation of presenting all sides of important public questions, fairly, objectively and without bias. The public interest—not the private—is paramount. These requirements are inherent in the conception of public*

interest set up by the Communications Act as the criterion of regulation. While the day to day decisions applying these *requirements* are
the licensee's responsibility, the ultimate duty to review generally the
course of conduct of the station over a period of time and *to take
appropriate action thereon is vested in the Commission.*[138]

The *Mayflower* decision is most well known for its nonadvocacy policy statement, subsequently called "the *Mayflower* doctrine." But the decision clearly sets forth part two of the fairness
doctrine, the obligation of a licensee who presents important public
questions to present different sides fairly. It emphatically states that
this is a legal requirement, based on the public interest standard of
the Communications Act, and that its fulfillment will be reviewed
by the Commission.[139]

The decision also appears to take the *Great Lakes* implication of a part one requirement one step further. A licensee "has
assumed the obligation of presenting all sides of important public
questions." This language can be interpreted to mean that licensees
have an affirmative obligation to program public issues as part of
their broadcast service.[140] It foreshadowed *United Broadcasting
Company,* decided four years later.

United Broadcasting,[141] a case largely ignored by fairness
doctrine commentators, represents the first definitive statement by
the FCC that broadcasters have an affirmative obligation to present
important public issues. Several labor groups in Columbus, Ohio,
had petitioned against the renewal of a license for the local radio
station, WHKC. The petition was based on the station's alleged
policy of not selling time to parties it disagreed with for programs
soliciting memberships or discussing controversial subjects.[142]

Subsequent to the petition, the labor groups and the station
worked out an agreement changing WHKC's policies, and they
filed a joint motion to adopt the new policy and dismiss the previous
proceeding. As part of the policy the station agreed to make time
available "primarily on a sustaining basis, but also on a commercial
basis, for the full and free discussion of issues of public importance,
including controversial issues . . . in order that broadcasting may
achieve its full possibilities as a significant medium for the dissemination of news, ideas, and opinions."[143] The station agreed to see
that its "broadcasts on controversial issues, considered on an overall basis, maintain a fair balance among the various points of view,

i.e., over the weeks and months it will maintain such a balance."[144] The station and labor groups thought the agreement set forth the duties of a licensee with respect to "the availability of time for discussion of issues of public importance" and "the maintenance of an overall program balance."[145]

The FCC agreed with the parties that such a policy did fulfill licensee responsibilities under the Act. The Commission explicitly stated that it was *"the duty of each station licensee to be sensitive to the problems of public concern in the community and to make sufficient time available, on a nondiscriminatory basis, for full discussion thereof,* without any type of censorship which would undertake to impose the views of the licensee upon the material to be broadcast."[146] Selling no time for "the discussion of controversial public issues" was "inconsistent with the concept of public interest established by the Communications Act as the criterion of radio regulations."[147]

These statements by the Commission mandating licensees to devote time (donated or sold) to public issues and its approval of a licensee policy that included such a provision culminate the implications of *Great Lakes* and *Mayflower*. The firm roots of part one of the fairness doctrine can thus be dated from 1945 and *United Broadcasting*.

United Broadcasting also reflects another major concept to be made more explicit in later cases. That is the Commission's looking at fairness in a licensee's "over-all" programming as opposed to a single show. WHKC would treat contrasting sides of issues over the "weeks and months" but not necessarily on any one show. This was acceptable to the Commission.

The requirement of affirmative public issue presentation was made even more explicit in a publication issued by the FCC in 1946 entitled PUBLIC SERVICE RESPONSIBILITY OF BROADCAST LICENSEES.[148] Popularly referred to as the "Blue Book," it reviewed program service requirements of licensees and spelled out procedural changes in license application and renewal. The Commission listed four program service factors relevant to the public interest that it would give "particular consideration to" in granting and renewing broadcast licenses.[149] Among the four was the airing of programs that discussed public issues.[150] The FCC emphasized that "one matter of primary concern . . . can be made by an overall

statement of policy. . . . This is the question of the *quantity* of time
which should be made available for the discussion of public issues."[151] The Commission realized that a vigorous presentation of a
viewpoint would offend some listeners. But to avoid such presentations completely would thwart the effectiveness of broadcasting in a
democracy. The Commission was particularly perturbed by a study
showing that, out of 842 stations during a five-month period in
1941, only 288 originated any programs dealing with major foreign
policy issues facing the nation.[152] The Commission warned that
"the *public interest clearly requires* that an adequate amount of
time be made available for the discussion of public issues; and the
Commission, in determining whether a station has served the public
interest, will take into consideration the amount of time which has
been or will be devoted to the discussion of public issues."[153] Part
one of the fairness doctrine had been firmly entrenched.[154]

Four months after the Blue Book was released, the Commission handed down another important fairness decision, *Robert
Harold Scott.*[155] In that case an atheist petitioned the Commission
to revoke the licenses of three San Francisco stations because they
refused to grant him time to broadcast views in opposition to their
religious programming, which he claimed directly and indirectly
attacked atheism. The FCC refused to rule on Scott's complaint,
because it considered the issue one of broad scope involving more
than just the three stations. However, it set down important dicta in
making three points. First, it incorporated into one statement the
two fairness doctrine concepts that had been developing. A licensee
has a "duty to make time available for the presentation of opposing
views on current controversial issues of public importance."[156]
Licensees have to both "make time available" and present "opposing views." The Commission also set down a definition of public
issues to be covered that survives to this day, i.e., "controversial
issues of public importance."

Second, the FCC made the important point that time should
be made available even for ideas that have a "high degree of unpopularity."[157] Freedom of speech over the radio "must be extended as readily to ideas which we disapprove or abhor as to ideas
we approve."[158] The fairness doctrine was not applicable only to
ideas held by sizable segments of the community. In fact, the Commission spoke in terms of "access" to broadcasting: "free speech

can be as effectively denied by denying access to the public means of making expression effective—whether public streets, parks, meeting halls, or the radio—as by legal restraints or punishment of the speaker."[159]

And third, the FCC indicated that an organization or idea could become a controversial public issue worthy of fairness air time if it was attacked by others.[160]

As the previous pages have shown, by 1949 the rationale underlying the doctrine had been substantially developed. Use of the airwaves had been established as a public trust, and it was decided that the scarcity of the airwave resource made it impossible for every applicant to control one frequency exclusively. This scarcity, it was argued, required that the frequency be used to broadcast the views of others. There was a fear of the power of any one broadcaster influencing public opinion for partisan ends, as well as a recognition of the public's right to hear diversified and controversial public affairs information and opinion.[161]

The requirement that, if a licensee chose to broadcast public issues, it could not air only one side of the issues originated in 1929 with *Great Lakes* and was made definitive in *Mayflower Broadcasting* in 1941. Although part one of the fairness doctrine, requiring affirmative public affairs presentation, had a later start than the balancing concept of part two, by the mid-1940s, with *United Broadcasting* and the Blue Book, it too had become a part of the regulatory constellation. Despite the fact that Congress had failed to pass fairness doctrine type provisions in 1927 and 1934, the FRC and FCC had proceeded to base their fairness mandates on the "public interest, convenience, or necessity" statutory authorization.

The 1940 *Mayflower* decision had created a "storm of controversy."[162] The National Association of Broadcasters, local stations, labor groups, and individual citizens opposed the supposed ban on editorializing as an invasion of free speech, and there were demands from all quarters for clarification of exactly what the *Mayflower* decision meant.[163] The Commission, reacting to the "apparent confusion" about licensee editorializing, held eight days of hearings in 1948 on its own motion. These hearings led to the issuance of a definitive and comprehensive statement on the fairness doctrine, the *Report on Editorializing by Broadcast Licensees*,[164] which was issued in 1949.

X. THE 1949 EDITORIALIZING REPORT

The *Report on Editorializing* included four major elements. First, it set forth the primary basis for the fairness doctrine. Second, it defined both parts of the doctrine. Third, it made clear that editorializing by broadcast licensees was permissible. And fourth, it set down a number of specifics on how the doctrine should be implemented.

The key reason for the doctrine was eloquently set forth in the following paragraph, and reflects the ideas Senator Howell had expressed over 20 years before:

> It is axiomatic that one of the most vital questions of mass communication in a democracy is the development of an informed public opinion through the public dissemination of news and ideas concerning the vital public issues of the day. Basically, it is in recognition of the great contribution which radio can make in the advancement of this purpose that portions of the radio spectrum are allocated to that form of radio communications known as radiobroadcasting. Unquestionably, then, the standard of public interest, convenience and necessity as applied to radiobroadcasting must be interpreted in the light of this basic purpose. The Commission has consequently recognized the necessity for licensees to devote a reasonable percentage of their broadcast time to the presentation of news and programs devoted to the consideration and discussion of public issues of interest in the community served by the particular station. And we have recognized, with respect to such programs, the paramount right of the public in a free society to be informed and to have presented to it for acceptance or rejection the different attitudes and viewpoints concerning these vital and often controversial issues which are held by the various groups which make up the community. It is this right of the public to be informed, rather than any right on the part of the Government, any broadcast licensee or any individual member of the public to broadcast his own particular views on any matter, which is the foundation stone of the American system of broadcasting.[165]

It is the right of the public to be informed on vital public issues in a democracy which requires the fairness doctrine. In fact, the informational function, and consequently the fairness doctrine, which is geared to ensuring that function, is described as the "foundation stone" of broadcasting and the reason for allocating air space to radio. This "paramount right" of the public has priority over any claims of the government, licensees, or particular individuals for access to express their viewpoints. The Commission recognized that radio licensees had First Amendment protection, but, in light of the scarcity of the airwave resource, some interference with this right was necessary. "Freedom of speech" would be enhanced by honoring the right of the American people to be informed over radio.[166] Thus, although the public right to know was based on the "public interest" standard, the Commission implied it would also further First Amendment interests.[167]

Inherent in the concept of preventing any one licensee or other party from controlling the radio frequencies is also the recognition and fear of an individual or group controlling the marketplace of ideas.[168] Thus inextricably linked with the objective of keeping the public informed was the goal of keeping any one entity from unduly influencing the public via the powerful radio medium.

Both parts of the fairness doctrine were directly set forth in the *Report.* Part one, calling for affirmative presentation of news and public issues programs, is explicitly discussed in paragraph six, excerpted above. The Commission repeated the part one obligation at four other places in its opinion,[169] including paragraph seven, which describes an "affirmative responsibility on the part of broadcast licensees to provide a reasonable amount of time for the presentation over their facilities of programs devoted to the discussion and consideration of public issues."[170] Broadcasters cannot simply adopt a policy of not refusing to air opposing views of public issues on request, but must "encourage and implement the broadcast" of, and play a "conscious and positive role" in presenting, opposing viewpoints on such issues.

The fairness doctrine part two obligation was just as explicitly set forth: "the Commission has made clear that in such presentation of news and comment the public interest requires that the licensee must operate on a basis of overall fairness, making his facilities available for the expression of the contrasting views of all responsible elements in the community[171] on the various issues which arise."[172]

A third element of the 1949 *Report* was its reversal of the supposed editorial ban imposed by *Mayflower.* The Commission considered licensee editorials—whether directly on behalf of a station or indirectly through use of a spokesman partial to station views—as just one of several types of public issue presentations. Those editorials, along with all public affairs programming, had to be balanced in accord with the two-fold fairness doctrine mandate. Station editorializing, when balanced by other programming, is "not contrary to the public interest."[173]

The fourth major element of the *Report on Editorializing* was its description of how licensees should enforce the fairness doctrine. There is a good deal of force in Commissioner Webster's "Additional Views" that a licensee reading the 1949 *Report* is left in a "quandary and a state of confusion in that he must follow with his own interpretation . . . an involved academic legal treatise to determine what he can or cannot do in his day-to-day operation."[174] The *Report* consists of 21 numbered but unlabelled paragraphs. Implementation steps are scattered throughout and mentioned in passing as parts of various paragraphs. A careful reading of the *Report*, however, reveals the following licensee instructions: the licensee cannot delegate his fairness doctrine responsibility to a network or other party;[175] it is the licensee who decides what issues are to be presented, the spokesman who will present them, and the format in which they will appear;[176] fairness balancing must be obtained in a licensee's overall programming as opposed to any one show;[177] a broadcast discussion originally thought not to be controversial may arouse opposition and require balancing;[178] an attack on a specific individual or group may require response time for the attacked party;[179] a licensee cannot "stack the cards" by selecting spokesmen of one view at the expense of another;[180] the news cannot be deliberately slanted or distorted;[181] licensees are protected from arbitrary action by procedural safeguards in the Communications Act and Administrative Procedure Act and by appeal to the courts;[182] and the public issues to be aired are variously described as "controversial," "public" and "of interest and importance to the community."[183] Of particular importance was the Commission's statement that there was no "all embracing formula" for ensuring fairness doctrine compliance, and that licensees would be judged on a standard of "reasonableness."[184] The standard of public interest is not so rigid that an honest mistake or error in judgment on the part of a licensee will be or should be condemned where his overall record demonstrates a reasonable effort to provide balanced presentation of comment and opinion on such issues."[185]

The Commission went no further in providing guidance to licensees than these general statements. Details would have to await case-by-case developments.

So in this four-to-one watershed decision,[186] the Commission reaffirmed the fairness doctrine obligation that had begun developing in *Great Lakes* 20 years before. There was no doubt that radio and television licensees[187] had a two-fold duty to present controversial public issues, and to do so fairly. And, for the first time, they had a packet of instructions to follow, even if they were vague and hard to pinpoint. In what was by now a familiar pattern, however, the Commission failed to analyze in any depth either the statutory basis for the fairness doctrine or the First Amendment implications; it settled for assertions that the doctrine was authorized under the "public interest, convenience, or necessity" standard, period.[188]

XI. 1949-59: SLOW DEVELOPMENT

Between 1949 and 1959, the year the Communications Act was amended with a fairness doctrine provision, the Commission slowly developed licensee fairness doctrine obligations. The language of the *Report on Editorializing* was constantly referred to, and the Commission did not stray far from what it had enunciated in 1949. However, there was expansion of the doctrine in several areas, and the doctrine was increasingly applied to the fast-growing medium of television.

Among the fairness developments during this period were Commission actions indicating that fairness required presentation of conflicting views on either the same evening or another evening shortly after the original broadcast and at approximately the same time;[189] that labeling a broadcast as a report to the people by elected representatives did not exempt the broadcast from fairness requirements, if controversial public issues were discussed;[190] that licensees cannot let a spokesman for one point of view veto the presentation of another point of view by not participating in a forum type program;[191] and that the establishment of a National Fair Employment Practices Commission constitutes a controversial issue of public importance.[192]

One theme that ran through many of the cases during the decade was a Commission emphasis that licensees were actively to implement the presentation of opposing views to rebut one side of a controversial issue that had already been broadcast.[193] In *WSOC Broadcasting Company*,[194] which exemplifies this emphasis, a North Carolina TV station had presented programming opposed to subscription television, including a half-hour skit entitled *Now It Can Be Tolled*, a 15-minute film clip of a U.S. Representative, and 43 spot announcements urging listeners to write their congressmen about the issue.[195] Approximately one month after this anti-subscription programming was completed, WSOC–TV sent a telegram to the three leading subscription television groups offering them joint use of its studios at a mutually agreeable time for a free broadcast presenting pro-subscription arguments. One of the three groups refused, and a show presenting opposing views was never broadcast.[196]

The Commission, on receipt of a listener complaint, reviewed the facts. It considered subscription TV a "matter of public controversy" requiring fairness treatment.[197] It concluded that WSOC–TV's efforts to present pro-subscription TV views were inadequate. It declared that a licensee has "an affirmative duty to seek out, aid and encourage the broadcast of opposing views by responsible persons" and that WSOC–TV "did not make any timely effort to secure the presentation of the other side of the issue by responsible representatives."[198] Thus, the 1949 *Report*'s call for licensees to play a "conscious and positive role" in presenting contrasting viewpoints was further elucidated. WSOC–TV had simply not presented a reasonable explanation of why it was unable to air pro-subscription views. It was necessary to do more than send telegrams to three potential opposing spokesmen one month after the original broadcasts.[199]

XII. THE 1959 FAIRNESS AMENDMENT: LEGISLATIVE HISTORY

Between 1934 and 1959 there had been congressional efforts to amend the Communications Act with fairness type provisions.[200] But it was not until 1959 that the act was changed to include such a provision. A key purpose of the fairness language eventually adopted was to warn broadcasters and the FCC that the new bill's exemption of news type programs from the equal time requirement did not disturb the Commission's fairness doctrine requirements for the news. However, my reading of the 1959 legislative history of this provision leads me to conclude that, in so doing, Congress gave statutory recognition and approval to the doctrine.

The proceedings leading to the 1959 amendments were prompted by the FCC's ruling in the *Lar Daly* case.[201] Lar Daly, a seemingly perpetual candidate for elective office in Illinois, was a legally qualified candidate for Mayor of Chicago, along with Mayor Richard Daley. Daly demanded equal time on a Chicago TV station, claiming that the station had allowed Mayor Daley to use its facilities, including exposure in a newsreel of the Mayor greeting the President of Argentina at the Chicago airport. The FCC, reviewing Lar Daly's complaint, decided that the newsreel depiction was a "use" of the broadcast station under section 315 and required it to offer Lar Daly equal time.[202] If the *Lar Daly* ruling was allowed to stand, TV and radio news operations might have to cease covering political candidates on news shows altogether during campaign periods, or they would be subject to an administrative nightmare. Senate hearings on section 315 amendments began less than a week after the Commission handed down *Lar Daly*.[203]

Emerging from the June 1959 Senate hearings, at which 35 witnesses testified, was S. 2424.[204] In essence, the bill exempted various kinds of news programs, such as the one Mayor Daley had appeared on, from equal time requirements. However, the Report from the Senate Committee on Interstate and Foreign Commerce bluntly stated on page 13:

Fear has been expressed that the adoption of legislation creating special categories of exemptions from section 315 would tend to weaken *the present requirement of fair treatment of public issues.* The Committee desires to make it crystal clear that the discretion provided by this legislation shall not exempt licensees who broadcast such news . . . from objective presentation thereof in the public interest. In recommending this legislation, the Committee does not diminish or affect in any way *Federal Communications Commission policy or existing law which holds that a licensee's statutory obligation to serve the public interest is to include the broad encompassing duty of providing a fair cross section of opinion in the station's coverage of public affairs and matters of public controversy.*[205]

On the floor, Senator William Proxmire was not content to leave the fairness obligation buried in Report language, and he offered an amendment specifying that nothing in the proposed legislation would change the intent of Congress under the act that "all sides of public controversies shall be given as equal an opportunity to be heard as is practically possible."[206] At the request of Senator Pastore, Chairman of the Subcommittee that had reported the bill, its floor manager, and Senate conferee at the House-Senate conference, the amendment was changed so that "as fair an opportunity" was substituted for "as equal an opportunity."[207]

The floor discussion of the amendment, like the Senate Report itself, makes clear that the Senate recognized the FCC's fairness doctrine as an existing requirement under the act's public interest standard. The amendment would simply reaffirm in explicit terms what was already law.

Senator Proxmire, in introducing the amendment, declared that the broadcaster should "consider all sides of public controversies, and make certain that not only the conservative, or not only the liberal viewpoints or ideas are expressed, but that the public has a chance to hear both sides, in fact all sides, and to be more specific so that this bill cannot be construed in any way to limit the responsibility of broadcasters to present all viewpoints, including the responsibility upon the appearances of qualified candidates on TV or radio."[208] He agreed with Senator Douglas that the purpose of the amendment was to make binding the fairness declaration at page 13 of the Senate Committee's Report.[209]

When Senator Pastore proclaimed, "I understand the amendment to be *a statement or codification of the standards of fairness.* I understand that the Commission is *now obliged by existing law and policy to abide by the standards of fairness,*"[210] there was no disagreement on the floor of the Senate.

The recognition of existing law as already requiring fairness is made even more plain in the following dialogue:

> Mr. Hartke: As I understand, this amendment does not deal with candidates, but deals with the general purpose and interpretation of the *Communications Act* itself.
> Mr. Pastore: *That is correct,* the amendment has nothing to do with legally qualified candidates, but is merely a requirement that

broadcasters shall live and shall abide by the rule of fairness in connection with all controversial issues, so as to bring them, in so far as possible, fairly to the attention of the public as a whole. *Of course, that is the law today.*[211]

H.R. 7985, which the House of Representatives substituted for S. 2424 and sent to conference, did not include a fairness provision.[212] However, there was some House recognition that the fairness principle was embodied in the Communications Act. In response to a query on what the House bill did with respect to broadcast editorials, Congressman Harris, Chairman of the House Committee that reported the bill and, like his counterpart in the Senate, its floor manager and representative in conference, stated: *"The Communications Act places the responsibility for fairness upon the broadcaster.* He has got to come back for his license every three years, and then he has to give an accounting as to whether or not he has operated that station in the public interest. If he has not done so and has been *unfair,* that could very well be held against him in connection with the renewal of his license."[213]

The bill reported from the House–Senate conference modified the Proxmire amendment. The relevant language, which was adopted by both houses and became part of section 315, stated:

> Nothing in the foregoing sentence shall be construed as relieving broadcasters, in connection with the presentation of newscasts, news interviews, news documentaries, and on-the-spot coverage of news events, from *the obligation imposed upon them under this Act to operate in the public interest and to afford reasonable opportunity for discussion of conflicting views on issues of public importance.*[214]

In interpreting this language, the Conference Report declared that, "It is a restatement of the basic policy of the 'standard of fairness' which is imposed on broadcasters under the Communications Act of 1934."[215]

In explaining the conference recommendations on the floor of the Senate, Senator Pastore reiterated that the fairness provision would be "a continuing reminder *to the Federal Communications Commission* and *to the broadcasters alike"* of *"giving the people the right to have a full and complete disclosure of conflicting views on news of interest to the people of the country."*[216] And Senator Scott, Senate conferee, stated:

We have maintained very carefully the spirit of the Proxmire amendment, and I ought to point out what I do not think has yet been
explained, that the phrase "To afford reasonable opportunity for the
discussion of conflicting views on issues of public importance" does
not refer merely to political discussions as such or to opposing views of
political parties or of candidates. It is intended to encompass all
legitimate areas of public importance which are controversial, and
there are many, as we know, which pertain to medicine, to education,
and to other areas than political discussion, and it is intended that no
one point of view shall gain control over the airwaves to the exclusion
of another legitimate point of view.[217]

On the House floor, Chairman Harris warned the FCC and
licensees to comply with the fairness doctrine: "Now, just in case
anybody in the broadcasting industry or in the *Federal Communications Commission* . . . should get the idea that 'reins are off, you
can do what you want to,' we have accepted in the conference
substitute a provision similar to what was referred to as the Proxmire amendment in the other body . . . [W]e . . . *reaffirmed the
'standard of fairness' established under the Communications Act.*
Anyone trying to take advantage will be held accountable to the
Federal Communications Commission for his action."[218] To a
fellow representative's query on whether the standard of fairness
still applied despite the section 315 changes, and applied not "only
to political candidates, but issues and editorializing by licensees as
well," Harris replied, "The gentleman is eminently correct." Every
one of the conferees "agreed that the standard of fairness must
prevail."[219]

XIII. ANALYSIS OF THE 1959 LEGISLATIVE HISTORY

What effect does the 1959 amendment have on the fairness
doctrine? As stated previously, legislative histories must be seen in
perspective. Seldom, if ever, are they precise guides to legislative
intent. And here, the legislative activity was motivated by an equal
time problem in the *Lar Daly* case, not a fairness doctrine issue.
There was no extensive discussion of the fairness doctrine, its history, and its implications in either the hearings, the congressional
debates, or the legislative documents. As Senators Pastore and
Proxmire indicated in the original debate on the Proxmire amend-

ment, as Representative Harris pointed out in reporting on the conference results, as shown in the Senate report on S. 2424, and most importantly as is obvious from the statutory language, a key reason for the 1959 fairness provision was to warn broadcasters that the new equal time exemptions did not release them from fairness obligations in the exempted news categories. But to state, as one distinguished authority in the field has done, that "probably, Congress intended neither approval nor disapproval of (the fairness doctrine) but merely intended to ensure that section 315 should not interfere with it,"[220] misses the mark. In its very warning to broadcasters that they had fairness obligations Congress was affirming those obligations. And explicit recognition of the fairness doctrine as a requirement under the Communications Act is found in the remarks of the Senate and House members who chaired the reporting committees, were floor managers, and were conference representatives for the bill, the statements of Senator Proxmire, remarks by other conferees who engaged in floor debate, the Senate Report on S. 2424, and the Conference Report. Nowhere in the documents or in the floor comments was an objection made to the numerous assertions that the Communications Act requires a presentation of views on public issues, and a fair presentation.

The language of the amendment itself refers to the obligation imposed under "this Act,"[221] recognizing an already existing Communications Act fairness doctrine requirement. The language was not restricted, as it could have been, to this "section" and only the news exemptions there discussed. Continual administrative practice by an expert agency interpreting a statute undisturbed by Congress through the years is subject to great weight in interpreting the statute.[222] Here, Congress not only left the practice as it stood, but also explicitly approved it as reflected in the statutory language and legislative history. It appears that in 1959 Congress, as Senator Pastore stated on the Senate floor, "ratified and codified" the fairness doctrine. After 1959, the FCC would be able to reverse the thrust of fairness doctrine policy only at the risk of violating a statutory mandate. Other procedural means, such as requiring access during specific times of the week, might be imposed legitimately to satisfy fairness doctrine objectives under the statute. But the 1959 legislation appears to dictate that licensees must reasonably present contrasting sides of controversial public issues.

XIV. RECENT CONTROVERSY OVER THE EFFECT
OF THE 1959 AMENDMENT

Despite this background, some still questioned the effect of the 1959 amendment. Thus John Dean, later to become a famed Watergate figure, warned that, "the self-limiting language used and the uncertainty of the legislative history should be an interpretive caveat."[223] The FCC disagreed with such doubting and boldly declared that the 1959 amendment "endorsed"[224] and gave "specific statutory recognition,"[225] to its fairness doctrine.[226]

The United States Supreme Court addressed the issue of the effect of the 1959 amendment in the case of *Red Lion Broadcasting Company v. FCC*.[227] The *Red Lion* decision is well known for its declaration that the fairness doctrine is constitutional and does not violate the First Amendment rights of broadcasters. Here, the relevance of the case to the meaning of the 1959 statute should be noted.

The focus of the two cases considered in *Red Lion* was the fairness doctrine's personal attack and political editorial provisions. A key question raised was the statutory basis for the doctrine and the component rules. The Supreme Court, after citing that part of the 1959 amendment dealing with the fairness doctrine, stated, "This language makes it very plain that *Congress* in 1959 announced that the phrase 'public interest' which had been in the Act since 1927 *imposed a duty on broadcasters* to discuss both sides[228] of controversial public issues. In other words, the amendment vindicated the FCC's general view that the fairness doctrine inhered in the public interest standard."[229] Congress, said the Court, had "ratified" the FCC's fairness doctrine "with positive legislation."[230] The FCC's fairness doctrine construction of the public interest standard had been "expressly accepted" by Congress.[231] However, the Court did acknowledge that, "When the Congress ratified the FCC's implication of a fairness doctrine in 1959 it did not, of course, approve every past decision or pronouncement by the Commission on this subject, or give it a completely free hand for the future. The statutory authority does not go so far."[232]

Despite the Court's language indicating that the 1959 amendment mandated a fairness doctrine duty on licensees to be enforced by the Commission, the Court also suggested at several points in the decision that the fairness doctrine, the personal attack rules, and the political editorial rules were merely a "legitimate exercise of congressionally delegated authority"[233] by the FCC. Whether by congressional mandatory compulsion on licensees or by congressional authorization of FCC mandatory compulsion on licensees, it is obvious that Congress in 1959 was approving of the Commission's fairness doctrine. But the distinction is important. If the amendment compels the fairness doctrine, then the FCC cannot remove it without congressional approval. Just such a move was suggested in 1975 by Chairman Richard Wiley who wanted to "experiment" with eliminating the fairness doctrine for radio in a few major markets.[234] If, by the 1959 amendment, the Commission is simply authorized, and not compelled, to impose the doctrine, then the Commission could indeed suspend its enforcement if it deemed this to be in the public interest.

Dicta in later cases reinforce the major thrust of the *Red Lion* interpretation of the amendment as codifying and thus mandating the doctrine. In 1973, the Supreme Court outrightly declared that Congress "has imposed on all broadcast licensees" an "affirmative and independent statutory obligation to provide full and fair coverage of public issues,"[235] and in 1975 the District of Columbia Court of Appeals declared that the "Fairness Doctrine finds its source of authority in the language of 47 U.S.C. sec. 315(a) *specifically.* . . ."[236] In a 1976 D.C. Circuit case Judge Wright, speaking for the Court, stated that the doctrine, "which originally evolved under the general provisions of the Communications Act calling for regulation in the 'public interest' . . . has since received *explicit statutory enactment,* in the 1959 amendment."[237]

Despite the merit of the Wiley proposal, it could not be implemented without congressional approval. The text of the 1959 amendment—which is addressed to each individual licensee[238]—the legislative history, and the thrust of court interpretations indicate that the fairness doctrine is required by statute. A simple renunciation of the doctrine by the FCC, at least without some other structural mechanism to assure fair presentation of important public issues by each individual licensee,[239] would be violative of the 1959 amendment.[240]

XV. CONCLUDING REMARKS

As the preceding pages have indicated, the fairness doctrine had an extensive history before the explosion of fairness doctrine activity in the 1960s and 1970s. Even before issuance of the definitive *Report on Editorializing* in 1949, both parts of the doctrine had been defined, and the rationale for its existence had been set forth in the context of radio broadcasting.

Part two of the doctrine, the balancing requirement, had its origins in *Great Lakes Broadcasting,* a ruling by the Federal Radio Commission in 1929, and was reaffirmed in *Mayflower Broadcasting,* decided by the Federal Communications Commission in 1941. Part one of the doctrine, requiring licensees to devote a reasonable percentage of broadcast time to controversial issues of public importance, had a later start. Its roots may be traced to *United Broadcasting* and the Blue Book in the mid-1940s. The 1949 *Report on Editorializing* combined both parts in the most comprehensive discussion of the doctrine until issuance of the 1974 *Fairness Report.* The legislative capstone of this early fairness doctrine development occurred in 1959 when Congress codified the doctrine in an amendment to the Communications Act, doing what it had failed to do in 1927 and 1934, despite the urgings of various congressmen.

In its evolving definition of the part one obligation, the Commission gave no sign of the double standard in enforcement that was to be set forth in the 1970s in cases such as *Public Communications, Inc.* and *Patsy Mink*.[241] The part one and part two obligations were not spoken of in terms of separate judgmental standards. A person reading the early decisions would assume that the same reasonableness, good faith standard that applied to the part two obligation applied to the part one obligation. There was no indication that issues had to be more critical for the FCC to mandate coverage under part one than to mandate balancing under part two.[242]

It should be stressed that, despite the emphatic fairness doctrine declarations issued by the FRC and the FCC throughout the early years, and the professed fairness obligations of licensees under the public interest standards of the Communications Act, there was an almost total lack of enforcement of the doctrine. Only in the most extreme situations, as when Dr. Shuler used his frequency to attack judges and the Board of Health, to influence trials, and to disparage religious groups, without allowing a word of reply, did the Commission take action. When the FCC occasionally focused on a situation where the licensee had presented only one side of an issue unfairly, as when WSOC-TV failed to adequately present pro-subscription-TV views, it simply pointed out the mistake. And complaints for the most part were reviewed at renewal time. There was no effective in-term Commission enforcement.

The Commission failed to describe in any detail the fairness doctrine parameters licensees were to follow. How did one determine whether an issue was controversial or of public importance? What kind of balance in terms of total time division, frequency of broadcast, and time of day presentation was reasonable in airing contrasting views? The Commission provided no answers to questions such as these, preferring to let guidelines develop on a case-by-case basis. Licensees were left adrift in a sea of uncertainty as to precisely what was expected of them under the fairness doctrine. Such vague guidelines also were relevant to those members of the public who wanted increased or fairer public issue coverage. Without any set of guidelines, it was difficult to argue that a licensee was not in compliance with the fairness doctrine. The FCC also failed to articulate in any depth the statutory basis for the doctrine. It just assumed it had the power to promulgate the doctrine's requirements and did so. Although its conclusion was undoubtedly correct, one would expect at least an explanation of its legal authority to impose so important a responsibility.

Enforcement and statutory problems aside, by 1950 the rationale for imposing the fairness doctrine on broadcasters had been set forth in national radio conferences, congressional debates, and decisions by the courts, the FRC, and the FCC. The factual predicates on which the doctrine was based were the scarcity of the airwave resource and the assumption that this resource was owned by the public, making the licensee a public trustee. These predicates, combined with the democratic need to inform the American people about important public issues in a "free marketplace of ideas," the potential for powerful broadcasters to monopolize or influence the marketplace and to bias the information received by the American people, and the desire to offer some broadcast access in a general way to parties to express their own views, provided the rationale for imposition of the fairness doctrine on broadcast licensees in the United States.

Notes

1. The lengthiest discussion occurs in John Paul Sullivan, *Editorials and Controversy: The Broadcaster's Dilemma*, 32 GEO. WASH. L. REV. 719 (1964). Despite its imposing title, Thomas J. Houser, *The Fairness Doctrine—an Historical Perspective*, 47 NOTRE DAME LAWYER 550 (1972), devotes fewer than ten pages to pre-1959 fairness developments. Neither of these pieces discusses the origins of the fairness doctrine's part one requirement.

2. FRED W. FRIENDLY, THE GOOD GUYS, THE BAD GUYS AND THE FIRST AMENDMENT: FREE SPEECH VS. FAIRNESS IN BROADCASTING (1976).

3. WALTER B. EMERY, BROADCASTING AND GOVERNMENT: RESPONSIBILITIES AND REGULATIONS 23 (1971).

4. LLEWELLYN WHITE, THE AMERICAN RADIO 129 (1947).

5. FRANCIS CHASE, JR., SOUND AND FURY 19 (1942).

6. EDWARD A. HERRON, MIRACLE OF THE AIRWAVE, A HISTORY OF RADIO 130 (1969). Descriptions of radio growth during this period by other authors is equally enthusiastic. "In broadcasting, euphoria was at the controls." 1 ERIK BARNOUW, A TOWER IN BABEL, A HISTORY OF BROADCASTING IN THE UNITED STATES 91 (1966). "The Advent of Radio Broadcasting created one of the most extraordinary booms in the history of the American people." GLEASON L. ARCHER, HISTORY OF RADIO TO 1926, 241 (1938).

7. Emery, *supra* note 3, at 24.

8. 36 Stat. 629 (1910).

9. 37 Stat. 199 (1912).

10. Radio Act of 1912 sec. 4, 37 Stat. 199.

11. Hoover v. City Intercity Radio Co., 52 App. D.C. 339, 286 F. 1003 (D.C. Cir. 1923). The Court did state, however, that the Secretary could exercise discretion "in selecting a wave length, within the limitations prescribed in the statute, which, in his judgment, will result in the least possible interference," *Id.* at 342, 286 F. at 1006.

12. United States v. Zenith Radio Corp., 12 F.2d 614 (N.D. Ill. 1926).

13. 35 OP. ATT'Y GEN. 126(a) (1926).

14. *Id.* 126(b).

15. *Id.* 126(c).

16. *Id.*

17. Emery, *supra* note 3, at 22–23, 25–26.

18. *Id.* 25.

19. *Id.* Erik Barnouw in his radio history trilogy related that radio was also blamed by citizens for such things as "dizzy spells, changes in weather, and creaky floorboards." Barnouw, *supra* note 6, at 103. In Louisville, Kentucky, a farmer walked into a local radio station and declared, "Yesterday afternoon I took a walk across my farm. A flock of black-birds passed over. Suddenly one of them dropped dead. Your radio wave must have struck it. [Pause] Suppose that wave had struck me?" CREDO FITCH HARRIS, MICROPHONE MEMOIRS OF THE HORSE AND BUGGY DAYS OF RADIO 99 (1937). According to Francis Chase, "Commerce officials were like keystone comedy cops directing present-day traffic in Times Square. Mailbags heavy with complaints were delivered to the department each day. Some days more than 12,000 such letters were received—but the department was unable to take any positive action," Chase, *supra* note 5, at 21.

20. Chase, *supra* note 5, at 20. Trying to "disentangle" signals from simultaneously broadcasting stations could be "an evening's occupation." Barnouw, *supra* note 6, at 94. Edward Herron in his popular history of radio states, "The interference between stations could be summed up in a stepladder of words: annoyance, irritation and nightmare." Herron, *supra* note 6, at 130.

21. Emery, *supra* note 3, at 26.

22. White, *supra* note 4, at 129. *See also* Barnouw, *supra* note 6, at 92.

23. Emery, *supra* note 3, at 25.

24. Chase, *supra* note 5, at 21.

25. White, *supra* note 5, at 131.

26. DOCUMENTS OF AMERICAN BROADCASTING 33 (2d ed. Frank J. Kahn 1973).

27. White, *supra* note 4, at 131.

28. Red Lion Broadcasting Co. v. FCC, 395 U.S. 367 (1969).

29. Edward F. Sarno, Jr., *The National Radio Conferences,* 13 J. BROADCASTING 189, 190 (1969).

30. *Id.* at 191.

31. *Id.* at 192.

32. First National Radio Conference, Minutes of Department of Commerce Conference on Radio Telephony 4-5 (1922) (mimeographed).

33. Sarno, *supra* note 29, at 191.

34. H.R. 13773, 67th Cong. 4th Sess., introduced and referred to the Committee on the Mercant Marine and Fisheries, 64 CONG. REC. 1617 (1923).

35. H. R. REP. No. 1416, 67th Cong. 3d & 4th Sess. vol. 1, at 2 (1922, 1923).

36. Sarno, *supra* note 29, at 194.

37. Bureau of Navigation, Department of Commerce, RADIO SERVICE BULLETIN, Apr. 2, 1923, at 9, 10.

38. H.R. 7357, 68th Cong., 1st Sess., introduced and referred to the Committee on the Merchant Marine and Fisheries, 65 CONG. REC. 3294 (1924).

39. Sarno, *supra* note 29, at 195.

40. *Id.* at 197. The ability of private partisan interests to influence public opinion and the trend of social thought by means of radio had been noted previously. The very first issue of the trade publication RADIO BROADCAST in 1922 had predicted that "some day in the future the popularity of a political party in office may hinge entirely upon the quality of broadcasting service." RADIO BROADCAST, May 1922. In 1924, both Democratic and Republican conventions were covered by live radio broadcasts. In the 1924 presidential campaign, "Radio was already recognized as a potent political medium" and was used extensively by both majority candidates. Archer, *supra* note 6, at 345. Francis Chase, Jr., in a chapter entitled *Seeds of American Fascism,* discusses how radio was instrumental in aiding Huey Long's election in Louisiana and in building the following of the racist Father Coughlin. Chase, *supra* note 5, at 80.

41. Sarno, *supra* note 29, at 195.

42. FOURTH NATIONAL RADIO CONFERENCE, PROCEEDINGS AND RECOMMENDATIONS FOR REGULATION OF RADIO 6 (Washington, D.C., November 9-11, 1925).

43. *Id.* at 7 (italics added).

44. *See* Schenck v. United States, 249 U.S. 47 (1919); Abrams v. United States, 250 U.S. 616, 624 (1919) (Holmes & Brandeis, JJ., dissenting), Gitlow v. New York 268 U.S. 652, 673 (1925) (Holmes & Brandeis, JJ., dissenting); Whitney v. California, 274 U.S. 357, 372 (1927) (Brandeis & Holmes, JJ., concurring).

45. FOURTH NATIONAL RADIO CONFERENCE, *supra* note 42, at 7.

46. Sarno, *supra* note 29, at 201.

47. H.R. 5589, 69th Cong., 1st Sess., introduced and referred to the Committee on the Merchant Marine and Fisheries, 67 CONG. REC. 901, debate at 5474, 5485, 5585.

48. The 1927 legislation was also spurred on by a presidential message to Congress in the winter of 1926. President Coolidge, in recommending passage of the new radio legislation, again stressed the scarcity theme: "many more stations have been operating than can be accommodated within the limited number of wave lengths available; further stations are in course of construction; many stations have departed from the scheme of allocation set down by the department, and the whole service of this most important public function has drifted into such chaos as seems likely, if not remedied, to destroy its great value. I most urgently recommend that this legislation should be speedily enacted." H.R. DOC. No. 483, 69th Cong., 2d Sess. 10 (1926).

49. 44 Stat. 1162, sec. 4 (1927). The Secretary of Commerce was to have the authority to enforce the Act one year after the Commission's first meeting, but this authority never was passed to the Secretary.

50. *Id.* sec. 1.

51. *Id.* sec. 4.

52. *Id.* sec. 91.

53. *Id.* sec. 29.

54. *Id.* sec. 18.

55. DOCUMENTS OF AMERICAN BROADCASTING, *supra* note 26, at 36.

56. 67 CONG. REC. 12335 (1926).

57. *Id.* The Senator later reinforced the scarcity concept by stating that there were only 89 channels available in the broadcasting band (an additional 6 were reserved for Canada) and that the Department of Commerce had managed to assign 528 stations to these 89 wavelengths. "Although there is considerable interference in some instances between various stations, the demand for broadcasting licenses has continuously increased until at this time there are approximately 650 applications for wavelengths on file with the Department of Commerce which have not been granted." *Id.* at 12336.

58. *Id.* at 12335.

59. *Id.* at 12356.

60. *Id.* at 12357.

61. Ironically, a later senator from Nebraska, Roman Hruska, in 1975 was the prime sponsor of S. 1178, a bill to abolish the fairness doctrine and other government controls over broadcasting content.

62. 67 CONG. REC. 12503 04 (1926).

63. However, under the present-day fairness doctrine, the commission has indicated that issues can have several contrasting sides that may need presentation, not just an "affirmative" and a "negative" side. *See* FCC, *Fairness Doctrine and Public Interest Standards, Fairness Report Regarding Handling of Public Issues,* 39 FED. REG. 26372, 26377 par. 38 (1974) [hereinafter cited as *Fairness Report*].

64. On March 12, 1926, he declared that combining existing stations and station applicants, there were 11 stations for each wavelength. 67 CONG. REC. 5479 (1926).

65. *Id.*

66. *See* remarks of Congressmen David and Blanton, *id.* at 5483.

67. Minority views of Representative Davis, H.R. REP. No. 464, 69th Cong., 1st Sess. 16 (1926). After proclaiming the dangers of radio propaganda, Davis stated, "There is nothing in this bill . . . to prevent a broadcasting station from permitting one party or one candidate or the advocate of a measure or a program or the opponent thereof, to employ its service and refusing to accord the same right to the opposing side."

68. 67 CONG. REC. 5480 (1926). Congressman White also stated, "I felt that we could go no further than the Federal Constitution goes in that respect." *Id.*

69. *Id.*

70. 67 CONG. REC. 5561 (1926) (italics added).

71. Eleven years later another congressman named Johnson was to be elected from Texas' Tenth District and eventually was to demonstrate a legislative skill not exemplified by his earlier Texas namesake in this episode. In the 1960s the campaign of then President Lyndon Johnson, however, used the substantive thrust of his Texas colleague, Luther Johnson, to excessive zeal. *See* Fred W. Friendly, *What's Fair on the Air?* N.Y. Times, Mar. 30, 1975, sec. 6 (Magazine), at 11.

72. 67 CONG. REC. 5558 (1926).

73. *Id.* at 5561. Another amendment making it criminal to broadcast a personal attack into a state where the attack would then constitute a defamation under local law was rejected by a wide margin. *Id.* at 5646.

74. S. REP. No. 772, 69th Cong., 1st Sess. (1926) (italics added).

75. 67 CONG. REC. 12503 (1926). The Senator continued, "We are not trying merely to place the privilege of broadcasting within the reach of all so far as cost is concerned, but we

want to place it within the reach of all for the discussion of public questions when one side or the other is presented." *Id.* at 12504.

76. The amendment read, "If any licensee shall permit a broadcasting station to be used by a candidate or candidates for any public office, he shall afford equal opportunities to all candidates for such public office in the use of such broadcasting station: Provided, that such licensee shall have no power to censor the material broadcast under the provisions of this paragraph and shall not be liable to criminal or civil action by reason of any uncensored utterance thus broadcast."

77. 67 Cong. Rec. 12358 (1926).

78. *Id.*

79. Senator Howell declared, "Are we going to allow these great interests to utilize their stations to disseminate the kind of publicity only of which they approve and leave no opportunity for the other side of public questions to reach the same audience? The Senator from Washington has left in the bill a provision respecting candidates. It is important, but it has not anything like the importance of the provision he has stricken out—the discussion of public questions." *Id.* at 12504.

80. *Id.*

81. *Id.* at 12358.

82. *Id.* (italics added).

83. H.R. Rep. No. 1886, 69th Cong., 2d Sess. (1927). Section 18 as finally enacted read: "If any licensee shall permit any person who is a legally qualified candidate for any public office to use a broadcasting station, he shall afford equal opportunities to all other such candidates for that office in the use of such broadcasting station, and the Commission shall make rules and regulations to carry this provision into effect; provided, that such a licensee shall have no power of censorship over the material broadcast under the provisions of this section. No obligation is hereby imposed upon any licensee to allow the use of its station by any such candidate."

84. Staff Study of the House Comm. on Interstate and Foreign Commerce, Legislative History of the Fairness Doctrine, 90th Cong., 2d Sess. 197 (Comm. Print 1968).

85. *Id.*

86. Over 40 years later another Commissioner named Robinson would be appointed to the Federal Communications Commission and hold a different view. Glen Robinson, who was appointed in 1974 and served until the summer of 1976, doubts the early origins of the fairness requirement and finds problems in its application. *See* Glen O. Robinson, *The Fairness Doctrine, the Law and Policy in Its Present Application*, Paper No. 3, *Hearings of the Special Subcommittee on Investigations of the House Committee on Interstate and Foreign Commerce*, 90th Cong., 2d Sess. (Comm. Print 1968).

87. H.R. Rep. No. 7716, 72d Cong., 2d Sess. (1933).

88. H.R. Rep. No. 2106, 72d Cong., 2d Sess. 4 (1933). As can be seen from the language, the amendment does not require affirmative presentation of public issues.

89. 75 Cong. Rec. 3681 (1932).

90. *Id.* at 3680. Congressman Lehlbach, also a member of the House Committee on Merchant Marine, Radio, and Fisheries that reported the bill, reiterated that "Every amendment in the bill has the support of the Federal Radio Commission," and that "This bill contains only matter that is absolutely uncontroversial." *Id.* at 3684.

91. S. 3285, sec. 315(a), 73d Cong., 2d Sess. (1934).

92. H.R. Rep. No. 1850, 73d Cong., 2d Sess. (1934).

93. The House managers of the bill who carried it to conference stated, "Section 315 on facilities for candidates for public office is the same as Section 18 of the Radio Act. The Senate provisions, which would have modified and extended the present law is [sic] not included in the substitute." 78 Cong. Rec. 10988 (1934).

94. *Id.* at 19316 (italics added).

95. Roscoe L. Barrow, *The Equal Opportunities and Fairness Doctrines in Broadcasting: Pillars in the Forum of Democracy*, 37 U. Cin. L. Rev. 447, 461 (1968).

96. STAFF STUDY, *supra* note 84, at 202.

97. However, it should be noted that the statutes do have provisions stating that the FRC and FCC shall not engage in "censorship" or interfere "with the right of free speech by means of radio communications." Radio Act of 1929, sec. 29; Communications Act of 1934, sec. 326. Congressman White referred to the bill giving the Secretary of Commerce "no power at all" to interfere with "freedom of speech in any degree," 67 CONG. REC. 5480 (1926), and Senator Dill pointed to the lack of government control over broadcasting stations, except for technical reasons, in giving background in consideration of the legislation, 67 CONG. REC. 12335 (1926). The issue is, of course, what does "censorship" mean? Requiring equal opportunities for political candidates was explicitly made a part of the statute. Its command of equal time and airing of specific individuals, that is, legally qualified candidates, appears to be as much an invasion of broadcasters' free speech as would be a fairness requirement of some reasonable balance if public affairs issues are presented. Since the former was not considered "censorship" by Congress, unless the statute is dramatically inconsistent it seems the latter would not be censorship under the statute either. Requiring the presentation of public affairs issues in the first instance, a later requirement of the fairness doctrine, appears to be more of a free speech burden, although even here the discretion afforded broadcasters on how to broadcast such issues and the scarcity and partisan control concerns mitigate against the "censorship" label. *See also* the text accompanying footnotes 88-90 discussing a bill passed by Congress in 1932 that included a fairness provision and was regarded as not changing the "substantive law."

98. Red Lion Broadcasting Co. v. FCC, 395 U.S. 367, 379 (1969).

99. *Id.* at 371.

100. *Applicability of Fairness Doctrine in the Handling of Controversial Issues of Public Importance,* app. B 29 FED. REG. 10416, 10425 (1969).

101. Houser, *supra* note 1, at 553. Mr. Houser was later appointed director of the Office of Telecommunications Policy.

102. Barrow, *supra* note 95, at 462.

103. DOCUMENTS OF AMERICAN BROADCASTING, *supra* note 26, at 370.

104. STAFF STUDY, *supra* note 84, at 205.

105. Johnathan O. Blake, *Red Lion Broadcasting Co. v. F.C.C., Fairness and the Emperor's New Clothes,* 23 FED. COM. B.J. 75, 79 (1969).

106. Robinson, *supra* note 86. *See also* Glen O. Robinson, *The FCC and the First Amendment: Observations on 40 Years of Radio and Television Regulation,* 52 MINN. L. REV. 67, 132 (1967).

107. Jerome A. Barron, *The Federal Communication Commission's Fairness Doctrine: An Evaluation,* 30 GEO. WASH. L. REV. 1, 2 (1969). *See also* Sullivan, *supra* note 1, at 728.

108. FEDERAL RADIO COMMISSION SECOND ANNUAL REPORT, SUPPLEMENT App. F(6), at 170 (1928).

109. *Id.* app. M(3), at 257.

110. FEDERAL RADIO COMMISSION THIRD ANNUAL REPORT 33 (1929).

111. *Id.* (italics added). In reiterating its opposition to propaganda stations, the FRC added, "the fact remains that the station is used for what is essentially a private purpose for a substantial portion of the time, and in addition, is constantly subject to the very human temptation not to be fair to opposing schools of thought and their representatives," *Id.* at 34.

112. In fact, later in the THIRD ANNUAL REPORT the Commission notes that the FRC legal division will conduct an examination of all license applicants, which will cover "any matters which tend to show that the granting of the application would not be in the public interest, convenience, or necessity." *Id.* at 53.

113. Professor John Sullivan, relying on only this balancing language in *Great Lakes,* states, "Here we have a clear expression of the fairness doctrine applied to controversial issues both political and nonpolitical." He apparently ignores the contemporary doctrine's emphasis on required presentation in part one of the doctrine in concentrating on the part two balancing requirement. Sullivan, *supra* note 1, at 728. Professor Sullivan also says the case leaves unclear the extent of the fairness obligation, and he implies that the obligation may have been a moral obligation as opposed to a legal obligation. Sullivan is certainly

correct in asserting that the fairness obligation had not been specifically delineated, but the general obligation to present opposing views on public issues was indeed framed in terms of a licensee's legal obligation to operate in the "public interest" under the statute, and a warning was given that the FRC would consider "future action" with respect to fairness complaints. According to Sullivan, *id.* at 728–29, the fairness doctrine became a legal obligation reinforced by threat of license forfeiture in Mayflower Broadcasting Corp., 8 F.C.C. 333 (1941).

114. Trinity Methodist Church, S. v. FRC, 62 F.2d 850 (D.C. Cir.), *cert. denied,* 284 U.S. 685 (1932).

115. KFKB Broadcasting Ass'n., v. FRC, 47 F.2d 670 (D.C. Cir. 1931).

116. Chicago Federation of Labor v. FRC, 3 F.R.C. 36 (1929).

117. 62 F.2d at 852.

118. *Id.*

119. *Id.* at 851. BROADCASTING magazine vehemently disagreed with the court's rationale and declared that the "Radio Commission may now muzzle a station simply because of the utterances heard over it." BROADCASTING, Jan. 15, 1933, at 18.

120. In a typical case, pointed to by the Court, Brinkley stated, "Sunflower State, from Dresden, Kansas. Probably he has gall stones. No, I don't mean that, I mean kidney stones. My advice to you is to put him on Prescription No. 80 and 50 for men, also 64. I think that he will be a whole lot better. Also drink a lot of water." 47 F.2d at 671.

121. *Id.*

122. *Id.*

123. *Id.* at 672.

124. 3 F.R.C. at 36.

125. *Id.* However, in an earlier case the Commission ruled that station WEVD in New York, which broadcast the doctrines of the Socialist Party, could keep its license. 2 F.R.C. ANNUAL REPORT at 154-55 (1928). "The commission will not draw the line on any station doing an altruistic work, or which is the mouthpiece of a substantial political or religious minority." *Id.* at 155. But the FRC warned that "Such a station must, of course . . . be conducted with due regard for the opinions of others." *Id.* So rhetoric on behalf of an owner's viewpoint could be broadcast, as long as the opinions of others were fairly aired. A seemingly inconsistent comment was later made by the Commission in a case involving the broadcasting of private disputes: "It is self-evident that the constitutional guaranty of freedom of speech applies to the expression of political and religious opinions, to discussions, fair comments, and criticisms on matters of general public interest, of candidates, of men holding public office, and of political, social, and economical issues. At no time has the commission considered that it had any right to chastise a station for its conduct in handling such matters if the station has observed the requirement of the law that it give rival candidates equal opportunities to use its microphone." 2 F.R.C. ANNUAL REPORT 160 (1928). If there could be no chastisement for discussion of such issues (except if opposing political candidates did not appear), why would a station have to have "due regard for the opinions of others"? Why could not a labor organization or a conservative minister broadcast what each wished? And how could the *Great Lakes* standards be legitimate?

One explanation for the inconsistency might be that the private dispute case was decided earlier than *Great Lakes, Chicago Federation,* or *Trinity,* and FRC policy may have changed over its tenure. A second explanation may be in defining the word "chastise." The FRC may not have considered license renewal review chastisement. Thus, in describing the pending litigation in *KFKB,* the FRC General Counsel's office defined the main issues as, "How far can the commission go in its *indirect censorship* of programs, determining what is or is not in the public interest?" KFKB Broadcasting Ass'n v. FRC, 4 F.R.C. ANNUAL REPORT 46 (1930). As noted in the text *supra,* the FRC had decided that refusing a license to Dr. Brinkley based on his program content was a legitimate exercise of its "public interest" authority. Chastisement may connote fines or some other "direct" form of interference. Violations of the equal opportunity provisions were clearly subject to fines of up to $500 and/or imprisonment for up to five years under section 33 of the Radio Act of 1927. A third explanation of the inconsistency of the statement with later FRC statements may simply be an acknowledgement that agencies do not always act in an ideal consistent pattern, and there is simply no reconciling the earlier declaration. Some comfort may be found in the fact that the case focused on private disputes, not public issues, and the statement may be regarded as dictum.

126. Chicago Federation of Labor v. FRC, 41 F.2d 422 (D.C. Cir. 1930). The Court of Appeals in affirming, however, placed its primary emphasis on the interference with two other existing stations that would be caused by granting WCFL its requested modification. *See* Toledo Blade Co., 25 F.C.C. 251 (1958), *infra* note 190, where labor interest in a station was not determinative, since contrasting viewpoints were aired.

127. It has been suggested that, despite these "extreme situations," "[f]rom the very beginning, radio broadcasters generally agreed that they had an obligation to be fair and to avoid bias," which was conceived, until *Mayflower* at least, as a "moral obligation." Sullivan *supra* note 201, at 728. An article appearing in BROADCASTING in 1933 proclaimed "Radio does not, and cannot, refuse its time to speakers on either side of any issue. Radio, by presenting arguments of both sides, in uncolored, unbiased fashion, leaves the decision squarely up to . . . the radio public." BROADCASTING, Apr. 15, 1933, at 14. The 1937 CBS ANNUAL REPORT indicated that "the great lesson of 1936 was that the broadcasters have been right in making their medium an impartial, non-partisan forum for the discussion and debate of public affairs, rather than seeking to exert editorial sway." CBS ANNUAL REPORT 2 (1937). The 1939 edition of the NAB, CODE OF STANDARDS OF BROADCASTING PRACTICE is the "earliest edition" of the Code, Letter from Jocelyn Kipnis, NAB researcher/writer, to Steven Simmons, Sept. 23, 1975, and suggests a two-part fairness doctrine obligation: "As part of their public service, networks and stations shall provide time for the presentation of public questions including those of controversial nature. . . . Broadcasters shall use their best efforts to allot such time with fairness to all elements in a given controversy." NAB, CODE OF STANDARDS OF BROADCASTING PRACTICE 3 (1939, amended 1941). Although no sanctions were imposed for violating the Code, the NAB represented 500 stations and more than 90 percent of the income of the broadcasting industry (387 stations were not members). Letter from Russell Place, NAB counsel, Jan. 28, 1941, to HARVARD LAW REVIEW, cited in Note, *Radio Regulation and Freedom of the Air*, 54 HARV. L. REV. 1220, 1225 n.42 (1941). The Code stated that time for the presentation of controversial issues, except for political broadcasts and sponsorship of regular public forum type programs under broadcaster control, would not be sold. The reasons suggested for this policy were the "public duty" of broadcasters to air public issue programming regardless of sponsorship, the difficulty of regulating the amount sold to differing sides, and especially the power of the wealthy to buy time and unfairly influence the public. NAB, CODE OF STANDARDS OF BROADCASTING PRAC-TICE, at 4. A similar controversial issue policy had been adopted by CBS in 1929. SUMMARY OF CBS POLICIES 2 (1929). Although NBC conformed to the NAB code after its adoption, it had previously allowed sponsorship of programs on controversial issues but reserved the right to require sponsors to air views of speakers opposed to the sponsor's speaker. BROADCASTING IN THE PUBLIC INTEREST (NBC pamphlet) 29, 35 (1939). The 1946 edition of the code dropped the 1939 language. It simply stated an affirmative obligation of licensees to present public questions by "straightforward statement" and declared that news should be presented with "fairness and accuracy." The prohibition against selling time for programs airing controversial issues was dropped. NAB, CODE OF STANDARDS OF BROADCASTING PRACTICE 3 (1945, amended 1946).

128. Young People's Ass'n for Propagation of Gospel, 6 F.C.C. 178 (1938).

129. *Id.* at 181.

130. *Id.* The Commission was also concerned with the interference that the proposed station would create with other stations.

131. An authoritative radio law text published in 1939, a year after *Young People's* was decided, declared that, "while pretending to exercise no direct censorship over the contents of communications by radio, the government's administrative body is possessed of a potent power of censorship over broadcast programs, which it exercises indirectly as part of its licensing powers." 2 WALTER A. SOCOLOW, THE LAW OF RADIO BROADCASTING 1013 (1939). It further stated that, "A broadcast station should provide equal opportunities for opposing points of view on public questions to be transmitted over its facilities. Whenever possible, a fair and non-partisan discussion should be permitted since the public interest will

thereby be best served. This result can be achieved by the assistance of impartial represen-tative groups of citizens who can function in relieving the station from the danger of reflect-ing its own private opinions in the creation of program standards." *Id.* at 1026.

132. FCC Sɪxᴛʜ Aɴɴᴜᴀʟ Rᴇᴘᴏʀᴛ 55 (1940) (italics added). A leading law review, approvingly commenting on the FCC's statement, suggested: "As radio facilities, unlike newspapers, comprise a narrowly limited commodity, this approach seems proper since it avoids the complexity of maintaining station and political beliefs." Note, *Radio Regulation and Freedom of the Air,* 54 Hᴀʀᴠ. L. Rᴇᴠ. 1220, 1223 (1941). Although the "duty" to present contrasting viewpoints is made explicit by the statement, it is not clear whether "well-rounded" discussions refers to a licensee's overall programming or the confines of a single show. As discussed *infra,* later cases would clarify any possible confusion: A licensee's fairness in presenting contrasting views would be based on its overall programming.

133. Mayflower Broadcasting Corp., 8 F.C.C. 333 (1941).

134. *Id.* at 339.

135. *Id.*

136. *Id.* (italics added).

137. *Id.*

138. *Id.* (italics added).

139. In fact, taken together with the nonadvocacy statement, the *Mayflower* decision is open to an interpretation different from the one commonly given it. A broadcaster's advocacy of a particular position may well have been justified and in the public interest, as long as it was fairly balanced with contrasting views. A station could not be "devoted" to partisan ends, but balanced presentation is arguably nonpartisan. For support of this position, *see* Note, *The Mayflower Doctrine Scuttled,* 59 Yᴀʟᴇ L.J. 759 n.27 (1950); Heffron, *Should Radio Be Free to Editorialize?* 47 Cᴏᴍᴍᴏɴᴡᴇᴀʟ 4 (1948). Former FCC Chairman Fly maintained that the decision was meant to ban editorials on behalf of stations but not editorials by licensees as individuals. Communication to the Yᴀʟᴇ Lᴀᴡ Jᴏᴜʀɴᴀʟ from James L. Fly, Apr. 4, 1950, cited in Note, *The Mayflower Doctrine Scuttled,* at 766 n.27. Others interpreted the decision to ban both licensee and station editorializing. *See* 23 Aɪʀ L. Rᴇᴠ. 785 (1948); Eʟᴍᴇʀ Sᴍᴇᴀᴅ, Fʀᴇᴇᴅᴏᴍ ᴏꜰ Sᴘᴇᴇᴄʜ ʙʏ Rᴀᴅɪᴏ ᴀɴᴅ Tᴇʟᴇᴠɪsɪᴏɴ 77 (1959). Commissioner Jones in the *Report on Editorializing* claimed that *Mayflower* "fully and completely suppressed and prohibited the licensee from speaking in the future over his facilities in behalf of any cause. . . . I cannot see how the *Mayflower* decision can be read in any other way but as a square holding that a licensee cannot use his microphone for personal advocacy. . . . This decision has hung like the Damocles' sword over every licensee to silence the licensee as an advocate." *Report on Editorializing by Broadcast Licensees,* 13 F.C.C. 1246, 1259, 1261 (1949) (separate views of Commissioner Jones) [hereinafter referred to as *Report on Editorializing*].

140. Soon after *Mayflower* was decided, Commissioner Fly emphasized "it should be remembered that the obligation in full, free, and two-sided discussion is imposed by law, that the broadcaster is under a legal duty to provide a competitive market in ideas." James Fly, *Regulation of Radio Broadcasting in the Public Interest,* 213 Aɴɴᴀʟs 102, 108 (1941).

141. United Broadcasting Co., 10 F.C.C. 515 (1945).

142. It was also charged that the station did not discuss "race, religion, and politics," and that scripts submitted by the labor groups were censored.

143. *Id.* at 517.

144. *Id.*

145. *Id.*

146. *Id.* (italics added).

147. *Id.* at 518. The Commission would not set down an "exact rule of thumb for provid-ing time" and admitted that it might be difficult to decide between applicants for the "sale or donations of time. . . . The fact that it places an arduous task on management should not be made a reason for evading the issue by a strict rule against the sale of time for any programs of the type mentioned." *Id.*

148. Rᴇᴘᴏʀᴛ ʙʏ Fᴇᴅᴇʀᴀʟ Cᴏᴍᴍᴜɴɪᴄᴀᴛɪᴏɴs Cᴏᴍᴍɪssɪᴏɴ (Mar. 7, 1946). It should also be noted that in 1946, the same year the Blue Book was released, the FCC for the first time explicitly indicated in dicta that broadcast advertising could involve controversial public

issues to which the fairness doctrine was applicable. Sam Morris, 11 F.C.C. 177 (1946). *See* Chapter Five for more on this development.

149. *Id.* at 55.

150. "The crucial need for discussion programs, at the local, national and international levels alike is universally realized. . . . Accordingly, the carrying of such programs in reasonable sufficiency, and during good listening hours, is a factor to be considered in any finding of public interest." *Id.* at 56. Aside from reflecting the affirmative presentation aspect of the fairness doctrine, the statement illustrates that public issues are not restricted to local questions. Indeed, they may be national or international in scope.

151. *Id.* at 40. The Commission made this statement after listing 19 questions that arise in connection with the broadcasting of public issues and saying these questions would be answered on a case-by-case basis as opposed to an "over-all statement of policy."

152. *Id.* There were, however, 217 relevant network programs made available to affiliates, although many of these were not carried by the affiliates.

153. *Id.* (italics added). The Commission also appeared to limit its interpretation of *United Broadcasting* unnecessarily in the Blue Book. Referring to *United,* the FCC stated, "While the Commission has recently held that an absolute ban on the *sale* of time for the discussion of public issues may under certain circumstances not serve the public interest, it is nevertheless clear that such broadcasts should be primarily of a sustaining nature." (Fn. omitted, italics added.) The station policy approved by the Commission in *United* stated that the public issue time made available would be "primarily on a sustaining basis," and the Commission spoke in terms of "sale or donation of time" for public issue discussion. So *United* dealt not only with banning the *sale* of time for public issue discussion, as the FCC suggests in the Blue Book, but also with the provision of time on a *sustaining* or *donated* basis.

154. Admittedly, the Blue Book did not speak of "controversial" issues of "public importance." But it did speak of a vigorous viewpoint offending some viewers and of public issues being discussed, obviously implying controversy. It explicitly declared its concern about the lack of American foreign policy issue discussion, certainly discussion involving controversy and public importance at that time. The Blue Book was issued right after *United Broadcasting* and right before *Robert Scott,* both of which speak of public issues in terms of controversy and public importance. If an issue is a "public" issue, by its very definition it should be an issue of some importance. The FCC in many fairness cases and statements speaks of the doctrine in terms of airing "public issues." It is simply assumed that in using the term the Commission is referring to controversial issues of public importance under the fairness doctrine. In the definitive 1949 *Report on Editorializing,* the Commission in several places used the words "public issues" without further modification in discussing a licensee's fairness obligation. Thus, the part one responsibility involves an "affirmative responsibility on the part of broadcast licensees to devote a reasonable amount of time for the presentation over their facilities of programs devoted to the discussion and consideration of public issues. . . ." *Report on Editorializing, supra* note 139, at 1249, par. 7. The comprehensive 1974 *Fairness Report* is subheaded *Fairness Report Regarding Handling of Public Issues. Fairness Report, supra* note 63, at 26372. *See also* the fairness doctrine definitions involving "public issues" given by the Commission and the Supreme Court in the text accompanying notes 2 and 3 of Chapter Two. The "public issue" requirement of the Blue Book is directly linked to the public issue requirement of the present-day fairness doctrine.

155. 11 F.C.C. 372 (1946).

156. *Id.* at 376.

157. *Id.*

158. *Id.* at 374.

159. *Id.* Later in the opinion it spoke of the need to "afford the listening audience that opportunity to hear a diversity and balance of views, which is an inseparable corollary of freedom of expression." *Id.* at 376. The Commission was thus acknowledging not only the public's First Amendment right to receive diverse information, but the First Amendment right of speakers to use the radio forum. The Commission also eloquently stated the need for a free flow of ideas to an effectively functioning democratic government and the danger to democratic institutions if they are immune from criticism. *Id.* at 375.

160. In a letter issued August 28, 1948, clarifying the *Scott* ruling, the Commission laid down an important fourth point: A licensee's fairness policy would be judged on the basis of "reasonableness." Letter to Edward Heffron from Wayne Coy, Chairman, 3 P & F RADIO REG. 264a (1948).

161. Although it was not articulated at the time, a key reason for allowing imposition of fairness doctrine obligations on radio and TV, and thus imposing different First Amendment standards on the electronic and the printed press, may have been the "lack of genuine journalistic effort in the beginning of telecommunication news." David L. Bazelon, *FCC Regulation of the Telecommunications Press*, 1975 DUKE L.J. 213, 219. *See also* Louis L. Jaffe, *The Editorial Responsibility of the Broadcaster: Reflections on Fairness and Access*, 85 HARV. L. REV. 768, 785 (1972).

162. Emlyn I. Griffith, *Mayflower Rule—Gone But Not Forgotten*, 35 CORNELL L. REV. 574 (1950).

163. *Id.* at 574-75; Smead, *supra* note 139, at 77; Note, *The Mayflower Doctrine Scuttled, supra* note 139, at 760. *See* note 139, *supra*, for various interpretations of the "ban." Actually, the NAB itself had a hand in preventing the airing of controversial material. Its first code, drafted as a guide for industry self-regulation but without any legal force, prohibited the sale of time for the discussion of controversial issues, except in the cases of political broadcasts and public forums, and banned the "coloring" of news broadcasts. NAB, CODE OF STANDARDS OF BROADCASTING PRACTICE 5 (1939). *See supra*, note 127. Discussion of vital public issues, aside from these excepted situations, was to be donated by the station. One of the main reasons for the Code provision was to prevent radio public affairs discussion from gravitating "almost wholly into the hands of those with the greater means to buy it." Note, *Radio Regulation and Freedom of the Air, supra* note 127, at 1227. However, "The effect of the Code was to encourage broadcasters to minimize discussion of public issues as suited their preference." Note, *The Mayflower Doctrine Scuttled, supra* note 139, at 763 n.23. The time sale code provision did not necessarily interfere with the evolving part two of the fairness doctrine, calling for balanced presentation if a broadcaster chose to air controversial public issues. But the effect of the provision clashed head-on with the part one affirmative responsibility to program public affairs issues, which was announced in *United Broadcasting* and the Blue Book. In fact, after *United Broadcasting, "The NAB hastily revamped its code to accord with the FCC's pronouncement." *Id.* at 764 n.23.

164. *Report on Editorializing, supra* note 139. The report was issued on June 1, 1949.

165. *Id.* at 1249, par. 6 (fn. omitted).

166. *Id.* at 1256, par. 20. The Commission bolstered its views by referring to language in Associated Press v. United States, 326 U.S. 1 (1945). The First "[A]mendment rests on the assumption that the widest possible dissemination of information from diverse and antagonistic sources is essential to the welfare of the public, that a free press is a condition of a free society. Surely a command that the Government itself shall not impede the free flow of ideas does not afford nongovernmental combinations a refuge if they impose restraints upon the constitutionally guaranteed freedom." *Id.* at 20, cited in *Report on Editorializing, supra* note 139, at 1257, par. 19.

167. Unfortunately, the Commission avoided any extended or insightful discussion of the First Amendment rights of the public.

168. The Commission reiterates later the "basic policy of the Congress that radio be maintained as a medium of free speech for the general public as a whole rather than as an outlet for the purely personal or private outlet of the licensee." *Id.* at 1257, par. 21. The *Mayflower* decision's asserted "ban" on licensee advocacy (at least without balancing views) was a reaction to fear of the effects such radio editorials would have on the public. The *Report on Editorializing*, as its name connotes, and as discussed in the text *supra*, was in large part a result of *Mayflower*. *See also id.* at 1253, par. 14, for a summary of witnesses' views before the FCC that express fear of licensee public opinion influence.

169. *Id.* at 1247, par. 3; 1249, par. 7; 1251, par. 21; 1257, par. 21.

170. *Id.* at 1249, par. 7. The Commission cited *United Broadcasting* to support this obligation. The Commission exaggerated when it added that the obligation was also "reaffirmed by this Commission in a long series of decisions." *Id.* As previously noted, the part

one obligation, although implied in *Great Lakes* and *Mayflower*, was born with *United*, which was just four years old.

171. In speaking of making time available for "expression" by people in the "community," the FCC plants the seed for another rationale for the doctrine, besides informing the public and the fear of partisan power. Allowing access for expression in and of itself is an objective. The Commission, earlier in the *Report on Editorializing*, makes another statement with access implications: "we think it is equally clear that one of the basic elements of any such operation is the maintenance of radio and television as a medium of *speech and freedom of expression* for the people of the Nation as a whole." *Report on Editorializing, supra* note 139, at 1248, par. 5 (italics added). "Freedom of expression" implies that individuals will have access to the radio to express their views. And, if licensees are required to present the different viewpoints on vital issues "held by the various groups which make up the community," *id.* at 1249, par. 6, it would logically follow that group members should have some access to air their views. A leading law review, in explaining the basis for the FCC's 1949 Report a year after it was released, saw both public information and individual expression objectives: "Fundamental to evaluation of the Commission's action is the principle that in a democratic society there should be a maximum opportunity to express diverse viewpoints on controversial issues and, equally important, maximum opportunity to hear and read the conflicting views of others." Note, *The Mayflower Doctrine Scuttled, supra*, note 139, at 760. As discussed *infra*, however, the Commission states in the *Report on Editorializing* that no individual has a specific right to speak over the radio. Access is seen as a generalized right of various viewpoints and is played in low key by the Commission. *See* note 159, *supra*, for more on early FCC discussion of access.

172. *Report on Editorializing, supra* note 139, at 1250, par. 7. The FCC put both parts together in a recapitulation at the end of its opinion: It is required "that licensees devote a reasonable percentage of their broadcasting time to the discussion of public issues of interest in the community served by their stations and that such programs be designed so that the public has a reasonable opportunity to hear different opposing positions on the public issues of interest and importance in the community." *Id.* at 1257-58.

173. *Id.* at 1253, par. 13.

174. *Id.* at 1258 (additional views of Commissioner E. M. Webster). Commissioner Jones, in addition to criticizing the majority failure to explicitly repudiate the *Mayflower* case and its asserted freedom of speech infringement, also thought the Commission's ruling was too vague. "I do not believe that the conditions imposed here are made clear enough to serve as an adequate guide to the conduct licensees will be required to follow if they are to avail themselves of the right to editorialize." *Id.* at 1264, par. 14 (separate views of Commissioner Jones). He thought that if the fairness implementation steps were to be discussed, they should have been issued as "clear and separately stated rules and regulations" pursuant to Administrative Procedure Act and Federal Register Act requirements. *Id.* at 1265-66.

175. *Id.* at 1248, par. 4.

176. *Id.* at 1251, par. 10.

177. *Id.* at 1255, par. 18; 1250, par. 8.

178. *Id.* at 1251, par. 8.

179. *Id.* at 1251, par. 10.

180. *Id.* at 1253, par. 14.

181. *Id.* at 1255, par. 17.

182. *Id.* at 1256, par. 18.

183. *Id.* at 1254, par. 16; 1258, par. 21. In addition, "the duty extends to all subjects of substantial importance to the community coming within the scope of the discussion under the first amendment without regard to personal view and opinion of the licensees on the matter, or . . . the possible unpopularity of the views to be expressed on the subject matter to be discussed among particular elements of the station's listening audience." *Id.* at 1250, par. 7.

184. *Id.* at 1255, par. 18. Commissioner Webster reiterated the flexible review standard, stating, "there can be no mechanical formula or test which can be prescribed to ensure the essential fairness." All a licensee has to do is to make "a sincere and reasonable effort." *Id.* at 1259 (additional views of Commissioner E. M. Webster).

185. *Id.* at 1256, quoting from Northern Corporation (WMEX), 12 F.C.C. 940, 945 (1948). The "reasonableness" standard had been mentioned in a 1948 case. *See supra* note 160.

186. FCC Chairman Coy and Commissioner Walker did not take part in the decision. The majority report represented the views of only two commissioners, Hyde and Skelling. Commissioner Webster filed an additional opinion in which he attempted to make more concise the majority opinion, including a one-paragraph statement reiterating licensees' public interest duty to provide a reasonable opportunity for presentation of conflicting views on controversial public issues. *Report on Editorializing, supra* note 139, at 1259. Commissioner Jones filed separate views in which he agreed with the majority that broadcast editorializing should be permitted but criticized the majority for not flatly reversing *Mayflower* based on First Amendment considerations. Although he stated that "licensees should be fair in the operation of their stations," *id.* at 1264, he disagreed with the majority's "prospective . . . doctrine of fairness," which he considered "too vague" and an inadequate "guide" for broadcasters to follow in this sensitive free speech area. Commissioner Jones felt that fairness and editorial obligations should be generated in the handling of specific problems as they arise, and not in some vague, a priori guide. Thus Commissioner Jones was the first commissioner to use the words "doctrine of fairness" in an FCC pronouncement, yet he actually rejected that doctrine as established in the 1949 *Report*. Commissioner Hennock agreed with the majority that fairness was necessary. *Id.* at 1270. But in her short dissenting opinion she stated that, in her judgment, the Commission did not have adequate powers to enforce fairness, and consequently partisan editorializing should be prohibited. Thus only three commissioners, Hyde, Skelling, and Webster, less than a majority of the seven-person commission, officially approved the 1949 *Report*'s prospective fairness doctrine.

187. Although television was yet to be fully developed on a commercial basis, the *Report on Editorializing* made reference to "television" service as part of the Commission's concern, along with radio. *Id.* at 1252, par. 11.

188. *Id.* at 1248, par. 5. The Commission mentioned "The legislative history" but failed to analyze it in any depth. *Id. See also* note 166, *supra*, and accompanying text.

189. Alabama Broadcasting System, Inc., 40 F.C.C. 461 (1958). Television station WABT, Birmingham, Alabama, had presented a program between 6:15 and 6:30 P.M. in which its news director presented views for "free television" and urged viewers to write Congress against a pending subscription TV bill. Three days later the station presented a 25-minute program on subscription television during the morning hours in which two station employees voiced pro-subscription-TV views and one station employee presented contrary views. After a complaint alleging unfair editorializing, the Commission en banc informed WABT that "A standard of reasonable fairness would call for the presentation by a proponent of subscription television during the same evening or at approximately the same time on a weekday shortly thereafter." *Id.* at 462. The Commission also felt that the licensee had not fulfilled its "affirmative duty to seek out, aid and encourage the broadcast of opposing views by responsible persons." *Id.* In light of Alabama Broadcasting's satisfactory operation, however, the Commission renewed its license to operate WABT and other stations. Despite the FCC's emphasis on presenting contrasting views soon after an initial broadcast and in the same time period, it has failed to follow this guideline in enforcing the doctrine in recent years.

190. *See* Paul E. Fitzpatrick, 40 F.C.C. 443 (1950), where New York Governor Dewey's *Report to the People* did not escape fairness scrutiny because of its label as a nonpolitical address, and Lamar Life Ins. Co., 18 P & F RADIO REG. 683 (1959), in which the broadcast of segregationist views by southern officials, following the suppression of a broadcast by Thurgood Marshall, then NAACP general counsel, was subject to fairness obligations. "The fact that the proponents of one particular position on such an issue are elected officials does not in any way alter the nature of the program or remove the applicability of our fair presentation policy." *Id.* at 685. Both cases also illustrate inadequate FCC enforcement policy. Despite the important issues addressed by Governor Dewey, and the outrageously unfair conduct of Lamar Life's WLBT, both station licenses were renewed. Lacking an intermediate sanction, the FCC would not refuse renewal, and in *Lamar Life* it referred to the mention, in the *Report on Editorializing*, of FCC tolerance of an "honest mistake or error in

judgment." *Id.* at 685. Interrupting a black spokesman with a sign saying, "sorry, cable trouble," *id.* at 684, and allowing a similar segregationist broadcast hardly seems an "honest mistake."

In Toledo Blade Co., 25 F.C.C. 251 (1958), surface characterization also was not determinative. Despite labor groups' interest in and identification with the station, the licensee had taken the necessary steps to be fair and present contrasting viewpoints. In that case the licensee's fairness doctrine obligation had been fulfilled. See note 126, *supra,* and accompanying text for a case where a labor group's interest in a station was ruled not in accord with fairness principles. *See also* Noe v. FCC, 260 F.2d 739 (D.C. Cir. 1958), where the District of Columbia Court of Appeals upheld the FCC's award of a license for a television channel to Loyola University, a Jesuit school in New Orleans. The competing applicants claimed that Loyola was anti-Protestant and that to grant it a license would violate the First Amendment. The Court ignored Loyola's characterization as a religious school and stated that the "prime consideration" in the comparative hearing was "whether the applicant, whatever his own views, is likely to give a 'fair break' to others who do not share them." *Id.* at 742. The Court of Appeals also held that the fairness doctrine was within the statutory power of the FCC and not a violation of the First Amendment. *But see* WORZ, Inc., 12 P & F RADIO REG. 1157 (1957), where the Commission said that a license applicant's plans to editorialize and to broadcast conflicting views were praiseworthy but did not merit "awarding a preference to the applicant." *Id.* at 1217.

191. Evening News Association, 40 F.C.C. 441 (1950). A licensee, admitting that a local Chrysler strike was a controversial issue of importance to the community, nonetheless refused to let the union present its views in a separate program. Since the Chrysler Corporation rejected the licensee's offer to participate in a joint appearance with the union, no views on the strike were broadcast. The Commission, in a letter to Evening News, suggested it was not acting in accord with the public interest, and should consequently review its action. In its emphasis on requiring some presentation of the important local issue, the Commission implies, even if indirectly, the part one fairness obligation. The case also demonstrates the Commission's willingness to interfere with a licensee's choice of broadcasting format, despite its emphasis in the 1949 *Report on Editorializing* on licensee discretion. In a later, seemingly contradictory case, the FCC stated that a licensee had met its public interest responsibility by "affording" spokesmen for one point of view "the opportunity to schedule a forum or debate type of program on which there would appear qualified representatives of the opponents and proponents." California Comm. Opposed to Oil Monopoly, 40 F.C.C. 450, 451 (1958). The cases may be distinguished in that the *California* licensee had in its overall programming offered the complainants and spokesmen for their cause other non-forum-type opportunities to air their views, and that it was the complainants, not the other side, who refused to participate in the forum. Unlike the situation in *Evening News,* the licensee and the opposing side were willing to participate in a forum broadcast, and it was the complainants who vetoed their own appearance. *See also Letter to Dominican Republic Information Center,* 40 F.C.C. 457 (1957), where the FCC made the statement that "the Commission has no authority to direct a licensee to present or to refrain from presenting a particular program."

192. New Broadcasting Co., 40 F.C.C. 439 (1950). The Commission regarded it as controversial because differing views were being "actively controverted by members of the public" and congressmen, and because the station's intensive programming on the issue over a 30-day period raised "the assumption that at least one of the purposes of the broadcasts was to influence public opinion," *Id.* at 440. In not taking steps to broadcast views opposed to the Fair Employment Practices Commission, the licensee had violated its "affirmative duty to seek out, aid and encourage the broadcast of opposing views on controversial questions of public importance." *Id.* The licensee was consequently asked in a letter to advise the FCC what corrective action it would take, hardly a sanction with much punch.

193. In Herbert Muschel, 18 P & F RADIO REG. 8 (1958), a licensee's lack of affirmative efforts to secure contrasting viewpoints was a factor (although not the critical one) weighed by the Commission in deciding frequency allocation. *Id.* at 33, par. 20. In John Dempsey, 40 F.C.C. 445 (1950), the Commission, responding to charges of a station's one-sided public affairs coverage, reiterated the licensee's "affirmative duty to seek out, aid and encourage

the broadcast of views on the other side." *Id.* at 445–46. *See also* Alabama Broadcasting System, Inc., *supra* note 189; Evening News Association, *supra* note 191; New Broadcasting Co., *supra* note 192.

194. 40 F.C.C. 468 (1958).

195. *Id.*

196. *Id.*

197. To substantiate this, the Commission pointed to ongoing congressional hearings on the topic. *Id.* at 469. It also mentioned that local newspapers, magazines, and direct mailings were discussing subscription TV.

198. *Id.* The Commission also rejected the station's contention that it could present only anti-subscription-TV views in light of the great amount of pro-pay-TV publicity afforded by other organs of the local media. "[T]he requirement of fairness applies to a broadcast licensee irrespective of the position which may be taken by other media on the issue involved . . . [T]he licensee's own performance . . . in and of itself, must demonstrate compliance with said policy." *Id.* However, the FCC renewed WSOC-TV's license despite the fairness violation, because its operation had been otherwise satisfactory.

199. Unfortunately, the FCC in its letter does not specify the other kinds of steps that the station might have taken, such as having its own staff prepare a pro-subscription program or making a much more intensive effort to recruit pro-pay-TV spokesmen.

200. *See,* for example, the discussion of bills in the 74th Congress in ROBERT S. MCMAHON, REGULATION OF BROADCASTING, HALF A CENTURY OF GOVERNMENT REGULATION OF BROADCASTING AND THE NEED FOR FURTHER LEGISLATIVE ACTION, STUDY FOR THE HOUSE COMM. ON INTERSTATE AND FOREIGN COMMERCE, 85th Cong., 2d Sess. 54 (1958), and *Hearings on Communications Act Amendments before a Subcomm. of the House Comm. on Interstate and Foreign Commerce,* 84th Cong., 2d Sess. 277, 323 (1956).

201. Columbia Broadcasting System, Inc., 26 F.C.C. 715 (1959).

202. The Commission's decision in Allen H. Blondy, 40 F.C.C. 284 (1957), just two years before, seemed in direct conflict with its *Lar Daly* ruling.

203. *Hearings on Political Broadcasting before the Communications Subcomm. of the Senate Comm. on Interstate and Foreign Commerce,* 86th Cong., 1st Sess. (1959).

204. S. REP. NO. 562, 86th Cong., 1st Sess. (1959).

205. *Id.* at 13 (italics added). The Senate Report also reiterated the standard scarcity and power of information rationales for broadcast regulation.

206. 105 CONG. REC. 14457 (1959).

207. *Id.* at 14457, 14462.

208. *Id.* at 14457.

209. *Id.*

210. *Id.* at 14462 (italics added). In light of the existing statutory requirement and reference to it in the Senate Report, Senator Pastore considered the amendment "surplusage," but nonetheless accepted it. *Id.*

211. *Id.* (italics added).

212. H.R. REP. NO. 802, 86th Cong., 1st Sess. (1959).

213. 105 CONG. REC. 16231 (1959) (italics added). There was also an amendment offered and defeated in the House that would have provided for equal time for "representatives of any political or legislative philosophy." *Id.* at 16245. The difficulty of providing precisely equal time to every such representative, and the consequent adverse effect on other programming, were mentioned as objections to the amendment in a very short floor discussion. *Id.* at 16246.

214. H.R. REP. NO. 1069, 86th Cong., 1st Sess. 5 (1959) (italics added). In the United States Code the word "Act" is changed to "Chapter," referring to a chapter of the Communications Act that covers "Wire or Radio Communication." 47 U.S.C. sec. 315(a) (1970).

215. H.R. REP. NO. 1069, 86th Cong., 1st Sess. 5 (1959).

216. 105 CONG. REC. 17830 (1959) (italics added).

217. *Id.* at 17831.

218. *Id.* at 17778 (italics added).

219. *Id.* at 17778, 17779.
220. Robinson, *The FCC and the First Amendment, supra* note 106, at 134.
221. This was later changed to "Chapter." *See* note 214, *supra.*
222. Zemel v. Rusk, 381 U.S. 1, 11, 12 (1965); Udall v. Tallman, 380 U.S. 1, 16–18 (1965); United States v. Burlington & M. R. Ry., 98 U.S. 334, 341 (1878).
223. John W. Dean, *Political Broadcasting: The Communications Act of 1934 Reviewed,* 20 FED. COM. B.J. 26, 31 (1966). *See also* Commissioner Robinson's comments in the text accompanying note 220, *supra.*
224. Metropolitan Broadcasting, 40 F.C.C. 491, 493 (1960).
225. *The History of the Fairness Doctrine, app. B, Applicability of the Fairness Doctrine in the Handling of Controversial Issues of Public Importance,* 29 FED. REG. 10425 (1964). In this particular interpretation, the FCC unduly restricts the statute's effect by focusing on the part two requirement "to be fair in the broadcasting of controversial issues," and by ignoring the part one affirmative presentation duty.
226. The Commission, in a letter to Congressman Harris, also noted that "the Communications Act imposes the specific obligation of fairness upon the broadcast licensee who permits use of his facilities for the presentation of programming dealing with controversial issues of public importance. . . . In short . . . there is a specific statutory obligation . . . to be fair in treating controversial issues." Honorable Oren Harris, 40 F.C.C. 582, 583 (1963).
227. 395 U.S. 367 (1969).
228. The Court actually misstated a broadcaster's obligation in declaring it has to discuss "both sides" of controversial issues of public importance. Many issues have more than just the two sides that the word "both" implies. A licensee must broadcast "conflicting views" on the issues, which may often include more than two.
229. *Id.* at 380 (italics added). The Court added that subsequent legislation declaring an earlier statute's intent is entitled to great weight, that the statutory construction of an agency that interprets a statute should be followed unless there are compelling indications that the construction is wrong, and that Congress had not altered the FCC's construction but in fact had approved it. *Id.* at 380-81.
230. *Id.* at 381–82.
231. *Id.* at 382.
232. *Id.* at 385.
233. *Id.*
234. Little more than a week before making his proposal, Chairman Wiley, at the end of a research interview, asked my opinion of lifting fairness obligations from radio in certain major markets. Interview with Richard Wiley by Steven J. Simmons, Sept. 8, 1975. My response was that, if done as an experiment with controls, the idea had merit. However, I pointed out that there would be severe statutory problems in light of the 1959 amendment and *Red Lion's* interpretation of the amendment. The Chairman immediately and perceptively acknowledged that this indeed would have to be considered. He made his proposal public in an address to the International Radio and Television Society on September 16, 1975. BROADCASTING, Sept. 22, 1975, at 22-24. After pointing to such large markets as Chicago, where "there are 65 commercial radio stations, or Los Angeles, where there are 29," the Chairman stated that "one might reasonably expect that an extensive range of viewpoints would be presented even with no government oversight." Mr. Wiley said the proposal should be the subject of an inquiry that would include a look at the "legal issues involved." *Id.* at 24. "Less than 24 hours later, Senator John Pastore (D—R.I.), Chairman of the Senate Communications Subcommittee before whom Chairman Wiley was testifying . . . indicated he doubted that the Commission has the authority to suspend the fairness doctrine without congressional action." *Id.* at 22.
235. Columbia Broadcasting Sys., Inc. v. Democratic Nat'l Comm., 412 U.S. 94, 129-30 (1973). The Court also states that Congress, in 1959, "amended section 315 of the Act to give statutory approval of the fairness doctrine," *Id.* at 110, n.18. The same interpretation is repeated at 113, n.12.
236. Accuracy in Media, Inc. v. FCC, 521 F.2d 288, 296 n.34 (D.C. Cir. 1975) (italics added). The quote continued, "and in the 'public convenience, interest, and necessity' provision of 47 U.S.C. sec. 303 (1970) generally."

237. Straus Communications, Inc. v. FCC, 530 F.2d 1001, 1007 n.11 (D.C. Cir. 1976) (italics added). It should be emphasized that the quoted dictum, like the dicta cited in the previous two footnotes, was set forth as general background information by the court. The issue of whether the 1959 amendment mandates the fairness doctrine was not an issue of law specifically decided by any of these cases. However, the remarks do indicate the trend of judicial thinking on the matter.

238. To say that there is adequate discussion of controversial issues of public importance over an entire market when viewed from the perspective of dozens and dozens of radio stations is not responsive to the statutory mandate. Ten stations cannot carry the ball for the other thirty in a market. Under the statute, *each* station must engage in public issue discussion.

239. Some sort of balanced access or minimum percentage of time scheme might suffice. In the *Columbia Broadcasting* case the Court, speaking through Chief Justice Burger, stated that "Congress has time and again rejected various legislative attempts that would have mandated a variety of forms of individual access. That is not to say that Congress' rejection of such proposals must be taken to mean that Congress is opposed to private rights of access under all circumstances. Rather, the point is that Congress has chosen to leave such questions with the Commission, to which it has given flexibility to experiment with new ideas as changing conditions require. . . . Conceivably at some future date Congress or the Commission—or the broadcasters—may devise some kind of limited right of access that is both practicable and desirable." Columbia Broadcasting Sys., Inc. v. Democratic Nat'l Comm., 412 U.S. 94, 122, 131 (1973). In a 1975 First Circuit Court of Appeals case, the court rejected petitioners' arguments that the 1959 amendment required the doctrine to be applied to standard broadcast commercials advertising snowmobiles. Public Interest Group v. FCC, 522 F.2d 1060 (1st Cir. 1975). The court, in an opinion by Judge Campbell, stated that petitioners' argument assumes a degree of legislative specificity that simply does not exist. "We cannot, merely from the generalized congressional endorsements described in *Red Lion,* say that the Commission acted contrary to statute when it struck the current balance between product advertising and the fairness doctrine. We think Congress left questions of application and accommodation to the Commission under the general public interest standard. . . ." *Id.* at 1066-67.

240. Indeed, in an opinion released March 24, 1976, the FCC indicated it had decided not to proceed with the Wiley proposal. Memorandum Opinion and Order on Reconsideration of the Fairness Report, 58 F.C.C.2d 691 (1976). Chairman Wiley, in a separate statement, still supported his proposal but declared that "[t]he question of the Commission's legal authority to adopt a fairness experiment is somewhat more difficult and complex. Prior to 1959, there would have been no doubt that we had the discretion to conduct such an experiment. In that year, however, the Communications Act was amended so as to refer approvingly to the standard of fairness in broadcasting. The literal wording of the statute indicates only that the Commission's fairness policies were left undisturbed, but the provision has, nevertheless, been widely interpreted to stand as a 'codification' or legislative enactment of the doctrine." *Id.* at 700 (separate statement of Chairman Wiley).

241. See Chapter Five.

242. However, the part one obligation was spoken of as requiring licensees to devote a "reasonable" or "sufficient" or "adequate" "percentage" or "amount" of time to controversial public issues. Thus it was a requirement to cover issues generally. Part two, on the other hand, was oriented to specific issues. Contrasting views were to be given to a specific issue initially presented by the licensee. Thus, FCC intervention to assure specific issue balancing may be viewed as more appropriate in the part two situation. The double standard that developed later can be seen as flowing to a large degree from the part one orientation toward covering issues generally, requiring less FCC intervention on behalf of specific issue coverage.

4

The FCC's
Personal Attack and Political Editorial
Rules Reconsidered

Under the personal attack and political editorial rules, an individual or group that is attacked during a discussion of a controversial issue of public importance or a candidate who is not favored in a broadcast licensee's political editorial is provided an opportunity to respond over the air.[1] Like the general fairness requirements, the personal attack and political editorial rules are geared, at least theoretically, to keeping the public informed of contrasting views on important public issues. Thus, a person who was attacked in a broadcast is not entitled to air time to respond unless the attack occurred during discussion of a controversial issue of public importance.[2] When a response is presented, the public is given the opportunity to hear that a person involved in a public controversy may not be as the attacker depicted him. Similarly, the candidate who was not endorsed or who was specifically opposed in an editorial gets the chance to present a different view on how the public should vote. In providing these reply opportunities, the FCC not only attempts to keep the public informed, but also tries to prevent any licensee from using the power of its scarce airwave frequency to influence the public unduly and allows some access for those who have been harmed by a broadcast to respond to it.[3] In the Commission's view, the personal attack and political editorial rules "serve to effectuate important aspects of the well established Fairness Doctrine. . . ."[4]

I. THE DEVELOPMENT OF THE RULES

A. PRE-1967 CASE LAW

Unlike the general fairness doctrine, the origins of which can be traced as far back as the Federal Radio Commission's 1929 decision in *Great Lakes Broadcasting*,[5] specific FCC involvement with personal attacks and political editorials had a later start. In the first definitive Commission report on the fairness doctrine, issued in 1949, the FCC stated: "[E]lementary considerations of fairness may dictate that time be allocated to a person or group which has been specifically attacked over the station, where otherwise no such obligation would exist."[6]

The personal attack and political editorial case law, however, did not begin to evolve seriously until the early 1960s. In *Clayton W. Mapoles*,[7] a group of state and county officials from Florida complained that Mr. Mapoles, licensee of radio station WEBY, had used the station to attack them personally. They alleged that station broadcasts had accused them of political tricks, dictatorial tactics, and using their offices for personal gain, and otherwise had denigrated their personal character and integrity. Mapoles, they charged, was doing all this primarily to promote his own candidacy for the state senate.

The Commission, after a series of on-the-spot interviews, found that the licensee indeed had attacked the petitioners. It concluded: "Where, as here, the attacks are of a highly personal nature which impugn the character and honesty of named individuals, the licensee has an affirmative duty to take all appropriate steps to see to it that the persons attacked are afforded the fullest opportunity to respond."[8] Finding, however, that Mapoles had offered the attacked individuals, in on-the-air announcements, an opportunity to respond over the station's facilities and had not used the station to promote his own candidacy for office, the Commission denied the petition for nonrenewal of Mapoles' license.

In a concurring opinion, FCC Chairman Newton Minow further delineated the kinds of "appropriate steps" that should be taken by licensees when personal attacks occur. "In many, if not most, cases," on-the-air statements offering response time to those personally attacked may not be enough. Rather, licensees may have to notify those to be attacked in advance of the broadcast, provide them with tapes or a verbatim text of the broadcast, or both.[9]

In *Billings Broadcasting Company*,[10] decided the same year as *Mapoles*, the general manager of the National Rural Electric Cooperative Association complained that a Montana radio station had broadcast at least 20 editorials vilifying him in connection with the Association's position favoring the creation of public utility districts in the state. He maintained that the station's offer allowing him to respond in an interview format was unfair and untimely because he had just arrived in town and could not prepare adequately. Although the Commission neither denied renewal of the license nor mandated absolutely the prior notice requirement advocated by Chairman Minow in *Mapoles,* it did state:

> [W]here, as here, a station's editorials attack an individual by name, the "fairness doctrine" requires that a copy of the specific editorial or editorials shall be communicated to the person attacked either prior to or at the time of the broadcast of such editorials so that a reasonable opportunity is afforded that person to reply.[11]

In failing to supply copies of the protested editorials, the Montana station had violated fairness doctrine requirements.

The broadcasts in *Mapoles* and *Billings* involved attacks on officials already elected or appointed to office. *Times-Mirror Broadcasting Company,*[12] on the other hand, focused on candidates seeking office. Two television commentators on KTTV in Los Angeles had made statements about the candidates and issues in the 1962 California gubernatorial campaign. In over 20 different broadcasts they had spoken either against incumbent Governor Brown and the Democratic Party or in favor of challenger Richard Nixon and the Republicans. Among their broadcasts were attacks on Brown such as one claiming "he is one of the greatest ignoramuses on Communism that ever lived or he is soft on it."[13] Their remarks apparently did not have much effect on the campaign's outcome; the former vice-president lost in his home state—ironically, he placed much of the blame on an alleged media bias against him.[14] The commentators' statements did have significance, however, in the development of evolving personal attack and political editorial case law.

In response to a complaint from the Democrats, the Commission telegrammed KTTV that the station's two broadcasts devoted to viewpoints opposed to those previously presented by the commentators did not adequately fulfill fairness doctrine requirements. KTTV's actions had violated "the right of the public to a fair presentation of views."[15] The Commission further asserted that if a station permits any person other than a candidate to attack one candidate or support another by direct or indirect identification, the station must "send a transcript of the pertinent continuity on each such program to the appropriate candidate immediately and should offer a comparable opportunity for an appropriate spokesman to answer the broadcast."[16] Responding to KTTV's objection that requiring such procedures might deter stations from covering election-period issues, the Commission sent a followup telegram a week later that exempted newscasts and news interviews, as well as discussion programs where contrasting spokesmen aired their views, from the personal attack notification procedures.[17]

Licensees were reminded of their personal attack responsibilities in a 1963 public notice[18] that summarized the three decisions just discussed. The notice stated that a licensee should send the text of the pertinent continuity to the attacked party and include a "specific offer" to use its broadcast facilities for response.[19] The 1964 *Fairness Primer*[20] also contained a section devoted to the "Personal Attack Principle"[21] that similarly digested the pertinent FCC decisions. It also cited the Commission's response to an inquiry letter sent in 1963 stating that, even if the attack is made by a party unconnected with the station, a station must follow personal attack procedures and that, if no tape or transcript is available, a licensee must send the most accurate summary possible to the party affected.[22]

In a *Fairness Primer* footnote, the FCC made four major points: the personal attack procedure is applicable only when statements are made "in connection with a controversial issue of public importance"; it is concerned only with attacks on a person's or group's "integrity, character, or honesty or like personal qualities"; it is not applicable to mere references to people or groups or mere disagreement about views on an issue; and it is not relevant to attacks on foreign leaders.[23]

During the same period that the FCC became active in the personal attack and political editorial area, legislative attention began to focus on the problem. The intense congressional concern about creating a viable remedial procedure for personal attacks, especially with respect to political candidates, was reflected in this 1963 statement addressed to FCC Chairman William Henry by Senator John Pastore, Chairman of the Senate Subcommittee on Communications:

> I think you ought to give the aggrieved party some immediate remedy.
> . . . All you have to do is worry about setting up the mechanism for

this person to bring his side to the public attention before it is too late. I would hope the Commission would get into this immediately.[24]

Agreeing with Senator Pastore, Chairman Henry, at hearings before the House and Senate Subcommittees on Communications, indicated that the Commission was considering issuing specific rules with respect to personal attacks over the airwaves and recommended that legislation not be passed in this area.[25] Nevertheless, it was almost three years before the FCC adopted a notice of proposed rulemaking to deal with the problem.[26]

B. THE 1967 RULES AND AMENDMENTS

The Commission finally issued specific rules on July 10, 1967.[27] The two primary reasons advanced for embodying personal attack and political editorial procedures in rule form were to make licensing procedures more precise and clear and to provide a basis for imposing sanctions in the event of noncompliance.[28] The rules are stated in three paragraphs:

Personal attacks; political editorials.

(a) When, during the presentation of views on a controversial issue of public importance, an attack is made upon the honesty, character, integrity or like personal qualities of an identified person or group, the licensee shall, within a reasonable time and in no event later than 1 week after the attack, transmit to the person or group attacked (1) notification of the date, time and identification of the broadcast; (2) a script or tape (or an accurate summary if a script or tape is not available) of the attack; and (3) an offer of reasonable opportunity to respond over the licensee's facilities.

(b) The provisions of paragraph (a) of this section shall be inapplicable to attacks on foreign groups or foreign public figures or where personal attacks are made by legally qualified candidates, their authorized spokesmen, or those associated with them in the campaign, on other such candidates, their authorized spokesman, or persons associated with the candidates in the campaign.

NOTE: In a specific factual situation, the fairness doctrine may be applicable in this general area of political broadcasts. See, section 315(a) of the Act (47 U.S.C. 315(a)); public notice: Applicability of the Fairness Doctrine in the Handling of Controversial Issues of Public Importance. 29 Fed. Reg. 10415.

(c) Where a licensee, in an editorial, (i) endorses or (ii) opposes a legally qualified candidate or candidates, the licensee shall, within 24 hours after the editorial, transmit to respectively (i) the other qualified candidate or candidates for the same office or (ii) the candidate opposed in the editorial (1) notification of the date and the time of the editorial; (2) a script or tape of the editorial; and (3) an offer of a reasonable opportunity for a candidate or a spokesman of the candidate to respond over the licensee's facilities: *Provided, however,* that where such editorials are broadcast within 72 hours prior to the day of the election, the licensee shall comply with the provisions of this subsection sufficiently far in advance of the broadcast to enable the candidate or candidates to have a reasonable opportunity to prepare a response and to present it in a timely fashion.[29]

In the text accompanying the announcement of the new rules, the Commission emphasized that the personal attack principle is part and parcel of the fairness doctrine and that the attack rules are applicable only when an attack occurs in the context of discussion of a controversial issue of public importance.[30] After brusquely rejecting arguments that the rules violate broadcasters' First Amendment rights,[31] the Commission stated that a licensee is responsible for what is broadcast over its facilities and must obey the personal attack rules even if the attack is made on a network show.[32] The Commission tempered its warning, however, by noting that the rule would not be used to sanction those who seek to comply with it in good faith.[33] It also stressed that personal attacks and political editorials were in no way prohibited; if such attacks or editorials were presented, however, the notification and reply opportunity requirements must be met.[34] The Commission concluded its remarks by pointing out that campaign attacks by candidates and their spokesmen against other candidates had been excluded because they usually fall within the equal time bailiwick[35] and, in offering a reply to a licensee political editorial, the licensee could air a candidate's spokesman instead of the candidate in order to avoid equal time obligations.[36]

Some of the procedures outlined in the new rules went further than the previous case law. For example, the new rules provided more specific time limits for notification and transmittal of the date and time of the broadcast and a more specific description of the proper form for an attack text reproduction.[37] The Commission also expanded the scope of the personal attack principle by failing to exempt from personal attack rules, in apparent repudiation of one of its previous rulings,[38] newscasts, news interviews, and

discussion programs including opposing speakers. At the same
time, the Commission loosened its requirements in some respects.
Although earlier cases had indicated that an attacked party should
be notified prior to or at the time of the broadcast containing the
attack,[39] the Commission did not require such advance or simultaneous notification in the rules.[40]

The news exemptions were reinstituted by two amendments
to the rules that came within a year of promulgation of the rules.
Less than a month after the rules were issued, the FCC exempted
bona fide newscasts and on-the-spot coverage of bona fide news
events from personal attack requirements[41] on the grounds that
requiring personal attack procedures for such programming might
be impractical and impede the news functions of licensees. Standard journalistic practices were thought adequate to assure the
broadcast of both sides of newsworthy personal attacks; in any case,
the general fairness doctrine provided an ultimate safeguard.[42] The
same considerations led the Commission later to exempt bona fide
news interviews and news commentary or analysis contained in any
newscast, news interview, or on-the-spot news coverage, after CBS
charged that the personal attack procedures inhibited journalism in
these areas.[43] The FCC added that it generally had not been faced
with personal attack problems in the news categories being exempted and that it was simply tracking the exemptions Congress
had made to the equal time requirements.[44] It reminded licensees,
however, that the general fairness doctrine still applied to the
exempt categories.[45]

Like the fairness doctrine generally, the personal attack and
political editorial rules on their face are applicable to both commercial and noncommercial broadcast stations and to origination
cablecasting under the control of cable system operators.[46] The
political editorial rules, however, do not have any real relevance for
noncommercial stations because Congress has forbidden such
broadcasters from editorializing or endorsing particular candidates
for political office.[47]

C. EMERGING GUIDEPOSTS IN POST-1967 DECISIONS

The most important post-1967 development involving the
personal attack and political editorial rules—and indeed the fairness doctrine itself—was the Supreme Court's decision in *Red Lion
Broadcasting Co. v. FCC*,[48] which held the rules and the underlying

fairness doctrine to be both statutorily authorized and constitutional. Aside from indicating that, as in general fairness doctrine cases, a licensee may not insist on payment from an attacked party for reply time, however, the case did not shed much light on how the rules were to be implemented.

A string of FCC decisions beginning in the late 1960s do provide some guidance. The FCC stated repeatedly that passing references to[49] or mere disagreement with[50] individuals or groups do not constitute attacks. It indicated that an attack can be made even when an individual is not named specifically, as long as he is sufficiently identified.[51] The Commission reaffirmed the attack rules' exemption of newscasts,[52] bona fide news interviews,[53] and attacks made on candidates by supporters of other candidates.[54] It stressed that, because the purpose of the rules is to inform the public on "vital issues of the day" and not to settle private disputes, for the personal attack rules to apply the attack must occur during discussion of a controversial issue of public importance.[55]

The Commission also emphasized the importance of the notification obligations. If there is any question whether statements made in a broadcast comprise a personal attack within the meaning of the rules, the licensee must retain a tape, script, or contemporaneously made summary of the remarks.[56] The FCC further declared that licensee inquiries to the Commission seeking advice on whether an attack has occurred should be made promptly and that, despite any uncertainty, the potentially attacked party should be notified within the prescribed seven-day period.[57]

FCC decisions further refined the meaning of "a reasonable opportunity to respond" in the personal attack context. As in the area of the general fairness doctrine, "what constitutes a reasonable opportunity to respond" is largely a "matter . . . for the good faith, reasonable judgment of the licensee."[58] This "good faith, reasonable judgment" must be made by the licensee with regard to both the placement of the response program and the amount of time afforded to the reply.[59] The Commission, however, tightened these loose-fitting fairness doctrine requirements by forbidding a licensee to insist that a reply to a personal attack be made as part of a round-table or panel discussion, where a moderator and questions or debate are involved.[60] Instead, the attacked party must be afforded a more direct opportunity to reply, although the licensee can insist that the reply be reasonably responsive to the attack.[61] The attacked party's reply may not be prefaced or followed by repetition or justification of the original attack,[62] nor may the licensee determine the reply spokesman—as it may in the ordinary fairness situation—because the person who responds ordinarily should be the person who was attacked or his designated spokesman.[63] If the attacked party is on the line of a radio phone-in show while the attack takes place and has an immediate opportunity to respond, however, the licensee has complied with the personal attack rules without doing anything more.[64]

"A reasonable opportunity to respond" has undergone similar case law definition in the political editorial context in the post-1967 period. The FCC held that if a candidate's response to a station's endorsement of another candidate is preceded by repetition of the endorsement, the reply opportunity is not reasonable and the licensee will incur additional reply obligations, unless the responding candidate either agrees to the repetition or is going to challenge the original endorsement by "specific mention thereof."[65] Moreover, the Commission tightened the parameters of what constitutes a reasonable opportunity to respond. Thus, total time ratios of approximately 4 to 1[66] and 2.7 to 1[67] (licensee editorial time to candidate reply time) were considered unreasonable, as were frequency of broadcast ratios of 4 to 1[68] and 7 to 2[69] (number of licensee editorial broadcasts to candidate reply broadcasts). Although precisely equal time has not been required under the political editorial rules,[70] greater equality is demanded than in the general fairness context.[71] The Commission declared: "In many instances a comparable opportunity in time and scheduling will be clearly appropriate" in the political editorial and personal attack situations.[72]

II. PROBLEMS IN IMPLEMENTATION OF THE PERSONAL ATTACK RULES

The FCC's rulings in the personal attack area have left an inconsistent and confusing trail of precedent on the critical questions of what constitutes a personal attack, what constitutes a controversial issue of public importance and how closely the attack must follow or precede discussion of the issue in order to be "during the presentation" of that issue. The precedent has generated other problems as well.

The following are demonstrative pairings of Commission rulings on what constitutes a personal attack under the rules.[73]

(1) Claiming that a County Board had " 'hoodwinked' a governmental agency" in part by using county vehicles for "taxi service" and had sold land in violation of the law, and accusing a county commissioner of taking a "champagne flight" for personal gratification when only authorized to fly on government business, do not constitute personal attacks;[74] but suggesting that the management of a local radio station may have dynamited the station transmitter to hoodwink the insurance company and fraudulently collect insurance proceeds, does.[75]

(2) Asserting that the Roman Catholic Church was illegally lobbying against abortion[76] and that a state legislator was projecting a conflict of interest image because of his private dealings[77] are not attacks; but implying that a political candidate might be receiving campaign contributions from crime figures, is.[78]

(3) Claiming that doctors and nurses in a hospital are "incompetent" is not an attack;[79] but suggesting that a female newspaper reporter obtained good interviews because of the way she positioned her legs and that she should get a job in a massage parlor, is.[80]

(4) Calling a person an "extremist" and a "patriotic extremist" is not an attack;[81] but asserting that an institute and its newsletter are "subversive," to the "Far Left," and run by a "Communist," is.[82]

(5) Stating that a university is a "breeding ground for Arab revolutionaries and terrorists," a "Guerrilla U.," and a "pipeline to the Palestinian guerrilla movement" is not an attack;[83] but claiming that the John Birch Society engages in "physical abuse and violence" and "local terror campaigns against opposition figures,"[84] and asserting that the United Church of Christ is "part of a conspiracy to cause prison unrest through illegal and violent means" and is financing "violent and/or subversive" groups, are.[85]

(6) Calling two United States senators "liberals and socialists" is not an attack;[86] but declaring that a university professor is a "Communist," is.[87]

(7) Declaring that a teacher federation was subjecting the public to "blackmail," that it was demanding "blood money," and in effect that its members were "unscrupulous criminals" is not a

personal attack;[88] but calling a congressman a "coward" for not appearing on an interview show, is.[89]

Many of these decisions, analyzed individually, do not appear unreasonable.[90] But, as Professor Benno Schmidt suggests, when rulings such as these "are read together, the decisions seem haphazard, and they hopelessly confuse any effort to figure out what general principles delineate the scope of the personal attack rules."[91] The Commission often fails even to provide rationales for its findings that particular comments constitute personal attacks.[92]

To be sure, some generalizations can be made. The Commission does not seem to consider mere policy disagreements[93] or charges of incompetence or bad judgment[94] to be personal attacks. Allegations of criminal activity,[95] moral turpitude, communist or subversive activity, or promotion of violence, on the other hand, generally are held to constitute such attacks. Nevertheless, as the above cases indicate, the pattern is extremely hard to follow and riddled with inconsistency. For example, in many cases, the line between charges of incompetence and bad judgment and those involving integrity or character seems very unclear and difficult to administer. Indeed, insofar as the purpose of the rules is to keep the public informed about important, controversial issues, it would seem that questions about certain individuals' competence and judgment often may be more important than other private, moral questions. Commission rulings, however, do not seem to be consistently sensitive to the purposes behind the rules.

B. WHAT IS A CONTROVERSIAL ISSUE OF PUBLIC IMPORTANCE?

As noted earlier,[96] an attack triggers the rules' obligations only if it occurs during discussion of a controversial issue of public importance. Therefore, the question of whether an issue raised is controversial and of public importance, so troublesome in the general fairness doctrine context,[97] must be answered. The Commission usually has failed to provide any rationale for why a particular issue is considered to be controversial or of public importance. The factors of media coverage, official and community leader attention, and impact that were stressed in the 1974 *Fairness Report*[98] are generally ignored. Thus, the radio discussion of a national organization's alleged association with Communists and alleged infiltration of the Methodist Church were found to be "clearly . . . controversial issues of public importance" in *WIYN Radio, Inc.*[99] Yet no evidence of controversy in the community or statements by officials or leaders indicating the issue's importance was offered by the Commission to support its "clear" conclusion. The same lack of analysis is evident in other Commission conclusions about the controversial nature and public importance of other issues, such as the role of the radical right[100] or whether the DuBois Clubs are being used by the Communist Party to subvert American youth.[101] The Commission's rejection of some pesonal attack complaints because the complainants had not "furnished the Commission with any information to indicate that there was a public debate or controversy in the community . . . so as to create a controversial issue of public importance,"[102] is absurd in light of its totally unsupported conclusions in other cases.

As might be expected from the Commission's failure to supply supporting rationales, the FCC's decisions on whether issues are controversial and of public importance display a lack of consistency. For example, the Commission found that the dismissal of an individual doctor from a city hospital was a controversial issue of public importance,[103] but an election between branches of two national labor unions involving 1,230 employees and affecting thousands of households was held not to involve such an issue.[104] A station management's alleged dynamiting of its transmitter in violation of public interest responsibilities was a controversial issue of public importance,[105] but a license renewal application, the success of which similarly determined whether the station could continue to broadcast, was not.[106]

C. THE "DURING THE PRESENTATION" REQUIREMENT

A significant question that has received very little attention is how close in time the personal attack must be to the discussion of the controversial issue of public importance in order for the attack to have been made "during the presentation" of that issue. The few Commission and staff statements on this question indicate that the FCC is taking an overexpansive view of when an attack is made during the presentation of an issue.

In *Richard S. Manne*,[107] an accusation that a rival station had intentionally dynamited its transmitter was considered a personal attack made during discussion of a controversial public issue even though the Commission had not received the "specific language of the discussion during which the statement was made.

. . ."[108] That the station making the broadcast had engaged in a "continuing discussion" of the construction and operation of the rival station was considered sufficient to establish that the "during the presentation" requirement had been met.

Three years later, in *Thomas O'Brien*,[109] this requirement was given a seemingly more restricted reading. Unnamed college professors were accused of treason in the first of a three-part program, and two were named in the second and third parts. The "during the presentation" requirement was met "even though the charge of treason and the naming of the professors took place in three different portions of the speech, since the three portions are so closely related as to constitute a continuing discussion of the same issue."[110] This result seems reasonable; all three parts dealt with the same topic and were explicitly presented by the broadcaster as interdependent segments.

Straus Communications, Inc.[111] is the most significant case dealing with this issue. The case involved a comment made by Bob Grant, the host of a phone-in show on radio station WMCA in New York City. On March 8, 1973, Grant began the phone-in program by reviewing the news of the day, including the nationwide meat boycott then in progress. Shortly after announcing that Benjamin Rosenthal, a local congressman and leader in the boycott, would soon be interviewed over the phone, Grant learned that Rosenthal had refused to be interviewed. Grant then told the audience of Rosenthal's refusal, suggested it might have resulted from past differences between the congressman and himself, and emphasized that he nonetheless agreed with the congressman on the boycott issue. Grant added that he could not believe the congressman "was afraid to come on" the program and that Rosenthal should lay aside his "prejudices" and discuss the "public issue."[112] At approximately 12:45 P.M., a full two hours after these comments were made, Grant was discussing with a caller some vaguely suggested improprieties involving mothballed government ships. In response to the caller's spontaneous outburst of praise for Grant, Grant stated: "[W]hen I hear about guys like Ben Rosenthal . . . I have to say I wish there were a thousand Bob Grants 'cause then you wouldn't have . . . a coward like him in the United States Congress. . . ."[113]

After Rosenthal filed a complaint, the Commission ruled that the "coward" comment was a personal attack, finding that the controversial issue of public importance was the nationwide meat boycott that Grant had discussed at 10:45 A.M. Most of those listening during the 12:45 lunch hour, when Rosenthal was called a coward, probably never heard the boycott issue discussed. For these listeners, the remark, thrown into an unrelated discussion of mothballed ships, must have made little sense. Those persons who did hear the earlier discussion doubtless would have realized that it was nothing more than Grant expressing frustration at Rosenthal's refusal to be interviewed. The Commission, however, supplying no further analysis, cited *Manne* and *O'Brien* to support its conclusion that the attack was made during the presentation of the boycott issue.[114] Both cases are arguably inapposite, however, because, in each, the attacks were made in the context of continuing discussions of the issue in question.

The case was appealed to the Circuit Court for the District of Columbia, which reversed the Commission's decision.[115] The court found that the station's arguments that Grant's remark did not occur during discussion of a controversial public issue "could hardly be called insubstantial,"[116] and concluded that the Commission had "made its own judgment, instead of judging the objective reasonableness of the licensee's determination."[117] That "[t]he Commission's decision amounted to a significant extension of the Personal Attack Rule to embrace instances where an alleged attack is separated by a substantial time lapse from the issue discussion to which it supposedly relates"[118] was considered a further demonstration of the reasonableness and good faith of the station.

The Commission must reconsider its position in future cases. The court, in a footnote, pointed out that its opinion would not necessarily bar the Commission's interpretation once that interpretation is communicated to broadcasters.[119] But when the relation of an attack to the underlying issue is as remote as it was in *Straus*, the policies underlying the attack rules—informing the public, providing access for the expression of views, and preventing stations from exercising undue political influence[120]—are not served by requiring the station to offer an opportunity to respond. In *Straus* the remarks simply had nothing to do with the issue being discussed—

mothballed ships—and were exceedingly remote in time from the identified controversial issue of public importance, the meat boycott.[121] The Commission's interpretation, at least as evidenced in *Straus* and *Manne,* seems so broad it practically reads the "during the presentation" requirement out of the attack rules.

D. OTHER PROBLEMS

Although the Commissoin has exempted bona fide newscasts, on-the-spot coverage of news events, and news interviews, as well as news commentary or analysis contained in any of these formats,[122] it has not exempted news documentaries or news commentary outside of the above contexts. If standard journalistic practices justify an exemption for other forms of news coverage,[123] they likewise should justify an exemption for news documentaries. Broadcasters surely do not lose their journalistic standards when they move from one form of news coverage to another.

The Commission has indicated that, in providing an opportunity to respond to an attack, total time and frequency ratios and time of day comparisons must be closer than in the general fairness context.[124] It has failed to go further, however, and define more precisely what constitutes a "comparative opportunity" for the attack victim.

Similarly, the Commission has not addressed the length of time a broadcaster may wait, after notifying the attack victim, before airing the response. In the political editorial situation, the election places a natural outer limit for responses, but no such easy answers exist in the personal attack context.

Finally, if a dispute erupts over whether a reply opportunity must be given, the Commission may take close to a year to rule on the matter—by which time the election may have been held or the attack forgotten. Of course, some administrative delay is inevitable, but the record indicates that the FCC has been lax in its administration of these disputes.[125]

III. THE ARGUMENT FOR REPEAL OF THE PERSONAL ATTACK RULES

Although the Commission's enforcement of the personal attack rule deserves criticism, the real problem lies in the rule itself.

The rule's failure to serve the policies underlying the fairness doctrine, the administrative complications the rule has spawned, its impingement on First Amendment freedoms, and the availability of alternative relief support the conclusion that the rule should be repealed *in toto*.

The attack rule, as part of the fairness doctrine, is justifiable only to the extent it furthers that doctrine's policies. The attack rules do not fulfill the objectives of informing the public and providing alternative viewpoints with media access on important issues. Response opportunities are required only when the discussion ceases to focus on issues and turns to *ad hominem* argumentation. The rules do not apply if a specific ballot issue is endorsed or attacked, a major controversial issue in the community is discussed, or a critical piece of legislation is criticized. What great democratic public benefit comes from knowing that a reporter may not have used her legs to get stories or that a radio station's managers may not have defrauded an insurance company? To a large extent, the personal attack rules generate name calling exercises, allowing those parties whose personalities are criticized to rebut the charges without requiring rebuttal opportunities on the more substantive issues.

Nor do the attack rules deal directly with the problem of broadcasters' undue influence on important public issues. Response opportunities must be extended only when remarks focus on personal qualities rather than on the underlying issues. Personal attack exchanges, however, do not really address the important public questions. Moreover, rather than resulting from a station management's deliberate decision to influence the public, the cases suggest that personal attacks usually result from a caller's comments, an interviewee's remarks, or a talk show host's getting carried away on the air.

Although the personal attack and political editorial rules were held to be constitutional in *Red Lion*,[126] the failure of the personal attack rules to serve fairness doctrine policies suggests that the rules deserve reconsideration. Although the *Red Lion* Court suggested that the rules do impose restraints on broadcasters' exercise of their First Amendment rights, it nonetheless determined:

> Because of the scarcity of radio frequencies the Government is permitted to put restraints on licensees in favor of others whose views

should be expressed on this unique medium. . . . It is the right of the viewers and listeners, not the right of the broadcasters, which is paramount. . . . It is the right of the public to receive suitable access to social, political, esthetic, moral, and other ideas and experiences which is crucial here.[127]

Now that it has become clear that the attack rules do not really provide an opportunity for spokesmen to address or for the public to be informed about important substantive public issues, *Red Lion*'s justification for the attack rules' restraints on broadcasters' rights is called into question.

Despite the FCC's declarations that the personal attack rules are meant only to inform the public further on important public issues, it is obvious that one of their key objectives is to protect the reputations of the individuals who are attacked. Given the burdens that the attack rules impose on broadcasters, such protection is poor justification for the rules, especially in light of the remedy for infringements of reputation provided by the law of defamation. Even were the personal attack rules to be justified in part as a defamation remedy, however, their provisions seem contrary to accepted principles of defamation law.

The personal attack rules stand the defamation standard on its head. As *New York Times Company v. Sullivan*[128] and its progeny have established, a higher liability standard protects newspapers when they attack a public figure[129] as opposed to a private person.[130] In the personal attack situation, however, broadcast media burdens are precisely the opposite: an attack on a public figure, someone involved with an important public issue, triggers a heavier broadcaster burden. The broadcaster must follow rigorous notification procedures and has limited discretion in creating a reply opportunity. If a private figure, one not connected with a public issue, is attacked, however, the attack rules are not brought into play, and the broadcaster need not notify that person or broadcast any reply.

One might argue that, insofar as *Sullivan* deprived public figures of a monetary damage remedy because their access to the media was, in effect, a sufficient alternative remedy, the personal attack rules serve to assure the effectiveness of that alternative remedy. A person involved in a controversial issue of public importance, however, is sufficiently assured of adequate media coverage

without the imposition of added burdens on broadcasters. The rationales that private individuals do not have these same "self-help" opportunities, that they have not chosen voluntarily public exposure as have public officials and figures,[131] and that the media need to be able to cover public issues and officials without being inhibited seem as relevant to broadcasters and personal attacks as they do to newspapers and defamatory statements.[132] The Commission has never explained these theoretical crosscurrents between the thrust of media burdens imposed under the personal attack rules and those imposed under defamation standards.

Ill-fitted to fulfill their purported goals, the personal attack rules also present large administrative difficulties for broadcasters. A personal attack may occur virtually any time someone speaks on the air. The licensee must decide whether an attack was made, whether there was a controversial public issue, and whether there was a sufficient nexus between the two. Once the licensee finds these three elements to exist, the victim(s) of the attack promptly must be notified and provided with a script, tape, or accurate summary. Finally, the licensee must decide what type of response opportunity is reasonable. Complex judgmental decisions must be made, with a possible fine or loss of license imposed if the FCC finds any of these decisions unreasonable. Such pressures may well inhibit the management and staff of stations from fully expressing their views and cause them to curtail the opportunities offered the public for broadcast expression.

In sum, the personal attack rules have not fulfilled fairness doctrine objectives, have generated severe administrative problems, and have raised constitutional concerns. For these reasons, they should be repealed.

IV. AN UNEASY CASE FOR RETENTION OF MODIFIED POLITICAL EDITORIAL RULES

The political editorial rules are distinguishable in terms of function, administration, and effect from the personal attack rules. The editorial rules do represent restraints on broadcasters' First Amendment rights[133] and do impose administrative burdens on broadcasters. On balance, however, they warrant retention.

In the political editorial situation the licensee not only condones the editorial, it uses its exclusive and powerful airwave frequency to explicitly advocate support of a candidate. There is no attempt to balance facts as in a typical news broadcast. Indeed, the licensee's objective is to bias the audience towards its point of view. A broadcast spokesman reflects the views of station management in a most direct way. The political editorial rules require that the broadcaster let its listeners hear other candidates with conflicting views. Thus, the political editorial obligations directly further the fairness doctrine goal of preventing powerful broadcasters from unfairly using their influence. The political editorial rules also further the other fairness doctrine objective of informing the public by granting access for spokesmen to discuss important public issues. Candidates are given the opportunity to address substantive campaign issues,[134] and such political responses come at a critical time for democratic debate—immediately before an election.

Administratively, the political editorial rules, though not unburdensome,[135] present fewer problems than the personal attack rules. The licensee does not have to determine whether a personal attack has occurred, what controversial issue of public importance has been raised, and whether that issue is so connected with the attack that the attack occurred during discussion of it. These difficult judgmental questions are simply not relevant to political editorials. The political editorial rules are triggered by a licensee's endorsement of a specific individual.[136] Once this easily discernible event occurs, the rules come into operation.

Finally, it should be noted that the political editorial rules do parallel existing equal time requirements.[137] As long as the latter are in effect, the political editorial rules seem a natural corollary. It would be inconsistent to require that broadcasters give candidates equal opportunities to appear on their stations, yet allow broadcasters to editorialize as much as they want in favor of or against a particular candidate. The personal attack rules, on the other hand, have no such connection with the statutory framework.

Although the political editorial rules should be maintained, some changes are desirable. The Commission could take much of the guesswork out of compliance with the rules by providing more precise guidelines on what constitutes a reasonable opportunity to respond. Reply parameters are tighter than in the traditional fairness setting, but they are still unnecessarily vague. The political editorial rules have also been greatly complicated by the FCC's invoking them whenever a station editorializes on an issue clearly identified with a particular candidate, even if the candidate is not directly opposed and the campaign is not mentioned.[138] One need only consider the great number of important campaign issues with which candidates often can be identified to appreciate the administrative problems inherent in applying this obligation. Such an obligation too often could result in inhibiting broadcasters who want to speak out on the issues. This interpretation also seems inconsistent with the FCC's failure to impose any reply requirements for editorials on ballot issues.

V. CONCLUSION

The personal attack and political editorial rules have historically been wedded, but the time has come to sunder the union. Although both were intended to serve the policies of the fairness doctrine, only the political editorial rules have furthered those goals. The failure of the personal attack rules is compounded by the burdens they impose on broadcasters both administratively and in the exercise of First Amendment rights.

The long-run solution to the problems raised by the personal attack and political editorial rules lies in expanding the number of electronic communications outlets available to the American people. The federal government must do more to promote cable, UHF, and public television as well as other means in order to increase the diversity of media access and public issue debate available to the American people. With such an abundance of communication opportunity, candidates, attack victims, and other parties will have little difficulty finding opportunities to reply to political editorials or personal attacks. Because frequency scarcity will be an outdated rationale, no need or justification will then exist for burdening licensees with the political editorial or personal attack rules.

In the short run, however, only the personal attack rules should be eliminated. Maintenance of such response opportunities is counterproductive and inimical to the public interest. The FCC can repeal the rules on its own initiative. Congress can, of course, eliminate them by statute.

Until creation of a communications system of abundance, there is greater justification for maintaining the political editorial rules. If these rules are to be retained, however, the Commission should reverse its decision to impose political editorial obligations whenever a broadcaster editorializes on an issue related to a campaign, because the ruling is difficult to administer, almost impossible to decipher intelligently, and especially inhibiting to licensees. In addition, the parameters for reply obligations in political editorials should be given further definition.[139] Both broadcasters and candidates should know their rights.

Notes

1. 47 C.F.R. secs. 73.123 (AM radio), 73.300 (FM radio), 73.598 (noncommercial educational FM radio), 73.679 (TV station), 76.209 ("origination cablecasting" over cable TV systems) (1976): Although much has been written about the Federal Communication Commission's fairness doctrine, the legal literature has largely ignored the Commission's articulation of that doctrine in its personal attack and political editorial rules. The exceptions are articles focusing on First Amendment issues raised by the rules. *See, e.g.,* Comment, *FCC's Formal Rules Concerning Personal Attacks and Political Editorials Contravene the First Amendment,* 44 NOTRE DAME LAWYER 447 (1969).

2. See text accompanying note 30, *infra.*

3. Although sharing many of the same objectives, the personal attack and personal editorial rules differ from the general fairness doctrine in several important ways. At the most obvious level, specific rules have been issued for personal attacks and political editorials, but not for the more general fairness doctrine situation. Unlike the general fairness situations, the licensee has no control over the reply speaker, must follow specific steps in notifying the reply speaker, has less control over the reply speaker's response format, and must pay a forfeiture if it is in violation of the rules. *See* text accompanying notes 5–72, *infra.* The licensee is also, of course, not obligated to air personal attacks in the first place, as it is to present controversial issues of public importance under the first part of the fairness doctrine.

4. FCC, PERSONAL ATTACKS; POLITICAL EDITORIALS, 32 FED REG. 10303 (1967). In pursuit of its fairness objectives and in order to make the public benefits of the rules more accessible to the citizenry, the Commission provided a format for filing a complaint with the FCC in the wake of what a complainant considers to be a personal attack: "If you file a complaint with the Commission, a copy should be sent to the station. The complaint should contain specific information concerning the following matters: (1) The name of the station or network involved; (2) the words or statements broadcast; (3) the date and time the broadcast was made; (4) the basis for your view that the words broadcast constitute an attack upon the honesty, character, integrity, or like personal qualities of you or your group; (5) the basis for your view that the personal attack was broadcast during the presentation of views on a controversial issue of public importance; (6) the basis for your view that the matter discussed was a controversial issue of public importance, either nationally or in the station's local area, at the time of the broadcast; and (7) whether the station within 1 week of the alleged attack: (i) Notified you or your group of the broadcast; (ii) transmitted a script, tape, or accurate summary of the broadcast if a script or tape was not available; and (iii) offered a reasonable opportunity to respond over the station's facilities." 39 FED. REG. 32290 (1974).

5. 3 F.R.C. 33 (1929). See Chapter Three for a history of the early development of the fairness doctrine. Although early, published Federal Radio Commission (FRC) or FCC cases focusing on personal attacks or political editorials are scarce, in at least one case a radio broadcaster's license was not renewed partially because of attacks made on judges, religious groups, a labor organization, and the Board of Health. Trinity Methodist Church, S. v. FRC, 62 F.2d 850 (D.C. Cir.), *cert denied,* 284 U.S. 685 (1932), 288 U.S. 599 (1933). In Mayflower Broadcasting Corp., 8 F.C.C. 333, 339-40 (1941), the FCC chastised a licensee for airing editorials in favor of political candidates and seemingly ordered licensees not to editorialize or advocate their personal views. The latter policy was reversed in *Report on Editorializing by Broadcast Licensees,* 13 F.C.C. 1246, 1252-53 (1949) [hereinafter cited as *Report on Editorializing*].

6. *Report on Editorializing, supra* note 5, at 1252.

7. 23 P & F RADIO REG. 586 (1962).

8. *Id.* at 591.

9. *Id.* at 593 (concurring statement of Chairman Minow).

10. 23 P & F RADIO REG. 951 (1962).

11. *Id.* at 953.

12. 24 P & F RADIO REG. 404 (1962).

13. 24 P & F RADIO REG. at 411.

14. New York Times, Nov. 8, 1962, at 1, col. 7.

15. 24 P & F RADIO REG. at 408.

16. *Id.* No fine was imposed. The FCC apparently was satisfied with KTTV's promise to follow the Commission's mandate between the telegram date and the election.

17. *Id.* at 406.

18. FCC, *Stations' Responsibilities Under Fairness Doctrine as to Controversial Issue Programming,* 28 FED. REG. 7692 (1963).

19. *Id.* In Springfield Television Broadcasting Corp., 45 F.C.C. 2083, 2085-86 (1965), the Commission cited the public notice in declaring that a Springfield television station's mailing of editorial transcripts to all persons attacked did not fulfill its fairness obligations, because a specific response offer was not transmitted.

20. FCC, *Applicability of the Fairness Doctrine in the Handling of Controversial Issues of Public Importance,* 29 FED. REG. 10415 (1964) [hereinafter cited as *Fairness Primer*].

21. *Id.* at 10420-21.

22. *Id.* (citing letter of Sept. 18, 1963, to Douglas A. Anello).

23. *Id.* at 10420 n.6.

24. *Hearings on S. 251, S. 252, S. 1696, and H.R.J. Res. 247 Before the Subcomm. on Communications of the Senate Comm. on Commerce,* 88th Cong., 1st Sess. 68 (1963). Pastore continued: "[A] small individual, what right of redress does he have? Take a person running for a school committee in the city of Providence. There is no remuneration for that position. And a local broadcasting station takes it upon itself, in a very spirited campaign for the school committee, which to the mothers of that community is just as important as the Presidency of the United States for the moment—the broadcaster comes along and endorses one candidate against the other. What protection does that little fellow have, unless you have something in the law that gives him protection?" *Id.* at 67-68.

25. *Id.* at 97-98; *Hearings on Broadcast Editorializing Practices Before the Subcomm. on Communications and Power of the House Comm. on Interstate and Foreign Commerce,* 88th Cong., 1st Sess., 89, 90 (1963) [hereinafter cited as *Hearings on Broadcast Editorializing Practices*].

26. FCC, *Personal Attacks: Political Editorials. Notice of Proposed Rulemaking.* 31 FED. REG. 5710 (1966).

27. 32 FED. REG. 10305-06 (1967), codified at 47 C.F.R. secs. 73.123, 73.300, 73.598, 73.679 (1976).

28. 32 FED. REG. 10303 (1967). The Commission stated that it would be able to impose forfeitures under 47 U.S.C. sec. 503(b) (1970) for willful or repeated violations. 32 FED. REG. 10303 (1967). In testimony before the House Subcommittee on Communications in 1963, Chairman Henry had stated that rules also would make available cease and desist

orders under section 312(b) and (c) and revocation under section 312(a)(4). He suggested that it might also be appropriate to require licensees to retain records of efforts to air opposing views. *Hearings on Broadcast Editorializing Practices, supra* note 25, at 89–90.

29. 47 C.F.R. secs. 72.123, 73.300, 73.598, 73.679 (1976).

30. 32 FED. REG. 10303–04 (1967). The Commission also said: "[T]he development of an informed public opinion through the public dissemination of news and ideas concerning the vital public issues of the day is the keystone of the Fairness Doctrine." *Id.* at 10303 (quoting *Report on Editorializing, supra* note 5, at 1249). The Commission stressed that private disputes involving personal attacks were not subject to the rules. *Id.* at 10304.

31. *Id.* at 10303.

32. *Id.* at 10304.

33. *Id.* The Commission said that sanctions would be applied only when the licensee does not comply and "there can be no reasonable doubt under the facts that a personal attack has taken place (e.g., a statement in a controversial issue broadcast that a public official or other person is an embezzler or a Communist)." *Id.* Licensees were also advised to consult the Commission promptly in appropriate cases. *Id.* at 10304 n.6. The Commission left the definition of "reasonable opportunity . . . to respond" up to the licensee's reasonable, good faith judgment. *Id.* at 10305.

34. *Id.* at 10303.

35. *Id.* at 10305; *see* 47 U.S.C. sec. 315 (Supp. V 1975).

36. 32 FED. REG. 10305 (1967). The Commission stated that, except in extraordinary circumstances, the candidate's spokesman should be chosen by the candidate. *Id.* at 10305 n.9. The FCC made two other significant points. First, it reaffirmed its ruling in John H. Norris, 1 F.C.C.2d 1587 (1965), *aff'd sub nom.* Red Lion Broadcasting Co. v. FCC, 395 U.S. 367 (1969), that the attacked party had to be given air time even if he could not pay for it. Secondly, the Commission noted that if a licensee decides that no personal attack has occurred, but it thinks that there may be some dispute over this conclusion, it should keep a record of the broadcast for a reasonable time and make it available for public inspection. 32 FED. REG. 10305 n.7 (1967).

37. "Foreign groups" were also added as an exempt category in addition to the "foreign leaders" category specified in the *Fairness Primer, supra* note 20, at 10420 n.6.

38. Times-Mirror Broadcasting Co., 24 P & F RADIO REG. 404, 406 (1962).

39. *See* Billings Broadcasting Co., 23 P & F RADIO REG. 951, 953 (1962); Clayton W. Mapoles, 23 P & F RADIO REG. 586, 593 (1962) (concurring statement of Chairman Minow).

40. The Commission did suggest that the one-week time limit "does not mean that such a copy should not be sent earlier or indeed, before the attack occurs, particularly where time is of the essence." 32 FED. REG. 10305 (1967). Such earlier notification, however, was not required in the text of the rules.

41. *Procedures in Event of Personal Attack or Where Station Editorializes as to Political Candidates,* 32 FED. REG. 11531 (1967).

42. *Id.* The Commission also noted that personal attacks occurring during on-the-spot news coverage would be rare. *Id.*

43. 33 FED. REG. 5362, 5364 (1968) (codified at 47 C.F.R. secs. 73.123(b), 73.300(b), 73.598(b), 73.679(b) (1976)): "(b) The provisions of paragraph (a) of this section shall not be applicable (1) to attacks on foreign groups or foreign public figures; (2) to personal attacks which are made by legally qualified candidates, their authorized spokesmen, or those associated with them in the campaign, on other such candidates, their authorized spokesmen, or persons associated with the candidates in the campaign; and (3) to bona fide newscasts, bona fide news interviews, and on-the-spot coverage of a bona fide news event (including commentary or analysis contained in the foregoing programs, but the provisions of paragraph (a) of this section shall be applicable to editorials of the licensee).

"NOTE: The fairness doctrine is applicable to situations coming within (iii), above, and, in a specific factual situation, may be applicable in the general area of political broadcasts (ii), above. See, section 315(a) of the Act, 47 U.S.C. 315(a); Public Notice: Applicability of the Fairness Doctrine in the Handling of Controversial Issues of Public Importance, 29 F.R.

10415. The categories listed in (iii) are the same as those specified in section 315(a) of the Act."

44. 33 FED. REG. 5362 (1968). The Commission refused to exempt licensee editorials, noting that there had been instances of failure to comply with the personal attack rules in the context of such editorials and news documentaries. The Commission distinguished its decision from the equal time news documentary exemption, which applies to incidental appearances by candidates. *Id.* at 5363; *see* 47 U.S.C. sec. 315(a)(3) (1970). The Commission stressed that the fairness doctrine obligation to present contrasting views of controversial public issues, including relevant personal attacks, still applied to the exempt news programs. 33 FED. REG. 5363 (1968). The Commission also buried in a footnote a significant exception to the personal attack rules: if the person attacked was given a fair opportunity to respond, at the time of an initial attack, to the substance of a later attack, compliance with the rules has been achieved. *Id.* at 5362 n.1.

45. *Id.* at 5363. If a personal attack occurs in an exempt news program during discussion of a controversial public issue, the licensee may present "the contrasting viewpoint on the attack issue" itself under the general fairness doctrine. *Id.* If the licensee has not and does not plan to do so, it is not appropriate for the licensee to make over-the-air offers of time to respond. "There is a clear and appropriate spokesman to present the other side of the attack issue—the person or group attacked." *Id.* The licensee should notify and allow "the person or group attacked a reasonable opportunity to respond." *Id.* In the latter situation, however, the precise time limitation and notification requirements of the personal attack rules do not apply. *See* Rev. Paul E. Driscoll, 40 F.C.C.2d 448 (1973) (fairness doctrine applicable to alleged attack on Rev. Driscoll and Catholic Church made during exempt bona fide news interview).

46. 47 C.F.R. secs. 73.123(a)(b) (AM radio, 73.300(a)(b) (FM radio), 73.598(a)(b) (noncommercial educational FM radio), 73.679(a)(b) (TV stations), 76.209(b)(c) (origination cablecasting over cable TV systems) (1976).

47. 47 U.S.C. sec. 399(a) (Supp. V 1975).

48. 395 U.S. 367 (1969); *see* text accompanying notes 125-26, *infra.* For discussions of *Red Lion,* see F. FRIENDLY, THE GOOD GUYS, THE BAD GUYS, AND THE FIRST AMENDMENT 32-77 (1976); Blake, *Red Lion Broadcasting Co. v. FCC: Fairness and the Emperor's New Clothes,* 23 FED. COM. B.J. 75 (1969); Firestein, Red Lion *and the Fairness Doctrine: Regulation of Broadcasting "in the Public Interest,"* 11 ARIZ. L. REV. 807 (1969); 15 S.D. L. REV. 172 (1970). One recent interesting allegation with First Amendment implications is the charge that the complainant in *Red Lion* was actually working with the Democratic Party as part of a secret national campaign on behalf of the Kennedy administration to use the personal attack rules and general fairness doctrine to silence or hamper right-wing commentators. *See* FRIENDLY, *supra,* at 33-42.

49. *See, e.g.,* Herschel Kasten, 39 F.C.C.2d 566 (1973).

50. *See, e.g.,* Port of N.Y. Auth., 25 F.C.C.2d 417, 418 (1970); Miners Broadcasting Serv., Inc., 20 F.C.C.2d 1061, 1063 n.6 (1970).

51. *See* Rev. Paul E. Driscoll, 40 F.C.C.2d 448 (1973). *Driscoll* can be read as implying that a person can be identified sufficiently for personal attack rule purposes without being specifically named because the FCC staff did not question complainant's assertion that the broadcast sufficiently identified him. The letter, however, did not directly comment on the identification issue, because it found that the comments were made during a bona fide news interview. *But see* Diocese of Rockville Centre, 50 F.C.C.2d 330 (1973) (charges that the men in the Roman Catholic Church were led into it "merely by ambition" and were "hypocritical and immoral" did not sufficiently identify the alleged attack victims).

52. Quechee Lakes Corp., 38 F.C.C.2d 1039 (1973) (accusation within news broadcasts that land development corporation used deceitful practices); Dorothy Healey, 24 F.C.C.2d 487 (1970), *aff'd,* 460 F.2d 917 (D.C. Cir. 1972) (broadcaster calling an individual a Marxist, Communist, and atheist in commentary part of news broadcast). *But cf.* Walker & Salveter, 32 P & F RADIO REG. 2d 839, 844 (1975) (the "Commission has not exempted the labeled station or network editorial, even if occurring in one of these exempt categories").

53. Rev. Paul E. Driscoll, 40 F.C.C.2d 448 (1973) (alleged attack made during bona fide news interview).

54. Thomas R. Asher, 38 F.C.C.2d 300 (1972) (accusation that President Nixon's supporters distorted Senator McGovern's welfare position and personally attacked him in campaign advertisements). Under the political editorial and the personal attack rules, the Commission looks to the definition of "legally qualified candidate" as interpreted under the equal time requirements of section 315 of the Communications Act of 1934, 47 U.S.C. sec. 315 (1970 and Supp. V. 1975). *See* Arthur W. Arundel, 14 F.C.C.2d 199 (1968) (editorial endorsement of Robert Kennedy for president required notification and opportunity to respond for other legally qualified candidates, but not for Senator Humphrey, who had not yet announced his candidacy); Senator Eugene J. McCarthy, 11 F.C.C.2d 511 (1968) (since personal attack rules are inapplicable to a legally qualified candidate's attack on another such candidate, alleged personal attack made by President Johnson must be based on assumption that Johnson was not yet a legally qualified candidate). An attack made by a legally qualified candidate on a person not a candidate or associated with a candidate is subject to the personal attack requirements, despite the fact that the licensee cannot censor comments by candidates under section 315. Capitol Cities Broadcasting, 13 F.C.C.2d 869 (1968) (candidate identified noncandidates as having been indicted for sedition, referred to their allegedly "subversive activities," and quoted excerpts from grand jury report).

55. National Ass'n of Gov't Employees, 41 F.C.C.2d 965 (1973).

56. Dr. Morris Crothers, 32 F.C.C.2d 864 (1971). The Commission stated that although the licensee "had no obligation to tape such remarks, under the circumstances of this case [it] should have retained a tape if one was made or, if a recording was not made, retained at least an accurate and contemporaneously made summary or transcript of the remarks, instead of relying on 'recollections' of [its] moderator. . . ." *Id.* at 865. *Crothers* involved a phone-in talk show, as many of the personal attack cases do.

57. Station WGGB, 41 F.C.C.2d 340, 342 (1973) ("A three months delay in seeking Commission advice obviously precludes any finding of a reasonable attempt of compliance with the rule").

58. John Birch Soc'y, 11 F.C.C.2d 790, 791 (1968).

59. *Id.* at 791. The Commission added that the licensee should consider "the time devoted to the attack and other pertinent considerations," and, in the "case of an attack in a program which is one of a series," a reasonable judgment may be demonstrated by "inclusion of the response during a portion of the time period regularly alloted to the series . . . if otherwise fair to the person attacked . . . and if effectuated by the licensee and not simply delegated to someone associated with the program series." *Id. See* Station WGCB, 41 F.C.C.2d 340, 342 (1973) (reasonable opportunity is "initially to be worked out by the licensee and the party"); John M. Slack, 26 F.C.C.2d 11 (1970) (three minutes' reply time on 6:00 and 11:00 P.M. news is reasonable); Dean C. Steele, 18 F.C.C.2d 661 (1969) (offering an attacked party precisely equal time is reasonable).

60. John Birch Soc'y, 11 F.C.C.2d 790, 791–92 (1968). Under the general fairness doctrine, a licensee may determine the format in which a spokesman will present the opposing views. FCC, *Fairness Doctrine and Public Interest Standards, Fairness Report Regarding Handling of Public Issues,* 39 Fᴇᴅ. Rᴇɢ. 26372, 26378, par. 42 [hereinafter cited as *Fairness Report*]; *Report on Editorializing, supra* note 5, at 1251 par. 10, 1258 par. 21. *See* Chapter Seven for a complete discussion of responding under the general fairness doctrine.

61. John Birch Soc'y, 11 F.C.C.2d 790, 792 (1968) (licensee's rejection of a general film about Robert Welch, offered as a rebuttal to attacks on the John Birch Society, upheld). A licensee's judgment on the responsiveness of a proposed reply to a personal attack may, of course, be deemed unreasonable. *See* Radio Albany, Inc., 40 F.C.C. 632, 634 (1965) (licensee's judgment that Rev. Martin Luther King, Jr.'s proposed reply to editorial attack was unresponsive to the attack found unreasonable).

62. Station WGCB, 41 F.C.C.2d 340 (1973).

63. *See* Radio Albany, Inc., 40 F.C.C. 632, 633 (1965).

64. Lew H. Cherry, 25 F.C.C.2d 887 (1970).

65. Mario Procaccino, 20 F.C.C.2d 451 (1969).

66. James Spurling, 30 F.C.C.2d 675 (1971) (unreasonable, in city council election, for licensee editorial to devote 25 lines to endorsement of two other candidates and opposition to complainant's candidacy, and allow only 6 lines for reply; 4 to 1 total time ratio assumption is based on 4 to 1 total line ratio).

67. Bill Bishop, 30 F.C.C.2d 829 (1971) (unreasonable for licensee to air seven editorial endorsements of one candidate for mayor totaling 11 minutes, 24 seconds, but allow opposing candidate's spokesman to reply in only two broadcasts totaling 4 minutes, 18 seconds).

68. George E. Cooley, 10 F.C.C.2d 969 (1967) (unreasonable for licensee to endorse candidate in 24 20-second editorials and offer candidate's opponent 6 20-second response broadcasts).

69. Bill Bishop, 30 F.C.C.2d 829 (1971).

70. 32 FED. REG. 10305 (1967). Moreover, the licensee may require appearance of a candidate's spokesman instead of the candidate himself to avoid equal time obligations. *Id.* "Barring extraordinary circumstances" the choice of spokesman is up to the candidate. *Id.* n.9. The licensee should look to equal time case law to define a "legally qualified candidate" in the political editorial context. Arthur L. Arundel, 14 F.C.C.2d 199 (1968). Unlike the equal time situation, in which the licensee can wait until the opposing candidates contact it for equal opportunities, the licensee must notify other candidates of its political editorials on its own initiative. *See* text accompanying notes 29 and 34, *supra*.

71. Total time ratios of 5.6 to 1 have been held reasonable under the general fairness doctrine, National Broadcasting Co., 16 F.C.C.2d 956 (1969), and frequency ratios of "4 or 5" to 1 similarly have been upheld, Wilderness Soc'y, 31 F.C.C.2d 729, 735 (1971) (concurring statement of Chairman Burch). *See* Chapter Seven.

72. 32 FED. REG. 10305 (1967).

73. The Commission has stressed that the truth or falsity of a statement is not determinative of whether there has been a personal attack and that the Commission makes no inquiry into the accuracy of the alleged attack. Lew H. Cherry, 25 F.C.C.2d 887, 888 (1970).

74. Senator Florian W. Chmielewski, 41 F.C.C.2d 201 (1973). The Commission added: "Criticism of a public official's wisdom, judgment or actions is not necessarily an attack upon his 'honesty, character, integrity or like personal qualities,' and we have stated that we shall not impose penalties in this area if the licensee could have had a reasonable doubt whether such an attack had taken place, or indeed in any case which does not involve a flagrant, clear-cut violation." *Id* at 207.

75. Richard S. Manne, 26 F.C.C.2d 583 (1970).

76. Rev. Paul E. Driscoll, 40 F.C.C.2d 448 (1973). The Commission declared: "[I]t should be clear that not all charges of illegality present attacks on honesty, character or integrity. One may assert that a person or group has in fact acted in violation of that law although the person or group assumed that such action was in full accord with the law's provisions. In such case, the charge is one of 'illegality,' but it is the judgment of the person or group in interpreting the law which is questioned, not their honesty, character or integrity." *Id* at 450.

77. John J. Salchert, 48 F.C.C.2d 346 (1974) (legislator chaired a legislative committee on nursing homes while working for several nursing homes).

78. Francis X. Bellotti, 40 F.C.C.2d 328 (1967).

79. Rome Hosp. 40 F.C.C.2d 452 (1973).

80. Charlotte Observer, 38 F.C.C.2d 522 (1972). The Commission rejected the station's assertions that the remarks were intended to be "humorous, . . . not malicious" and may only have demonstrated "questionable taste." *Id.* at 523.

81. Columbia Broadcasting Sys., Inc., 21 P & F RADIO REG. 2d 497 (1971). The Commission added: "Mere mention of groups of persons, or even certain types of unfavorable references thereto, do not constitute personal attacks as defined by the Commission." *Id.* at 497.

82. WIYN Radio, Inc., 35 F.C.C.2d 175 (1972).

83. J. Allen Carr, 30 F.C.C.2d 894 (1971).

84. John Birch Soc'y, 11 F.C.C.2d 790, 791 (1968).

85. Station WGCB, 41 F.C.C.2d 340, 342 (1973).

86. Thomas O'Brien, 42 F.C.C.2d 1106 (1973). The Commission added: "Comments of this nature refer to political ideological beliefs and do not constitute character denunciation." *Id.* at 1107. In light of the FCC's affording personal attack replies to those termed "Communist," this statement is astounding.

87. Brandywine-Main Line Radio, Inc., 24 F.C.C.2d 18, 26 (1970), *aff'd,* 473 F.2d 16 (D.C. Cir. 1972), *cert. denied,* 412 U.S. 922 (1973); *cf.* William M. Kunstler, 11 F.C.C.2d 678 (1973) (characterizing a club as a Communist organization is an attack).

88. Philadelphia Fed'n of Teachers, 48 F.C.C.2d 507, 510 (1974).

89. Straus Communications, Inc., 51 F.C.C.2d 385 (1975), *vacated and remanded,* 530 F.2d 1001 (D.C. Cir. 1976). Commissioner Robinson, in dissent, made the following telling comments on *Straus* in light of *Philadelphia Federation of Teachers:* "No differences in the dictionary definition of the vituperative words used, and nothing in common sense can make these two cases consistent. I can find no principle that justifies them. It may be, of course, that these are among the species of cases for which principles do not really suffice, and that must consequently be decided according to the length of the Chancellor's foot. If a certain amount of arbitrariness is necessary to finish important business in realms where mere language will not carry us, so be it. But in such cases, it is the Chancellor's duty at least to try to keep his foot from changing size like Alice in Wonderland." 51 F.C.C.2d at 390 (Commissioner Robinson, dissenting) (fn. omitted).

90. For examples of other comments held not to be personal attacks, *see* Thaddeus Kowalski, 42 F.C.C.2d 1110 (1973) (making "Pollack jokes"); John Cervase, 42 F.C.C.2d 613 (1973) (calling an individual a "political opportunist"); Dewey M. Duckett, Jr., 23 F.C.C.2d 872 (1970) (calling an individual a "spook").

Consistently with the general fairness doctrine (*see* text accompanying note 5 of Chapter Two), the FCC claims to use a "reasonableness" standard in assessing licensee determinations of when personal attacks have been made. *See, e.g.,* Senator Florian W. Chmielewski, 41 F.C.C.2d 201, 208 (1973) ("the question . . . is not what our initial view might be . . . but rather whether the licensee could reasonably judge the allegations not to involve personal attacks"). This flexible view might seem to explain the Commission's inconsistent holdings outlined in the text accompanying notes 74-89, *supra.* The question, however, then becomes: "What sorts of determinations will be found 'reasonable'?" The answers to that question are no more coherent and provide no more guidance than the answers to the original question: "What sorts of remarks will be found to constitute personal attacks?" In other words, the problem remains however the question is formulated.

91. B. SCHMIDT, JR., FREEDOM OF THE PRESS VS. PUBLIC ACCESS 171 (1976).

92. *See, e.g.,* Francis X. Bellotti, 10 F.C.C.2d 328 (1967); note 78, *supra,* and accompanying text.

93. The distinction between policy differences and charges of dishonesty, moral turpitude, or criminal conduct, however, may be extremely tenuous. *See, e.g.,* Sidney Willens, 33 F.C.C.2d 304, 306 (1972) (a charge that judges handed out illegal sentences found not to be an attack, the Commission stating that there "is an important distinction . . . between contending that a judge has exceeded his discretion in the legal sense . . . and charging that he has decided a case because of improper or corrupt motives"); John B. Walsh, 31 F.C.C.2d 726 (1971) (a charge that county supervisors engaged in mental gymnastics and were inconsistent in providing free office space to senator and enacting a tax increase found not to be an attack); Port of N.Y. Auth., 25 F.C.C.2d 417, 418 (1970) (a charge that Port Authority Commissioners were secretive and developed port in a way "most profitable to them" found not to be an attack, the Commission noting that "strong disagreement, even vehemently expressed, does not constitute a personal attack, in the absence of an attack upon character or integrity"); notes 74, 76, 88, *supra,* and accompanying text.

94. *See, e.g.,* Herschel Kasten, 39 F.C.C.2d 566 (1973) (calling a person unqualified to be head of a college); Robert B. Choate, 29 F.C.C.2d 73 (1971) (charge that individual's conclusions about biology topics were childish and that he was not suited for any work not an attack).

95. *See, e.g.,* Joseph A. Gillis, 43 F.C.C.2d 584 (1973) (claims that a doctor is a convicted abortionist, had "paid off police officers" to continue his "abortion racket," and had gone to jail rather than describe his payoffs to the grand jury is an attack); Dr. John Gabler, 40

F.C.C.2d 579 (1973) (accusing doctor of unethical conduct in deaths of two boys and of having been convicted for the death of one boy is an attack).

96. *See* text accompanying notes 1, 30, *supra.*

97. The FCC itself has stated, "One of the most difficult problems involved in the administration of the fairness doctrine is the determination of the specific issue or issues raised by the particular program." *Fairness Report, supra* note 60, at 26376, par. 32. The Commission has laid down a series of inconsistent decisions on what issue is raised in a broadcast and whether it is controversial and of public importance. *See, e.g.,* Accuracy in Media, Inc., 40 F.C.C.2d 958 (1973), *remanded with direction to vacate order and dismiss complaint sub nom.* National Broadcasting Co. v. FCC, 516 F.2d 1101 (D.C. Cir. 1974), *cert. denied sub nom.* Accuracy in Media, Inc. v. National Broadcasting Co. 424 U.S. 910 (1976); National Broadcasting Co. v. FCC, 516 F.2d 1101, 1156 (1974) (Bazelon, C.J., dissenting); for a discussion of the Commission's record, *see* Chapters Five and Six.

98. *Fairness Report, supra* note 60, at 26376 pars. 30, 31.

99. 35 F.C.C.2d 175, 180 (1972).

100. John Birch Soc'y, 11 F.C.C.2d 790 (1968).

101. William M. Kunstler, 11 F.C.C.2d 678 (1968).

102. National Ass'n of Gov't Employees, 41 F.C.C.2d 965, 966–67 (1973).

103. Dr. John Gabler, 40 F.C.C.2d 579 (1973). The licensee apparently admitted, however, that the dismissal involved a controversial issue of public importance. *Id.* at 580.

104. *Id.*

105. Richard S. Manne, 26 F.C.C.2d 583 (1970). The conclusion, typically, was reached without any supporting evidence or rationale.

106. Duane Lindstrom, 26 F.C.C.2d 373 (1970). *Lindstrom* was a general fairness doctrine case; newspaper articles submitted by complainant did "not demonstrate that the license renewal of one or more specific stations is a controversial issue of public importance." *Id.* at 375 n.4.

107. 26 F.C.C.2d 583 (1970).

108. *Id.* at 584.

109. 42 F.C.C.2d 1106 (1973).

110. *Id.* at 1108–09.

111. 51 F.C.C.2d 385 (1975), *vacated and remanded,* 530 F.2d 1001 (D.C. Cir. 1976).

112. *Id.* at 385.

113. *Id.*

114. *Id.* at 387.

115. Straus Communications, Inc. v. FCC, 530 F.2d 1001 (D.C. Cir. 1976).

116. *Id.* at 1010.

117. *Id.* at 1011.

118. *Id.*

119. *Id.* n.28.

120. *See* text accompanying notes 1–4, *supra.*

121. Even had the remarks borne a closer relationship to the controversial issue of public importance, in terms of the articulated purposes of the rules one must wonder what purpose would have been served by requiring an opportunity to respond. What additional public knowledge about the boycott would have been gained by hearing Congressman Rosenthal's reaction to being called a coward for not appearing on Bob Grant's phone-in show? *See* text accompanying notes 126–132, *infra.*

122. *See* text accompanying notes 41–43, *supra.*

123. *See* note 42, *supra,* and accompanying text.

124. *See* note 71, *supra,* and accompanying text.

125. A study of all fairness cases considered during the first half of 1973 found an "average delay of about eight months between broadcast and ruling." The study also revealed a "number of cases in which several years elapsed." HENRY GELLER, THE FAIRNESS DOCTRINE IN BROADCASTING 37 and app. D (Rand R-1412 FF, Dec. 1973). In Francis X. Bellotti, 10 F.C.C.2d 328 (1967), for example, the original complaint was made on October 20, 1966, a few weeks before the November election; the Commission's ruling was delivered on September 27, 1967.

126. 395 U.S. 367 (1969); *see* text accompanying note 48, *supra*.

127. *Id.* at 390.

128. 376 U.S. 254 (1964).

129. A public official cannot recover damages "for a defamatory falsehood relating to his official conduct unless he proves that the statement was made with 'actual malice'—that is, with knowledge that it was false or with reckless disregard of whether it was false or not." *Id.* at 279–80. *See also* Time, Inc. v. Hill, 385 U.S. 374 (1967) (*Sullivan* standard applies to right of privacy action against magazine by private individuals involved in incident of public interest); Rosenblatt v. Baer, 383 U.S. 75 (1966) (criticism of former supervisor of county-owned ski resort); Garrison v. Louisiana, 379 U.S. 64 (1964) (criticism of state criminal court judges).

130. Gertz v. Robert Welch, Inc., 418 U.S. 323, 345–46 (1974): "[P]rivate individuals are not only more vulnerable to injury than public officials and public figures; they are also more deserving of recovery. . . . [W]e conclude that the States should retain substantial latitude in their efforts to enforce a legal remedy for defamatory falsehood injurious to the reputation of a private individual."

131. *See id.* at 344–45.

132. *See* New York Times Co. v. Sullivan, 376 U.S. at 270–83.

133. *See* Miami Herald Publishing Co. v. Tornillo, 418 U.S. 241 (1974) (a right of reply for political candidates statutorily imposed by Florida on *newspapers* inhibited newspaper journalists and violated the First Amendment).

134. The need to supply every qualified candidate who was not favored in an editorial the right to reply, however, undoubtedly inhibits some broadcasters from airing political editorials. In the usual editorial or other fairness situation, only one or two reply spokesmen need be presented. In the political editorial situation, many more may be necessary, resulting in burdensome notification requirements and the offering of much free time.

135. *See* note 138, *infra*, and accompanying text (reply obligations resulting from editorials on an issue closely associated with a candidate). Complications also may arise in determining when broadcast statements are the "official opinion" of the licensee and thus subject to the political editorial rules. That editorial-type statements by broadcast announcers are "made with the approval of the management of the station, does not necessarily mean that the statements were intended or represented on the air as the official opinion of the management of the station." Peter H. Beer, 48 F.C.C.2d 1067, 1068 (1974).

136. *But see* note 135, *supra*.

137. 47 U.S.C. sec. 315(a) (Supp. V 1975). The equal time rule itself has been the deserving object of criticism. *See, e.g.,* Derby, *Section 315: Analysis and Proposal,* 3 HARV. J. LEGIS. 257 (1965–66); Erbst, *Equal Time for Candidates: Fairness or Frustration?* 34 SO. CAL. L. REV. 190 (1961). Although it is beyond the scope of this chapter to explore the hotly debated equal time rule, 42 U.S.C. sec. 315 (1970 and Supp. V 1975), equal time also should be subject to reevaluation. The inhibitory effect of the free time aspects of this rule may be even greater than the effects of the political editorial rule. An improved structure might eliminate equal time requirements for any program on which a candidate appears but does not pay for his broadcast as he does for political commercials. In light of the public's great need to hear issues discussed by candidates during campaign periods, the major party candidates, at least in the presidential elections, might be given free back-to-back periods of time to discuss the issues (perhaps a half hour per candidate) each week for five or six weeks before an election. Minor qualified candidates might be given less time in accord with a pre-arranged formula based on previous vote tallies or petition. These broadcasts would be devoted to discussions of issues in detail and would be in addition to any presidential debates the networks might arrange (without any equal time requirements if the debates were aired without payment from the candidates). During these periods the candidates could discuss or present the issues as they wished, without editorial interference. Such a scheme would fulfill the critical democratic need for extended discussion of important public issues during campaign periods and get away from the limited coverage of presidential issues inherent in short newscasts and broad-ranging presidential debates. It would also mitigate many of the inhibitory effects of the present equal time law and be simple to administer. Licensees would be

free to cover any candidates they chose, in any format they desired, without having to give time to every other qualified political candidate. Unlike the political editorial situation, where broadcasters are consciously trying to bias the public toward their point of view about a candidate, the assumption would be that good journalistic practices would cause licensees to be fair in their candidate coverage. Equal time requirements still would prevail for paid political advertising, an arrangement that has a lesser inhibitory effect.

138. *See* Taft Broadcasting Co., 33 P & F RADIO REG. 2d 1260 (1975). Even when a candidate is not opposed expressly or the election directly referred to, "a licensee editorial gives rise to the affirmative obligations of the political editorial rule if it takes partisan position on a politically significant issue which is readily and clearly identified with a legally qualified candidate." *Id.* at 1268.

139. Thus, candidates responding to a licensee's editorial endorsement of an opponent should be entitled to a similar time period for reply. A 6:00 P.M. licensee editorial on a Tuesday night should require a reply between 5:00 and 7:00 P.M. on a similar week night. At the least, a prime-time editorial should require prime-time responses. Candidates should be offered at least roughly equal total time to reply to licensee editorials. Further, frequency of broadcast must be given adequate attention. If a licensee's political editorials are twice as frequent as a candidate's reply, the allocation formula should be considered inherently suspect; the licensee should be asked to justify the 2 to 1 frequency ratio with a demonstration that the total time ratio largely offsets the frequency differential.

CHAPTER 5

Commercial Advertising and the Fairness Doctrine: The New FCC Policy in Perspective

During the past decade, the charge has increasingly been made that commercial advertising broadcast by television and radio stations raises important consumer, environmental, and public health issues. Complainants attempting to air another viewpoint on these issues have used the fairness doctrine as the basis for demanding broadcast time for countercommercials and other balanced programming. This chapter analyzes how the fairness doctrine has been applied to commercial advertising by the Federal Communications Commission and the courts, and examines the FCC's latest in-depth pronouncement on commercial advertising and the fairness doctrine, the 1974 *Fairness Report*.[1] A suggested interpretation of the Report's language with respect to institutional advertising and an assessment of the new FCC policy to remove standard product advertising from fairness obligations follow.

I. COMMERCIAL ADVERTISING AND BROADCASTING: THE BACKGROUND

In 1901 when Guglielmo Marconi first succeeded in transmitting a Morse code radio signal across the Atlantic Ocean, few persons thought the new medium would be the basis for a profit-making venture. Fewer still expected radio's profits to come from advertising.[2] In fact, during radio's infant days, stations were built and operated mainly to stimulate the sale of radio receivers. General Electric, Westinghouse, and the Radio Corporation of America, the major radio receiver manufacturers, had hoped that receiver sales would support broadcast service.[3] Rising construction and production costs caused the manufacturers to reevaluate their balance sheet projections, and it became clear that some other source of revenue would be necessary to support broadcasting. Private contributions,[4] a self-imposed industry tax,[5] and a government tax on receiver sets[6] were all proposed. The rejection of a government-supported broadcasting system[7] and the industry's own conclusion that those who use broadcasting to carry their message should pay for it[8] "led naturally to selling time to advertisers who wanted to reach a large audience."[9]

WEAF,[10] a New York AT&T station, broadcast the first advertisement over the air waves on August 28, 1922,[11] and in less than ten months it had a list of 35 sponsors. "It was evident AT&T had found an effective way of supporting broadcasting."[12]

Although additional stations immediately followed WEAF's lead,[13] 1927 has been called the year "in which American radio became really 'commercial',"[14] for it was the first full year of operation of permanent commercial radio networks that regularly sold advertising time.[15] Revenue from the sale of radio time jumped from less than $200,000 in 1926 to roughly $26.8 million in 1929.[16] Advertisers became so involved in the broadcast industry that during the 1930s over 50 percent of sponsored network programs were actually produced by advertising agencies.[17] Buttressed by advertising sales of $150 million a year, radio in 1940 had expanded to include four national networks and more than 700 commercial stations transmitting to almost 30 million home receivers and 7 million car receivers.[18] By 1972 annual radio advertising sales had skyrocketed to over $1.4 billion, supporting more than 6,800 commercial radio stations and 129 regional radio networks.[19]

Commercial television was first introduced in 1941 when the FCC announced it would issue commercial licenses.[20] "Television broadcasting from the beginning was entirely dependent on advertising revenues for its support and the few years of uncertainty that characterized radio's infancy were absent. Commercially oriented, television sought mass audiences to attract billings from sponsoring advertisers and to entice new customers as well."[21] Five television stations were issued commercial licenses in 1941. Despite the limited number of television receiving sets then in existence, WNBT[22] of New York began its first week of broadcasting with four commercial sponsors.[23] The other stations also had commercial backing.[24]

As television sales increased and World War II drew to a close, television advertising support expanded. Its time sales climbed from under $9 million in 1948 to $1.8 billion in 1966, at which point its total time sales were double those of radio—$912 million.[25] Between 1949 and 1952 the number of television sets in American homes rose by over 500 percent—from 2.8 million to 15 million.[26] By 1973, 97 percent of American homes had television sets, over 80 million Americans were reached by television each day, and yearly television advertising sales exceeded $3.1 billion. Over 700 commercial stations were on the air.[27]

It has been charged with a good degree of force that advertisers today adversely affect broadcast programming, by promoting bland shows that appeal to the least common denominator and by constantly interrupting programs with offensive and often ludicrous commercials.[28] Yet, for better or for worse, it is undeniable that in the United States "advertising is the lifeblood of broadcasting,"[29] and it has provided the critical financial support necessary to develop, distribute, and sustain television and radio service throughout the country.

II. COMMERCIAL ADVERTISING AND THE FAIRNESS DOCTRINE: THE CASE HISTORY

In 1946 the FCC first explicitly considered the applicability of fairness doctrine principles to commercial advertising. In *Sam Morris*,[30] a case involving a radio station's refusal to sell commercial time for broadcast of advertisements advocating abstinence from alcohol,[31] the Commission clearly indicated that advertising could involve controversial public issues. As discussed on p. 41, before 1946 the Commission had considered broadcasting different sides of controversial public issues as part of a licensee's public interest obligations.[32] Analyzing the advertising issue in light of this "criterion of the public interest," the Commission in *Morris* stated:

> Difference concerning the relative merits of one product over another does not usually divide the community by raising basic and important social, economic, or political issues. But it must be recognized that under some circumstances it may well do so . . . [and] this controversy . . . may assume the proportions of a controverted issue of public

importance. The fact that the occasion for the controversy happens to be the advertising of a product cannot serve to diminish the duty of the broadcaster to treat it as such an issue.[33]

Licensees were thus warned in 1946 that as part of their public interest obligations, it might be necessary for them to broadcast viewpoints contrasting with commercial advertising claims.[34] A somewhat more explicit warning on the question of advertising came with the Commission's 1963 notice to licensees advising them of fairness doctrine responsibilities: "In determining compliance with the fairness doctrine the Commission looks to substance rather than to label or form. It is immaterial whether a particular program or viewpoint is . . . a paid announcement."[35]

Despite the *Morris* dicta and the 1963 notice, the first FCC decision to rule directly on advertising and the fairness doctrine was handed down in 1967. This decision on cigarette advertising started the fevered debate over advertising and the doctrine in the late 1960s and early 1970s, which eventually led to adoption of the FCC's 1974 guidelines.[36]

A. CIGARETTES: A UNIQUE PRODUCT?

John Banzhaf III, in a fairness doctrine complaint to the Commission, asserted that, after airing a number of cigarette commercials, a television station had refused to allow responsible opposing spokesmen to speak on the inadvisability of smoking and had consequently violated the fairness doctrine.[37] The Commission agreed, in *WCBS-TV*. It held that the fairness doctrine was applicable to cigarette advertising and that balanced—but not equal time—presentation was necessary.[38] Since the Commission had defined the controversial issue of public importance to be the desirability of smoking, portrayed in the commercials, despite the fact that the commercials made no affirmative health claims,[39] the decision's sweep could have been enormous. The desirability of using any product might be contested. Indeed, the complainant's opponents claimed that the ruling would apply to such items as automobiles and high cholesterol foods.[40] But the Commission, emphasizing the government's concern with cigarette health hazards, referred to cigarette advertising as a "unique situation."[41] The Commission also naively declared that it knew of no other advertised product that would arouse the same government health concerns and that "instances of extension of the ruling to other products upon consideration of future complaints would be rare, if indeed they ever occurred."[42]

Commissioner Loevinger, in a reluctant concurring opinion, perceptively foresaw the future difficulty of distinguishing cigarettes from other products, such as automobiles.[43] But Commissioner Johnson found Loevinger's "slippery slope" fears uncalled for in view of the Commission's "sound and durable" limitation of its ruling to cigarettes.[44] The Court of Appeals for the District of Columbia Circuit eventually affirmed the Commission's decision.[45]

B. THE CASES AFTER *BANZHAF:* A CRAZY QUILT

Banzhaf and the succeeding decisions at least indicate that commercial advertisements can raise issues requiring a response over the airwaves under the fairness doctrine.[46] But the applicability of fairness responsibilities to advertising is clear only in the simplest situation in which the broadcaster allows a commercial sponsor to advocate a position on an issue outright, for example, where a gasoline retailers' association opposed to higher gas taxes has paid for time explicitly to urge rejection of such a federal policy.[47] This kind of case is similar to explicit public affairs programming traditionally covered by the fairness doctrine. But with respect to advertisements without this explicit connection with controversial issues of public importance, the Commission's stance on the applicability of the fairness doctrine to advertising has followed a tortured course during the years following *Banzhaf,* and Commissioner Loevinger's "slippery slope" fears have proved well founded.

Institutional Advertising. Institutional advertising—that is, advertising that promotes the overall image of its sponsor and indirectly its product[48]—may raise issues subject to the fairness doctrine when it tracks arguments being made in the community on one side of an issue.

In the *National Broadcasting*[49] case, for example, two environmental groups filed a complaint against NBC for the airing of Esso commercials that concerned oil development in Alaska. They alleged that the advertisements raised the issue of the need for fast Alaskan oil development and the capability of transporting Alaskan oil via pipeline without environmental damage.[50] Although the advertisements did not explicitly mention the need for quick construction of an Alaskan pipeline or road, that very issue was before the courts and the executive branch and was being hotly debated by the public.[51] The FCC rejected the television network's interpretations of the advertisements and its claim that they were noncontroversial "institutional advertising."[52] Even though the advertisements did not explicitly discuss the Alaskan pipeline, the Commission found the issues discussed did have a "cognizable bearing" on the pipeline controversy.[53] The Commission also found that NBC had reasonably presented viewpoints contrasting with those expressed in the advertisements. Chairman Burch, in his concurring opinion, declared that, "The Commission has affirmed that product commercials *can* raise fairness obligations and that these commercials do so."[54] The problem is that the decision did not lay down any guidelines for when other commercials might also raise such obligations.[55]

In several actions that challenged military recruitment commercials, the FCC refused to reason so expansively.[56] The commercials were televised while the Vietnam war was raging, young men were fleeing the country to avoid the draft, and intensive debate on the war and military service persisted throughout the country. One stated: "Ask him (a Marine lieutenant) what it takes to lead a Marine platoon . . . a fighting man just doesn't come any finer than a Marine," and another declared, "This is Frank Blair speaking to young men facing a military obligation. As a father, I was pleased when my sons . . . told me they wanted to become Marines."[57] One licensee had concluded that the only issues raised by the recruitment advertisements were whether the United States "at this time should maintain armed forces" and should have "voluntary recruitment" and that these issues were not controversial. The FCC, in *Green*,[58] held that these conclusions were not unreasonable. Although the Commission admitted that the war and the draft were controversial, it contended that these issues were not raised by the advertisements and that, in any case, no evidence had been produced indicating that the stations had failed in their general obligation to serve community needs by presenting contrasting sides of these issues.[59] The District of Columbia Circuit affirmed the Commission's ruling.[60]

The distinction between the connection of the recruitment advertisements in *Green* to the war issue and the connection of the advertisements in *National Broadcasting* to the pipeline issue is not

readily apparent. Although the oil advertisements' texts more closely paralleled a viewpoint being expressed in the community on a
controversial issue, the military commercials also mimed arguments
made by one side on the draft and Vietnam issues. The Commission's and the court's implosive reasoning is explicable not in terms
of a considered development of precedent, but rather in terms of
the traditional deference to national security needs, the intensely
political nature of the war issue, the huge administrative problems
potentially connected with monitoring complaints based on the
advertisements, and the fact that a public sponsor was involved.
This is highlighted in the fact that the FCC shifted back to vigorous scrutiny of institutional advertising in the *Media Access Project* case.[61]

In *Media,* the complainant contended that two Georgia television stations were broadcasting advertisements for the Georgia
Power Company that raised the issue of the Company's request for
a rate increase. Public hearings were being held on the rate increase
request, the Georgia courts were reviewing the rate matter, and
many groups opposed the increase.[62] The Commission ruled that at
least two of the advertisements did raise one side of the issue and
required the stations to air the opposing side.[63] In so ruling, the
Commission used a test[64] centered on whether the advertisement
"clearly" presented one side or "position" on an issue.[65] Ironically,
the two advertisements that the Commission found "clearly presented"[66] the Power Company's position did not explicitly mention "rate increase" or the connected proceedings at all. But they
did parallel arguments the Company was making at the proceedings. And, the Commission noted, it was "arguable" that four
other advertisements, which only asserted the need for an increase
in generating capacity, also advocated one side of the rate increase issue.[67]

The FCC tightened its approach once again in its first consideration of the advertisements challenged in the *Neckritz* case.[68]
The commercials, possessing the attributes of both institutional and
ordinary product advertisements, involved gasoline with an additive
called "F-310"—"Chevron with F-310 turns dirty smoke into good,
clean mileage. There isn't a car on the road that shouldn't be using
it."[69] The Commission ruled that the fairness doctrine did not apply
to these commercials, even though they were the subject of a

Federal Trade Commission (FTC) complaint[70] and despite Commissioner Johnson's protestation that they "practically shout that they are dealing with a controversial issue of public importance."[71] According to the Commission, the advertisements did not "deal directly with an issue of public importance."[72]

The problem with these institutional advertising cases is that the standards for judging the relationship between the advertisement and the controversial issue of public importance, and consequently for judging whether a fairness obligation has been incurred, are confused. *Neckritz* states the advertisement must deal "directly" with the issue; *National Broadcasting* speaks of advertisements' "inherently" raising and having a "cognizable bearing" on the issue; and *Media Access* focuses on an advertisement that "clearly presents" the issue. What do these terms mean? In *National Broadcasting* there was no direct discussion of the Alaska pipeline, but, in discussing the need for Alaskan oil development and the ecological effects of such development, the pipeline controversy was raised.[73] In *Neckritz*, which admittedly involved a product with institutional promotional overtones, problems of air pollution were explicitly discussed, yet the Commission held that a controversial public issue was not raised. *Green*, like *National Broadcasting*, involved an institution trying to promote its image through advertising. The advertisements, even if they did not raise the issues of the Vietnam war and the draft, certainly focused on the desirability of serving in the military, a topic of intense public debate at that time. But the Commission did not find this issue implicitly raised, much less controversial and of public importance. Finally, the advertisements in *Media Access* contained text that reflected the arguments its sponsor was making elsewhere, but they still did not mention the rate proceedings, which were the controversial issues of public importance that the FCC said the advertisements raised. If the Commission itself, unburdened by a priori guidelines, was interpreting this kind of advertising in such a seemingly inconsistent manner, how could it hold licensees to a consistent standard of behavior?

Product Commercials. The cases demonstrate an even more confused approach to product commercials—that is, commercials that attempt to convince the public to purchase a specific product by making it seem desirable.[74] *Sam Morris*[75] set the stage for product commercial controversy. In the context of radio commercials for beer and wine that did no more than advertise the beverages, the Commission clearly stated that product commercials under certain circumstances would raise controversial issues of public importance. Those circumstances arose in *Banzhaf*, in which the Commission aggressively applied the government's policy against smoking to impose a fairness duty on broadcasters to counter cigarette advertising.[76]

But after *Banzhaf* there emerged a clear attempt by the Commission to close the gate on product commercials.[77] Time after time it referred to the cigarette case as unique. In not one case[78] after *Banzhaf* did it apply the fairness doctrine to an ordinary product commercial.[79]

The first indication that *Banzhaf* would be confined to its facts came with the military recruitment cases.[80] If military service is viewed as a product being sold by the military sponsor, the battlefield health dangers connected with the product are certainly more severe than those connected with cigarette smoking. Indeed, Commissioner Johnson in his dissent, bending the "durable" line he had declared in the cigarette case,[81] forcefully argued that *Banzhaf* should be applicable to the recruitment advertisements. But both the Commission and the Court of Appeals rejected the *Banzhaf* analogy.[82]

The Commission eventually confronted the *Banzhaf* problem squarely in *Friends of the Earth*.[83] At issue in the case were advertisements carried over a television station for large engine cars and leaded gasolines.[84] The Commission disagreed with the contention that the advertisements represented only one side of the air pollution issue with respect to cars and gas, and supported the licensees' refusal to grant time for countercommercials. The Commission did acknowledge that the fairness doctrine was fully applicable[85] if a commercial dealt "directly with an issue of public importance," but "general product" advertisements were excluded.[86]

The Court of Appeals for the District of Columbia Circuit reversed the Commission, finding it impossible to distinguish the air pollution case meaningfully from the cigarette case.[87] As in *Banzhaf*, there was ample evidence of government concern for the health problems caused by automobile air pollution, including declarations by the President of the United States, Congress, and state officials.[88] The experts, with a report from the Surgeon General at the top of the list, seemed united on the dangers of car-generated air pollution. Like the cigarette advertisements, the automobile advertisements did not affirmatively discuss health problems; but just as the very use of cigarettes posed health problems and raised controversial issues of public importance, so did the use of large cars and high-test gasoline. The court, per Judge McGowan, stated:

> When there is undisputed evidence, as there is here, that the hazards to health implicit in air pollution are enlarged and aggravated by such products, then the parallel with cigarette advertising is exact and the relevance of *Banzhaf* inescapable.[89]

It should be noted that *Friends of the Earth* was not the first case in which the Court took issue with the Commission about the implications of *Banzhaf*. In *Retail Store Employees Union, Local 880 v. FCC*,[90] the court reversed the FCC's refusal to hold a hearing on a radio station's license renewal despite a fairness complaint lodged against the station. The station had discontinued airing a union's advertisements explicitly supporting a union boycott of a department store but had continued broadcasting the store's regular product advertising. The court, per Chief Judge Bazelon, stated that the product advertisements inherently raised one side of the controversial and important boycott issue, and read the FCC *Banzhaf* decision to mean that some advertisements could "carry an implicit as well as an explicit message."[91] The court also stated that the overall obligation of the FCC to regulate broadcasting in the "public interest" should cause the Commission to question whether licensee refusal of the labor union's advertisements was consistent with national policy favoring equalization of labor-management bargaining powers.[92]

The court's reversal of *Friends of the Earth* prompted the Commission to rehear the "F-310" case, *In re Neckritz*.[93] But notwithstanding the Court of Appeals' indications to the contrary in *Retail Store* and *Friends of the Earth*, the Commission again declined to extend *Banzhaf*. Affirming its earlier refusal to impose fairness balancing, the Commission distinguished *Friends of the Earth* by stating that there was no evidence indicating F-310 "enlarges or aggravates hazards to the public health" like the use of high-powered cars or leaded gas, and that, even if a hazard was involved, the expert opinion was much more divided.[94] It then cited a series of reasons for its holding that were essentially the same as those it had put forward in its original *Friends of the Earth* decision. Among them were the need for the Commission not to interfere with licensee discretion, the opinion that the advertisements did not argue a position,[95] and the potential for an administrative and economic nightmare if the Commission were to rule otherwise.[96]

Like previous decisions,[97] the *Neckritz* decision illustrates the Commission's loose handling of the *Banzhaf* precedent. In *Banzhaf*, the FCC, relying on the cigarette health hazard and the unanimous government policy against smoking, held that a fairness obligation was incurred. Yet in *Friends of the Earth*, when again faced with products involving a health hazard and government policy, the Commission ruled that no fairness balance was required. *Neckritz*, although distinguishable on the grounds that it involved a product whose use did not aggravate a health hazard and did not involve a unified negative government policy, nonetheless involved commercials that were more explicit than *Banzhaf*'s in discussing a controversial issue. Here too, however, the Commission avoided fairness treatment.

The District of Columbia Circuit, on the other hand, repeatedly frustrated the Commission's attempt to rid itself of *Banzhaf*. Not only did it reverse *Friends of the Earth*, finding the analogy with *Banzhaf* too close to ignore, but in *Retail Store* it expanded the potential for application of the fairness doctrine to product commercials. In that case, no health hazard was involved. But the court held that, in the context of an employer-employee conflict and a government policy favoring increased economic equality, an ordinary product commercial called for fairness scrutiny.

From one perspective, the District of Columbia Circuit's opinions may be viewed as a reflection of the court's traditional deference to critically important government policies. Such strong policies were clearly involved in *Banzhaf* and *Green*, and *Retail Store*'s mention of government labor policy may also be viewed in this light. Conceivably, the FCC obligation to see that broadcast licensees operate in the "public interest" could be stretched to include furtherance of these interests. However, an approach that allows established government policies to determine what positions should or should not be open to fairness rebuttal does not seem appropriate for a doctrine whose purpose is to create robust, open debate. In fact, the government's position might be the very one contested, as it was in *Green*.

From another perspective, the Court of Appeals' opinions, particularly *Friends of the Earth*, simply reflect a judicial attempt to gain closer FCC adherence to the *Banzhaf* precedent and a refusal to allow the FCC to escape the import of that decision by drawing unconvincing distinctions.[98] Support for this view can be found in the court's affirmance of the FCC's ruling in *Neckritz*.[99] In *Neckritz v. FCC*, the court agreed with the Commission that the F-310 commercials should be distinguished from the commercials in *Banzhaf* and *Friends of the Earth* on the ground that "the [F-310] commercials made no attempt to glorify conduct or products which endangered public health or contributed to pollution."[100] Significantly, Judge Bazelon, in explaining his vote denying petitioner's request for a rehearing of the case, stressed the importance of the FCC's 1974 *Fairness Doctrine Report*, which was issued shortly after the court's decision.[101] This statement may perhaps be viewed as an indication that the court will defer to the FCC's approach to *Banzhaf* if it is coherently developed. The *Fairness Report* indeed represents the Commission's effort to deal with the *Banzhaf* precedent in a convincing and rational manner.

III. THE 1974 FAIRNESS REPORT

Faced with increasing criticism of its fairness decisions with respect to commercial advertising, severe questioning of many aspects of its overall fairness doctrine policies, and demands for citizen access to the airwaves, the FCC in 1971 initiated a far-reaching inquiry into the doctrine.[102] On July 12, 1974, the Commission released the results of its inquiry and declared a major change in its policy on the fairness doctrine and commercial advertising.[103] The 1974 Report divides commercials into three categories:[104] those that are clearly and explicitly editorials; institutional advertising that implicitly raises controversial issues of public importance; and advertising for commercial products or services. The Report does not substantially alter FCC policy toward the first two types of advertising, but it announces a significant change in policy toward the last.

A. EDITORIAL ADVERTISING

The FCC says that "overt editorial"[105] advertisements consist of "direct and substantial commentary on important public issues" and "should be recognized for what they are—editorials paid for by the sponsor."[106] As an example of such an editorial advertisement the Commission describes a 30- or 60-second announcement prepared and sponsored by an anti-abortion group that urges adoption of a constitutional amendment to override the Supreme Court's abortion decision. Such explicit discussion of a controversial public issue unquestionably would have required fairness balancing in a licensee's programming before the 1974 Report.

B. INSTITUTIONAL ADVERTISING

The Commission refers to *National Broadcasting* for an example of advertising that is not so overt. Esso's advertisements in that case "did not explicitly mention that pipeline, but they did present what could be termed arguments in support of its construction."[107] Implicit advocacy, says the Commission, is most likely to occur in the "context of promotional or institutional advertising; that is, advertising designed to present a favorable public image of a particular corporation or industry rather than to sell a product."[108] Such institutional advertising may appear to discuss a public issue but may not "explicitly address the ultimate matter in controversy."[109] The advocacy in such advertisements may be particularly difficult to identify, since the sponsor is not normally considered to be engaged in controversial debate.[110] But, when such discussion implicitly occurs in advertising, fairness doctrine obligations accrue.

The Commission attempts to set a standard for judging institutional advertising. It rejects Professor Jaffe's suggestion that broadcasters in essence become mindreaders,[111] and states that it is only concerned with "an obvious participation in public debate and not a subjective judgment as to the advertiser's actual intentions."[112] The Commission expects licensees

> to do nothing more than to make a reasonable, common sense judgment as to whether the "advertisement" presents a meaningful statement *which obviously addresses, and advocates a point of view* on, a controversial issue of public importance. This determination cannot be made in a vacuum; in addition to his review of the text of the ad, the licensee must take into account his general knowledge of the issues and arguments in the ongoing public debate. Indeed, this relationship of the ad to the debate being carried on in the community is critical. If the ad bears only a tenuous relationship to that debate, or one drawn by unnecessary inference . . . the fairness doctrine would clearly not be applicable. . . . The situation would be different, however, if that relationship could be shown to be both *substantial and obvious.* For example, if the arguments and views expressed in the ad closely parallel the major arguments advanced by partisans on one side or the other of a public debate, it might be reasonable to conclude that one side of the issue involved had been presented thereby raising fairness doctrine obligations.[113]

This language can be interpreted as giving broadcasters and advertisers increased leeway in determining if institutional advertising raises fairness doctrine obligations. An advertisement must be a "meaningful statement which obviously addresses and advocates" a position and bears "both a substantial and obvious" relationship to a controversial issue of public importance. The words appear to demand a more clear-cut connection with public issues than did the phrases in the cases that described commercials "inherently," "directly," or "clearly" raising, or having a "cognizable bearing" on, public issues.[114] As precedent for the 1974 Report's wording, the FCC cited *Media Access Project,* which involved institutional advertisements that were far more obvious than advertisements in other FCC cases.

Several other points should be noted with respect to the Commission's institutional advertising guidelines. First, institutional advertisements that raise controversial issues of public importance in their textual and visual components are not frequently broadcast. The bulk of commercial advertising consists of standard product commercials. A limited survey supervised by the author revealed that fewer than 1 percent of the commercials broadcast were institutional advertisements that could be said potentially to raise a controversial issue of public importance.[115] Thus, the institutional guidelines are important, but they must be seen in perspective. They will not have a major impact on programming.

Second, because the guidelines emphasize that the advertisements must have an "obvious" relationship to the public issue, institutional advertisements that may attempt subtly to convey one side of a controversial issue may escape fairness scrutiny. Yet, imaginative use of visual imagery, the true genius of television, can be particularly effective in presenting a point of view. One telephone advertisement, for example, visually depicted the many kinds of telephone equipment available to the customer. It generated sympathy for the telephone company and the job it was doing by demonstrating the diversity of service available.[116] In light of the simultaneous antitrust court proceedings focusing on telephone company monopoly of equipment supply, and the public and media debate over the issue, such advertising subtly raises one side of the controversy. But if such advertisements are without a text obviously addressing a point of view, they will pass muster under the guidelines, even if they have a greater impact on the viewer than more obvious advertising.

However, if the FCC is not to act as a continuous censor, the exclusion of less obvious advertisements from FCC scrutiny is necessary and appropriate. Interpretation of such advertisements would always be open to differing conclusions, and licensees would have to act with even less certainty in assessing commercials for fairness doctrine purposes.

Third, the guidelines are not entirely clear even for those commercials that more obviously address controversial issues of public importance. The FCC itself, referring to the assessments that broadcasters must make of the fairness implications of these commercials, states, "We fully appreciate that in many cases, this judgment may prove to be a difficult one and individual licensees may well reach differing conclusions concerning the same advertisement."[117] Commissioner Hooks, in his separate opinion concurring and dissenting in part, is perhaps closer to the mark when he states: "We have not articulated a fully satisfactory distinction between controversial ads not falling into the majority's category of 'obvious-

and-meaningful' and the precedent established in the *Banzhaf* case and later expanded."[118] Given the very general guidelines the Commission has set forth, the FCC as well as the courts should sustain broadcasters' judgments except in the most blatant of cases.

Fourth, in light of the *Green* decision,[119] it would have been helpful if the FCC had specifically stated that institutional advertising may raise a controversial issue of public importance, regardless of sponsor.[120] A government-sponsored advertisement like that in *Green* may call for balancing. In fact, the need to balance viewpoints is particularly acute when the government acts to propagate its own message, since that is where potential First Amendment infringement and abuse of the airwaves is greatest.

In the same vein, the FCC should have explicitly rejected reliance on government policy in determining what advertisements raise controversial issues of public importance, whether or not the government itself sponsors the advertising in question. In its initial Notice of Inquiry, the Commission pointed to *Retail Store*'s reliance on "pertinent national policies" in determining whether an advertisement raises a controversial issue of public importance, and asked for comment.[121] The 1974 Report does not fulfill the original Notice's call for discussion of the pertinence of such government policy to institutional advertising. For the same reasons mentioned in the preceding paragraph, I submit that judgment on whether commercials raise controversial issues of public importance should not be biased toward established government policy, labor or otherwise. Although such policy is relevant, of course, it should not be the sole determining factor. The existence of controversial debate in the community and its importance to community members, even if the viewpoints conflict with government policy, should be the guiding criteria.

Despite these shortcomings, the Report's institutional advertising guidelines do provide increased protection for the broadcaster. If the FCC does continue the fairness doctrine in its present form, the FCC's new "substantial and obvious" wording should be strictly construed. Deciding whether an institutional advertisement raises an issue of public importance is simply too difficult a task, and the potential for increased FCC interference with broadcaster's freedom is too great a danger to tolerate a loose and activist construction of the new definition.

C. PRODUCT COMMERCIALS

Although the FCC had not applied the fairness doctrine to a standard product commercial since *Banzhaf*,[122] it had never rejected the *Banzhaf* precedent. The possibility existed that in the right circumstances a product commercial might raise a controversial issue of public importance, even without affirmative discussion of one side of that issue beyond simple depiction of the product as desirable. This possibility encouraged numerous complaints, one of which succeeded in the *Friends of the Earth* court decision.[123]

In the 1974 Report, the FCC closes the door on this possibility. Referring to *Banzhaf*, the Commission states in no uncertain terms that

> [w]hile such an approach may have represented good policy from the standpoint of the public health, the precedent is not at all in keeping with the basic purposes of the fairness doctrine [to facilitate the development of informed public opinion] . . . We believe that standard product commercials, such as the old cigarette ads, make no meaningful contribution toward informing the public on any side of any issue.[124]

Should a case similar to the cigarette controversy confront the Commission, it indicates that it may find it more appropriate to refer the matter to Congress for solution.[125]

The Commission offers four reasons for not applying the doctrine to standard product commercials. The greatest emphasis is placed on an idea illustrated in the quotation above: these commercials do not meaningfully contribute to the public debate to which the First Amendment and the fairness doctrine are addressed. The texts of such advertisements do not include any affirmative discussion on one side of an issue.[126] Moreover, applying the doctrine to such commercials would, at best, provide the public with but one articulated side of a controversial issue of public importance.[127] The standard product advertisement only makes use of the product appear desirable. If balanced programming is required, however, the rebuttal programming would provide an explicit discussion of the negative side of the underlying product use issue. Third, in determining if balancing is required with advertisements containing no text discussing one side of an issue, the Commission is forced to impose its view on the controversy in question.[128] And fourth, the process of applying the fairness doctrine to such advertisements involves licensees and the Commission in the "trivial task" of balancing commercials that "contribute nothing to public understanding,"[129] and significantly diverts broadcasters from their public trustee responsibility of meaningfully informing the public.[130]

A critical consideration underlying the FCC's switch in policy appears with the Commission's reference to advertising's role in providing economic support for broadcasting. In its consideration of the fairness doctrine's applicability to advertising, the Commission does not want to undermine "the economic base of the system."[131] As will be discussed below, the opposite conclusion on *Banzhaf's* relevance to standard product commercials could have had disastrous economic consequences for broadcasting.

Economic consequences were also explicitly mentioned by the FCC in its rejection of a proposal made by the Federal Trade Commission.[132] The FTC advocated a right of access to respond to certain types of commercials. In addition to advertisements explicitly and implicitly raising controversial issues, the FTC suggested that advertisements making claims based on disputed scientific premises as well as those remaining silent about products' adverse effects should require responses.[133] But the FCC foresaw "a predictable adverse economic effect on broadcasting" if such a plan were adopted.[134]

Thus, under the 1974 Report, unless commercials for products or services contain material in their auditory or visual components that obviously and meaningfully addresses a controversial issue of public importance, they are not subject to the fairness doctrine. Controversies surrounding a product's use, scientific basis, or harmful effects are simply not relevant for fairness doctrine purposes. Simple advocacy of product use does not raise fairness questions. A product's advertisement, like institutional advertising, can affirmatively discuss controversial issues of public importance that call for fairness balancing. But without such discussion in the advertisement's spoken text or visual segment, the fairness doctrine does not impose obligations. The *Banzhaf* precedent is reversed.[135]

The courts, of course, may reject the FCC's "reformulation" in this area. However, this seems unlikely. In *Friends of the Earth v. FCC,*[136] the District of Columbia Circuit referred to the FCC's fairness doctrine inquiry and left open the question of the effect that it would have:

> We do not, of course, anticipate what the result of that proceeding will prove to be, nor do we minimize either the seriousness or the thorny nature of the problems to be explored therein. Pending, however, a reformulation of its position, we are unable to see how the Commission can plausibly differentiate the case presently before us from *Banzhaf.*[137]

Given the FCC's intensive three-year study of the advertising issue, and the deference to the proceeding indicated in the above dicta, the Commission's rejection of *Banzhaf* in the 1974 Report probably foreshadows a changed Court of Appeals stance.[138]

D. REMOVING PRODUCT-SERVICE ADS FROM DOCTRINE OBLIGATIONS: THE RIGHT POLICY

The FCC's decision to remove standard product and service commercials from fairness doctrine obligations is wise policy, and a number of arguments can be offered in support of this viewpoint.

1. *The First Amendment Interests of Broadcasters.* As the FCC itself suggests, applying the fairness doctrine to standard product and service advertisements would unnecessarily infringe the First Amendment interests of broadcasters. That radio and television are protected by First Amendment speech and press guarantees is well established.[139] Restrictions on licensee use of the airwaves should not unreasonably infringe broadcasters' First Amendment interests.

Extensive advertising regulation would have a significant effect on broadcaster programming decisions. Since commercials constitute a large segment of broadcast time[140] and since most product commercials can be considered to raise some controversial public issue,[141] there would have to be constant daily programming adjustment to allow for countercommercials or other balanced programming. Other broadcast scheduling would be affected. The Commission would be looking over licensees' shoulders to ensure sufficiently balanced programming. The FCC would, in essence, become an ex-officio member of the staffs of licensees' editorial and programming departments in order to review the dozens of commercials broadcast each day that would be the subject of fairness complaints, and to ensure balanced programming. Broadcasters would be denied the freedom to use much of their air time in a manner they deem best. This kind of FCC involvement, necessary to apply the fairness doctrine effectively to ordinary product-service commercials, would entail a far greater intrusion on broadcasters' First Amendment interests than now exists.

In recent years, in *Virginia State Board of Pharmacy v. Virginia Citizens Consumer Council, Inc.*[142] and *Bigelow v. Virginia,*[143] the Supreme Court ruled that commercial advertising is entitled to First Amendment protection, reversing the precedent of *Valentine v. Christenson.*[144] In *Virginia Board of Pharmacy* the Court struck down a state statute that forbade any pharmacist from advertising drug price information "in any manner whatsoever."[145] In *Bigelow* the Court ruled unconstitutional a statute that forbade advertising in any manner the opportunities for a woman to have an abortion.[146] The criminal conviction of a newspaper editor who had published an ad about low-cost New York abortion treatment was reversed. However, these two rulings do not mean that standard product commercials must be treated exactly the same as public affairs programming under the fairness doctrine.[147]

First, in both cases the Court was careful to explicitly distinguish its holding from bearing on regulation of the broadcast media, which were said to have "unique characteristics."[148]

At a more fundamental level,[149] however, the balancing of government interests against First Amendment interests involved in fairness doctrine regulation does not tip the same way as the balancing in *Virginia Board of Pharmacy* or *Bigelow.*[150]

The government has several interests in the fairness doctrine context. Thus there is a compelling governmental interest in not unduly infringing on the First Amendment freedoms of broadcasters, jeopardizing the industry's economic base, imposing a difficult administrative burden on broadcasters, paving the way for further fairness incursions on entertainment programming, and further accentuating the differences between the broadcast and print press. The government has alternative, less burdensome means to police broadcast commercials that will meet most of the demands of those who criticize commercials. These governmental interests are far more compelling and significant than Virginia's professed interests in preventing price competition (which theoretically leads to inferior pharmaceutical services) and protecting pharmacists' professional image.[151] As the Court concluded, the Virginia advertising ban did not accomplish these objectives and only kept the public in ignorance of price terms of competing pharmacists.[152]

On the other side of the equation, whose First Amendment rights are involved? In *Virginia Board of Pharmacy,* they were the rights of consumers to receive price information and certain pharmacists to advertise. The First Amendment rights of an editor to publish or broadcast what he or she wants were not involved.[153] In the fairness doctrine context the First Amendment imperative as far as the broadcaster is concerned is for precisely the governmental decision made; *i.e.,* no interference with standard broadcast ads. Indeed, in light of the interference with journalistic discretion and the potential economic harm to broadcasting, the First Amendment interests of the viewing public as a whole to receive unfettered, diverse information might suffer from an activist application of the doctrine to standard product ads. And, in the fairness doctrine situation, even those who want to voice their views freely in opposition to broadcast commercials can do so in a variety of ways.[154] There is not an absolute prohibition of communication about commercial products, as there was in *Virginia Board of Pharmacy*[155] and *Bigelow.*[156]

2. *Economic Consequences.* Application of the fairness doctrine to ordinary product commercials could have adverse economic consequences for licensees.[157] There are no data available on the precise economic effect of applying the doctrine to product commercials, and different views have been expressed on the subject.[158] Such an action, however, could severely affect the industry by requiring licensees to give up valuable free time for rebuttal programming, driving advertisers away from the electronic media, and subjecting licensees to additional administrative and legal costs.

In projecting the economic impact of this application of the fairness doctrine, one starts from the premise that the *Banzhaf-Friends of the Earth* rationale can be applied to the very large percentage of advertised products whose effect on the environment and public health is at least as controversial as that of large cars and leaded gasoline. As stated in an intensive study,[159] "There are relatively few advertised products whose normal use does not involve some significant issue: automobiles (large or small), gasoline (leaded or unleaded), any type of medication, beer, airplanes, any product that does not have a biodegradable container, any foreign product—the list is virtually endless."[160]

The fairness doctrine would require reply time to such advertisements in the form of either countercommercials or other programming. Under the *Cullman Broadcasting* principle, the cost of reply programming must be borne by the licensee if paid sponsorship is not forthcoming.[161] Since few consumer and environmental groups would have the funds to sponsor any counterprogramming, even at reduced rates, the licensee would have to pay for most of this programming. And, of critical importance, it would have to give up air time that other, standard advertisers might buy.

The potentially severe impact of such time displacement was pointed out by the Columbia Broadcasting System in a brief submitted for the Commission's Fairness Inquiry proceedings.[162] CBS assumed that *Banzhaf* at least would apply to cereals, gasoline, oil, drugs, and detergents—which accounted for 26 percent of all 1970 television network advertising revenues.[163] If countercommercials were required on a one-to-five basis, as the Commission required with cigarette commercials, CBS calculated that $68 million, or $18 million more than 1970 pretax profits for all three networks, would have to be donated by the networks. Network bankruptcy was predicted.[164]

Even if these figures are only half correct,[165] they make the point: giving up time for counterprogramming potentially could have a very adverse effect on broadcasting's economic base. And the CBS figures focused on consequences for the more profitable networks only. The outlook would be even grimmer for the hundreds of less successful local licensees.

In fact, to be even-handed in applying the doctrine, a very strong case could be made for requiring countercommercials to the countercommercials.[166] Ordinary product advertisements do not discuss the health or other problems that might be associated with the product. The advertisements go only to the desirability of the product. Countercommercials or other counterprogramming, on the other hand, does affirmatively and explicitly discuss the product's alleged problems and the controversial public issue involved. Product commercial sponsors could rightfully argue that they deserve reply time to address the issues explicitly discussed in the counterprogramming. They could forcefully argue that per the *Cullman* principle, they should not have to pay for such rejoinder time. Even if the product sponsors did not request reply time for themselves, they, or others, could well maintain that the licensees were required to provide counterprogramming on their own if other spokesmen could not be found.

Counterprogramming would also be likely to drive a good deal of advertising from the electronic media to newspapers, magazines, and billboards. The only figures available on this issue are those that show the trend of cigarette advertising after counter-commercials were broadcast. Although these figures do show some loss in cigarette television advertising revenue, it is not major.[167] The problem with generalizing from these statistics, as at least one commentator has attempted to do,[168] is that cigarettes, unlike cars and detergents, are addictive products. It is much harder to "break the habit." Well-designed advertisements against a particular detergent or car, however, might produce far greater consumer reaction, and, in consequence, industry might become reluctant to involve itself with broadcast advertising at all. If a businessman's product is going to be continually attacked on national television and radio as long as he advertises through that medium, it may be assumed that he will seek the safer haven of printed advertising. In fact, spokesmen for national advertisers have announced that if counteradvertising is limited to broadcasting, they will switch to the other media.[169] Although former Commissioner Loevinger is overstating the case, there is a good deal of truth to his assertion that "there can be no reasonable doubt that counter-advertising would drive most, if not all, advertisers away from broadcasting to more hospitable media."[170]

Licensees would also suffer economically from the cost of constantly responding to fairness inquiries and complaints. For example, in the *KREM-TV* case, in which the FCC staff found that the licensee had acted reasonably despite fairness complaints from local groups,[171] the station's executive and supervisory personnel spent approximately 480 man-hours dealing with the matter in addition to secretarial and clerical time.[172] A station executive stated, "This represents a very serious dislocation of operational functions."[173] The licensee also incurred well over $20,000 in legal, travel, and other expenses connected with the complaints.[174] Considering that the total 1972 profits for all three television stations in the licensee's area was $494,000,[175] the expenses were most considerable.

The KREM expenses were incurred for just one fairness incident, based on one controversial issue, and KREM was not an exceptional case. There would be many such incidents if numerous product commercials were subject to the fairness doctrine, and expenses would rise accordingly. As one author puts it, "endless litigation of individual fairness complaints directed at specific advertisements and products is costly, chaotic and a poor substitute for regulation."[176]

3. *Difficulties with Administration and Enforcement.* Imposing the fairness doctrine on product commercials would lead to increased administrative burdens for the FCC and would compound all of the fairness doctrine problems inherent in the non-advertising context. The FCC has a small staff to deal with fairness complaints.[177] Applying the fairness doctrine to commercials would significantly increase the number of complaints with which the Commission must deal, requiring additional staff time and personnel. Additional time and effort would also have to be devoted by the full Commission.

A fairness doctrine–product commercial link would bring to the realm of advertising all of the administrative-enforcement problems discussed in Chapter Six, which occur when the doctrine is applied to regular public affairs programming. The difficult question of determining what issue is raised by a broadcast again would be present. In the product advertising context, the question is compounded, for no explicit text guides the licensee or the Commission. With what criteria would licensees or the FCC decide which allegedly negative aspect of a product should be addressed, what factual assertions are controversial enough to require rejoinder, or what larger socioeconomic issues are inherently raised by product commercials? The absence of explicit text would require the Commission to intrude with its own values. As already mentioned, instead of having a controversy explicitly delineated by the programming, the Commission must read into a commercial its own opinion of underlying controversy surrounding the advertised product. Such imposition of agency opinion would represent a dangerous expansion of governmental power into the "marketplace of ideas."

The product commercial area also has the administrative problems discussed in Chapter Seven connected with it.[178] How many countercommercials must be run in opposition to a particular product commercial? Is the total time devoted to a product commercial the revelant criterion, is the individual advertisement's frequency more important, or is some combination of both factors necessary to determine the proper balance? What relevance has the time of day in which the broadcasts were made? How does one balance a prime time advertisement with a daytime advertisement? How does one figure in other licensee news and public affairs programming that might touch on the product commercial issue? The spectre of the FCC and licensees endlessly working out such intricate formulas is administratively frightening.

Inextricably linked with the problem of balancing contrasting viewpoints is the problem of developing adequate guidelines for licensees to follow. The FCC would have to offer guidance on how licensees are to determine whether an advertisement demands reply time, what issue must be addressed, how the licensee is to present the contrasting view, what remedial action the FCC may take, and other fairness questions.[179] A declaration of policy applying the doctrine to commercials followed by weak or nonexistent enforcement by the FCC would only increase public skepticism of the Commission and defeat, at least partially, consumer and environmental goals. Finally, adequate notice of governmental requirements should be a cornerstone in regulating any industry affected with First Amendment interests. Yet the administrative difficulties inherent in the application of the fairness doctrine to product commercials leads to a state of uncertainty in which licensees are not given sufficient warning of what is required of them.

4. *The Exemption of Entertainment Programming.* It would be inconsistent to apply the doctrine to product advertising but not to the important controversies inherently raised by entertainment programming. One might ask why consumer issues should demand countercommercials and balanced programming,

but not the violence that is part of so many programs. Does not a television movie glorifying a war hero's deeds inherently raise the issue of violence against fellow man, which may be far more important and controversial than whether detergents pollute? One commentator has seriously suggested that programs such as "All in the Family," "The FBI," westerns, and even football games be subject to fairness doctrine balancing.[180] While theoretically consistent, this course of action would in essence replace broadcaster freedom with almost complete government monitoring of the airwaves. The FCC has sensibly steered clear of such a course.[181] Television entertainment unquestionably needs improvement, but the fairness doctrine is not the way to achieve it. Applying the doctrine to product commercials could push the FCC and the courts toward a different conclusion.

5. *The Exemption of the Print Medium.* Applying the doctrine to broadcast advertising but not newspaper advertising would accentuate the fairness policy inequity that already exists between the two media. In the past five years the Supreme Court has demonstrated the dichotomy in its approach.[182] The Court has struck down a statute mandating access to present opposing views in newspapers,[183] but has let stand the fairness doctrine as applied to broadcasters.[184] An expansion of the fairness doctrine to broadcast product advertising in the face of court rulings that might well prohibit its application to print product advertising would draw the explanation for the broadcast–print media difference into question and leave broadcasters with even less protection in comparison with their media brethren.

6. *Alternative Means of Achieving the Ends of the Fairness Doctrine.* There is a critical need for television and radio to dramatically increase coverage of pressing consumer, environmental, and social issues and to ensure that its advertising is honest. But there are other, less harmful, and more effective ways to police product commercials and cover the issues they raise than using the fairness doctrine.

If an advertisement is misleading about a product's effect, the FTC can ban the advertisement from the airwaves. Under the Federal Trade Commission Act it is unlawful to disseminate false advertisements[185] or use unfair or deceptive practices in commerce.[186] In addition to FTC cease and desist orders,[187] injunctive relief may be obtained[188] and in certain circumstances criminal penalties may be imposed.[189] Although the FTC's record in this area has been very poor,[190] in the last few years the FTC enforcement has become more vigorous, and corrective advertising has been required.[191] The FTC also has recently created an advertisement substantiation program that requires advertisers to document product claims before advertising and to produce these claims at the FTC's request.[192] If documentation is not sufficient the FTC can have the advertisement withdrawn[193] and compel corrective advertising.[194]

It remains to be seen how forceful and effective the FTC will be in this area. Congress undoubtedly should allocate it additional resources to do the job, and the public can play an increasing role in monitoring advertisements and notifying the FTC, FCC, and licensees of advertisements it considers deceptive.[195] FTC-FCC-licensee cooperation in removing deceptive advertisements from the airwaves seems a much more direct and effective way of protecting consumers against such advertising than fairness debates. Rather than imposing the fairness doctrine, and all the problems it brings to licensees and the public, on misleading advertisements, they should simply be taken off the airwaves.[196] Thus in *Neckritz,* instead of protracted fairness proceedings, a speedy FTC procedure to remove the F-310 advertisements should have been commenced.[197]

Licensees already have the responsibility "to take all reasonable measures to eliminate any false, misleading, or deceptive matter" from their broadcasts,[198] and to help them fulfill this responsibility they receive the FTC's "Advertising Alert" on pending complaints.[199] Cooperation of this sort should be improved, and the intensity of FTC activity increased.[200]

Other methods can also be used to further consumers' interests. Public service announcements giving consumers buying tips and referring them to local consumer information sources could be aired on a nationwide basis under FTC auspices or at the behest of local groups. Station news shows could take increasing advantage of interesting consumer programming such as that now produced and offered by CONSUMER REPORTS, or they could create their own consumer hotlines.[201] The advertising industry itself could continue to expand its efforts at self regulation.

Beyond this, major changes in public affairs programming, such as requiring a fixed percentage of broadcast time to be devoted to important social issues,[202] would result in much wider coverage of consumer and other social issues. If citizens take advantage of the participation opportunity, the recent alterations in FCC requirements, allowing for increased involvement of the public in determining licensee programming, can cause a more intensive broadcaster focus on consumer issues.[203] An expanded Public Broadcasting System, and the development of cable and UHF television, should also allow the public to receive an increasing flow of vital consumer and environmental information and should be strongly supported.

CONCLUSION

During the late 1960s and early 1970s, the FCC began to apply the fairness doctrine to broadcast advertising. The Commission and the courts set down a string of inconsistent and confused precedents as they attempted to grapple with a growing number of fairness complaints directed at commercial advertising.

In 1974, the Commission completed a reevaluation of the fairness doctrine and issued its *Fairness Report*. The Report states that institutional advertising may raise fairness doctrine issues only if the issues are explicitly and meaningfully addressed. The Report's language can be interpreted to mean that it will be more difficult to file successful fairness complaints based on institutional advertising, and it has been suggested in these pages that it should be so narrowly construed. The difficulty of interpreting these advertisements, the lack of clear guidance, and the First Amendment rights of broadcasters all call for such a conclusion.

The 1974 Report also signalled a major change in FCC policy by exempting ordinary product and service advertisements from fairness doctrine obligations. This policy change should be applauded by even the severest critics of product advertisements. At its best, the fairness doctrine–product advertising marriage attempted only to replicate other, more effective means to police product commercials and give the American people vital consumer and environmental information. At its worst, it created a quagmire

of precedents that potentially undermined the economic foundation
of the broadcasting industry and threatened the First Amendment
interests of broadcasters and the public alike.

Notes

1. FCC, *Fairness Doctrine and Public Interest Standards, Fairness Report Regarding
Handling of Public Issues*, 39 FED. REG. 26372 (1974) [hereinafter cited as *Fairness Report*];
see notes 102–35, *infra*, and accompanying text. The conclusions in the *Fairness Report* with
respect to product commercials and the fairness doctrine were reaffirmed in *Fairness Doctrine and Public Interest Standards. Reconsideration of Fairness Report Regarding Handling of Public Issues*, 58 F.C.C.2d 691 (1976) [hereinafter referred to as *Reconsideration
Fairness Report*]. The First Circuit has held that the Report's conclusion on product advertising is rational, authorized by statute, and constitutional. Public Interest Research Group
v. FCC, 552 F.2d 1060 (1st Cir. 1975). *See* note 147, *infra*. *See also* note at end of this
chapter for the District of Columbia Court of Appeals' decision on the Report.
2. D. SANDMAN, D. RUBIN & D. SACHSMAN, MEDIA, AN INTRODUCTORY ANALYSIS OF
AMERICAN MASS COMMUNICATIONS 138 (1972).
3. J. PENNYBACKER & W. BRADEN, BROADCASTING AND THE PUBLIC INTEREST 5 (1969).
4. *Id.*
5. *Id.*
6. R.E. SUMMERS & H.B. SUMMERS, BROADCASTING AND THE PUBLIC 38 (1966).
7. *Id.* at 38.
8. J. PENNYBACKER & W. BRADEN, *supra* note 3, at 6.
9. *Id.*
10. WEAF's present-day call letters are WNBC.
11. A real estate firm on Long Island paid $50 for approximately 50 minutes of advertis-
ing spread over a consecutive five-day period to advertise a new subdivision it was developing. At present WNBC rates, 50 minutes of advertising, spread out in morning, afternoon,
and evening slots over a one-week period, would cost approximately $60 per minute, or
$3,000. Telephone interview with Susan Segal, account executive, WNBC, by Steven J.
Simmons, May 4, 1975. The 60-fold increase in price bears testimony to the huge expansion
in radio's audience.
12. J. PENNYBACKER & W. BRADEN, *supra* note 3, at 6.
13. R.E. SUMMERS & H.B. SUMMERS, *supra* note 6, at 38.
14. *Id.*
15. "During January 1927, the weekly schedules of the two networks operated by the
National Broadcasting Company included a total of 22 hours of evening programs of which
16 hours were sponsored." *Id.* at 43.
16. R.E. SUMMERS & H.B. SUMMERS, *supra* note 6, at 44.
17. *Id.*, at 123. Today almost all network programming is produced by network personnel
or independent production companies. *Id.*
18. *Id.* at 50.
19. 1974 BROADCASTING YEARBOOK, 80, 12. By 1972, 98 percent of American homes,
excluding those in Hawaii and Alaska, had at least one radio, and 97 percent had at least one
television set. *Id.* at 68. The main reason radio's growth rate slowed from that of its early
days was the public's intense interest in the new medium of television. R.E. SUMMERS &
H.B. SUMMERS, *supra* note 6, at 69.
20. R.E. SUMMERS & H.B. SUMMERS, *supra* note 6, at 62.
21. H. SCHILLER, MASS COMMUNICATION AND AMERICAN EMPIRE 26 (1969). Other
commentators note: "Throughout the 1930's and 1940's, advertisers produced almost every
radio program broadcast. The job of the station was merely to sell the time and man the
transmitter; the sponsor and its ad agency handled everything else. When commercial

television was introduced in the late forties, this pattern of advertiser control and advertiser production was accepted from the very start. By the late 1950's the cost of even a single prime-time network television show had grown too big for all but the largest advertisers to afford. . . . By 1962 it was rare for a sponsor to produce its own show. Some continue to sponsor particular network-produced programs. . . . Advertisers no longer write their own shows, but they still decide where to put their ads." D. SANDMAN, D. RUBIN & D. SACHS-MAN, *supra* note 2, at 139.

22. WNBT's present call letters are WNBC-TV.

23. R.E. SUMMERS & H.B. SUMMERS, *supra* note 6, at 63.

24. *Id.*

25. H. SCHILLER, *supra* note 21, at 26–27, quoting figures from TELEVISION FACT BOOK 51a, 55a (1968–69).

26. R.E. SUMMERS & H. B. SUMMERS, *supra* note 6, at 75.

27. 1974 BROADCASTING YEARBOOK 68, 69, 80. The figure for percentage of American homes excludes Alaska and Hawaii.

28. *See* D. SANDMAN, D. RUBIN & D. SACHSMAN, *supra* note 2, at 134–42, and F. WOLF, TELEVISION PROGRAMMING FOR NEWS AND PUBLIC AFFAIRS, A QUANTITATIVE ANALYSIS OF NETWORKS AND STATIONS (1972), for a discussion of advertiser control of the media. Wolf, referring to a survey of nonnews programming, stated (at 136): "The advertisers' aversion to controversy was clear, and this made it difficult for contentious issues and problems to reach the air. When they did, the advertisers sought presentations that did not risk offending people. But the public record of advertisers' attempts to intervene in programming was inconclusive. To the extent that advertisers' aims limited programming, they appear to have done so more by their program sponsorship policies than by direct action."

29. R.E. SUMMERS & H.B. SUMMERS, *supra* note 6, at 100. As one popular magazine put it, "Viewers may bemoan the clutter of spots before their eyes—commercial spots, that is, brashly punctuating their programs—but if the spots weren't sold, there'd be no money, no show, no networks, no TV," TV GUIDE, Jan. 11–17, 1975, at 11.

30. 11 F.C.C. 197 (1946).

31. The FCC, calling the issue one of "industry wide proportions," refused to consider it in the context of a single station and denied Morris's petition. *Id.*

32. The "public interest requires ample play for the free and fair competition of opposing views, and the Commission believes that the principle applies . . . to all discussions and issues of importance to the public." Great Lakes Broadcasting Co., 3 F.R.C. ANNUAL REPORT 32 (1929), *rev'd on other grounds,* 37 F.2d 993 (D.C. Cir.), *cert. denied,* 281 U.S. 706 (1930).

33. 11 F.C.C. at 198, 199.

34. The *Report on Editorializing by Broadcast Licensees,* 13 F.C.C. 1246 (1949) [hereinafter referred to as *Report on Editorializing*], issued three years after *Morris,* did not explicitly discuss advertising. It did state that some material thought to be noncontroversial when originally broadcast may subsequently arouse opposition and controversy. *Id.* at 1251. Advertising could theoretically consist of such material.

35. *Controversial Issue Programming,* 40 F.C.C. 571, 572 (1963).

36. *Fairness Report, supra* note 1, at 26380–83.

37. WCBS-TV, 8 F.C.C.2d 381 (1967) (the *Banzhaf* case).

38. *Id.* at 381–82.

39. WCBS-TV, 9 F.C.C.2d 921, 938, 939 (1967) (this was a second opinion, issued in response to numerous petitions and requests for reconsideration of the initial cigarette advertising decision).

40. *Id.* at 942. They also included "alcoholic beverages, fluoride in toothpaste, pesticide residue in food, aspirin, detergents, candy, gum, soft drinks, girdles, and even common table salt." *Id.* at 952–53.

41. *Id.* at 953.

42. *Id.* The Commission continued, "In short, our ruling applies only to cigarette advertising, and imposes no Fairness Doctrine obligation upon petitioners with respect to other product advertising." *Id.*

43. *Id.* at 954 (Loevinger, concurring opinion).

44. *Id.* at 958 (Johnson, concurring opinion).

45. Banzhaf v. FCC, 405 F.2d 1082 (D.C. Cir. 1968), *cert. denied,* 396 U.S. 842 (1969). Judge Bazelon, speaking for the court, declared that, because cigarette smoking posed a "unique danger authenticated by official and congressional action," 405 F.2d at 1099, the FCC's action was authorized under the Commission's statutory obligation to regulate broadcast licenses in the "public interest," 47 U.S.C. sec. 307(a)(d) (1964). The court also held that the First Amendment rights of broadcasters and advertisers were not violated, because, among other reasons, cigarette advertising was only "marginal 'speech'," and the ruling would result in additional information being provided to the public. 405 F.2d at 1102–03.

46. For more on the problem of deciding what issues are raised by programming under the fairness doctrine, see Chapter Six.

47. *See* Alan F. Neckritz, 29 F.C.C.2d 807, 812 n.6 (1971), for an FCC pronouncement on such advertising. These explicitly political advertisements have been called "advertorials" by one commentator. Note, *Constitutional Law—Freedom of Expression—Violation of First Amendment for Radio and Television Stations to Deny Completely Broadcasting Time to Editorial Advertisers When Time Is Sold to Commercial Advertisers,* 85 HARV. L. REV. 689, 692 (1972). This Note used the term to refer to antiwar advertisements, which a group of sponsoring businessmen wanted aired. *See also* Business Executives' Move for Vietnam Peace v. FCC, 450 F.2d 642 (D.C. Cir. 1971), *rev'd* Columbia Broadcasting System, Inc. v. Democratic National Comm., 412 U.S. 94 (1973). In *Columbia Broadcasting,* the Supreme Court held, in a seven-to-two decision, that "responsible" groups do not have a constitutional or statutory right to purchase time for the presentation of advertisements supporting their view of a controversial issue of public importance. The Court left open, however, the possibility of the FCC's imposing, on its own initiative, a mandatory advertising access system on licensees.

48. This category of advertising may be contrasted with advertising that directly promotes purchase of a specific product by making the product seem more desirable for one reason or another. Of course, in some cases the line dividing institutional advertising from simple product commercials, *see* text accompanying note 74, *infra,* may be fuzzy.

49. 30 F.C.C.2d 643 (1971).

50. The groups complained about three specific advertisements. In part, these advertisements stated: "I. Here on the North Slope of Alaska it takes 30 days to erect an oil rig, compared with a few days in Texas. Roads scarcely exist. In winter when sea lanes are choked with ice, all equipment must be flown in. The freight bill for the first North Slope wells was nearly a million dollars, with no guarantee of finding oil. Is it worth the risk? We at Jersey think so, both for us and for you. The Alaskan oil strikes are big, but so is America's need for energy. At the rate this country is now using oil, the Alaskan strikes probably represent little more than three years' supply. If America's energy supply is to be assured in this unpredictable world the search for domestic oil must go on and fast.

"II. This is the Canadian Arctic near Alaska . . . Jersey's Canadian affiliate, Imperial Oil, made its first discovery in the Arctic fifty years ago. Experience since then has shown them not only how to look for oil in the far North, but to look for ways to preserve the ecology. . . . By balancing demands of energy with the needs of nature they're making sure that when wells are drilled or pipelines built, the life that comes back each year will have a home to come back to.

"III. The Arctic wilderness is not always frozen . . . Jersey's affiliate, Humble Oil, is exploring and drilling for oil in the Arctic. In constructing roads and living quarters they can't avoid disturbing some of the Tundra and if it isn't replanted it can turn into a permanent sea of mud. . . . Now we believe we know how to restore disturbed Tundra to help create a better balance between the need for oil and needs of nature." *Id.*

51. *Id.* at 644, 645.

52. *Id.* at 644. The Commission agreed with petitioners that the advertisements "appear to" raise the issues of the need for immediate Alaskan oil development, the ecological effects of the developments, and "inherently" raised the pipeline-ecology issue. *Id.* at 646. But in an

opinion issued pursuant to NBC's petition for reconsideration, the Commission unnecessarily narrowed the issues in dispute. While it referred in its first opinion to the timeliness of
the oil development itself, the overall ecological problem thereby created, and the pipeline
controversy, in the second opinion it focused almost entirely on the pipeline controversy.
Although the pipeline issue was obviously central to the discussion of Alaskan oil, other
issues were important, such as how fast the oil should be developed and whether oil drilling
as opposed to oil transportation would damage the environment.

53. Wilderness Society, 31 F.C.C.2d 729, 733 (1971). If the pipeline controversy is
regarded as the topic at issue, the advertisements certainly cannot be called "clearly
editorial" as at least one commentator suggests. *See* Comment, *A Proposed Statutory Right
to Respond to Environmental Advertisements: Access to the Airways After* CBS v. Democratic National Comm., 69 Nw. U.L. REV. 234, 248 (1974). A prerequisite of any editorial
would certainly be mentioning the subject of that editorial.

54. Wilderness Society, 31 F.C.C.2d at 734 (emphasis added).

55. The Commission's unclear attitude toward institutional advertising can also be seen in
a 1969 opinion, Anthony R. Martin-Trigora, 19 F.C.C.2d 620 (1969). Among complainants'
contentions in that case was that certain television stations had aired advertising promoting
the ABC network. It was also alleged that other broadcast advertising, sponsored by the
National Association of Broadcasters (NAB), praised the television industry. With respect to
the former contention, the Commission ruled that the ABC promotional advertisements did
not raise fairness issues. "Were we to rule otherwise, the institutional or promotional
advertisements of many companies would be regarded as stating one side of a controversial
issue." *Id.* at 621. Despite complainants' forceful contention that the NAB advertisements
were obviously advocating one side of the raging pay television controversy, the Commission
ruled that the pay television controversy was not at issue. The Commission noted that there
was no "reference to pay television" in any of the NAB commercials and "praise of
commercial television . . . cannot be regarded as clear criticism of pay television or a claim of
supremacy over pay television for purposes of the fairness doctrine." *Id.* at 622. But in
National Broadcasting as well, there was no "clear criticism" of the environmentalists'
position on the Alaska pipeline. There was only "praise of the oil companies' " efforts to
protect the environment, as there was praise of "free, privately owned and operated television," *id.*, in the NAB commercials. The rationale for finding one side of the pipeline
controversy implicit in the *National Broadcasting* commercials, but not finding one side of
the pay television controversy implicit in the *Martin-Trigona* commercials is entirely unclear.

56. San Francisco Women for Peace, 24 F.C.C.2d 156 (1970); David C. Green, 24
F.C.C.2d 171 (1958); Alan F. Neckritz, 24 F.C.C.2d 175 (1970).

57. Green v. FCC, 447 F.2d 323, 324, 325 nn.1, 2 (D.C. Cir. 1971).

"SPOT NUMBER ONE

"Are you a young man who likes a challenge and who likes to do his best at anything he
does? Well, if you are . . . the United States Army needs you. Life in the Army demands the
very best you have . . . travel . . . good pay . . . and most important . . . the opportunity to
make a really worthwhile contribution to the security of your country. For all the facts . . .
visit your local Army recruiter. Your future . . . your decision . . . choose Army.

"SPOT NUMBER SEVENTEEN

"Ask a Marine officer what it means to be a Marine lieutenant. Ask him what it takes to
lead a Marine platoon. He'll tell you it's about the toughest post-graduate course a college
man ever had. He'll tell you it takes every ounce of leadership you've got, because a fighting
man just doesn't come any finer than a Marine. And if you can lead a platoon of Marines,
you can lead anybody. Anywhere, anytime. Refrain: Ask a Marine."

The full text of the one spot announcement alluding to the draft reads: "This is Frank
Blair speaking to young men facing a military obligation. As a father, I was pleased when my
sons Thomas and John told me they wanted to become Marines. They told me that there was
more than one way to look at an obligation: to consider it something you have to do, or as an
opportunity to grow as an individual. How about you? Are you ready to develop in body,
mind and spirit? Find out the details from your Marine Corps representative today." *Id.*

58. 24 F.C.C.2d at 172.

59. *Id.* at 172, 173.

60. Green v. FCC, 447 F.2d 323 (D.C. Cir. 1971).

61. Media Access Project, 44 F.C.C.2d 755 (1973).

62. The controversy surrounding the Georgia Power Company rates was still raging in 1975, including a $1 million damage suit filed against the company by an Atlanta couple, other consumer groups' legal actions, and intense community debate. Kent, *Soaring Power Bills Upset Georgians,* Los Angeles Times, Feb. 16, 1975, sec. 1, at 1, col. 1.

63. The Commission rejected outright as unreasonable one station's contention that advertisements that were "institutional in nature" could not incur fairness obligations. 44 F.C.C.2d at 758.

64. This test was mentioned before in an institutional advertising case. *See* Anthony R. Martin-Trigona, 19 F.C.C.2d 620 (1969); note 55, *supra.*

65. 44 F.C.C.2d at 761.

66. Excerpts from the texts of the two advertisements follow:

"[A-1] By 1978, our customers will need twice as much electric power. And we must build to supply it.

"Every year, you're increasing your use of electricity. We're busy keeping up with your present needs, and getting ready for the future.

"But it costs money. We'll spend nearly $2 million every working day this year, just for construction.

"Most of that money must be borrowed. And interest rates are steep.

"Environmental protection adds millions of dollars to our costs, too. For instance, one tower to cool and recirculate water is about $4 million.

"All these things affect the price of your electricity. So does inflation. *In today's economy, it just isn't possible to provide electricity at pre-inflation prices.* But your needs keep growing . . . and construction can't wait. We're building . . . to serve *you.*" 44 F.C.C.2d at 765 (app. I) (emphasis added).

"[A-10] . . . [T]o continue providing the power needed by Georgia homes and industries, we must be able to build. Which means borrowing money. Lots of it. An increase in price will help us borrow the money that's needed, and keep power flowing. To *your* home and *your* job. Electricity. What would you do without it?" *Id.*

67. 44 F.C.C.2d at 761-62. The Commission did not rule on these advertisements in light of its ruling on the first two.

68. Alan F. Neckritz, 29 F.C.C.2d 807 (1971), *reconsidered,* 37 F.C.C.2d 528 (1972), *aff'd,* 502 F.2d 411 (D.C. Cir. 1974). For a discussion of the FCC's reconsideration of the case, *see* notes 93–96, *infra,* and accompanying text.

69. 29 F.C.C.2d at 807.

70. The FCC declared, "The merits of any one gasoline, weight reducer, breakfast cereal, or headache remedy—to name but a few examples that come readily to mind—do not rise to the level of a significant public issue." *Id.* at 812. However, the Commission did state: "This is not to say that a product commercial cannot argue a controversial issue raising fairness responsibilities. For example, if an announcement sponsored by a coal-mining company asserted that strip mining had no harmful ecological results, the sponsor would be engaging directly in debate on a controversial issue, and fairness obligations would ensue. Or, if a community were in dispute over closing a factory emitting noxious fumes and an advertisement for a product made in the factory argued that question, fairness would also come into play." *Id.* at 812 n.6. The Commission, however, did clearly hold that the fact that an advertisement is the subject of an FTC complaint does not, by itself, invoke fairness scrutiny, and this position was affirmed by the court. Neckritz v. FCC, 502 F.2d 411, 418 (D.C. Cir. 1974).

71. Alan F. Neckritz, 29 F.C.C.2d at 817. In setting forth an argument to be used later in its 1974 *Fairness Report,* the Commission's opinion also stated: "The Chevron F-310 announcements do not argue a position on a controversial issue of public importance. . . . [M]aking such a claim for a product is not the same thing as arguing a position on a controversial issue of public importance. . . . It would ill suit the purposes of the fairness doctrine,

designed to illuminate significant controversial issues, to apply it to claims of a product's efficacy or social utility." *Id.* at 812.

72. *Id.* at 812, *quoting* Friends of the Earth, 24 F.C.C.2d 743, 749 (1970). One commentator has stated that the Commission was applying a "new standard of directness." Ira Mark Ellman, *And Now a Word Against Our Sponsor: Extending the FCC's Fairness Doctrine to Advertising,* 60 CALIF. L. REV. 1416, 1426 (1972). The concept of "directness" had been implied by the FCC in *Friends of the Earth,* where the Commission stated that "a commercial could deal directly with an issue of public importance," and if it did ". . . the fairness doctrine is fully applicable." 24 F.C.C.2d at 749. In *Neckritz,* however, the F-310 commercials were found not to break the "directness" threshold. 29 F.C.C.2d at 812.

73. As discussed at note 52, *supra,* if the topics at issue were the need for Alaskan oil development and the potential ecological harm caused by such development, these were indeed directly discussed. But the Commission in its second, more definitive, opinion focused on the pipeline controversy.

74. A case involving a commercial that was difficult to categorize confused things even more. United People, 32 F.C.C.2d 124 (1971). At issue were public service announcements and other program material broadcast by a local television station advocating contribution to the local United Appeal. In a sense, the advertisements were promoting a product or service, that is, the use of a particular charity to distribute donations. The advertisements also had an institutional flavor, in promoting the image of United Appeal by discussing the many good things the organization was doing. A group called United People disagreed with the utility of the United Appeal, and claimed that it was controlled by local business leaders and did not allocate money to the community's most important needs. Contending that anti-United Appeal views were not sufficiently aired by the station, United People complained to the FCC and submitted numerous newspaper articles outlining the local charity controversy as well as evidence of coverage on other local radio and TV stations. Surprisingly, the FCC held unreasonable the licensee's judgment that views in favor of United Appeal were not controversial and of public importance. Complainants' victory, however, was somewhat illusory, for the United Appeal campaign they complained about was long over by the time the Commission rendered its decision. The Commission did note that it had some evidence that a similar controversy was arising in connection with the current United Appeal campaign, and that its decision would "assist [the licensee] in determining . . . fairness doctrine obligations. . . ." *Id.* at 127. Here was an advertisement whose text did not appear to raise any controversy and that did not affirmatively argue or track one side of an issue in the community. It was the very use of the service advertised that was controversial and of public importance.

Like the post-*Banzhaf* product commercials, *see* text accompanying notes 77-101, *infra,* the issue was implicit. Unlike the FCC decisions on those commercials, however, the fairness doctrine was held applicable.

75. *See* notes 29-33, *supra,* and accompanying text.

76. *See* notes 37-45, *supra,* and accompanying text.

77. *But see* United People, 32 F.C.C.2d 124 (1971), discussed in note 74, *supra,* which was a quasi-product-service commercial.

78. One commentator, after discussing *Neckritz,* declared, "the Commission is opposed to any extension of the fairness doctrine." Comment, *supra* note 53, at 253. This overstates the Commission's position but is correct with respect to product advertising.

79. One author has proclaimed that, "disastrous results, from the F.C.C.'s point of view, . . . followed the Commission's cigarette ruling." Comment, *The Regulation of Competing First Amendment Rights: A New Fairness Doctrine Balance After CBS?* 122 U. PA. L. REV 1283, 1311 (1974); and another stated that the *Banzhaf* decision has "haunted the Commission." Louis L. Jaffe, *The Editorial Responsibility of the Broadcaster: Reflections on Fairness and Access,* 85 HARV. L. REV. 768, 775 (1972).

80. David C. Green, 24 F.C.C.2d 171 (1970); San Francisco Women for Peace, 24 F.C.C.2d 156 (1970), *aff'd sub nom.* Green v. FCC, 447 F.2d 323 (D.C. Cir. 1971).

81. 24 F.C.C.2d at 162-64.

82. 447 F.2d at 332–33 (D.C. Cir. 1971).

83. 24 F.C.C.2d 743 (1970), *rev'd,* 449 F.2d 1164 (D.C. Cir. 1971).

84. Among the advertisements was one suggesting "moving up to" a larger car, such as one of Ford's with "up to 429 cubic inches," and one encouraging "high-test leaded gasoline for cold weather starting." Friends of the Earth v. FCC, 449 F.2d 1164, 1165 (D.C. Cir. 1971).

85. 24 F.C.C.2d at 749.

86. *Id.* As further examples of general product advertisements the Commission recited " 'Join the Dodge Rebellion,' 'Put a Tiger in your tank,' etc." *Id.* The Commission also indicated that large cars and leaded gasoline could be distinguished from cigarettes because the issues involved in air pollution were "more complex," and that "broadcast educational campaigns" were one of the few means to combat cigarette smoking whereas other means were available to deal with air polluting products. *Id.* at 746–47. However, the government and expert spokesmen were straightforward in pointing out the dangers of automobile-induced air pollution. And there appears to be no reason why Congress could not directly require that only less dangerous brands of cigarettes be sold. The FCC's distinctions are tenuous.

87. Friends of the Earth v. FCC, 449 F.2d. 1164 (D.C. Cir. 1971).

88. *Id.* at 1165, 1166.

89. *Id.* at 1169. On remand, the FCC, as could be expected, read the Court of Appeals decision narrowly. Friends of the Earth, 33 F.C.C.2d 648 (1972). In comments submitted to the Commission after the Court of Appeals decision, Friends of the Earth urged that advertisements for any kind of gasoline or car required rebuttal time. 33 F.C.C.2d at 650. The FCC maintained that Friends was changing its position from its original emphasis on only large engine car and leaded gas commercials. The Commission "read the opinion of the Court of Appeals as holding . . . it is the advertising of large engine cars (and leaded gasolines)" that constituted the controversial issue of public importance. *Id.* at 650–51. It also stated that NBC did not have to meet its fairness obligations by spot announcements but could balance its overall programming in other ways. *Id.* at 651. Ultimately, the case was settled when the station agreed to participate in a New York City campaign to focus public attention on the air pollution problem, and the FCC on motion of the parties terminated the proceedings. Friends of the Earth, 39 F.C.C.2d 564 (1973).

In March 1974 the FCC reaffirmed its narrow reading of *Friends of the Earth.* The Sierra Club and the National Council of Jewish Women complained that two Los Angeles television stations were not living up to their fairness obligations. Sierra Club, 45 F.C.C.2d 833 (1974). They contended that the stations were airing commercials for automobiles and gasolines that, in the context of the Los Angeles automobile pollution problem and the need to reduce local use of gas and private automobiles, raised a controversial issue of public importance. Complainants relied on the *Friends of the Earth* Court of Appeals opinion, 449 F.2d 1164, and the Commission's Interim Memorandum Opinion and Order on Remand, 39 F.C.C.2d 564, in demanding presentation of the other side of this issue. The Commission staff ruled that such reliance was not well founded, since the commercials at issue were not for large engine cars and leaded gasoline, and it dismissed the complaint. 45 F.C.C.2d at 836. The staff also stated that "the product advertisement" does not "per se" raise a fairness issue, and that the National Environmental Policy Act, 42 U.S.C. secs. 4321 *et seq.* (1970), does not alter the scope of the fairness doctrine. *Id.* at 836.

The Commission denied the complainants' Application for Review and affirmed the staff's ruling in Sierra Club, 51 F.C.C.2d 569 (1975). The Commission declared "that we 'will not extend the fairness doctrine to "general product advertisements such as those making claims regarding a product's efficacy or social utility" unless the advertisements directly or by necessary inference address a controversial issue of public importance,' despite the fact that the use of that product might be related to a controversial issue of public importance." *Id.* at 573, *quoting* Peter C. Herbst, 48 F.C.C.2d 614, 615 (1974), *quoting* (in turn) NBC (Wilderness Society Esso), 30 F.C.C.2d 643, 645 (1971). It cited the *Fairness Report* language, discussed in the text accompanying notes 123–31, *infra,* which rejected fairness treatment for "standard advertisements such as those involved in . . . Friends of the Earth." Sierra

Club, 51 F.C.C.2d at 572, *quoting Fairness Report*, 48 F.C.C.2d 1, 26 (1974). Since complainants submitted no material showing that the car and gas advertisements addressed the issue of the need for reduction in Los Angeles private automobile use, they failed to meet their burden of showing that the broadcast material had presented one side of the issue. 51 F.C.C.2d at 573.

90. 436 F.2d 248 (D.C. Cir. 1970).

91. *Id.* at 258.

92. *Id.* at 259. The court held that further FCC examination of the union's complaint was in order and that renewal of the license without a hearing was not supported by the record.

The case is similar to *Banzhaf* in that the text in the commercials did not directly discuss the controversial issue. Rather, the controversial issue of public importance was implicit in the very use of the products being advertised.

93. 37 F.C.C.2d 528 (1972).

94. *Id.* at 531.

95. Although the ads, unlike those in *Friends of the Earth*, did explicitly state that F-310 was "[a] major breakthrough to help solve one of today's critical problems" and would help achieve "cleaner air," Alan F. Neckritz, 29 F.C.C.2d at 807, they also referred to "the problems of controlling our environment . . . and solving a growing national problem." *Id.* at 817.

96. 37 F.C.C.2d at 531-32.

97. In two other cases decided within six months of each other in 1970 and 1971, the Commission was asked to rule on commercials for detergents and trash compactors. In William H. Rodgers, Jr., 30 F.C.C.2d 640 (1971), the complainants asserted that the danger of phosphate-based detergents was even greater than that of cigarettes, since the physical as well as the human environment was severely affected. A mass of government material describing the dangers of such detergents, including reports advocating their absolute ban, was presented. The Commission's letter in response to the complaint made no attempt to distinguish *Banzhaf* and simply stated that complainants had "cited no examples of commercial announcements which deal directly with controversial issues of public impor- tance." *Id.* at 642. The Commission assumed this same ostrichlike posture in John S. MacInnis, Consumers Arise Now, 32 F.C.C.2d 837 (1971), where complainants stated that advertisements for trash compactors were extolling a product that was antithetical to recy- cling, and thereby raised a controversial issue of public importance. They cited language from the National Environmental Policy Act of 1969, 42 U.S.C. secs. 4321 *et seq.* (1970), call- ing for the federal government to use all practical means to obtain maximum recycling of resources. The Commission's staff reply again contained no lengthy analysis. Its simple answer was: "The Commission has consistently refused to apply the fairness doctrine to the broadcast of ordinary product commercials, and the commercials herein do not come within the exception to that policy enunciated in *Banzhaf v. FCC.*" 32 F.C.C.2d at 838.

An FCC staff decision rendered less than three weeks after *MacInnis* reached a different conclusion on a product commercial. Center for Auto Safety, 32 F.C.C.2d 926 (1972). The two-minute advertisement at issue described the buckle start system designed to ensure greater consumer safety. Twelve seconds of the advertisement discussed the alternative air bag system, calling it "costly" and "unreliable." *Id.* at 929. Complainants filed against two networks and two local stations and pointed to several ongoing federal government actions that might critically affect automobile airbag requirements, a statement by over 80 congress- men on the airbag system, other news media coverage, and the manufacturers' print media campaign against air bags. The Commission staff concluded that the subject of air bags was indeed a controversial issue of public importance, and that the 12 second nonneutral refer- ence in the advertisements raised fairness obligations. In the end, however, complainants' tack lost wind, for the staff ruled that the licensees had broadcast enough contrasting viewpoints on the issue in their overall programming to fulfill their fairness mandate. The case can be distinguished from *Banzhaf, Rodgers,* and *MacInnis* in that the wording of the text in *Center's* advertisements explicitly argued one side of a controversial issue being debated in the community. Not only was the use of the product at issue, as in the other cases, but the affirmative discussion of that use was in the commercial itself. The staff ruling, in a typically brief opinion, unfortunately did not make this distinction between textual and use issues.

98. Friends of the Earth v. FCC, 449 F.2d 1164, 1170 (D.C. Cir. 1971); *see also* text accompanying notes 87-89, *supra.*

99. Neckritz v. FCC, 502 F.2d 411 (D.C. Cir. 1974).

100. *Id.* at 418. For a discussion of how *Neckritz* may be viewed as inconsistent with *Banzhaf,* see text accompanying notes 73 and 94-96, *supra.* The District of Columbia Circuit contribution to furthering FCC consistency is thus questionable.

101. See note at the end of this chapter on the Court of Appeals decision reviewing the 1974 *Fairness Report.*

102. *Notice of Inquiry, In the Matter of the Handling of Public Issues Under the Fairness Doctrine and the Public Interest Standards of the Communications Act,* 30 F.C.C.2d 26 (1971). "Access to the Broadcast Media as a Result of Carriage of Product Commercials," was one of the inquiry's major topics. The 1971 announcement of the inquiry mentioned the very broad policy questions being raised by recent fairness complaints related to commercials, and discussed some of the fundamental questions raised by the court in *Retail Store.* It called for comments from interested parties on four specific questions, as well as any other relevant issues having to do with the fairness doctrine and commercial advertising and broadcasting.

The Commission invited interested parties to address the following four questions:

"I. Ought there be some public interest responsibility behond that of fairness to carry material opposing or arguing the substance of product commercials? If so, should time be afforded free or only on a paid basis?

"II. What account should be taken of the court's observation (in *Retail Store*) that spot announcements may not add substantially to public knowledge and, on the other hand, that repetition is a significant factor to be considered?

"III. What should or must be the licensee's area of discretion in this entire matter—and is there some workable standard for distinguishing various categories of commercials, some of which would give rise to fairness or public interest duties and some of which would not?

"IV. Finally, what would be the predictable effect of any new policy adopted here on the carriage of product advertisements and thus on the continued growth and health of the commercial broadcasting system?" *Id.* at 32.

It noted that, "The foregoing by no means exhausts the possible issues that are involved in the area of product commercials." *Id.* at 33. Other topics included "The Fairness Doctrine Generally," *id.* at 27, "Access Generally to the Broadcast Media for the Discussion of Public Issues," *id.* at 33, and "Application of the Fairness Doctrine to Political Broadcasts," *id.*

103. The report was printed in the FEDERAL REGISTER on July 18, 1974. *Fairness Report, supra* note 1. Outside of the broadcast advertising area, the Report does not make any major changes in fairness doctrine policy. Despite increasing criticism of the fairness doctrine, the Commission reaffirms the doctrine's basis and utility, describes how it functions, and for the present rejects mandated public access to the broadcast media. *Id.* The Report does provide additional guidance on how to determine whether an issue is controversial and of public importance. *Id.* at 26376, pars. 29-31; *see* Chapter Six, pp. 154-55. It also suggests a lessening of the broadcast monitoring burden for complainants attempting to establish a prima facie fairness doctrine violation. *Id.* at 26379 pars. 52, 53; *see* Chapter Seven, p. 209.

104. *Id.* at 26380.

105. *Id.* at 26380 par. 61.

106. *Id.* par. 60.

107. *Id.* par. 63.

108. *Id.* par. 62.

109. *Id.* par. 63.

110. *Id.* par. 62.

111. Professor Jaffe, a distinguished fairness doctrine commentator, had urged in a law review article that licensees should be required to give advertisements fairness doctrine balancing whenever the advertiser "by implication . . . intends to speak to a current, publicly-acknowledged controversy." Jaffe, *supra* note 79, at 777-78, quoted in the *Fairness*

Report, supra note 1, at 26380 par. 64. A standard based on advertiser implication and intention offers licensees little if any guidance. A stronger and more obvious connection between the advertisement and the controversy, as discussed in the text accompanying notes 117-18, *infra,* should be necessary to trigger the fairness doctrine.

112. *Fairness Report, supra* note 1, at 26380-81 par. 64.

113. *Id.* pars. 64-65 (emphasis added).

114. *See* Public Media Center, 59 F.C.C.2d 494, 513-14 pars. 34-37 (1976), for an example of commercials that address the issue of nuclear power in a way that the FCC decided fit the new criteria. One ad claimed, "the safety record of commercial nuclear power plants is unmatched in industrial history. There has never been a nuclear caused death . . . not even significant injury." *Id.* at 514 par. 36. This language presented a viewpoint on the safety of nuclear power.

The Commission's definition of "issue" appears to restrict the licensee's fairness obligations to issues of *current* significance. See Chapter Six, pp. 159-60.

115. The survey was supervised by the author and included the prime time programming of three network-affiliated and two independent local stations. It was conducted from Tuesday, February 4, through Saturday, February 9, 1975, in Newport Beach, California, which, for the most part, receives Los Angeles television programming. Each night one station was continuously viewed from 6:30 to 10:30 P.M., and all advertisements were tape recorded and analyzed. The stations were KNXT, Channel 2 (CBS affiliate, viewed 2/4), KABC, Channel 7 (ABC affiliate, viewed 2/5), KNBC, Channel 4 (NBC affiliate, viewed 2/8), KTLA, Channel 5 (independent, viewed 2/6), and KCOP, Channel 13 (independent, viewed 2/7), all located in the Los Angeles area. A total of 456 commercials were broadcast. Of these, 3 commercials or .7 percent were considered institutional advertising that potentially raised a controversial issue of public importance (97.1 percent were product or service commercials, and 2.2 percent were very explicit editorials).

The survey was informal, and there was no extensive research design. An extensive research project in this area would be most welcome. But this informal survey does give some idea of the small amount of institutional advertising with implicit controversial, public issue messages that would be seen by a viewer tuning in to one of the stations surveyed on an average night.

116. "The telephone: it comes in all sizes, colors, and combinations. If you're going to have one installed, find out what's available. There's a lot to choose from, so plan carefully. I'm a telephone service representative. Call me. I'll send you a free planning guide. It will help you get what you want the first time, and we won't have to come back. When we don't have to come back a second time, you save $12." Pacific Telephone Company advertisement heard Jan. 31, 1975, on Channel 13.

117. 39 FED. REG. at 26381, par. 65 (1974).

118. *In the Matter of the Handling of Public Issues Under the Fairness Doctrine and the Public Interest Standards of the Communications Act,* 48 F.C.C.2d 1, 55 (1974) (Commissioner Hooks, concurring and dissenting).

119. David C. Green, 24 F.C.C.2d 171 (1970), *aff'd,* 447 F.2d 323 (D.C. Cir. 1971).

120. *See* text accompanying notes 56-60, *supra.*

121. 30 F.C.C.2d at 30. *See* text accompanying notes 90-92, *supra.*

122. *But see* United People, 32 F.C.C.2d 124 (1971), discussed in note 74, *supra,* which involved a quasi-product-service commercial appealing for charitable contributions.

123. *See* notes 87-89, *supra,* and accompanying text.

124. 39 FED. REG. at 26381 pars. 67-68 (1974) (footnotes omitted).

125. *Id.* at 26381 n.22.

126. The Commission inserted the following to reinforce its point: "Promoting the sale of a product is not ordinarily associated with any of the interests the First Amendment seeks to protect. As a rule, it does not affect the political process, does not contribute to the exchange of ideas, does not provide information on matters of public importance, and is not, except perhaps for the ad-men, a form of individual self-expression. . . . Accordingly, even if . . . [such] commercials are protected speech, we think they are at best a negligible part of any exposition of ideas, and are of . . . slight social value as a step to truth. . . . Banzhaf v. FCC,

405 F.2d 1082, 1101–02 (D.C. Cir. 1968), *quoting* Chaplinsky v. New Hampshire, 315 U.S. 568, 572 (1942)." *Id.* par. 67. It concluded: "it seems to us to make little practical sense to view advertisements such as these as presenting a meaningful discussion of a controversial issue of public importance." *Id.*

127. *Id.* at 26381 par. 68.

128. The Commission thus takes Commissioner Loevinger's position that, in *Banzhaf,* as opposed to encouraging debate, the FCC only imposed its view of what health practices were in the public interest.

129. *Id.* par. 69.

130. *Id.* par. 70.

131. *Id.* at 26380 par. 59. In its *Reconsideration Fairness Report, supra* note 1, at 699 par. 30, the Commission, reacting to charges that it had not used adequate economic data, backtracked and stated, "the economic impact on the broadcasting industry was only one of many factors contributing to our choice of policy."

132. *Id.* at 26382 par. 71.

133. *Id.*

134. *Id.* par. 72. The Commission also stressed the "serious" diversion of "attention and resources of broadcasters from the traditional purposes of the fairness doctrine." *Id.* This, plus the potential adverse economic consequences, led the Commission to conclude that "[w]e are therefore not persuaded that the adoption of these proposals would further 'the larger and more effective use of radio in the public interest. . . .' 47 U.S.C. sec. 303(g), or contribute in any way to the promotion of genuine debate on public issues."

135. Two months after the Report's standard product declaration, the Commission reaffirmed the demise of *Banzhaf* in rejecting the demands of several complainants that a Maine television station afford fairness balancing time to counter snowmobile advertising. Peter C. Herbst, 48 F.C.C.2d 614 (1974), *reconsideration denied,* 49 F.C.C.2d 411 (1974). A group claimed that snowmobiles were harmful because of their effect on wildlife and vegetation, their trespassing on private land, noise generation, and possible injury from their operation. Peter C. Herbst, 40 F.C.C.2d 115 (1973). Because of the ongoing debate in Maine over their use, print media coverage of the issue, and state legislative hearings on snowmobiles, complainants claimed that a controversial issue of public importance was raised by the snowmobile advertisements and that fairness balancing was required. The Broadcast Bureau staff ruled that since the advertisements "do not deal explicitly with one side of the controversial issue . . . the issue is squarely the application of the fairness doctrine to ordinary product commercials . . . we decline to apply the fairness doctrine to those ordinary product commercials." *Id.* at 117, 118. The Commission later rejected the staff's finding that the complainants' television monitoring had not been extensive enough to establish a prima facie fairness case, but it upheld the staff's key ruling on product advertising. Citing and quoting from its recent *Fairness Report,* the Commission concluded: "While hazardous operation, adverse environmental effects, and interference with private property rights by snowmobilers may constitute controversial issues of public importance in the complainants' area, it cannot be said that the announcements in question 'are devoted in an obvious and meaningful way to the discussion of those issues.' " 48 F.C.C.2d at 615, 616. On appeal the First Circuit Court of Appeals affirmed the Commission's decision. Public Interest Research Group v. FCC, 522 F.2d 1060 (1st Cir. 1975). The court said the decision was neither arbitrary nor capricious, *id.* at 1066, and was constitutional. It also declared, "Given the necessity of product advertising in American broadcasting, and the administrative difficulties and costs of determining when a product is so controversial as to trigger fairness obligations, we cannot . . . say that the Commission acted contrary to statute when it struck the current balance between product advertising and the fairness doctrine." *Id.* at 1067. *See also In re* Sierra Club, 51 F.C.C.2d 569 (1975), discussed *supra,* note 89, where the Commission quoted at length from the *Fairness Report* in a decision rejecting application of the doctrine to automobile and gasoline advertisements.

136. 449 F.2d 1164 (D.C. Cir. 1971).

137. *Id.* at 1170. *See also* Neckritz v. FCC, 502 F.2d 411 (D.C. Cir. 1974), discussed in notes 100–01, *supra,* and accompanying text.

138. Further support for this prediction may be found in the Supreme Court's reversal of the District of Columbia Circuit's access decision, Business Executives Move for Vietnam Peace v. FCC, 450 F.2d 642 (D.C. Cir. 1971), *rev'd*, Columbia Broadcasting Sys., Inc. v. Democratic Nat'l Comm., 412 U.S. 94 (1973). *See* note 47, *supra. See* note at the end of this chapter on the Court of Appeals decision reviewing the 1974 *Fairness Report.*

139. United States v. Paramount Pictures, Inc., 334 U.S. 131 (1948).

140. The National Association of Broadcasters sets a maximum allowable prime time limit for commercials at 9½ minutes per hour for network affiliated stations and 12 minutes per hour for independent stations. (Prime time is described as a 3½-hour continuous period designated by the station between 6:00 P.M. and midnight.) The limit for both types of stations during non-prime time is 16 minutes per hour. NATIONAL ASS'N OF BROADCASTERS, TIME STANDARDS FOR NON-PROGRAM MATERIAL, in 14 TELEVISION CODE 14, 15 (17th ed. 1974). Many stations do broadcast below this maximum. KNBC in Los Angeles, for instance, airs an average of 7 to 8½ minutes of commercials during prime time. Interview with William Emerson, manager, Broadcast Standards, KNBC, by Steven J. Simmons, May 6, 1975.

141. *See* text accompanying notes 159–61, *infra.*

142. 96 S. Ct. 1817 (1976).

143. 421 U.S. 809 (1975).

144. 316 U.S. 52 (1942).

145. 96 S. Ct. at 1819.

146. 421 U.S. at 812.

147. *Cf.* Susan T. Edlavitch, Note, *The Fairness Doctrine and Access to Reply to Product Commercials,* 51 IND. L.J. 756 (1976).

148. "Nor need we comment here on the first amendment ramifications of legislative prohibitions of certain kinds of advertising in the electronic media, where the 'unique characteristics' of this form of communication make it especially subject to regulation in the public interest." 421 U.S. at 825 n.10. "Finally, the special problems of the electronic broadcast media are likewise not in this case." 96 S. Ct. at 1831.

149. It should be noted that the Court did say that "some forms of commercial speech regulation are surely permissible" even in the nonbroadcast context. 96 S. Ct. at 1830. *See also* 421 U.S. at 828. It pointed to "time, place, and manner restrictions" as well as regulation of "deceptive or misleading" advertising. 96 S. Ct. at 183.

An argument can be made that it is perfectly reasonable for the FCC to conclude that a standard product ad that simply pushes the desirability of a product does not amount to "discussion" of differing "views" on important public issues under the statutory mandate, 47 U.S.C. sec. 315(a) (1970). Because such an ad does not amount to discussion, it does not necessarily mean that commercial speech is being given wholly unequal treatment with political affairs intercourse. Like entertainment or sports programming, see Chapter Six, pp. 151–54, the content of such programming does not amount to "discussion" under the statute. Indeed, as mentioned above, if there is such explicit discussion even in the confines of a commercial, the FCC has ruled that the fairness doctrine does apply.

150. In *Bigelow,* Justice Blackmun, speaking for the Court, stated "a court may not escape the task of assessing the first amendment interest at stake and weighing it against the public interest allegedly served by the regulation." 421 U.S. at 826. *See also* Pittsburgh Press Co. v. Pittsburgh Comm'n on Human Relations, 413 U.S. 376, 389 (1973).

151. 96 S. Ct. at 1828–29.

152. In *Bigelow,* the state's asserted interest in preventing women from seeking abortion services from parties interested only in financial gain was really "an interest in regulating what Virginians may hear or read about New York" abortion services. 421 U.S. at 827. This state interest was entitled to little weight in comparison with the First Amendment interest of the newspaper editor to publish what he wants and the interests of the public in receiving the information about abortion treatment.

153. As discussed *supra,* note 152, in *Bigelow,* when a newspaper editor's rights were involved, the government ruled unconstitutional the state's interference with those rights. A broadcaster could maintain that, just as Bigelow's right to publish an advertisement was

protected, so its First Amendment rights in airing product-service commercials of its choosing should not be interfered with by the government's fairness doctrine. In fact, in *Bigelow* the Court declared, "We know from experience that 'liberty of the press is in peril as soon as the Government tries to compel what is to go into a newspaper.' " 421 U.S. at 829.

154. A person who wants to criticize the product can buy an ad in any newspaper or magazine, can seek news coverage in any print or broadcast outlet, can try to interest any print or broadcast editor in the merits of a story, or can distribute his or her own publicity. Indeed, a broadcaster may directly air the views of the person in a countercommercial or editorial reply context. The general public may also receive views about the product from just as diverse sources.

155. "A pharmacist licensed in Virginia is guilty of unprofessional conduct if he (3) publishes, advertises, or promotes, directly or indirectly, in any manner whatsoever, any amount, price, fee, premium, discount, rebate, or credit terms for any drugs which may be dispersed only by prescription" 96 S. Ct. at 1819, quoting from Va. Code Ann. sec. 54-524.35 (1974).

156. Under Va. Code Ann. sec. 18.1-63 (1960), "If any person, by publication, lecture, advertisement, or by the sale or circulation of any publication, or in any other manner, encourage or prompt the procuring of abortion or miscarriage, he shall be guilty of a misdemeanor."

157. The programming most likely to be severely affected by economic setbacks would be the less profitable public affairs type. *See.* R. Noll, M. Peck & J. McGowan, Economic Aspects of Television Regulation 12, 69 (1973), for a description of the unprofitable nature of public affairs documentaries. This is precisely the kind of programming most in need of expansion to inform the public on a variety of controversial issues of public importance. In fact, the objective of part one of the fairness doctrine is to promote such programming. Application of the fairness doctrine to product commercials would thus be "cutting the doctrine's nose to spite its face."

158. *See, e.g.,* the dire predictions of former Commissioner Loevinger in *The Politics of Advertising,* 15 Wm. & Mary L. Rev. 1, 8-10 (1973), and Commissioner Hooks, concurring and dissenting, in *Fairness Report, supra* note 1, 48 F.C.C.2d at 52 (1974), in comparison with the more optimistic forecasts of Ira Mark Ellman, *And Now a Word Against Our Sponsor: Extending the F.C.C.'s Fairness Doctrine to Advertising,* 60 Calif. L. Rev. 1416, 1446-49 (1972), and Tom A. Collins, *Counter Advertising in the Broadcast Media: Bringing the Administrative Process to Bear on a Theoretical Imperative,* 15 Wm. & Mary L. Rev. 799 (1974).

159. Henry Geller, The Fairness Doctrine in Broadcasting: Problems and Suggested Courses of Actoin (Rand R-1412 FF, Dec. 1973) (prepared under a Ford Foundation grant).

160. *Id.* at 85. The study concludes, "There is thus no way to limit the cigarette advertising rule to few products or to some commercials." *Id.* Referring to the *Banzhaf* case, Professor Jaffe has stated: "Its logic can be expanded to justify so many demands for free time as to threaten broadcasting's advertising base. It can be argued that almost all advertising places a product in its most favorable light and does not communicate its significant and controversial countervailing costs. Automobiles pollute the air and overcrowd the cities. Drugs may induce too much reliance on drugs. Cereals may not be as nourishing as some think they should be, quite apart from whether false claims are made." Jaffe, *supra* note 79, at 775.

161. Cullman Broadcasting Co., 40 F.C.C. 576 (1963).

162. Heading III: "Access to the Broadcast Media as a Result of Carriage of the Product Commercials," Notice of Inquiry, *supra* note 102, at 20.

163. Brief for CBS at 13, 14.

164. *Id.* at 14-15.

165. Former Commissioner Loevinger, however, who has made accurate predictions before in this area, puts faith in them. *See* Loevinger, *supra* note 158.

166. *But see Formulation of Appropriate Further Regulatory Policies Concerning Cigarette Advertising and Antismoking Presentation,* 27 F.C.C.2d 453 (1970), *aff'd sub nom.*

Larus & Bros. Co. v. FCC, 477 F.2d 876 (4th Cir. 1971), in which the Commission, even though it had originally ruled pro-smoking commercials did require countercommercials, ruled that the anti-smoking commercials in question in the case did not require countercommercials.

167. The figures do indicate a drop of over $15 million in annual television cigarette advertising revenue from 1967, when *Banzhaf* was decided, to the 1968-70 period before cigarette ads were banned. But there was still heavy cigarette television advertising support of around $200 million. Figures from chart supplied by Television Bureau of Advertising and reprinted in Ellman, *supra* note 72, at 1446 n.172.

168. *See id.* at 1446-49.

169. Loevinger, *supra* note 158, at 9.

170. *Id.* at 10.

171. H. GELLER, *supra* note 159, at 40-41. The case involved an editorial in favor of Expo 74 and a supporting bond issue. *Id.* at 40.

172. Letter to Roger J. Wallenberg from Jay Wright, Office of the Vice-President, Engineering, King Broadcasting Co., *reprinted in* H. GELLER, *supra* note 159, app. E, at 134.

173. *Id.*

174. H. GELLER, *supra* note 159, at 41.

175. *Id.*

176. C. Delos Putz, Jr., *Fairness and Commercial Advertising: A Review and a Proposal,* 6 U. SAN FRANCISCO L. REV. 215, 250 (1972). Putz suggests FCC regulations requiring that licensees make available a certain percentage of the licensee's total paid commercial advertising time for free countercommercial type advertising as a substitute for standard fairness doctrine requirements in this area. *See also Fairness Report, supra* note 1, at 26381 par 67.

177. See Chapter Two, note 26.

178. Especially *see* the discussion at pp. 197-200 of Public Media Center, 59 F.C.C.2d 494 (1970), which involved the airing of power company "advertorials" by California licensees.

179. The 1974 *Fairness Report* should have discussed whether product commercials that explicitly discuss the controversy surrounding a product's use and the charges made against it require fairness balancing. Suppose a detergent advertisement not only urges use of a detergent and makes claims for the nonpolluting nature of a particular ingredient but also actually discusses and disputes environmental groups' charges that the particular product pollutes. Does this demand airing of the contrasting viewpoint? There would seem to be a point at which a product advertisement goes beyond the simple "F-310" type of claim and actually engages in debate on the controversy surrounding its use. Under the present fairness doctrine rationale this should require fairness balancing. The *Fairness Report*, however, provides licensees with no additional guidance.

180. Note, *The Fairness Doctrine and Entertainment Programming: All in the Family,* 7 GA. L. REV. 554, 561, 562 (1973). The author states: "In general, any position which might reasonably be inferred from an entertainment program, whether through outright statement or through innuendo, would trigger the application of the doctrine." *Id.* at 562.

181. See Chapter Seven, pp. 151-54.

182. *Id.*

183. Miami Herald Publishing Co. v. Tornillo, 418 U.S. 241 (1974).

184. Red Lion Broadcasting Co. v. FCC, 395 U.S. 367 (1969).

185. 15 U.S.C. sec. 52(a) (1970). Under this section it is unlawful to disseminate, or cause to be disseminated, false advertising inducing a purchase of food, drugs, devices, or cosmetics.

186. 15 U.S.C. sec. 45(a) (1) (1970).

187. 15 U.S.C. sec. 45(b) (1970). A violation of such an order can be remedied with a fine up to $5,000. *Id.* sec. 45(l). The order does not become final until complete court review, *id.* sec. 45(g), and this may take years.

188. 15 U.S.C. sec. 53(a) (1970). The Federal Trade Commission may also require the affirmative disclosure of a negative fact about a product in order to better inform the consumer. J.B. Williams Co. v. FTC, 381, F.2d 884 (6th Cir. 1967).

189. 15 U.S.C. sec. 54(a) (1970). Under the section, violation of 15 U.S.C. sec. 52(a) (1970), *supra* note 185, constitutes a misdemeanor punishable by a maximum penalty of $5,000 and six months' imprisonment if the violation occurred with intent to defraud or mislead, or if the commodity advertised may be injurious to health. A second conviction under the section may result in a maximum fine of $10,000 and one year's imprisonment.

190. In the *Carter Pills* case, for example, 13 years elapsed between the first FTC cease and desist order and final removal of the deceptive commercials from the air. *Adoption of Standards Designed to Eliminate Deceptive Advertising From Television,* 32 F.C.C.2d 360, 363 (1971) [hereinafter cited as *Adoption of Standards*]. The FTC's policy has been called one of "delay, ineffective sanctions, and the inability to reach those most responsible," by one group of researching law students. *Id.* at 363. One commentator asserts that "[o]ver the years . . . the F.T.C. has gained notoriety for its lack of effectiveness in enforcing the provisions of the [Federal Trade Commission] Act," Note, *Advertising, Product Safety, and a Private Right of Action Under the Federal Trade Commission Act,* 2 HOFSTRA L. REV. 669, 672 (1974). *See* E. COX, R. FELLMETH & J. SCHULZ, THE NADER REPORT ON THE FEDERAL TRADE COMMISSION (1969), for more on the Commission's past inadequacies.

191. Wasem's, Inc., 3 TRADE REG. REP. par. 20,536, at 20468 (FTC Feb. 22, 1974); Amstas Corp., 3 TRADE REG. REP. par. 20.356, at 20240 (FTC Oct. 2, 1973); Ocean Spray Cranberries, Inc., 80 F.T.C. 975 (1972); ITT Continental Baking Co., 79 F.T.C. 248 (1971).

192. *See* 36 FED. REG. 12058 (1971). Numerous companies have been ordered to produce substantiating documentation under the program. *See also Developments in Program,* 2 TRADE REG. REP. sec. 90, par. 7573, at 12181-83 (1974). "Although the program has not been an unqualified success, it has forced major ad agencies to introduce new review procedures to assure that they will not be embarrassed or prosecuted for making unsupported claims." Note, *The F.T.C. Ad Substantiation Program,* 61 GEO. L.J. 1427 (1973).

193. 36 FED. REG. 12058 (1971).

194. *Id.*

195. The FTC encourages the public's help in notifying it of advertisements that should require substantiation, and hopes that "the Commission can be alerted by consumers, businessmen and public interest groups to possible violations of Section 5 of the Federal Trade Commission Act." 36 FED. REG. 12058 (1971). One method of increasing consumer input would be a private right of action directly against the manufacturer for deceptive advertising under federal legislation. The specific procedures for such a lawsuit could be outlined in an amendment to the Federal Trade Commission Act, 15 U.S.C. secs. 41 *et seq.* (1970). *See* Note, *supra* note 192, at 1447-52. It also has been suggested that the courts can imply such a right of action directly from the existing Federal Trade Commission Act. *See* Note, *supra* note 190; Note, *Private Judicial Remedies for False and Misleading Advertising,* 25 SYRACUSE L. REV. 74.7 (1974).

196. And if a product is considered too dangerous, Congress should forbid broadcast advertising entirely, as was done with cigarettes, or the appropriate agency or Congress should ban its use altogether, as was done with thalidomide.

197. In fact, the FTC did finally act. Finding "that the F-310 advertisements . . . were false, misleading and deceptive in violation of Section 5 of the Federal Trade Commission Act," it issued a cease and desist order. Standard Oil of California, 3 TRADE REG. REP. par. 20,789, 20,646 at 20658 (Nov. 26, 1974). The Commission stated: "The challenged F-310 advertisements are examples of the type of advertising which focuses on serious anxieties of consumers resulting from heated public discussion of issues such as environmental protection; individual and public health; job, home and auto safety; economic woes such as shortages and inflations, etc. . . . In our opinion, it is incumbent upon advertisers who seek to advance their own interests in even partial reliance on such serious consumer concerns to exercise an extra measure of caution in order to be certain that their representations to consumers will not deceive or mislead." *Id.* at 20656. However, the Commission did not think the state of the record justified corrective advertising. *Id.* at 20658. An extension of the FTC's injunctive powers in the food and drug area to other product advertising, including commercials thought to be unsubstantiated, would allow advertisements like those for F-310 to be removed from the airwaves more quickly. *See* Glen E. Weston, *Deceptive Advertising*

and the Federal Trade Commission: Decline of Caveat Emptor, 24 FED. B.J. 548, 561 n.111 (1964).

198. *Adoption of Standards, supra* note 190, at 1551.

199. *Id.*

200. *See* Note, *supra* note 192, for a good discussion of FTC activity in this area and suggestions for improvement.

201. According to CONSUMER REPORTS, published by Consumer's Union of United States, Inc., "As part of CU's goal of bringing education and counsel about consumer goods and services to the widest possible audience, our Broadcast/Film division is producing a series of short news features for television. Most of the features are based on material researched by the CONSUMER REPORTS technical and editorial staff." CONSUMER REPORTS, July 1974, at 50. As of June 19, 1974, "Consumer Reports of the Air" had been purchased for broadcast twice weekly on the evening news in at least 30 major cities. *Id.*

202. *See* Chapter Seven, pp. 225–27.

203. *See* Richard Kurnit, *Enforcing the Obligation to Present Controversial Issues: The Forgotten Half of the Fairness Doctrine,* 10 HARV. CIV. LIB-CIV. RIGHTS L. REV. 137, 158–70 (1975), for an excellent discussion of the ways individual citizens and public interest groups can use FCC regulations to affect licensee programming, especially *Formulation of Rules and Policies Relating to the Renewal of Broadcast Licenses, Final Report and Order,* 43 F.C.C.2d 1 (1973); *Broadcast Procedure Manual,* 37 F.C.C.2d 286 (1972), *Primer on Ascertainment of Community Problems by Broadcast Applicants,* 27 F.C.C.2d 650 (1971); and *Availability of Locally Maintained Records for Inspection by Members of the Public,* 28 F.C.C.2d 71 (1971).

Editorial Note: After this book was in the hands of the printer, the D.C. Court of Appeals handed down its decision reviewing the 1974 *Fairness Report* and the FCC's decision therein to exempt standard product commercials from fairness doctrine treatment, *National Citizens Committee for Broadcasting, et al. v. FCC,* 46 U.S.L.W. 2264–65 (11/11/77, McGowan, Wright, Tamm, JJ.). The court found the FCC policy change constitutional and consistent with the recent Supreme Court cases affording commercial speech more protection. The court also found the FCC decision to be consistent with the Communications Act and supported by reasoned decision making and substantial evidence. In the second part of its decision the court remanded for additional FCC review of petitioner's proposals for an optional public access scheme and an annual listing of the ten controversial, public issues most aired by a licensee along with response offers and representative programming for each issue (as well as other possible proposals for achieving fairness compliance). Commission rejection of a proposal for fairness doctrine review only at license renewal time was upheld.

6
The Problem of "Issue"
in the Administration of the
Fairness Doctrine

Almost all of the administrative and judicial activity involving the fairness doctrine has concerned the second part of the doctrine, requiring a licensee who has aired views on one side of an issue to air contrasting views. Resolution of fairness complaints has focused on the problem of "issue," and two key questions: What issues have been raised in a broadcast? Are these issues controversial and of public importance? Complainants, licensees, the FCC, and the courts have wrestled with the problem of interpreting programs to isolate and define the issues raised. Once it is determined that a particular issue has been raised in a broadcast, and that it is a controversial issue of public importance, the fairness doctrine's balancing requirement applies.[1]

Only a handful of FCC rulings have dealt with the first part of the doctrine, requiring a broadcast licensee to devote a reasonable percentage of its programming to the coverage of controversial issues of public importance. The problem of issue is also critical to the resolution of part one complaints, since the complainant attempts to define the issue ignored by the licensee and describe its importance and controversiality in the community. If a complainant can demonstrate both that a particular issue is critically important and controversial and that the licensee has failed to cover it, the licensee has violated its obligation under part one of the fairness doctrine.

This chapter first examines the difficult threshold question faced in the typical part two fairness cases: what issue is raised in a broadcast? Then it explores the FCC's inquiry into whether an issue is controversial and of public importance. Case law, the 1974 *Fairness Report*,[2] and the Commissioners' own comments are critically analyzed to understand how the FCC determines whether a licensee has been reasonable in its decision on an issue's controversiality and importance. Next, *Accuracy in Media, Inc.* (the *Pensions* case),[3] is discussed at length to illustrate the problems experienced by the FCC and the courts in administration of the fairness doctrine.

The following section discusses the problem of issue in part one fairness cases. The alternative standard developed by the FCC in part one cases is examined, as are the problems and dangers inherent in enforcing the part one obligation.[4] Finally, the issue problems hampering the administration of the fairness doctrine are reviewed, and several recommendations for policy changes are offered.

I. WHAT ISSUE IS RAISED?

Determining what issues have been raised in a contested broadcast is "one of the most difficult problems . . . in the administration of the fairness doctrine. . . ."[5] Controversial public issues may be raised in programming ranging from newscasts and documentaries to commercials and entertainment shows. The ultimate issue being addressed will not always be clearly labelled or explicitly discussed. There may be several perfectly reasonable opinions about which issue requires a response. In addition, the parameters of the issue may not be readily apparent. Most major issues involve a multiplicity of subissues, and the decision about which subissues require a response is not always easy.

The FCC precedent in this complex area can best be viewed as focusing on the reasonableness of a licensee's treatment of "explicit" and "implicit" issues. Where controversial issues of public importance have been explicitly discussed in programming, cases have centered on whether the subissues addressed or the brief references made to other issues require separate treatment under the fairness doctrine. Implicit controversial issues of public importance—issues not clearly discussed yet implied by a broadcast—have generated precedent focusing on commercial advertising, entertainment shows, and broadcasts that track arguments made in the community.

A. EXPLICIT ISSUES: SUBISSUES AND PASSING REFERENCES

The case most frequently cited by the FCC as precedent in determining whether a broadcast raises a subissue worthy of fairness doctrine application is *National Broadcasting Company.*[6] In that case, the Aircraft Owners and Pilots Association (AOPA) complained that a three-part presentation on the nightly Huntley-Brinkley news show, entitled "Air Traffic Congestion and Air Safety," had raised the subissue of whether private pilots are a major safety hazard. The Broadcast Bureau of the FCC, after reviewing the three shows, agreed that the issue of private pilots' contributions to midair collisions and near misses had been explicitly raised in the first night's presentation. The Bureau pointed to the fact that the show had actually "focused" on one private pilot with little flying time, who related his experiences flying over Kennedy Airport without a radio and over Shea Stadium during the World Series. The NBC commentator had added that the pilot was " 'a potential danger to passenger jets and himself when and if he flies in the congested airspace around airports.' "[7] In comparison, a commercial pilot was presented, described as a family man with 25 years' experience and 14,000 hours' flying time. The staff concluded that the "clear import of the presentation was that both pilots were typical examples of their class: the private pilot was depicted as inexperienced and ill-trained, with a somewhat carefree attitude . . . the commercial pilot was depicted as responsible."[8] NBC, according to the Bureau, would have to program pro-private-pilot views on the issue to counter the anti-private-pilot statements made in the Huntley-Brinkley shows.

The full Commission reversed the Bureau, finding the *"thrust of the program* is the congestion over large airports."[9] The Commission declared: "If every statement, or inference from statements or presentations, could be made the subject of a separate and distinct fairness requirement, the doctrine would be unworkable."[10] The Commission added the caveat that a licensee "could not cover an issue, making two important points in his discussion of that issue; afford time for the contrasting viewpoint on one of these two points; and on the other point, reject fairness requests on the ground that it is a 'subissue.' "[11]

In *David I. Caplan,*[12] the Commission continued its refusal to recognize the raising of subissues. It held reasonable a licensee's judgment that an editorial stating that Governor George Wallace was shot by a "cheap, Saturday Night Special" did not raise a separate issue as to which type of gun should be banned under proposed legislation. Rather, the type of gun question was "part and parcel to the real issue of gun control."[13]

More troublesome is the Commission's judgment that the program "Hunger: A National Disgrace" could reasonably be said not to raise the issue posed by its very title—whether hunger in the United States is indeed a national disgrace.[14] The Commission, stating that it was looking at the thrust of the program, offered no rationale for its decision, and seemed to be deliberately ignoring an obvious point.[15] In *Bernard T. Callan*,[16] the Commission ruled that, even though the majority of total time over a series of eight broadcasts had been devoted to discussion of a famous New York adoption case, it was reasonable to assume that the broadcasts in their entirety had not raised the issue of the adoption case for fairness doctrine purposes.[17] The "thrust" doctrine of *National Broadcasting* apparently had little relevance in *Callan*, at least if time devoted to a topic has anything to do with "thrusting" toward that topic.

It is difficult to reconcile these holdings with *Accuracy in Media, Inc.*[18] Accuracy in Media, Inc. complained that a program entitled "Justice," aired over the Public Broadcasting Service (PBS), had raised the trials of Angela Davis and of the Soledad Brothers as an issue and had provided unfair coverage of those trials. PBS responded that the only issue raised by "Justice" was the functioning of the American "law enforcement system, including courts and prisons,"[19] an issue on which its overall programming was balanced. The Commission, after reviewing the program, rejected the contentions of both sides. Instead, it concluded sua sponte that the program had raised two subissues: (1) whether blacks can receive justice in American courts, prisons, or postprison life; and (2) what the penal institutions and the correctional system are doing to rehabilitate those whom society has judged to be wrong.[20] The Commission offered neither a rationale nor a supportive program text to justify this conclusion.[21]

These cases illustrate the difficulty of determining whether subissues are raised by broadcasts. The Commission has talked of the "thrust" of a program to ascertain whether the subissue is really subordinate to the main theme of a particular program. It has asked whether an asserted subissue is just "part and parcel" of the broader issue covered by a broadcast. These terms are vague, offering little guidance. Not surprisingly, the precedent is inconsistent and lacks a clear rationale. This inconsistency does not suggest that the Commission was wrong in any of its individual decisions.

Rather, the lack of clear guidelines only underscores the inability of both the licensee and a potential complainant to predict the Commission's attitude toward the subissues allegedly raised in a broadcast.

Although the FCC has failed to develop a reasoned line of precedent when dealing with major subissues, it has been more consistent in its treatment of passing references to issues made in programs. For its "passing reference" policy, the FCC usually cites the language of *National Broadcasting*: "[E]very statement, or inference from statements or presentations," cannot require fairness balance, for this "would involve this agency much too deeply in broadcast journalism."[22] The "statements" at issue in *National Broadcasting* were certainly not passing; they involved a substantial part of one show's programming.

In attempting to follow *National Broadcasting*, however, the Commission has effectively removed passing references from fairness doctrine treatment. In *Gary Lane*,[23] it was held to be reasonable for NBC to conclude that David Brinkley's brief remarks about the Subversive Activities Control Board during a commentary on the retirement of Mr. Otepka, a member of the Board, did not raise the Control Board issue under the fairness doctrine. Similarly, in *Clinton R. Miller*,[24] three sentences discussing fluoridation during a 60-sentence discussion of dental care did not raise the flouridation issue. A passing reference to school prayers in a Red Skelton record did not raise the issue of school prayers in *Martin-Trigona*.[25] As the Commission stated in its 1974 *Fairness Report*, "a fairness response is not required as a result of offhand or insubstantial statements."[26]

In essence, the passing reference policy is a part of the subissue doctrine. Passing references are subissues that do not cross the threshold of becoming an important point requiring fairness balancing. They are merely "junior subissues," not worthy of treatment. Although a passing reference may address a distinct and controversial issue of public importance, the Commission has chosen to ignore the content of brief references in favor of a quantitative measurement. The Commission has focused on the broadcast time or script space devoted to the reference in terms of the relevant program. This analysis has been applied consistently, resulting in a predictable line of precedent.

B. IMPLICIT ISSUES: ARGUMENTS, ADVERTISING, AND ENTERTAINMENT

Ultimate issues or subissues need not be explicitly discussed in a broadcast to be subject to the fairness doctrine. Rather, they might be depicted in a fictional setting, or be present only by process of viewer association.[27] In its 1974 *Fairness Report,* the FCC set forth guidelines for dealing with a broadcast that avoids explicitly mentioning the ultimate issue in controversy, yet clearly makes arguments supporting one side or the other. According to the Commission, the licensee should:

> exercise his good faith judgment as to whether [a broadcast] had in an obvious and meaningful fashion presented a position on the ultimate controversial issue . . . whether [a] statement in the context of the ongoing community debate is so obviously and substantially related to the [ultimate] issue as to amount to advocacy of a position on that question.[28]

When substantial arguments have clearly been made in a program, and these arguments are obviously linked to a position on one side of an ultimate issue being debated in the community, the Commission has consistently found the ultimate issue to be raised. For example, in *Thomas M. Slaten,*[29] an editorial that was critical of judges raised the issue of the quality of local judges; and in *John Birch Society,*[30] a specific description of abuses by and criticism of the John Birch Society raised the issue of the radical right. These programs "obviously and substantially" related to an ultimate issue being debated in the community.[31]

The difficulty of determining the implicit issues raised by a broadcast are acutely seen in the advertising area. As discussed in Chapter Five,[32] in most standard product commercials and institutional advertisements[33] there is no explicit discussion of a controversial issue of public importance. Even where there is some commentary that arguably presents views being expressed in the community regarding an issue, it is extremely difficult to determine whether the commentary is "obviously and substantially" related to that issue. As analyzed in previous pages,[34] in the 1974 *Fairness Report* the Commission rejected its past policy of finding implicit issues raised in certain standard product commercials.[35] The administrative difficulties of applying the doctrine to ordinary product and service ads and a host of other reasons make this Commission decision a wise one.[36]

Entertainment programming[37] may also present controversial issues of public importance. The programming may depict an incident or story that relates to a recognized issue; or it may contain dialogue that actually discusses the issue. Suppose, for example, there is an ongoing community debate over the safety of nuclear reactors, and the potential for terrorist attacks on such reactors is a principal point made by those favoring expenditures to make reactors more secure. In the middle of this debate, a TV movie portrays a fictional terrorist attack on a nuclear reactor. In realistic fashion the drama depicts terrorists taking over a reactor and holding a city hostage. Has the show, a pure adventure drama containing no explicit discussion of any issues, raised the issue of nuclear reactor safety for the purposes of the fairness doctrine? Suppose further that several minutes of the film are devoted to a town meeting prior to the terrorist takeover at which community leaders adamantly present a series of arguments for increasing expenditures to protect the reactor. Does this explicit discussion of the nuclear safety issue within the confines of an entertainment show raise the issue under the fairness doctrine?

The Commission, perhaps realizing the drastic implications of a contrary path, has avoided ruling that a fictional, satirical, comical, or other entertainment presentation raises a controversial issue of public importance. The FCC has declared that, if entertainment programming merely depicts an issue, as in the first version of the terrorist attack TV movie, it does not raise that implicit issue under the fairness doctrine. Although it has proclaimed that entertainment programming can raise an issue subject to fairness doctrine application if, as in the second version of the movie, the program explicitly discusses that issue, the Commission has always found licensees to have been reasonable in concluding that fairness doctrine issues were not raised by entertainment programming.

In a 1975 case, the National Organization for Women (NOW) challenged the renewal of a TV license based in part on the licensee's alleged portrayal of women in stereotyped female roles, including being dependent on men and valued only as a sex object.[38] NOW asserted that the TV station had thereby raised the important and controversial issue of the role of women in society, and had failed to present diverse views on the issue. The FCC rejected the licensee's rejoinder that entertainment programming could never raise a fairness issue. But it did side with the licensee against NOW because "fairness doctrine obligations are rooted not in the mere depiction of any role by a women [*sic*], but rather in the discussion—the dialogue—that occurs. . . . [The] programming NOW identifies contained no true *discussion* of the role of women in society."[39]

An Alabama complainant received the same treatment when he declared that ABC, in presenting the movie, "The Gun," an episode of "That's My Mama," and an episode of "Streets of San Francisco," had raised the issue of gun control.[40] The programming had shown the tragic events that followed purchase of a gun, and the complainant thought that this demonstrated one side of the gun control issue, which needed fairness balancing. The Commission disagreed, stating that many TV police dramas portray crime involving handguns. The complainant had simply not shown that the programs in question had "addressed the issue of 'handgun control' in such an 'obvious and meaningful fashion.' "[41]

In a 1972 case, the Commission received a complaint that three Boston television stations were, by airing programs containing violent scenes, raising the issue of the effect on children of violence in television programming.[42] Discounting the analogy to cigarette commercials and their effect on health,[43] the FCC rejected the complaint for failure to point out how violent programming in and of itself raises a controversial issue of public importance.[44]

The FCC was confronted with entertainment dialogue that actually discussed a viewpoint on a controversial issue of public importance in a case involving the comedy series "Maude."[45] Following the discovery that Maude, a middle-aged mother, was pregnant, a family discussion about an abortion took place during which family members expressed various pro-abortion arguments. Faced with a complaint demanding that the "pro-life" viewpoint be presented, the FCC neatly escaped answering whether the Maude dialogue had raised the abortion issue for fairness doctrine purposes; "assuming arguendo that the program did so," the Commission ruled that the complainants had nonetheless failed to show that in its overall programming the television station had not presented contrasting views on abortion.[46]

The FCC's efforts to shelter entertainment from scrutiny under the fairness doctrine are commendable because of the administrative chaos and the infringement of First Amendment rights of broadcasters that would result from application of the fairness doctrine. Entertainment programming constitutes the bulk of radio and television time;[47] because many programs depict controversial issues, the broadcast schedule of licensees would be subject to constant readjustment to allow for balanced programming.[48] The problems connected with the application of the doctrine to conventional public affairs programming would be magnified and expanded in the area of entertainment programming. The question of which issue and possible subissues are raised would be particularly complex since "successful controversial fictional characters are often different things to different people."[49] Broadcasters might well avoid airing any entertainment programs containing potential controversial issues of public importance; if self-censorship did not occur, the FCC would have to play an unprecedented role as a fairness adjudicator, creating a serious risk that the editorial and creative freedom of the broadcaster would be reduced. In either event, the critically important right of the public to receive an unfettered, robust supply of diverse views of controversial public issues would suffer.[50]

The FCC's declaration that dialogue in entertainment shows can raise fairness issues is ominous. The Commission would do well to treat issues presented in entertainment programming as it does passing references and avoid applying the fairness doctrine. At the very least, this rule should be strictly construed in future decisions and applied to only the most blatant cases.

II. IS THE ISSUE CONTROVERSIAL AND OF PUBLIC IMPORTANCE?

Once the issues raised in a broadcast have been identified, it still must be determined whether they are "controversial" and of "public importance." The 1949 *Report on Editorializing*[51] left these terms completely undefined. The 1964 *Fairness Primer*[52] provided some help, but only by offering brief synopses of cases illustrating isolated examples of controversial issues of public importance. No decisional rationale was offered. The 1974 *Fairness Report* represented the first policy statement by the FCC designed to provide some guidance to the Commission, its licensees, and potential complainants.[53] The report reaffirmed the FCC's reliance on licensees' reasonable, good faith judgment and rejected the idea of issuing detailed criteria in favor of suggesting guidelines in the form of "general observations."[54] Dividing the definitional task into two separate questions, the Commission first focused on how to determine "public importance." It pointed to three factors: the degree of media coverage; the degree of attention given the issue by government officials and other community leaders; and the principal test, a "subjective evaluation of the impact that the issue is likely to have on the community at large."[55]

The Commission asserted that the controversiality of an issue can be determined in a more objective manner, apparently because there is no need to evaluate the issue's impact on the community. The less significant factors in defining "public importance" —the degree of media coverage and the attention given the issue by government officials and community leaders—become critical in defining "controversial." The licensee should be able to tell whether the issue is the subject of vigorous debate, with substantial elements of the community in opposition to one another.

The Commission's "general observations" are general indeed. As with the question of what issues are raised, the FCC's most important decision-making principle is deference to the reasonableness and good faith of the licensee.[56] The vagueness in standards and deference to licensee judgment do not create problems where, as is often the case, the proper judgment as to an issue's controversiality and public importance is obvious.[57] It is hard to find fault with the FCC's conclusions that bullfighting in Spain,[58] the theories of curved space,[59] and electronic speech compression[60] did not present controversial issues of public importance, while the Vietnam war,[61] racial integration,[62] and sex education in the public schools[63] did.[64] Where the determination has not been so obvious, however, the FCC has decided cases inconsistently and has often failed to offer an explanatory rationale for its decisions, relying instead on conclusory statements and boiler plate language.[65]

A. GIVING CONTENT TO FUZZY GUIDELINES

Despite the substantive inconsistency of some FCC decisions, and the lack of explanatory rationale in a great many, there are certain discernible trends in the cases. The most important guideposts in determining whether an issue is controversial and of public importance remain those enumerated in the *Fairness Report*: media coverage, attention by government officials and community leaders, and a subjective evaluation of community impact. In a case decided just six months after the *Fairness Report* was issued, however, the Commission stated that there are no "quantitative standards against which one could measure the applicability of any or all of these three factors to any particular issue." According to the Commission, these factors did not "constitute an absolute test of the importance of any issue," but instead were to be "some of the factors which could be considered on a case-by-case basis in evaluating the importance of an issue."[66]

Although the Commission has often failed to mention media coverage and official attention, these factors have played a part in many FCC opinions. In examining the media factor, the FCC has rejected arguments that media coverage alone makes issues controversial and of public importance.[67] Similarly, the Court of Appeals for the District of Columbia has held, in affirming a Commission decision, that media coverage by itself does not determine whether an issue is a controversial issue of public importance.[68] Media coverage may, however, help make an issue controversial and of public importance.

The kind of coverage that has been most persuasive with the Commission is coverage that reports on actual debate in the community over the issue. Thus, articles in Seattle newspapers that described organized community opposition to a school levy proposition were used by the Commission to determine whether the levy was a controversial issue.[69] Similarly, newspaper and broadcast coverage of the conflict between a variety of interest groups over the United Appeal campaign in Dayton, Ohio, was considered by the FCC as evidence that the Appeal was a local controversial issue of public importance.[70] A major newspaper story about a Communist housewife,[71] a sports commentator's mention of a private pension dispute between retired and active football players,[72] and even letters to the editors discussing a licensee's programming on evolution,[73] however, were held to be insufficient evidence of controversial issues of public importance.

Whether attention is given to an issue by community leaders has been an important and sometimes critical factor in determining whether that issue requires fairness balancing.[74] If an issue is the subject of a public election, this will be relied on by the FCC in calling it a controversial issue of public importance.[75] Federal legislative and executive issues, such as the National Fair Employment Practices Commission,[76] and unemployment compensation laws,[77] have required fairness treatment, and various actions of state and local government, such as the tax and planning policies of a state legislature and county board,[78] have also been considered controversial issues of public importance.

The 1974 *Fairness Report* indicated that the most important factor in determining an issue's public importance (although not its controversiality) was a subjective evaluation of its impact on the community.[79] Impact on the community, however, from either a subjective or an objective perspective, is almost never discussed in the case law but is simply assumed. Because there is no impact rule that can be divined from the precedent, use of impact as a guidepost in new situations is difficult.

A serious problem with using the guideposts provided by the *Fairness Report* is that the separate questions of controversiality and public importance have been merged by the cases into a single question. With one exception,[80] cases decided after issuance of the 1974 *Report* ignore its two-step definitional approach. The Commission often determines only that an issue is controversial and concludes that it is thus a controversial issue of public importance; occasionally it determines only that an issue is important to the public and reaches the same result. There often is no discussion of either question; the Commission simply declares that an issue is or is not a controversial issue of public importance.[81]

B. PUBLIC ELECTIONS AND PRIVATE DISPUTES

FCC and judicial case law substantiate the conclusion of Milton Gross, the person in charge of the initial review of all fairness complaints brought to the FCC, that "practically . . . anything that's on the ballot would be a controversial issue of public importance."[82] In a case involving a vote for increased school funds in Seattle, the Commission stated: "The existence of an issue on which the community is asked to vote must be presumed to be a controversial issue of public importance, absent unusual circumstances not here present."[83] Issues that have been considered controversial issues of public importance because they have been the subject of an election include such items as a town charter,[84] party primary elections for the United States Senate,[85] and an initiative on the death penalty.[86] The Commission has yet to find those "unusual circumstances" in an election situation that would negate fairness doctrine application.

In contrast, the FCC has declared that purely private disputes or other private matters do not require fairness doctrine balancing.[87] Termination of a licensee's employee,[88] a dispute over ownership of a radio station's sign,[89] and conflict over whether retired professional football players should share in a pension program[90] were all considered private matters, and thus not controversial issues of public importance.

C. NATIONAL AND INTERNATIONAL ISSUES

The Commission has ruled that in addition to the basic obligation of balancing contrasting views on issues that are controversial and of importance in the local service area, licensees must balance differing opinions on national controversial issues of public importance. The Commission has failed to explain this policy adequately, however. It has implied that, if an issue is controversial and important nationally, it simply would be unreasonable to conclude that it was not so in the local service area, despite local evidence to the contrary,[91] but it has also asserted that there is an obligation to inform the local community on national controversial issues, regardless of the extent of local debate on such issues.[92] Whatever the rationale, the FCC has indicated that if one side of an important, nationally debated issue is presented by a local licensee, contrasting sides must be presented.[93] The licensee cannot escape this obligation by arguing that the issue is not controversial or important locally.[94] A corollary doctrine is that, if a licensee presents one side of an issue that is controversial and of importance on a statewide basis, it must also present contrasting sides regardless of the extent of local service area debate.[95]

With respect to broadcast coverage of events occurring in foreign countries, the FCC has qualified the fairness requirement. For the doctrine to apply, a foreign event must not only constitute a controversial issue of public importance in this country but also involve "the question of United States relations or involvement."[96]

If a complainant can show that there is controversy about the foreign event in this country, and that the event directly involves the United States, fairness balancing is necessary. Thus, coverage of the struggle for minority rights in Northern Ireland[97] and internal development problems and plans in Israel[98] could reasonably be said not to involve United States policy directly and thus not to require fairness doctrine balancing.[99]

The problem here, of course, is attempting to demarcate those foreign events that involve United States relations. Internal Irish and Israeli events today may have a major impact on United States policy tomorrow. Such events are indeed carefully monitored by the American foreign policy apparatus. To conclude that the Vietnam war[100] or the nuclear test ban treaty[101] were controversial and involved United States relations in an important manner appears eminently reasonable. To deny the same conclusion with respect to the overthrow of President Allende and subsequent military control of the Chilean government seems questionable.[102] Programming that does not cover an "event," but contains background information on a foreign internal situation that may be relevant to domestic United States problems raises a similar problem. The fairness doctrine obligation apparently does not apply, despite the doctrine's avowed purpose of informing the American public on vital public issues.[103]

D. THE EXCLUSION PROBLEM

In attempting to define a controversial issue of public importance, the Commission has looked to vigorous debate between substantial elements in the community, thus excluding the ideas of the small minority. Obviously there is a tension between the 1949 *Report on Editorializing* command that licensees ignore the "possible unpopularity" of a viewpoint,[104] and the case law and 1974 *Fairness Report*, which look to debate among a community's "substantial elements."[105] Ideas must be popular to some degree to merit the doctrine's application. If a lone pariah's ideas or those of a small group are scoffed at by the rest of the community, there is no debate and therefore no fairness requirement.

Because fairness issues must be the subject of ongoing debate, they must also be current. No matter how far ahead of the times an advocate may be, if his or her ideas are not currently controversial and important, the fairness doctrine does not apply. Thus, if three years before the energy crisis a party had demanded fairness doctrine reply time to dispute a program that discussed the boundless supply of energy in the United States, he would have been denied by the FCC. The energy supply would not have been the subject of a current controversial debate in the community.

These restrictions seem antithetical to the fairness doctrine's principal purpose of generating debate on issues vital to American democracy. Yet currency and substantial debate are necessary cutoff points in light of the significant First Amendment and administrative problems that would arise in requiring broadcasters to foresee issues of future concern to society and to master every idea's potential public importance regardless of controversy. To penalize a broadcaster for failing to possess such foresight or understanding would be tantamount to imposition of government thought on the licensee as well as the public. Nonetheless, the limitations of the fairness doctrine caused by these cutoff points should be recognized and understood.

III. PENSIONS: A CASE IN POINT

A recent case, *Accuracy in Media, Inc.*[106] (the *Pensions* case), illustrates well the problems involved in isolating the issues raised in a broadcast and determining whether those issues are controversial and of public importance. *Pensions* further demonstrates the potential inhibiting effects of the doctrine on the broadcasters it seeks to regulate.

A. THE CASE AND THE DECISIONS

The case centered around a one-hour documentary, "Pensions: The Broken Promise," presented by NBC and narrated by NBC correspondent Edwin Newman. The documentary began with statements by men and women about troubles they had encountered with their own private pension plans and comments on problems with the private pension system in general.[107] Newman's narration then began at the Department of Labor, where the annual pension reports required by law are filed. He stated:

> There are millions of hopes and dreams in these files. If experience is any guide, very many of the hopes will prove to be empty and dreams

will be shattered and the rosy promises of happy and secure retirement and a vine covered cottage will prove to be false.[108]

Interviews with various public officials who criticized the operation of private pension funds followed.[109] Toward the end of the program several critics recommended changes in the private pension system. Ralph Nader declared: "I think time is running out [on the private pension systems]. And [if] its abuses continue to pile up . . . it might collapse of its own weight, and social security will have to take up the slack."[110]

In concluding the program, Mr. Newman remarked:

> This has been a depressing program to work on but we don't want to give the impression that there are no good private pension plans. There are many good ones, and there are many people for whom the promise has become reality. That should be said.
>
> There are certain technical questions that we've dealt with only glancingly . . . [portability, vesting, funding, and fiduciary relationship].
>
> These are matters for Congress to consider and, indeed, the Senate Labor Committee is considering them now. They are also matters for those who are in pension plans. If you're in one, you might find it useful to take a close look at it.
>
> Our own conclusion about all this, is that it is almost inconceivable that this enormous thing has been allowed to grow up with so little understanding of it and with so little protection and such uneven results for those involved.
>
> The situation, as we've seen it, is deplorable.[111]

Accuracy in the Media, Inc. complained to the FCC that NBC had violated the fairness doctrine by presenting " 'a one-sided documentary that created the impression that injustice and inequity were widespread in the administration of private pension plans,' " and that emphasized " 'the need for new regulatory legislation.' "[112] NBC countered by arguing that it had only presented a " 'broad overview of some of the problems involved in some private pension plans.' "[113] Since there was no question that some problems existed with some private pension plans, it declared that it had not presented a documentary that raised a controversial issue of public importance.

The full Commission affirmed its staff's ruling that NBC was being unreasonable when it contended that the "program was confined in scope to only some problems in some pension plans."[114]

The documentary's "overall thrust was general criticism of the entire pension system, accompanied by proposals for its regulation."[115] Since NBC also indicated that it had not broadcast any other programming dealing with this issue, and did not plan to do so, it was held to be in violation of the fairness doctrine; a reasonable opportunity to present the contrasting view would have to be presented.[116] NBC's contention that the program itself was balanced because of two allegedly pro-pension-plan statements was rejected.[117]

Responding to this intrusion into its programming prerogatives, NBC moved for and was granted an expedited appeal and stay in the District of Columbia Circuit Court of Appeals after its petition for a stay of enforcement pendente lite was refused by the Commission.[118] Initially the Court of Appeals reversed the FCC ruling. Judge Leventhal, writing for the court, indicated that the Commission's major error was to substitute its judgment on the question of what issue was raised by the pensions documentary for that of NBC. He reasoned that, even though the Commission admitted that NBC was reasonable in viewing the subject of the program as "some problems in some pension plans," the Commission had found the network in violation of the fairness doctrine because the FCC staff had formed a different opinion of what issue the program had in fact addressed.[119] The FCC had thus violated the applicable law that licensee judgments are not to be disturbed unless unreasonable or in bad faith and that licensees are to be given wide discretion in their primary responsibility for enforcing the fairness doctrine.[120]

The court went on to state that in light of First Amendment considerations and congressional concerns about the public's right to know, it had a greater responsibility in reviewing agency action in fairness doctrine cases than in more ordinary matters. It would have to take a "hard look" when engaging in such judicial review.[121] In taking that hard look, the court concluded that the record sustained NBC's judgment as reasonable and made in good faith.[122]

B. A CRITIQUE

Several problems with Judge Leventhal's opinion underscore the confusion surrounding the fairness doctrine and the tension between the courts and the FCC in enforcement of the doctrine's requirements. First, as Judge Bazelon and Judge Tamm point out in powerful dissents,[123] the court simply misread the legal standard applied by the Commission. The Commission did not ignore the standard of reasonableness or substitute its judgment for NBC's; the FCC had to look at what "in fact" was presented in the documentary in order to determine whether NBC's judgment on the issue was reasonable. Only after reviewing the broadcast did the FCC conclude that the licensee's judgment strained "the most 'permissive standard of reasonableness' past the breaking point."[124]

The court seemed to enter an Alice-in-Wonderland world in its analysis of explicit comments made on the overall performance of private pension plans;[125] it simply ignored numerous comments in the documentary that were adverse to the overall performance of private pension plans, including the critically important opening and closing narratives by Newman.[126] In looking at favorable comments on overall performance, it took statements out of context, making them seem more favorable than they really were.[127] Its strained view of the facts was undoubtedly related to the court's desire to conclude that a reasonable balance of pro and con views was presented on the issue of overall performance.[128] A quick perusal of the documentary transcript contained in the Appendix to the opinion,[129] however, strongly indicates that the unmistakable thrust of the commentary was criticism of the private pension system generally.

The court also concluded that the issue of whether reform legislation should be enacted was not controversial. This conclusion was based principally on the Commission's asserted failure to document that a controversial issue existed as well as a letter from NBC that all of the groups testifying in Washington hearings had supported some form of remedial legislation. The Commission had indeed failed to document extensively the controversial nature and public importance of the issue. There was no mention of news media coverage, for example. Such a failure of documentation has been a consistent FCC pattern, and the Commission was finally caught. But the issue itself presented a classic situation of a controversial issue of public importance, a situation that FCC precedents repeatedly have held to involve a controversial issue of public importance: the need for passage of a statute pending before a legislature. Despite the fact that the complainant had submitted documents indicating that various major interest groups opposed legislation in the area,[130] the movement for legislative reform was found not to present a controversial issue.

Finally, the court failed to answer the question raised by its own conclusion that the issue raised was some problems with some pension plans. Why was this not a controversial issue of public importance? Lack of dispute over the general fact that problems do exist with respect to some plans does not mean that there are not divided and hotly debated viewpoints on those particular plans under discussion. Indeed, there were very partisan views expressed about these problems throughout the documentary. Why was the case not remanded to the Commission to see if fairness doctrine balancing was necessary on this more limited issue? In previous cases the court had divided issues into subissues to see if fairness doctrine balance was achieved.[131] It is ironic that a hard-hitting investigative documentary, winner of the Peabody and other awards, was characterized as a documentary that did not cover a controversial issue of public importance.

In the final analysis, NBC was clearly unreasonable in concluding that "Pensions: The Broken Promise" did not raise the issue of the overall performance of the private pension industry and the need for legislative reform of that industry. The Commission's decision that this was the issue raised and that NBC had not provided a reasonable balance on the issue was justified by more than substantial evidence. It would appear to be an open and shut fairness case, based on precedent and existing policy. But the court's tortured interpretation of the legal standard applied by the Commission, its distorted view of the balance of comments made on overall performance, its tenuous justification for finding that the need for reform legislation is not a controversial issue, and its failure to recognize the controversial nature of the more limited issue of the problems with some pension plans can only serve to further undermine predictability in the judicial handling of fairness doctrine cases. One is inclined to agree with Judge Tamm's observation that the court was stalking "bigger game" with "an obvious antipathy to the fairness doctrine suggesting that, given a free hand, it would have struck down the doctrine as unconstitutional."[132]

C. THE IMPACT ON THE BROADCASTER

One cannot help but think that the result of the court's *Pensions* decision in terms of its meaning for NBC was correct,[133] despite the misapplication of existing law. NBC had invested time and money in a first-rate, award-winning job of investigative journalism. It informed the American people about a pressing social problem affecting millions of persons. This investment and effort by NBC appears especially laudable given the financial burden of the program; public affairs documentaries receive notoriously low Nielsen ratings and are comparative money losers for the networks. Undoubtedly, NBC could have made more money by showing a police story or a game show.

For its efforts, the network became the defendant in a major lawsuit requiring legal expenditures of over $100,000 and hundreds of hours of network personnel time.[134] If the Commission's ruling had not been disturbed, contrasting views to those presented in "Pensions: The Broken Promise" would in all likelihood have had to be presented free of charge by the network, inflicting still further financial damage.[135] How could such a sequence of events help but create a disincentive against future public affairs documentaries? Such documentaries deserve encouragement designed to offset commercial pressures; instead the fairness doctrine's balancing requirements, as interpreted by the FCC, discourage television networks from presenting controversial public issues. This disincentive is magnified for a local licensee who desires to produce a public affairs documentary locally. The burdens on financial resources and personnel time have a far more drastic disincentive effect on the less profitable local stations.[136]

In the context of scarce airwave frequencies, the Supreme Court has held that the public has a right to be informed about important and controversial public issues by each individual licensee.[137] But, as mentioned above, licensees also have First Amendment rights that must be respected.[138] It is in the delicate balance of licensees' First Amendment speech and press rights and the right of the public to be informed that the public interest is best served. Unfortunately, the fairness doctrine, held constitutional by the Supreme Court, inevitably leads to unhealthy Commission intervention in broadcast journalism and healthy yet tortured court decisions, such as *Pensions,* to rectify the First Amendment balance. This type of judicial review would be far less likely if the Commission by regulation, or Congress by statute, changed the fairness doctrine fiat, as discussed in the next chapter. Assuming that broadcasters are required to present a minimum percentage of public issue and news programming,[139] the public can be best informed by ensuring that professional broadcast journalists have maximum editorial freedom over how that programming is handled. Government encroachment on such editorial freedom poses a far greater danger to the public good than an occasional broadcaster who may incorrectly determine the issue raised by a broadcast, and government encroachment is precisely what occurs when the FCC must determine what issue is raised by a broadcast and whether or not it is controversial and of public importance. Such decisions may be difficult to make, as there may be several reasonable interpretations; but deciding what issues to cover and how to cover them is uniquely within the training of a journalist. The increasing involvement of government in a powerful mass communications system may well prove intolerable.

IV. THE PART ONE OBLIGATION

The fairness doctrine's part one obligation demands that licensees devote a reasonable amount of their programming time to controversial issues of public importance. The question of issue in this context relates to determining which issues must be covered by a licensee under this mandate.

As both the courts and the FCC have recognized, "the essential basis for any fairness doctrine . . . is that *the American public must not be left uninformed.*"[140] In achieving this goal, the doctrine's part one obligation should theoretically be of immense importance, since the part two obligation, calling for the balancing of contrasting views, can be triggered only if there is an initial presentation of views on an issue. Until 1975, however, the part one obligation had "never been enforced."[141] In not a single case had the FCC held that a licensee had violated the part one obligation. In fact, numerous stations have had their licenses routinely approved without proposing any public issue programming for their broadcast schedules.[142] The part one obligation had become "The Forgotten Half of the Fairness Doctrine."[143]

A. DEVELOPMENT OF THE ISSUE DOUBLE STANDARD

Despite the lack of enforcement, the FCC had nonetheless outlined the part one requirement in its decisions before 1975. The obligation was implied in *Great Lakes Broadcasting*[144] in 1929, and was made explicit in *Mayflower Broadcasting Company,*[145] *United Broadcasting Company,*[146] the *Blue Book,*[147] and the *Report on Editorializing* in the 1940s. Since then, court and Commission decisions have routinely referred to the part one obligation.[148]

Although the same standard of reasonableness and good faith that applies to the part two obligation had been assumed to apply to the part one obligation, dicta in *Friends of the Earth*[149] appeared to undermine that assumption. In *Friends of the Earth,* the Commission ruled that broadcast commercials for large engine cars and leaded gasolines did not implicitly raise the issue of air pollution and did not require balanced programming under part two of the fairness doctrine. The Commission emphasized, however, that in light of the part one obligation it would be unreasonable, and therefore improper, for licensees not to air programming that covered the *"burning* issues of the seventies,"[150] or issues of *"great* importance"[151] such as air pollution, Vietnam, or racial unrest.[152] The Commission thus appeared to hold that the issues that must be covered under the part one obligation must be of greater significance than those required to activate fairness balancing under part two, where the Commission had spoken only of a controversial issue of public importance. Thus, an issue that would require balancing under part two might reasonably escape coverage altogether under part one if it did not reach a sufficient level of importance.

Although in the 1974 *Fairness Report* the Commission characterized the part one obligation as the "most basic requirement of the fairness doctrine,"[153] it nonetheless declared that the individual broadcaster is the party responsible for choosing which news items and issues to cover. Referring to *Friends of the Earth,* the Commission stated:

> We have, in the past, indicated that some issues are so *critical* or of such *great public importance* that it would be unreasonable for a licensee to ignore them completely. . . . But such statements on our part are the rare exception, not the rule, and we have no intention of becoming involved in the *selection of issues* to be discussed, nor do we expect a broadcaster to cover each and every important issue which may arise in his community.[154]

In *Public Communications, Inc.,*[155] decided a few months after the 1974 *Fairness Report* was released, the Commission made good on its pledge to avoid involvement with licensees' initial selection of issues. The complainant maintained that the three commercial networks and various Los Angeles television stations had not given adequate coverage to broadcasting license renewal legislation then before the United States Senate. In a well-researched complaint,[156] Public Communications, Inc., demonstrated the impact that the legislation would have on the American public by pointing out the significant effect of the proposed law on the "allocation of what may be the country's most valuable resource—the airwaves," and "our must influential private institution—our broadcasting system."[157] Attention paid to the legislation by numerous government officials, community leaders, public interest groups, and the broadcast industry press was also documented, as was the substantial controversy surrounding the legislation.[158] The issue, if measured under the 1974 *Fairness Report*'s three factors for judging part two complaints,[159] certainly would have required balancing. But the Commission rejected the complaint, despite the admission by the networks and local television stations that they had broadcast no programming whatsoever on the license renewal legislation. The FCC stressed that the complainant "apparently fails to recognize the essential distinction which must be drawn by the Commission in enforcing these two separate requirements"[160] of the fairness doctrine. According to the Commission, the part one obligation "imposes a general obligation on licensees to carry [programming on controversial issues of public importance] and it has only a very limited application to the programming of specific issues."[161] The FCC left to the broadcasters the discretion to choose which issues they will cover; it held "there is no requirement that a licensee address any particular issue merely because the issue is controversial and of public importance."[162]

The three factors pointed to in the 1974 *Fairness Report* as indicators of whether an issue is controversial or of public importance under part two could, indeed, also be used to demonstrate that an issue was critical and of great public importance, therefore requiring coverage under part one of the doctrine. But these factors, the Commission believed, do not constitute an absolute test of an issue's importance, and they are to be considered on a case-by-case basis. In the view of the FCC, a "large number of issues" exist that a licensee could readily classify as "important and controversial enough in their initial presentation to require subsequent presentation of contrasting views, but which could not be said to be 'so critical or of such great public importance' as to justify Commission intrusion on the discretion afforded the licensee in the selection of issues to cover."[163] The Commission concluded that it must "very sparingly invoke the 'critical issue' responsibility of licensees if we are not to take over their rightful programming function."[164]

The double standard for part one and part two complaints thus became firmly entrenched.[165] For a licensee to be judged unreasonable in not covering the issue, that issue must be far more important than an issue requiring balanced presentation under part two. The Commission, after *Public Communications,* was much more hesitant to order issue coverage under part one than to order issue balancing under part two, and until April 13, 1976, there still was no case in which the Commission had ruled against a licensee on a part one complaint. The double standard insulating a licensee's part one decisions stood as a formidable barrier.

B. THE *PATSY MINK* DECISION

The Commission took an initial step toward changing its hands-off treatment of part one cases in its decision in *Representative Patsy Mink.*[166] The case developed in the summer of 1974, when Representative Patsy Mink wrote to a number of broadcast stations asking them to air an 11-minute tape containing her views on pending strip mining control legislation. She said the tape would provide contrasting opinions to those expressed in a United States Chamber of Commerce program, which had been aired by hundreds of stations. Among those stations responding to Mink was station WHAR in Clarksburg, West Virginia. WHAR rejected her request, claiming that it had not broadcast the chamber's program, or any other programming, on the strip mining controversy.[167]

Representative Mink, joined by two other complainants and represented by lawyers from the Media Access Project, developed a strong case, including extensive documentation to demonstrate that the issue of strip mining was of " 'extraordinary controversiality and public importance to WHAR's listeners,' "[168] and that strip mining legislation then being debated in Congress " 'was *probably the single most important issue to arise in several decades*' "[169] in the county. WHAR admitted that it had not originated any local programming on strip mining.[170]

The FCC agreed with the complainants that the strip mining issue was an issue of such importance to the licensee's service area that the station was, under the part one obligation, required to provide coverage.[171] The Commission cautioned that it had "no intention of intruding on licensees' day-to-day editorial decision making."[172] Instances requiring such remedial action would be "rare," intervention being reserved for "vital issues of public importance,"[173] issues that have a "tremendous impact within the local service area," or issues that have a "significant and possibly unique impact on the licensee's service area."[174]

In concluding that strip mining was such an issue, the Commission relied on the documentation supplied by the complainants. The complainants had shown the "extreme importance" of the strip mining issue by supplying congressional testimony, numerous newspaper and magazine articles, and even a research study that demonstrated the "enormous impact" of strip mining on the air and water quality and the economy of the region. These materials also revealed that Clarksburg and its vicinity had the highest percentage of strip-mined land of any county in the state. Long-range environmental and employment developments were shown to be directly linked to strip mining legislation being debated in Congress. Moreover, WHAR had admitted that strip mining was important to many people in Clarksburg. The "highly controversial nature" of the strip mining issue was shown by reference to citizen protests, numerous front-page stories in the local newspaper, and the lengthy debate in Congress.[175] The complainants had also demonstrated the great amount of attention paid to the issue by community leaders and government officials.[176] Clearly, some programming on strip mining would have to be aired.[177]

If the FCC was not to completely abdicate its role and responsibility in the part one area under the present enforcement structure, WHAR had to be found in violation of its part one obligation. Strip mining was obviously a critical issue in Clarksburg and WHAR's programming was woefully inadequate on that issue.

The Commission's decision in *Patsy Mink* represents a first step toward significant change in enforcement of the part one obligation. Several unsolved problems remain, however.

Patsy Mink illustrates the timing problems encountered when enforcement is carried out through responses to specific complaints. Such a system risks overlooking an issue until the time for public action on the issue is past. For example, the original complaint against WHAR was filed on September 25, 1974.[178] It made specific reference to strip mining legislation then being debated in Congress, and it charged that the licensee had failed "for at least a four-month period when Congress was considering strip mining legislation to air *any* programming on the strip mining controversy."[179] The Commission's ruling on the complaint was adopted on June 8, 1976—more than one year and nine months later. During that period, the strip mining legislation was passed by Congress and vetoed by the President. Since similar legislation had been introduced in late 1975, the Commission ultimately concluded that the "issue of reclamation of strip mined land has continued to be controversial up to the present date."[180] Had the legislation not been vetoed, however, but become law—or had similar legislation not been introduced at the later date—the Commission's order would have come a year after the critically important strip mining legislation issue had become moot. The time for informed public discussion about the issue among citizens is before and during legislative debate—not after the question has been resolved.

The part one cases reemphasize the administrative problems, tinged with First Amendment considerations, evident in fairness doctrine disputes. The Commission speaks of issues that are "burning," "critical," "vital," "rare," of "great importance," of "great public importance," and of "extreme importance," or that have a "tremendous" or "unique" impact within the licensee's service area. What do these terms mean? How is a licensee to distinguish between such issues and other issues that are merely controversial and of public importance? And what if an issue is "burning" and "critical" on a national level, but not within the local service area? Are such national issues automatically ruled out of the part one requirement?

The "issue raised" question becomes particularly troublesome in part one cases. Neither the 1974 *Fairness Report* nor FCC case law provides any guidance. If it is difficult to determine the issue raised when an initial broadcast has triggered a part two obligation, it is much more difficult to determine the specific issue that needs addressing when there has been no previous broadcast. In *Patsy Mink*, the Commission failed to clarify whether the specific issue that had to be covered was the strip mining legislation being considered in Congress, the local ramifications of strip mining, or the issue of strip mining generally.

Finally, the question of how much programming on the issue must be aired comes into play. The Commission offered absolutely no instruction on how much broadcast time on the strip mining question had to be presented. No precedent exists on the matter, and *Patsy Mink* gives no guidance.

These general and more particular problems are perhaps unavoidable under present enforcement procedures. From this perspective, the development of the issue double standard and the reluctance to enforce the part one obligation can be viewed as attempts to differentiate the Commission's role in part one and part two situations. As Commissioner Robinson stated in *Patsy Mink*: "[E]nforcement of the first obligation constitutes a somewhat greater degree of government interference than enforcement of the second inasmuch as it is not triggered by the *licensee*'s program choice."[181] In part two cases, the licensee has already exercised its First Amendment choice by airing programming on an issue. It has already decided that an important and controversial topic is involved that needs coverage. If the government then finds the licensee's programming wanting, it asks that the licensee give more coverage on a topic that the licensee has already chosen to air.

In the part one situation, the licensee has chosen not to cover the issue at all. Many factors may have prompted this decision, ranging from an editorial choice based on time limitations to the licensee's judgment that the issue simply does not merit coverage. Federal government action forcing a broadcaster to cover a particular issue therefore involves a more intrusive First Amendment infringement than part two enforcement in that it does not parallel a broadcaster's initial issue decision. Part one intervention thus raises the spectre of government using the media to cover issues that the government deems important, *i.e.*, in its interest.

Under the "double standard" procedure, the Commission gets involved in precisely those circumstances in which its involvement is least necessary. In communities where issues are "burning," and of "critical importance," those issues will most likely receive thorough coverage by other organs of the media. In fact, intense coverage by the media and attention by community and government leaders is necessary to show that the issue is critical enough to break through the part one portion of the double standard and gain FCC remedial action. One cannot help but wonder if the significant interference with broadcasters' First Amendment rights and the potential for government abuse are worth whatever marginal advantage might be gained by FCC action on part one complaints.

This analysis suggests that the Commission should evaluate a licensee's part one performance on an overall rather than an issue-by-issue basis—whether annually or as part of the license renewal procedure. The FCC might ask several questions as part of such review. What average percentage of time has the licensee devoted to news and public affairs? Have a certain number of important issues been covered? How has the licensee ascertained the important issues in the community? Such questions would provide a more satisfactory basis for the assessment of a licensee's performance under part one of the fairness doctrine.

V. CONCLUSION

A. THE PROBLEMS REVIEWED

As the preceding discussion has demonstrated, severe problems have developed under part two of the fairness doctrine in determining what issue is raised by a broadcast and whether that issue is controversial and of public importance. In defining the issue raised, the FCC usually works from written documents, ignoring the television image. The Commission's use of a "thrust doctrine" to determine what subissues are raised in a broadcast has resulted in a string of inconsistent precedent, offering little rationale for the conclusions reached. It has been more consistent in refusing to apply the fairness doctrine to passing references and entertainment programming, although entertainment shows have not been completely exempt from the doctrine's coverage.

In determining whether an issue is controversial and of public importance, the FCC has offered some guidelines by pointing to media coverage, attention by government and community leaders, and impact on the community. But this guidance is vague indeed, as the Commissioners' own words substantiate, and the FCC has decided cases inconsistently, generating confusion about what is required of licensees. The case law has been marked by the Commission's failure to provide any rationale for deciding that an issue is or is not controversial and of public importance. The FCC has virtually ignored its own suggestion that the definitional task be divided by determining controversiality and public importance separately. Moreover, the definition of the controversial-public importance standard excludes views that are "ahead of their time" and not currently controversial.

It must also be emphasized that the issue problems are just part of the difficulties that inhere in applying the fairness doctrine's second part. The critical problem of how to ensure a reasonable opportunity for presentation of contrasting views must ultimately be faced. The FCC must determine the reasonableness of the balance in terms of the frequency, total air time, and hour of broadcast given to views on each side of the issue. In decisions on these questions, like the issue problems, the Commission has set forth a series of inconsistent rulings, with little supporting rationale, and confusing guidelines.[182]

In applying the part one requirement of the fairness doctrine, the Commission has in recent years given licensees additional protection from government interference. Under part one, licensees are obligated to cover only "critical," "vital" issues of "great importance." They need not cover all the issues that would ordinarily need balancing under part two.

Welcome as the additional part one licensee protection is, one wonders whether that protection goes far enough. Any activist enforcement of part one on an individual complaint basis would magnify the existing issue problems in the part two situation. With no previous broadcast to guide the licensee or the Commission, a cacophony of conflicting voices in the community would have to be deciphered to determine exactly which issues require broadcast coverage. Once an issue is isolated, it still must be decided whether the issue is "critical," "vital," or of "great importance." What do these terms mean? How does a licensee meaningfully distinguish between such issues and ones that are merely controversial and of public importance? The Commission offers little guidance.[183] Beyond this, an issue-by-issue part one enforcement policy is effective exactly when additional coverage of that issue is least necessary.

Even with the double standard protection, present part one issue enforcement threatens encroachment on the journalistic judgment of the broadcast press. Despite the irresponsibility of WHAR in *Patsy Mink*, the concept of the federal government telling a West Virginia licensee what issue to cover smacks of government interference alien to a free press. The licensee has chosen not to cover that issue, and the government should hesitate to instruct it otherwise, because of the enormous potential for abuse.

B. FUTURE POLICY STEPS

The House Communications Subcommittee will be examining the 1934 Communications Act during the 95th Congress. The Subcommittee will consider recommendations for revision of the Act, and as part of its study, will scrutinize the continued viability of the fairness doctrine.[184] Regardless of what Congress does, however, the FCC may act on its own to alter fairness doctrine administration.

One short-term way to meet the concerns addressed in this chapter would be to drop the fairness balancing requirement of part two[185] and require that a relatively high minimum percentage of programming be devoted to news and public affairs. The federal government would then be out of the business of telling broadcasters which issues to cover and how to cover them. There would be no part two intervention to determine which issue was raised by a broadcast, whether it was controversial or of public importance, and whether a proper balance had been presented. There would be no part one intervention to force a broadcaster to cover a particular issue because it is "vital" and "burning." These questions would be left to the journalistic practices of the broadcast press. But at license renewal time, every three years, licensees would be required to demonstrate that they had broadcast a certain amount of public issue programming as part of their news and public affairs coverage.[186] This proposal is discussed more fully at the end of the next and concluding chapter.

Notes

1. *See* FCC, *Fairness Doctrine and Public Interest Standards, Fairness Report Regarding Handling of Public Issues,* 39 FED. REG. 26372, 26376-77 par. 36 (1974) [hereinafter cited as *Fairness Report*].

2. *Id.*

3. 40 F.C.C.2d 958, *application for review denied,* 44 F.C.C.2d 1027 (1973), *rev'd sub nom.* National Broadcasting Co. v. FCC, 516 F.2d 1101, *reversal vacated and rehearing en banc granted,* 516 F.2d 1155, *rehearing en banc vacated,* 516 F.2d 1156, *second reversal vacated as moot and remanded with direction to vacate initial order and dismiss complaint,* 516 F.2d 1180 (D.C. Cir. 1974).

4. *See* Representative Patsy Mink, 59 F.C.C.2d 987 (1976).

5. *Fairness Report, supra* note 1, at 26376 par. 31. Much reliance is placed on the issue set forth in the initial complaint. Interviews with Milton Gross, Chief, FCC Fairness/Political Broadcasting Branch, Complaints and Compliance Division, by Steven J. Simmons, Sept. 3, 9, 1975, Dec. 8, 1976; interview with Commissioner Glen Robinson by Steven J. Simmons, Sept. 3, 1975; interview with Larry Secrest, Administrative Assistant to Chairman Richard Wiley, by Steven J. Simmons, Sept. 4, 1975.

The Commission must often pinpoint the specific issue or issues involved without the aid of a transcript or tape of the relevant program. This necessitates reliance on the memories of listeners and station employees. *Fairness Report, supra* note 1, at 26376 par. 33.

6. 19 P & F RADIO REG. 2d 137 (1970), *petition for reconsideration granted and complaint denied,* 25 F.C.C.2d 735 (1970).

7. 19 P & F RADIO REG. 2d at 139.

8. *Id.*

9. 25 F.C.C.2d at 737 (emphasis added). The Commission also inexplicably appeared to redefine the subissue to be "that the private pilot is a hazard because of the nature of his training." *Id.*

10. *Id.* at 736.

11. *Id.* at 737.

12. 38 F.C.C.2d 1027 (1973).

13. *Id.* at 1031. It should be noted that in this case, as in *National Broadcasting,* the Commission was doing exactly the opposite of what one law journal writer suggested was its practice. Rather than revealing a "tendency to limit the 'issue raised' as narrowly as possible," Note, *The FCC Fairness Doctrine and Informed Social Choice,* 8 HARV. J. LEGIS. 333, 337 (1971), it expanded the issue greatly in order to encompass the alleged subissue, and thereby declare the licensee's judgment reasonable. The Commission would have done better to analyze the *Caplan* decision as a "passing reference" case. See text accompanying notes 21–26 *infra.* The Commission, however, chose to focus on whether the subissue (the types of guns that are the subject of proposed legislation) was separable from the issue (gun control) and not on the brevity of the initial remark.

14. American Conservative Union, 23 F.C.C.2d 33 (1970).

15. The Commission concluded that "the thrust of the programs and the overwhelming majority of views expressed were on the subject of how to end hunger, rather than discussing whether hunger is a national disgrace." *Id.*

16. 30 F.C.C.2d 758 (1971).

17. For other cases where the Commission ruled that subissues were not raised or had a differing interpretation of the broadcast from that of a complainant, *see* Metromedia, Inc., 23 P & F RADIO REG. 2d 610 (1972) (proper role of public officers as part of a series entitled "Criminals and the Courts"); National Sportsman's Club, Inc., 30 F.C.C.2d 636 (1971) (role of hunting in wildlife management as part of a program on the extinction of animal species).

18. 39 F.C.C.2d 416 (1973), *aff'd on other grounds,* 521 F.2d 288 (D.C. Cir. 1975). *See also* Brandywine-Main Line Radio, Inc., 24 F.C.C.2d 18 (1970), *petition for reconsideration denied,* 27 F.C.C.2d 565 (1971), *aff'd,* 473 F.2d 16 (D.C. Cir. 1972), *cert. denied,* 412 U.S. 922 (1973), where the Commission lists seven topics, under headings such as "Issue—The Vietnam War," and then lists various subissues, such as "the United States should do everything in its power to achieve a triumphant military victory," that needed a balancing of broadcast viewpoints under the fairness doctrine. 24 F.C.C.2d at 35. Other headings use the plural "issues" such as "Issues Relating to the Loyalty of Federal Officials," and list

separate issues, essentially subissues of the topic heading, such as the allegation that "many high ranking federal officials . . . were . . . disloyal to the United States." *Id.* at 36.

19. 39 F.C.C.2d at 418.

20. *Id.* at 422. It went on to find the overall programming of PBS balanced on both of these subissues. *Id.* at 423.

21. The conflict with precedent is even more glaring when one considers that, in such cases as *National Broadcasting* and *Callan,* complainants had asked for subissue division and had been rejected. In *Accuracy in Media, Inc.,* however, the Commission created subissues sua sponte.

It is also difficult to square precedent with Tri-State Broadcasting Co., 3 P & F RADIO REG. 2d 175 (1964), which focused on a 30-minute dramatization of the "Communist threat." In response to a complaint that the program was only a vehicle for "ultra rightist dogma," the Commission found that the film raised the issue of "the most effective and proper method of combating Communism and Communist infiltration." *Id.* at 176. Rather than airing the "communist viewpoint," the licensee would have to air other views on how to combat communism. *Id.*

Assuming that the issue raised was how to combat communism, why was this not considered a subissue of the broader issue of communism? If a specific method of combating handgun proliferation was part and parcel of gun control in *Caplan,* and an alleged contributing factor to unsafe air conditions was a subissue of air congestion in *National Broadcasting,* it seems inconsistent to isolate methods of combating communism from the overall issue of communism.

22. 25 F.C.C.2d at 736.

23. 26 P & F RADIO REG. 2d 1185 (1973).

24. 26 F.C.C.2d 920 (1970).

25. Anthony R. Martin-Trigona, 19 F.C.C.2d 620 (1969), *reconsidered and relief denied,* 22 F.C.C.2d 683 (1970). *See also* Stambler & Shrinsky, 33 P & F RADIO REG. 2d 931 (1975) (mention of broadcast properties to be acquired in purchase of Washington Star); Elsie Bradberry, 21 P & F RADIO REG. 2d 379 (1971) (mention of God); Robert H. Scott, 25 F.C.C.2d 239 (1970) (mention of "God is great," and "God is good," and "under God").

26. *Fairness Report, supra* note 1, at 26376 par. 35. Even with passing references, however, there may be difficult problems of line-drawing. *See* Boalt Hall Student Ass'n 20 F.C.C.2d 612 (1969), where the complainant association asserted that in a 30-minute broadcast California Governor Reagan had talked not only about the issue of student unrest, as the licensee asserted, but also about subissues such as the faculty's alleged permissiveness toward obscenity and an allegedly unfit instructor. The Commission was unclear about why it ruled that the licensee's definition of the broader issue was reasonable, but among the reasons it set forth were that the statements complained of "were of extremely brief duration." *Id.* at 616. Apparently, however, they were major points made by the Governor. Compare this decision with Phillip H. Schott, 25 F.C.C.2d 729 (1970), where, on a complaint involving another broadcast by Governor Reagan about student unrest and the closing of college campuses, the Commission apparently reached a contrary and inconsistent conclusion. It listed in an appendix to the decision seven subissues (six of which were based on short Reagan statements) that were covered in the Governor's address, and it found the fairness doctrine "applicable to the issues." *Id.* at 730.

27. At least one licensee has also suggested that viewpoints on issues have been raised and balanced under the fairness doctrine by balancing commentators with different political philosophies. But the Commission stated: "The fairness doctrine is applicable to specific controversial issues of public importance, and therefore, in the absence of a showing as to the specific viewpoints presented, reliance on the general philosophy or bent of a commentator does not adequately answer the question whether a licensee has discharged its affirmative duty to encourage and implement the broadcast of opposing viewpoints on such specific issues." Lamar Life Broadcasting Co., 38 F.C.C. 1143, 1148 (1965). Just as the Commission will look beyond philosophies to specific issues, so it will look beyond broadcast formats. Thus, whether a broadcast raises a controversial issue of public importance "is determined

by the content of the presentation, and not upon the placing of any label such as 'editorial,' or 'commentary,' or 'opinion,' on that presentation." WNCN Listener's Guild, 53 F.C.C.2d 149, 155 (1975).

28. *Fairness Report, supra* note 1, at 26376 par. 34.

29. 28 F.C.C.2d 315 (1971).

30. 11 F.C.C.2d 790 (1968).

31. *See also* Richard B. Wheeler, 6 F.C.C.2d 599 (1965) (program clearly criticizing abuses in debt-adjusting business raises issue of debt-adjusting business).

32. *See* Chapter Five, pp. 115–16, 125–26.

33. For a definition of these terms, *see* note 48 and accompanying text in Chapter Five.

34. *See* Chapter Five, pp. 118–20.

35. *Fairness Report, supra* note 1, at 26380–82 pars. 60–76.

36 *See* Chapter Five, pp. 120–29.

37. For purposes of this discussion, entertainment programming includes all television (or radio) programming other than news, documentaries, interview shows, other programming focused on public affairs, commercial advertising, public service announcements, and religious, agricultural, and other such specialized programming. Thus, fictional series, movies, dramatic presentations based on fact, comedies, musical shows, satires, game shows, and sports may be considered the standard fare of such entertainment programming.

38. American Broadcasting Co., 52 F.C.C.2d 98 (1975).

39. *Id.* at 115 (emphasis in original). *See also* Rudolph P. Arnold, 52 F.C.C.2d 405 (1975); National Broadcasting Co., 52 F.C.C.2d 273 (1975).

40. Thomas E. Mitchell, 54 F.C.C.2d 593 (1975).

41. *Id.* at 395. One legal justification the FCC might have asserted for excluding much entertainment programming from fairness treatment would rely on the language of section 315. Under the statute, licensees must "afford [a] reasonable opportunity for the *discussion* of conflicting views on issues of public importance." 47 U.S.C. sec. 315(a) (4) (1970) (emphasis added). Mere depiction of an event, as in the first terrorist-atomic plant hypothetical, arguably does not constitute "discussion" of that issue.

42. George D. Corey, 37 F.C.C.2d 641 (1972). Corey asked that the stations broadcast the following public service announcement or its equivalent in order to comply with the fairness doctrine: "*Warning:* Viewing of violent television programming by children can be hazardous to their mental health and well being." *Id.*

43. Commissioner Johnson's dissent convincingly refuted the Commission's attempt to distinguish cigarette commercials from violent programming and its effect on children. *Id.* at 644.

44. "It is simply not an appropriate application of the fairness doctrine to say that an entertainment program—whether it be Shakespeare or an action-adventure show—raises a controversial issue if it contains a violent scene and has a significant audience of children." *Id.* at 643. The Commission correctly pointed out: "[W]ere we to adopt your construction that the depiction of a violent scene is a discussion of one side of a controversial issue of public importance, the number of controversial issues presented on entertainment shows would be virtually endless." *Id.* at 643–44. The same fate awaited complainants charging that implicit controversial issues of public importance were raised by how Indians were treated in the "Daniel Boone" series, David Hare, 35 F.C.C.2d 868 (1972), and by "depictions of 'Indians, Latinos, Blacks, Jews, and others' in motion pictures," Flower City Television Corp., 57 F.C.C.2d 112, 116 (1975). In *Flower City,* the fairness issue came up in a challenge to renewal of a television station's license. The Commission, after admitting that entertainment programming could raise a fairness issue, declared that the "Fairness Doctrine does not enter the picture unless the program contributes to or constitutes a discussion. The petitioner has failed to show us that any of the dialogues of the cited motion pictures could reasonably be considered 'discussions' of an on-going community debate such that they would amount to advocacy." *Id.* at 117 (citations omitted). *See also* Rose Sodano, 40 F.C.C.2d 972 (1973) (complaint alleging that reference to Al Capone in Alistair Cooke's "America" series disparaged Italian-Americans); Robert S. Gelman, 29 F.C.C.2d 34 (1971)

(complaint alleging that references in "All in the Family" disparaged New York Jewish attorneys and asking reply under the personal attack doctrine).

45. Diocesan Union of Holy Name Societies, 41 F.C.C.2d 297 (1973).

46. *Id.* at 298-99.

47. *See, e.g., Types of Network TV Shows and Their Audiences,* 1976 BROADCASTING YEARBOOK C-300.

48. The almost unlimited potential for such application is asserted by one law review writer who sees fairness issues implicit not only in the portrayal of violence in televised westerns, movies, and football games, but also in the FBI series' favorable treatment of the Bureau. Comment, *The Fairness Doctrine and Entertainment Programming: All in the Family,* 7 GA. L. REV. 554, 561-62 (1973). The author argues: "In general, any position which might reasonably be inferred from an entertainment program, whether through outright statement or through innuendo, would trigger the appliation of the doctrine." *Id.* at 502. As another commentator points out, such application would place the Commission "in a position of drama critic." Michel Rosenfeld, *The Jurisprudence of Fairness: Freedom Through Regulation in the Marketplace of Ideas,* 44 FORDHAM L. REV. 877, 902 (1976).

49. Rosenfeld, *supra* note 48, at 904.

50. Many of the other arguments against application of the doctrine to commercial advertising made in Chapter Five (pp. 120-29) are relevant to entertainment programming. Thus there would also be an adverse economic effect on broadcasting if the doctrine were applied to entertainment shows, although possibly not as severe as in the advertising context. The First Amendment concerns would also be magnified.

51. FCC, *Report on Editorializing by Broadcast Licensees,* 13 F.C.C. 1246 (1949) [hereinafter cited as *Report on Editorializing*].

52. FCC, *Applicability of the Fairness Doctrine in the Handling of Controversial Issues of Public Importance,* 29 FED. REG. 10415 (1964) [hereinafter cited as *Fairness Primer*].

53. Various commentators have urged that the FCC develop more definite standards in determining the reasonableness of a licensee's judgment on controversy and public importance, and some have even suggested decisional criteria. *See* Comment, *The Regulation of Competing First Amendment Rights: A New Fairness Doctrine Balance After CBS?* 122 U. PA. L. REV. 1283, 1320-22 (1974); Note, *The FCC Fairness Doctrine and Informed Social Choice,* 8 HARV,. J. LEGIS. 333, 345-46 (1971). Others have disagreed. Interview with John Goldhammer, Program Director for television station WTOP-TV, Washington, D.C. by Steven J. Simmons, Sept. 8, 1975; Interview with Ben Raub, Vice President and Assistant General Attorney, who oversees legal responses to all fairness matters for NBC, by Steven J. Simmons, Aug. 26, 1975. *See also* Roscoe Barrow, *The Equal Opportunities and Fairness Doctrines in Broadcasting: Pillar in the Forum of Democracy,* 37 U. CIN. L. REV. 447, 490 (1968).

54. *Fairness Report, supra* note 1, at 26,376 par. 30. The Commission states that, "given the limitless number of potential controversial issues and the varying circumstances in which they might arise, we have not been able to develop detailed criteria which would be appropriate in all cases. For this very practical reason, and for the reason that our role must be one of review, we will continue to rely heavily on the reasonable, good faith judgments of our licensees in this area." *Id.* par. 29.

55. *Id.* par. 30.

56. The lack of definitional standards is well illustrated by the commissioners' own words. Commissioner Charlotte Reid candidly admitted that whatever "controversial-public-importance" guideposts exist "are pretty nebulous. It's a matter of feeling and reaction." Interview with Charlotte Reid, by Steven J. Simmons, Sept. 16, 1975. Commissioner Hooks has declared that it is "almost like pornography. I may not be able to define it, but I know it when I see it." Interview with Benjamin Hooks by Steven J. Simmons, Sept. 14, 1975. The commissioner added, "It just seems to me that a controversial question of public importance is a question that apparently a great deal of people have some concern about and not a unanimous viewpoint. I don't have any fixed or pat answer, it's just a matter of recognizing it." *Id.* Commissioner Wells told one interviewer that he "had no clear standard," although

there were some indicia. John L. Swartz, *Fairness for Whom? Administration of the Fairness Doctrine, 1969-70,* 14 B.C. IND. & COM. L. REV. 457, 461 (1973). The indicia were "coverage by other media, legislative or executive action, and the existence of concerned community organizations." *Id.*

Other commissioners have commented on the lack of standards. Commissioner Glen Robinson asserted, "there are no guidelines. . . . It's pretty murky." Interview with Glen Robinson by Steven J. Simmons, Sept. 3, 1975. The Commissioner indicated that the Commission generally handled complaints by indicating that the complainant has not met the "burden of proof."

Commissioner James Quello does not "know of any yardstick I'd provide." Interview with James Quello by Steven J. Simmons, Sept. 8, 1975. The Commissioner added that coverage by television, newspapers, and magazines and whether the issue was to be voted on by the public are factors he considers. *Id.*

Commissioner Robert Lee has suggested "a great deal of visceral reaction on my part." Interview with Robert Lee by Steven J. Simmons, Sept. 15, 1975. And Chairman Richard Wiley, while pointing to the 1974 *Fairness Report*'s guidelines, has referred to judges' disagreement over a famous and complicated torts case: "You look at the *Palsgraf* case and see how these guys wrangled around on what a reasonable man is, or a zone of danger—anything you put to a microscope when you come right down to it—they all have certain difficulty seeing it all the way through . . . you have to make some common sense judgments. Everybody defines it slightly differently." Interview with Chairman Richard Wiley and Administrative Assistant Larry Secrest by Steven J. Simmons, Sept. 14, 1975. Secrest continued: "That's why the reasonableness standard is so important in here, because there is so much of a subjective element in judgment. It's necessary that the Commission avoid any close second guessing because the standards just aren't that mechanical." *Id.*

57. It should also be noted that fairness complainants will frequently fail to provide any information, even of media coverage of officials' comments, to substantiate whether an issue is controversial or of public importance. Complaints are very frequently returned to the complainants by the FCC staff for further information, often never to reemerge.

58. The Clarin, 28 F.C.C.2d 313 (1971).

59. Morton Schwartz, 52 F.C.C.2d 596 (1975).

60. Christopher S. Riley, 53 F.C.C.2d 190 (1975).

61. American Friends of Vietnam, Inc., 6 P & F RADIO REG. 2d 126 (1965). *See also* Accuracy in Media, Inc., 39 F.C.C.2d 558 (1973); Horace P. Rowley III, 39 F.C.C.2d 437 (1973); Richard B. Kay, 24 F.C.C.2d 426 (1970), *aff'd,* 443 F.2d 638 (D.C. Cir. 1970).

62. Lamar Life Broadcasting Co., 38 F.C.C. 1143 (1965).

63. Accuracy in Media, Inc., 39 F.C.C.2d 416 (1973), *aff'd,* 521 F.2d 288 (D.C. Cir. 1975), *cert. denied,* 425 U.S. 934 (1976).

64. In many of those cases (*e.g., American Friends, Lamar Life,* and *Accuracy in Media*), however, the Commission simply assumed that the issue was a controversial issue of public importance without offering any explanatory rationale. If the Commission is simply to take "administrative notice" of an issue as being controversial and of public importance, it should at least state that it is doing so.

65. One sequence of inconsistent cases commenced with Living Should Be Fun, 33 F.C.C. 101 (1962). Listeners complained to the FCC that a daily radio program offering discussions on diet and health matters had presented one-sided views of controversial issues of public importance. Among these issues were the fluoridation of water, the value of krebiozen in the treatment of cancer, the nutritive qualities of white bread, and the use of high potency vitamins without medical advice. The FCC agreed that these issues did deserve treatment under the fairness doctrine, and that the licensee would have to air contrasting viewpoints. No explanation of why the issues were controversial and of public importance was given beyond the assertion that the program's narrator had "emphasized the fact that his views were opposed to many authorities in these fields." *Id.* at 107.

In 1975, the FCC was confronted with a complaint alleging that discussion of the hotly debated drug Laetrile, used in the treatment of cancer, raised a controversial issue of public importance. Thomas N. Lippitt, 53 F.C.C.2d 1195 (1975). Despite the submission of newspaper articles on Laetrile, court cases concerning its licensing and use, and controversy about it within the medical profession, the Commission ruled that the complainant had not shown that it was a controversial issue of public importance. There seems to be no rational reason for concluding that krebiozen use in treatment of cancer should be any more controversial or important in *Living Should Be Fun* than Laetrile should be in *Lippitt*. If anything, Lippitt demonstrated more controversy and importance in his complaint, even describing media coverage and official action as the *Fairness Report* suggests. The difference of opinion among expert authorities that seemed to be dispositive in *Living Should Be Fun* had little effect in *Lippitt*.

Living Should Be Fun also seems to conflict with *American Vegetarian Union,* 38 F.C.C.2d 1024 (1972), in which the complainant alleged that disparagement of a vegetarian diet and advocacy of an all-animal-protein diet, including statements that vegetarians lack vitamin B-12, raised a controversial issue of public importance. Despite the complainant's description of a pending Food and Drug Administration ruling on antibiotics injected into animal foods, relevant congressional bills on meat products, and a considerable divergence of opinion among nutritionists on the effects of meat diets, the Commission ruled that the issue did not involve a public controversy. No rational distinction was expressed to explain why the nutritional value of white bread and the use of vitamins in *Living Should Be Fun* presented controversial issues of public importance, while the nutritional value of animal products and lack of vitamins in a vegetarian diet in *American Vegetarian Union* did not.

Cases focusing on employee-employer relations also present a conflicting line of precedent. *Compare* National Ass'n of Gov't Employees, 41 F.C.C.2d 965 (1973), *with* Communication Workers of Am., 31 F.C.C.2d 841 (1971); *and* Big Bend Broadcasting, 20 P & F RADIO REG. 2d 93 (1970), *with* Retail Store Employees Union Local 880, 436 F.2d 249 (D.C. Cir. 1970).

66. Public Communications, Inc., 50 F.C.C.2d 395, 400 (1974).

67. In the 1974 *Fairness Report,* the FCC declared that it is "obvious that an issue is not necessarily a matter of significant 'public importance' merely because it has received broadcast or newspaper coverage." *Fairness Report, supra* note 1, at 26376 par. 30.

68. Healey v. FCC, 460 F.2d 917 (D.C. Cir. 1972). "Our daily papers and television broadcasts alike are filled with news items which good journalistic judgment would classify as newsworthy, but which the same editors would not characterize as containing important controversial public issues." *Id.* at 922. The Court reasoned that a "57-year old Communist housewife and her PTA activities, her children, and their friends" did not qualify as a controversial issue of public importance, and reaching an opposite decision in such a case would "swamp" the FCC with fairness complaints. *Id.* at 923. Television and radio would be discouraged from commenting on any newspaper editorials or items, and the robust public debate that the doctrine was designed to foster would thereby suffer. *Id.*

69. Ted Bullard, 23 F.C.C.2d 41, 43 (1970). The community controversy plus the fact that the levy was the subject of an election made the issue a controversial issue of public importance. Typically, however, the conclusion as to controversy has not been separated from the conclusion as to public importance.

70. United People, 32 F.C.C.2d 124, 125–27 (1971). *See also* Thomas M. Slaten, 28 F.C.C.2d 315 (1971).

71. Dorothy Healey, 24 F.C.C.2d 487 (1970), *aff'd,* 460 F.2D 917 (D.C. Cir. 1972).

72. National Football League Players Ass'n, 39 F.C.C.2d 429 (1973).

73. Mrs. H.B. Van Velzer, 38 F.C.C.2d 1044 (1973). *See also* Douglas J. Allam, 36 P & F RADIO REG. 2d 443 (1976) (local newspaper article discussing broadcast); Thomas W. Lippitt, 53 F.C.C.2d 1195 (1975) (newspaper articles and other publications discussing Laetrile "battle"); Thaddeus L. Kowalski, 46 F.C.C.2d 124 (1974) (news coverage of complaint to FCC); Illinois Citizens Comm., 26 F.C.C.2d 373 (1970) (newspaper coverage of license renewal controversies in other cities). Note that the alleged bias of the news media may itself be a controversial issue of public importance. *See* Brandywine-Main Line Radio, Inc., 24 F.C.C.2d 18, 36 n.6 (1970).

74. The Commission's reliance on government attention to tell it when an issue is important seems alien to a doctrine attempting to create a free marketplace of ideas. Debate in a community may concern whether the government should take action on a particular issue. To exclude such an issue from fairness doctrine obligations because it has not been stamped with the seal of government attention in the form of a ballot measure or legislative proposal seems contrary to the doctrine's stated purposes.

75. See text accompanying notes 82–86, *infra*.

76. *Fairness Primer, supra* note 1, at 10416–17.

77. *See* Brandywine-Main Line Radio, Inc., 24 F.C.C.2d 18, 36 n.2 (1970). In the *Report on Editorializing, surpa* note 51, at 1256 par. 18, the FCC offers the example of a "controversial bill pending before the Congress of the United States" to exemplify when fairness balancing would be necessary.

78. Senator Florian W. Chmielewski, 41 F.C.C.2d 201 (1973). *See also* Democratic State Cent. Comm., 19 F.C.C.2d 833 (1968).

79. *See* text accompanying note 55, *supra*.

80. Public Media Center, 59 F.C.C.2d 494, 514-15 par. 37 (1976). In discussing public importance, however, the Commission failed to mention either media coverage or comment by community or government spokesmen as suggested in the 1974 *Fairness Report*. Rather, the social choice involving public safety, potential environmental harm, and insurance considerations made nuclear power and nuclear power plants an issue of public importance. To establish controversiality, the Commission relied on debate between significant community groups, a petition signature drive to place the issue on a statewide referendum ballot, and congressional concern. *Id.* at 495 par. 3.

81. *See, e.g.*, Committee to Elect Jess Unruh Our Next Governor, 25 F.C.C.2d 726, 727 (1970).

82. Interview with Milton Gross, *supra* note 5, Sept. 3, 1975. In its 1974 *Fairness Report*, the Commission states: "If the issue involves a social or political choice, the licensee might well ask himself whether the outcome of that choice will have a significant impact on society or its institutions." *Fairness Report, supra* note 1, at 26376 par. 30. This language appears to temper the case law discussed in notes 83–86, *infra*, in which the FCC declares that, if a political choice involves a voting situation, the issue should be presumed to be controversial and of public importance. The quoted language may mean that, where a measure is subject to popular vote, an inquiry is necessary only to rule out unusual situations, and the decision to rule out must run upstream against a presumption of controversiality and public importance.

83. Ted Bullard, 23 F.C.C.2d 41, 43 (1970). The Commission continued: "It is precisely within the context of an election that the fairness doctrine can be best utilized to inform the public of the existence of and basis for contrasting viewpoints on an issue about which there must be a public resolution through the election process." *Id.* No explanation is given of the "unusual circumstances" in which an election issue would not require fairness treatment. Since the Commission in *Bullard* goes on to discuss controversy in the community over the school levy, presumably one such circumstance might be where no controversy surrounded a ballot issue. Another might be found where the issue involved had no significant impact on the community. See note 82, *supra*. These circumstances both directly contradict what is presumed when an issue is reflected in a ballot measure—that the issue is controversial and important because of its significant impact on the community.

84. Lincoln Smith, 23 F.C.C.2d 45 (1970). *See also* Citizens for Responsible Gov't, 25 F.C.C.2d 73 (1970) (vote on a city charter is a controversial issue of public importance); Dowie A. Crittenden, 18 F.C.C.2d 499 (1969) (assumed sub silentio that advocating placing voter district incorporation issue on ballot is advocacy of controversial issue of public importance).

85. Richard B. Kay, 24 F.C.C.2d 426 (1970), *aff'd*, 443 F.2d 638 (D.C. Cir. 1970).

86. Timothy K. Ford, 57 F.C.C.2d 1208 (1976) (assumed sub silentio to be a controversial issue of public importance). *See also* Public Media Center, 59 F.C.C.2d 494, 514 (1976) (signature petition effort to place nuclear power issue on statewide referendum cited to

indicate issue was a controversial issue of public importance); Miami Beach Betterment Ass'n, 27 F.C.C.2d 350 (1971) (advisory referendum on legalized gambling).

87. The 1974 *Fairness Report* states that the fairness doctrine was not created to provide "a forum for the discussion of mere private disputes of no consequence to the general public."*Fairness Report, supra* note 1, at 26376 n.11. Line-drawing between public and private disputes can become difficult, however.

88. Women Strike for Peace, 25 F.C.C.2d 890 (1970).

89. Lincoln County Broadcasters, Inc., 51 F.C.C.2d 65 (1975). This case is unusual in that the licensee claimed that the matter it broadcast was of public interest and not a private dispute. *Id.* at 68. It claimed to have offered reply time on the issue and thus to have obeyed the fairness doctrine, but the Commission disagreed, ruling that the licensee had used its station to further its private interests in the dispute. *Id.* at 69.

90. National Football League Players Ass'n, 39 F.C.C.2d 429 (1973).

91. Mary Sinclair, 26 F.C.C.2d 594 (1970).

92. Spartan Broadcasting Co., 33 F.C.C.2d 765 (1962). *See also* Cullman Broadcasting Co., 40 F.C.C. 576 (1963). Note that with respect to national issues the job of determining which issues need balanced treatment may become particularly difficult. If the licensee cannot exclude such issues from fairness treatment due to the lack of controversy and debate in its local service area, then it must presumably look to controversy and debate on the national level. In all likelihood every national issue will have received media coverage and be the subject of comment by national leaders or government officials. Does every national issue then require balancing? Does the decision come down to the question of impact on the local service area, or does impact on the national polity satisfy the "community impact" requirements of the 1974 *Fairness Report?* The Commission has not supplied answers to such questions. In fact, the Commission has added to the confusion by making the remarkable statement that a licensee could not avoid its fairness obligations "on the ground that members of the general public had little knowledge of the subject and hence were not engaged in any discussion of or debate on that issue." Accuracy in Media, Inc., 40 F.C.C.2d 958, 966 (1973). What relevance do the precedents and 1974 *Fairness Report* have in helping to define controversy in terms of vigorous debate and news media coverage if "discussion or debate" on the issue is immaterial?

93. For cases indicating that a fairness complainant may show an issue to be controversial and of public importance either in the local service area *or* nationally, *see* Honorable M. Gene Snyder, 49 F.C.C.2d 493 (1974); Diocesan Union of Holy Name Societies, 41 F.C.C.2d 297 (1973).

94. *See* cases cited in notes 92–93, *supra*. Of course, if an issue is controversial and important locally but not nationally, contrasting viewpoints must still be presented. *See* United People, 32 F.C.C.2d 124 (1971).

95. Committee to Elect Jess Unruh Our Next Governor, 25 F.C.C.2d 726 (1970). *See also* Media Access Project, 44 F.C.C.2d 755 (1973).

96. J.F. Branigan, 31 F.C.C.2d 490, 491 (1971).

97. *Id.*

98. Miss Geri Tully, 6 P & F RADIO REG. 123 (1975). In this case, however, the FCC fails to indicate whether it has concluded that United States policy is not directly involved or that the licensee has adequately balanced its Israel coverage. *Compare* J. Allan Carr, 30 F.C.C.2d 894 (1971), where the Commission stated, without further explanation, that "when the Arab-Israeli conflict involves the question of U.S. relations with respect to Israel and the Arab countries, that question is clearly a controversial issue of public importance in this country." *Id.* at 896; *accord* Federated Organizations on Am.-Arab Relations, 30 F.C.C.2d 892 (1971).

99. *Branigan* and *Tully,* discussed in notes 96, 98 and accompanying text, *supra,* apparently conflict with at least one part of Brandywine-Main Line Radio, Inc., 24 F.C.C.2d 18, 36 n.4 (1970), in which the Commission held that a broadcaster's stance "favoring the separatist government of Rhodesia" involved a controversial issue of public importance. The Commission did not note any connection between the internal Rhodesian problems and United States foreign policy.

100. *See* cases cited in note 61, *supra.*

101. Cullman Broadcasting Co., 40 F.C.C.2d 576 (1963).

102. Accuracy in Media, Inc., 51 F.C.C.2d 219 (1974) (complainant had not satisfied burden of showing that a controversial issue of public importance existed at time of broadcast, a little more than a month after the Allende overthrow).

103. For further discussion of the foreign affairs dilemma, see Comment, *The Regulation of Competing First Amendment Rights: A New Fairness Doctrine Balance after CBS?* 122 U. PA. L. REV. 1283, 1300-01 (1974).

104. *Report on Editorializing, supra* note 51, at 1250 par. 7.

105. *Fairness Report, supra* note 1, at 26376 par. 31.

106. 40 F.C.C.2d 958 (1973), *application for review denied,* 44 F.C.C.2d 1027 (1974), *rev'd sub nom.* National Broadcasting Co. v. FCC, 516 F.2d 1101, *reversal vacated and rehearing en banc granted,* 516 F.2d 1155, *rehearing en banc vacated,* 516 F.2d 1156, *second reversal vacated as moot and remanded with direction to vacate initial order and dismiss complaint,* 516 F.2d 1180 (D.C. Cir. 1974).

107. *E.g.,* "The pension system is essentially a consumer fraud"; "I think it's a terrible thing in this country where men who work forty-five years have to eat yesterday's bread." 516 F.2d at 1134.

108. *Id.* at 1135.

109. During a discussion of specific plans, individuals also made statements of a more general nature: "Pensions in the private area are a mockery. They're a national disgrace." *Id.* at 1141. "Pension funds have outgrown the laws regulating them." *Id.* at 1144.

110. *Id.* at 1145.

111. *Id.* at 1146.

112. 40 F.C.C.2d at 963. The complainant also alleged that the documentary had omitted various facts, thus presenting "distorted" and "inaccurate" information. The FCC rejected these allegations of "deliberate distortion and slanting," indicating that without extrinsic evidence of such activity it would not investigate or consider such complaints. *Id.* at 962.

113. *Id.* at 963.

114. *Id.* at 965. This was the "first case" in which a broadcaster had "been held in violation of the fairness doctrine for the broadcasting of an investigative news documentary that presented a serious social problem." 516 F.2d at 1125. Some feared that *"Pensions* may well mark the beginning of a more interventionist stance by the FCC in the area of program content." Note, *Radio and Television—Fairness Doctrine—Network Documentary Presenting Only One Side of a Controversial Issue of Public Importance Violates the Fairness Doctrine,* 52 TEXAS L. REV. 797, 805 (1974). *See also* Bagdikian, *Pensions: The FCC's Dangerous Decision Against NBC,* COLUM. JOURNALISM REV. March/April 1974, at 16, 18.

115. 40 F.C.C.2d at 966.

116. *Id.* at 968. The Commission did not elaborate on its remarkable statement that a licensee could not avoid its fairness obligations "on the ground that members of the general public had little knowledge of the subject and hence were not engaged in any discussion of or debate on that issue." *Id.* at 966. Such statements complicate the application of the fairness doctrine by suggesting that an issue need not be controversial on a local *or* a national basis, *i.e.,* not controversial among the "general public," to require fairness balancing. See note 92, *supra.*

117. 40 F.C.C.2d at 967.

118. 44 F.C.C.2d at 1045.

119. 516 F.2d at 1117-18. The FCC staff had made the mistake of saying that because *it* had found that the program raised the entire pension plan issue, NBC's contrary judgment could not be reasonable. The Commission recognized the broadcaster's discretion to make reasonable good faith judgments as to its fairness doctrine responsibilities, but it indicated that such discretion is not unlimited. 44 F.C.C.2d at 1034-35.

120. 516 F.2d at 1117-22. The court summarized the legal standard to be used by the FCC in reviewing a licensee's "issue raised" decision: "A substantial burden must be overcome before the FCC can say there has been an unreasonable exercise of journalistic discretion in a licensee's determination as to the scope of issues presented in the program. Where,

as here, the underlying problem is the thrust of the program and the nature of its message, whether a controversial issue of public importance is involved presents not a question of simple physical fact, like temperature, but rather a composite editorial and communications judgment concerning the nature of the program and its perception by viewers. In the absence of extrinsic evidence that the licensee's characterization to the Commission was not made in good faith, the burden of demonstrating that the licensee's judgment was unreasonable to the point of abuse of discretion requires a determination that reasonable men viewing the program would not have concluded that its subject was as described by the licensee." *Id.* at 1121 (footnote omitted). The court added that, where specific personal attack and political editorializing rules are involved, the Commission has a "more ample role." But in reviewing the "general obligation concerning controversial issues of public importance," the FCC had to rely on a licensee's journalistic discretion and correct only for "*abuse* of discretion." *Id.* at 1120 (emphasis in original).

121. *Id.* at 1122.

122. *Id.* at 1125–32. After the case was initially decided on September 27, 1974, the court ordered on December 13, 1974, that the case be reheard en banc and that the decision of September 27 be vacated. *Id.* at 1155. After considering the FCC's suggestion of mootness, on March 18, 1975, the court vacated its December 13 order for rehearing en banc and reinstated the initial decision. The court then referred the question of mootness to the panel of judges that had rendered the initial decision. *Id.* at 1156. The panel, per Judge Fahy, remanded the case to the FCC on July 11, 1975, and ordered the FCC to vacate its original order and dismiss the complaint. *Id.* at 1180. The three judges on the panel, however, did not agree on the grounds for remanding the case. Judge Fahy based his vote for remand on the equity powers of the court, *id.*, and Judge Tamm, noting that the relevant congressional pension legislation had already been passed, based his vote on mootness, *id.* at 1184. Judge Leventhal dissented from the order to remand the case. However, he agreed that, if the case was to be remanded, then remand should not be based on mootness, as Judge Tamm suggested, but on the equitable principles suggested by Judge Fahy. *Id.* at 1201.

123. Chief Judge Bazelon was not a member of the panel of three judges that originally heard the case; his thorough and incisive dissent was actually made in reaction to the court's order vacating its decision to hear the case en banc. *Id.* at 1156. Judge Tamm was a member of the panel and did dissent from its decision. *Id.* at 1153. But the bulk of his views were contained in an expansion of his opinion on remanding the case to the Commission. *Id.* at 1184.

124. 44 F.C.C.2d at 1040.

125. As an analytical aid, the court also gave much weight to the comments of print media columnists who reviewed the documentary. The court used a few brief excerpts from reviewers characterizing the program as a study of problems with "some pension plans" to indicate that NBC was not unreasonable in its description of the issue raised. *Id.* at 1126–27. Thus, print media comment, in addition to helping define whether an issue is controversial and of public importance, now may play a part in defining what issue is raised by a broadcast. Judge Tamm expressed skepticism about the court's reliance on such excerpts prepared by a licensee. *Id.* at 1189. If the excerpts were to be relied on, it should be noted that there were even more excerpts that described the program as focusing on problems with the overall pension industry. *See, e.g.,* excerpts from the Chicago Sun-Times, *id.* at 1147.

126. *See id.* at 1160–62 (Bazelon, C.J., dissenting opinion).

127. *Id.* at 1163.

128. The court's distortion is further exemplified by its discounting of comments by various people that addressed overall performance. The court stated that these comments were really comments on subissues of overall performance, subissues that had not been shown to be controversial or of public importance. But the Commission had explicitly refused to break the overall performance issue into subissues, and these comments should have been seen as comments on the issue of overall performance. *See id.* at 1162–63. The court's treatment of these comments as subissues was inconsistent with the FCC precedent that had consistently refused to recognize the raising of subissues. Chief Judge Bazelon remarked: "Once this concept of inseparability is recognized, all the statements in the

broadcast relating to the overall need for reform must be considered as comments on the controversial issue defined by the Commission." *Id.* at 1166.

129. *See id.* at 1147–51.

130. 44 F.C.C.2d at 1034 n.3. The court's reliance on NBC's assertion that there was no meaningful opposition to reform legislation seems misplaced, since it is a standard legislative practice for interest groups opposed to legislative action to suppart weak legislation as an alternative to a statute that will bring significant reform. Also hearings are often arranged so that only supporters of legislation testify.

131. *See* Healey v. FCC, 460 F.2d 917, 921–22 (D.C. Cir. 1972). In this case, however, the court did not rule that the broadcast specifically raised the three subissues suggested in the pleadings; it only indicated that, even if two of the three subissues had been raised, there was no substantiation of whether the licensees' overall programming was unfair with respect to those two. *See also* Green v. FCC, 447 F.2d 323, 329–32 (D.C. Cir. 1971). *Green* may be distinguished in that it dealt with subissues that were "implicit" in military recruitment ads and that could only be raised by a process of viewer association with the ad, as opposed to subissues that are "explicitly" raised in a broadcast. But for purposes of analysis the court did consider the five implicit subissues separately, and for four of them ruled that unfair overall programming coverage had not been demonstrated.

132. 516 F.2d at 1191.

133. The decision considerably limits the ability of the Commission to rule that licensees' judgments on the issue raised and whether it is controversial and of public importance are unreasonable under the fairness doctrine. Although the decision of the panel to vacate its initial judgment, *see* note 122, *supra,* means that the decision technically is not binding precedent, it does indicate the thinking of at least two judges on the court of appeals and will undoubtedly influence the FCC.

134. Interview with Marshall Wellborn, Assistant General Attorney, and Russell Tornabene, Public Relations, NBC, by Steven J. Simmons, Aug. 26, 1975.

135. *See* Cullman Broadcasting Co., 40 F.C.C. 576 (1963).

136. As noted in Chapter Five, pp. 124–25, in one fairness case that the local TV licensee eventually won, it reported spending $20,000 in legal expenses in addition to other expenses, such as travel. Even more detrimental in the licensee's view was the estimated 480 man-hours of executive and supervisory time spent on the matter. *See* HENRY GELLER, THE FAIRNESS DOCTRINE IN BROADCASTING, 40–43, 133–34 (Rand R–1412 FF, Dec. 1973).

137. Red Lion Broadcasting Co. v. FCC, 395 U.S. 367, 390 (1969).

138. United States v. Paramount Pictures, Inc., 334 U.S. 131 (1948).

139. See Chapter Seven, pp. 225–27.

140. Green v. FCC, 447 F.2d 323, 329 (D.C. Cir. 1971) (emphasis in original), quoted in Representative Patsy Mink, 59 F.C.C.2d 987, 993 (1976). *See also* Columbia Broadcasting Sys., Inc. v. Democratic Nat'l Comm., 412 U.S. 94, 129–30 (1973); *Report on Editorializing, supra* note 51, at 1249 par. 6.

141. Interview with Commissioner Glen Robinson by Steven J. Simmons, Sept. 3, 1975.

142. *See, e.g., Renewal of Standard Broadcast Station Licenses,* 7 F.C.C.2d 122 (1967). *See also Broadcast Licenses for Ark., La., & Miss.,* 42 F.C.C.2d 3, 16–22 (1973); *Renewal of Standard Broadcast & Television Licenses for Okla., Kan., & Neb.,* 14 F.C.C.2d 2, 12–13 (1968); Herman C. Hall, 11 F.C.C.2d 344 (1968).

143. Kurnit, *Enforcing the Obligation to Present Controversial Issues: The Forgotten Half of the Fairness Doctrine,* 10 HARV. CIV. LIB.-CIV. RIGHTS L. REV. 137 (1975).

144. 3 FEDERAL RADIO COMMISSION THIRD ANNUAL REPORT 32 (1929).

145. 8 F.C.C. 333 (1941).

146. 10 F.C.C. 515 (1945).

147. FCC, PUBLIC SERVICE RESPONSIBILITY OF BROADCAST LICENSEES (1946).

148. *See, e.g.,* Columbia Broadcasting Sys., Inc. v. Democratic Nat'l Comm., 412 U.S. 94, 111, 129–30 (1973); Red Lion Broadcasting Co. v. FCC, 395 U.S. 367, 369, 377 (1969); 1974 *Fairness Report, supra* note 1, at 26375 pars. 23–26. However, the Commission has contributed to the lack of awareness about the part one obligation and caused confusion by

occasionally speaking about the doctrine in terms of only part two obligations. *See, e.g.,* the unclear description in the introduction to the important 1964 *Fairness Primer, supra* note 52, at 10416.

149. 24 F.C.C.2d 743 (1970), *rev'd on other grounds,* 449 F.2d 1164 (D.C. Cir. 1971).

150. 24 F.C.C.2d at 750 (emphasis added).

151. *Id.* at 747 (emphasis added).

152. *Id.* at 750–51.

153. 1974 *Fairness Report, supra* note 1, at 26375 par. 23.

154. *Id.* at par. 25 (emphasis added).

155. 49 F.C.C.2d 27, *application for review denied,* 50 F.C.C.2d 395 (1974).

156. Fairness Doctrine Complaint: License Renewal Act of 1974, submitted by Marsha Lynn Jones & Tracy A. Westen, for Public Communications, Inc., to William B. Ray, Chief of the FCC's Complaints and Compliance Division (Aug. 29, 1974).

157. *Id.* at 29.

158. The complaint noted the lack of coverage by nonbroadcast industry media, but emphasized the self-interest motivations of "many licensees, the networks, and the many newspaper owners with television holdings" in not covering the legislation, and argued that lack of such media coverage by itself was not determinative. *Id.* at 26–27.

159. See text accompanying notes 54–55, *supra.*

160. 50 F.C.C.2d at 399.

161. *Id.*

162. *Id.* at 400.

163. *Id.* The Commission continued: "If the complainant's argument on this point were correct, any issue which might be controversial and important enough to require presentation of contrasting viewpoints *once the licensee had made the initial decision to present programming on the issue,* would also automatically be 'so critical or of such great public importance' that the licensee would have had an obligation to present initial programming on that issue." *Id.* (emphasis in original).

164. *Id.*

165. For a later case, see Council on Children, Media, & Merchandising, 59 F.C.C.2d 448 (1976) (children's advertising and its effects are not critical or of great public importance).

166. 59 F.C.C.2d 987 (1976).

167. Although the station did broadcast a tape from another congressman who was opposed to uncontrolled strip mining, the Commission found that neither strip mining legislation nor the environmental impact of strip mining were discussed on the tape. *Id.* at 996.

168. *Id.* at 987–88.

169. *Id.* at 991 (emphasis in original).

170. *Id.* at 989.

171. *Id.* at 995.

172. *Id.* at 994.

173. *Id.*

174. *Id.* at 997.

175. *Id.* at 995.

176. *Id.* at 991–92.

177. *Id.* at 995–97.

178. *Id.* at 987.

179. *Id.* (emphasis in original).

180. *Id.* at 996 n.2.

181. *Id.* at 998 n.1 (concurring statement of Commissioner Robinson) (emphasis in original). Robinson concludes, however, that "the first and second obligations differ more in degree than in kind. Enforcement of either obligation requires us to scrutinize licensee judgment, . . . compelling a licensee to carry some program which it has chosen not to air." *Id.* Yet, the part one cases offer no rationale for evaluating licensee treatment of issues differently from the evaluation done in part two cases.

182. See Chapter Seven, pp. 194-205.

183. In large part, the issue problems noted above are the inevitable result of the government's attempt to second-guess broadcasters' editorial judgments. What is needed is a delicate balancing between the rights of broadcast journalists to exercise their freedom of press and speech as they see fit, and the right of the public to a diversity of opinion on important public matters. This right of the public to hear a diversity of views is crucial. Ultimate good, according to Justice Holmes, "is better reached by free trade in ideas—that the best test of truth is the power of the thought to get itself accepted in the competition of the market, and that truth is the only ground upon which [the people's] wishes may safely be carried out. That at any rate is the theory of our Constitution." Abrams v. United States, 250 U.S. 616, 630 (1919) (Holmes, J., dissenting). Presently, however, the field upon which the airwave marketplace transacts business is walled. The large networks and powerful television licensees determine the list of ideological players. Other countries have kept this scarce broadcasting privilege and power under government control. In the United States, this power has been granted free of charge to private entities for private profit.

184. BROADCASTING, Nov. 22, 1976, at 20.

185. An exception to dropping the part two balancing requirement should be made for explicit licensee editorials. See Chapter Seven, pp. 223-24.

186. As long as the FCC continues to ensure that licensees "afford reasonable opportunity for discussion of conflicting views on issues of public importance," 47 U.S.C. sec. 315(a) (1970), it will be in accord with the statutory mandate. The proposals outlined in the next chapter would provide such a "reasonable opportunity." A complete elimination of the fairness doctrine without any alternative scheme to fulfill the legislative goal would raise statutory compliance problems.

7
The "Unfairness Doctrine" —Balance and Response Over the Airwaves

The development of the fairness doctrine was based on noble objectives. It was predicated on the asserted scarcity of the airwave resource, on public ownership of that resource, and on the federal government's award of an airwave frequency to a licensee relatively free of charge. The doctrine was an attempt to ensure that the American public receives a supply of diverse information on important public issues essential to democratic government, that broadcasters do not selfishly use their powerful monopoly positions to further only their own views, and that various parties have access, in a general way, to the airwaves to communicate their differing points of view.[1]

Despite these noble objectives the doctrine has taken on an "unfairness" quality. Because of the competing interests it must resolve and the way it has been administered, the doctrine has been unfair to the public, to broadcasters, to parties seeking access to the media, and ironically, to the Federal Communications Commission (FCC) itself.

Three critical questions that have been at the center of fairness doctrine activity are: (1) What issue has been raised in a broadcast that may require response under part two of the doctrine;[2] (2) is that issue "controversial and of public importance";[3] and (3) what issues must be covered under part one of the doctrine?[4] The difficulties encountered in resolving these important questions were discussed at length in Chapter Six.

But suppose these questions have been resolved. Suppose, in the typical part two case,[5] the issue has been specified and the licensee has determined it is a controversial issue of public importance. What must a licensee do to ensure presentation of contrasting viewpoints on the issue? When are its efforts in this regard considered reasonable by the FCC?

This chapter confronts these questions. FCC case law and policy guidelines for determining which contrasting viewpoints and spokesmen must be aired are first critically analyzed. Problems involved in FCC decisions on how licensees are to balance formats, total time, frequency of broadcast, and time of day between contrasting speakers' presentations are explored next. The administrative problems involved in trying to deal with balance problems, including stop-watch and elapse time concerns, and cases illustrating how administration of licensees' balance obligations may be counterproductive and harmful to the public interest, are then addressed. The next two sections focus on the Commission's less-than-vigorous enforcement record and the potential for abuse of any enforcement under the doctrine as it presently exists. The chapter concludes with an examination of how the doctrine has resulted in unfairness and a proposal for change that will mitigate many of the doctrine's detrimental effects.

I. OVERALL PROGRAMMING

A critical concept, and one that is often overlooked by fairness doctrine complainants, is that the licensee's fairness is ordinarily judged on the basis of its overall programming, not on the basis of any one show.[6] A single documentary or a particular editorial may be totally biased toward one point of view on an issue. This does not amount to a violation of the fairness doctrine if, in other programming, the licensee has presented a reasonable balance of contrasting viewpoints. The Commission insists that fairness complainants substantiate that contrasting viewpoints have not been presented in a licensee's total programming.[7]

The licensee cannot avoid its overall balancing obligation by pointing a finger at the networks. Even if an initial biased viewpoint was presented on a network program, it is the licensee's ultimate responsibility to ensure balance.[8] The FCC's determinations on how to ensure balance, however, are typically vague, inconsistent, and at times ill advised.

II. THE CONTRASTING VIEWPOINT

If one side of a controversial public issue has been aired, the licensee must determine which contrasting viewpoint is to be pre-

sented. Although the Commission sensibly declared in its 1974
Fairness Report that for many issues a variety of contrasting viewpoints may need broadcast coverage,[9] it has never found a licensee
unreasonable for presenting only two viewpoints.[10] In fact, the
Commission has reinforced the "two viewpoint" perspective by frequently referring to the licensee's obligation to present "both" sides
of issues[11] instead of "contrasting sides."[12] Given the complexity of
many controversial issues of public importance and the obvious
truth of the *Fairness Report*'s declaration, the FCC's reinforcement
of a licensee's bipolar orientation appears antithetical to the doctrine's stated objective of informing the American public.

In outlining which contrasting viewpoints must be aired, the
Commission has clearly stressed only "major viewpoints and shades
of opinion."[13] Although the FCC has declared that a licensee cannot keep a viewpoint off the air simply because it disagrees with that
view,[14] the Commission will not require the "coverage of every
possible viewpoint or shade of opinion regardless of its significance."[15] In deciding which shades of opinion are to be presented in
a reply broadcast, licensees are to look to the standard utilized in
determining which political parties or candidates are to be covered
under the fairness doctrine. That standard, set forth in *Lawrence
M.C. Smith*[16] in the vaguest of terms, calls for "a good faith judgment" about whether there is a need or interest in the community in
hearing the candidate or party, and if so, the extent of that need.
The enforcement effect of the standard was demonstrated in 1972
when Dr. Benjamin Spock, who was nominated as a presidential
candidate at a national convention by the People's Party and appeared on the ballot in ten states, attempted to get air time via a
fairness complaint to the FCC. Despite the facts that Spock was a
significant minority candidate,[17] that during the last three critical
weeks of the campaign not one of the three national networks gave
Spock a second of air time, and that massive coverage had been
given to Richard Nixon and George McGovern, the Commission
ruled that there was not enough evidence to show a fairness doctrine
violation.[18]

In essence, the standard gives great discretion to the licensee
to determine what contrasting viewpoint is important enough to
merit reply time and reinforces the notion that only major opinions
need be presented. Nonestablishment, minority viewpoints—no
matter what their worth—simply do not need airing. And even if

there are a number of major "establishment" viewpoints on an issue, the licensee will probably be safe from reprimand if it presents only two.

III. THE REPLY SPOKESMAN

The question of which contrasting viewpoint must be presented is directly linked to the question of how spokesmen are to be selected to present that viewpoint. Licensees cannot simply sit back and follow a policy of not refusing to broadcast reply viewpoints when reply time is demanded. The Commission has stated emphatically that licensees have an obligation to actively and affirmatively encourage the presentation of contrasting viewpoints.[19] In the 1974 *Fairness Report*[20] the Commission reaffirmed its *Cullman* doctrine,[21] first enunciated in 1963, that if paid sponsorship is unavailable to support presentation of a contrasting viewpoint, an otherwise acceptable reply spokesman cannot be rejected for lack of funds to pay for his or her presentation. It is more important to leave the public informed than to leave the licensee's pocket full.

Except in personal attack, political editorial, and *Zapple* situations,[22] the Commission has not set down a specific formula for how broadcasters should find a spokesman and who that spokesman should be.[23] It has left this implementation strategy to the good faith, reasonable discretion of licensees.[24] No specific individual, group, or organization has any "right" to be the reply spokesman presenting a contrasting view to one that has already been broadcast.[25] The broadcaster, although not compelled to, may present the contrasting view or views itself.[26] However, the Commission has warned that licensees must take reasonable steps to ensure "presentations by genuine partisans who actually believe in what they are saying,"[27] and cannot "stack the cards" toward one point of view in selecting spokesmen.[28]

Although the Commission has used forceful rhetoric to emphasize a licensee's obligation to pursue the search for a contrasting spokesman vigorously,[29] it has in the past been satisfied with less-than-vigorous efforts. Simple over-the-air announcements inviting responsible reply speakers to air their views have been deemed sufficient.[30] In the *Fairness Report*, the Commission appeared to stiffen these solicitation requirements. It declared that there may be occasions, especially where "major issues" are "discussed in depth," when a licensee will have to demonstrate that it made "specific offers of response time to appropriate individuals in addition to general over-the-air announcements."[31] However, the year before, in *Ronald E. Boyer*,[32] the Commission had been satisfied with only over-the-air announcements by a licensee who had presented one side of a county government pay raise issue in more than fifty five-minute editorials spread over a two-week period. The 1974 *Fairness Report*'s new mandate has yet to be enforced.

The Commission has held that, when a spokesman offers to make a reply presentation to a viewpoint already broadcast and the licensee rejects that spokesman as inappropriate, more intensive solicitation efforts must be undertaken. In this situation, over-the-air announcements are not enough, and specific offers to other parties must be made.[33] However, if the over-the-air announcements and specific offers do not elicit a responsible reply spokesman, the licensee need not present any contrasting viewpoint.[34] This is so even if the broadcaster's side of the issue is presented in a number of different broadcasts.[35] The Commission has also held that if an appropriate reply spokesman is chosen by a commercial licensee, it is still reasonable for the licensee not to supply him with a tape or transcript of the original broadcast.[36]

The FCC has reversed itself in judging the amount of effort required of licensees to assure presentation of contrasting viewpoints when the licensee has a personal or financial interest in the issue. A number of cases had held that a more extensive attempt would have to be made than in the ordinary fairness situation to ensure fairness.[37] As late as 1971 the Commission indicated that "licensees who editorialize on matters of personal concern which involve controversial issues of public importance should exercise extraordinary diligence to achieve fairness."[38] However, cases in the mid-1970s changed this policy. The Commission's standard of review presently remains the same in all fairness cases and does not vary if a licensee has a financial or other personal interest in a conltroversial issue of public importance.[39] The same degree of reasonableness and good faith is demanded of all licensees, and the initial burden of proof remains with the fairness complainant.[40]

IV. THE BALANCE–FORMAT DYNAMIC

Nowhere under the fairness doctrine is the licensee's discretion more apparent than in its capacity to determine the timing balance afforded to contrasting viewpoints and the format in which those viewpoints will be presented. The Commission has set some parameters, but even these are wide, allowing licensees a large amount of scheduling freedom.

It has already been noted that a licensee need not present contrasting viewpoints in the same broadcast, or even in the same series of programs.[41] The FCC has also declared that the licensee may determine the format for presenting contrasting views, including the techniques of production and presentation.[42] In *Boalt Hall Student Association,*[43] for example, the complainants argued that the only fair way for them to respond to California Governor Ronald Reagan's 30-minute, uninterrupted broadcast of his views on campus unrest was to have a comparable uninterrupted period of time. The Commission disagreed, stating that it was reasonable for the licensee to present the complainants' or other parties' contrasting views in question-and-answer formats, in standard editorials, or in features and news stories. Other parties attempting to secure a format allowing uninterrupted presentations of their views to balance the uninterrupted presentation of the telegenic and articulate Governor fared no better than the *Boalt* complainants.[44] Contrasting viewpoints to standard television station editorials ordinarily may be presented as items on news shows or as part of interview shows.[45] Spot announcements do not have to be balanced with other spot announcements.[46] Licensees may also delete and edit material offered by contrasting spokesmen before it is aired.[47]

There are some format limits beyond which licensees cannot "reasonably" go. When contrasting viewpoints are presented, they must not be presented in a hostile atmosphere, as in a phone-in show where the moderator encourages callers to ridicule the views of previous callers,[48] or where the moderator harasses callers with whom he disagrees by such techniques as cutting them off and insulting them.[49] A moderator for an interview program cannot interrupt with hostile questions a guest whose views he does not share, and allow those interviewees with whom he agrees to speak without interruption.[50] A licensee may not set down conditions for a reply spokesman that unreasonably censor that spokesman, such as requiring that his comments not subject any party to ridicule, not contain personal attacks, and not create further fairness doctrine obligations.[51] Presenting contrasting viewpoints in a brief news item where station staff merely categorize the reasons for opposing a particular ballot measure is not an adequate format for rebutting numerous editorials and a feature program that vigorously supported the measure.[52] Nor can a licensee escape its fairness doctrine obligations by choosing a label for a particular format, such as calling an elected official's talk a "Report to the People."[53] It is the substance of the broadcast that counts, not the label.[54]

Despite these limitations, it should emphasized that, by manipulating format, a licensee can favor one spokesman or viewpoint over another and be deemed reasonable by the FCC. This need not be a deliberate, vindictive effort on the licensee's part. The Commission tells the licensee that it is reasonable if it presents a short interview with a spokesman on one side of the issue and then gives the other side a lengthy and uninterrupted period of broadcast time. The licensee might scrupulously and in good faith follow the law, but the views presented by an interviewee are likely to have far less impact than views presented by a spokesman who can methodically, forcefully, and dramatically present them without interruption. A short documentary, with cameras on location, illustrating one side of an issue may have far more impact than a contrasting spokesman in any studio format.[55] Punchy spot announcements may be far more influential than other types of programming. Yet in these situations balance requirements under the fairness doctrine may be satisfied.

V. BALANCE AND THE 1974 *FAIRNESS REPORT*: TOTAL TIME, FREQUENCY, AND AUDIENCE (TIME OF DAY)

The wide discretion afforded licensees and the difficulty encountered by the FCC in fairness cases are vividly illustrated in the "timing" decisions made by the Commission. Timing decisions are those that determine the amount of time the licensee must devote to contrasting viewpoints, the number of times each viewpoint is to be presented, and the time of day during which the viewpoints must be presented.[56] The key question is: What amounts to a reasonable balance with respect to these three factors?

In its 1974 *Fairness Report,* the Commission reemphasized its long-standing procedure of not setting down any "precise mathematical formula" for the time that should be allocated to contrasting viewpoints; it shunned any "mathematical ratio, such as 3-to-1 or 5-to-1 to be applied in all cases."[57] Privately, the Commissioners reaffirm the lack of exact guidelines in this area. As Benjamin Hooks suggests: "We don't have a written rule." Pointing to the "reasonable man" standard, he states, "Nobody has ever defined that standard with exactitude, and yet we have existed for two hundred years in the courts, using that standard."[58]

Despite the Commission's refusal to set down a precise formula for an appropriate balance it has, as in discussing a controversial issue of public importance, offered some vague indicators of reasonableness. As Milton Gross, Chief of the FCC's Fairness/ Political Branch, states: "You have to look at the entire picture. There's no one thing." But, "time of day, frequency, things like that . . . are taken into consideration."[59]

"Things that are taken into consideration" are discussed in more detail in the *Fairness Report.* Although the popular press and the general public continually confuse fairness requirements with equal time, the licensee clearly is not required to provide equal time for the various points of view under the fairness doctrine.[60] In its most complete statement to date on the timing balance dilemma, the Commission stated:

> While the road to predicting Commission decisions in this area is not fully and completely marked, there are, nevertheless, a number of signposts which should be recognizable to all concerned parties. We have made it clear, for example, that 'it is patently unreasonable for a licensee consistently to present one side in prime time and to relegate the contrasting viewpoint to periods outside prime time. Similarly, there can be an imbalance from the sheer weight on one side as against the other.' . . . This imbalance might be a reflection of the total amount of time afforded to each side, of the frequency with which each side is presented, of the size of the listening audience during the various broadcasts, or of a combination of factors.[61]

Thus, total amount of time devoted to differing viewpoints, frequency of broadcasts, and size of audience (which is related to the time of day of the broadcast) are all elements the Commission says it considers. But the standard is still vague. What division of total time between contrasting sides is too imbalanced? Precisely how much prime time airing of one viewpoint versus non-prime-time broadcasting of another is unreasonable? What frequency comparison is acceptable? The "signposts" in the *Fairness Report* do not offer any answers.[62]

VI. BALANCE AND THE CASE LAW:
TOTAL TIME, FREQUENCY, AND AUDIENCE (TIME OF DAY)

Unfortunately, the FCC case law does not provide much help in determining when opposing viewpoints have been sufficiently balanced. The Commission has steadfastly avoided setting down any "ideal" balance ratio that will be reasonable in every circumstance. The inconsistent, confusing, and sparse guidance offered by the Commission, as well as the wide discretion given licensees, can be seen in *National Broadcasting,*[63] *Public Media Center,*[64] and *Committee for Fair Broadcasting.*[65]

In 1969 in *National Broadcasting* the Commission decided whether a New York television station was in compliance with the *Banzhaf*[66] cigarette decision, which required that anti-cigarette programming be aired to balance pro-cigarette advertising. Despite the fact that the total time devoted to cigarette commercials was five times as great as the total time devoted to anti-smoking messages, the station's overall performance was not deemed deficient.[67] Although the Commission ignored the frequency of broadcasts in making the determination, it did consider audience size. Thus, insufficient anti-cigarette material had been programmed in prime time, when the largest number of viewers had been watching television. The Commission requested that the station take action to correct the prime time imbalance, although absolutely no guidance was given as to how much more prime time programming was necessary. Giving one side of an argument five times as much time to present its view hardly correlates with traditional notions of fairness, and the FCC's ruling gives licensees a great deal of discretion.[68] But a 5 to 1 ratio parameter is better than none at all in offering licensees guidance and complainants a basis to increase airing of contrasting viewpoints.[69]

In *Public Media Center,* decided in 1976, the Commission addressed complaints that thirteen California licensees had aired power company advertisements urging the immediate construction of nuclear power plants and use of nuclear power but did not adequately broadcast contrasting views.[70] The Commission ruled that eight of the licensees had been unreasonable and would have to present additional contrasting programming. Never before had so many stations been found in violation of the fairness doctrine in a single case.

When one looks beneath the apparent enforcement toughness of the FCC in this case, however, it becomes clear that the Commission actually granted licensees wide discretion in terms of frequency of broadcast. Total time division is a far more important signpost than the number of broadcasts on contrasting sides of an issue. Thus radio station KATY,[71] with a nearly equal total time division, was deemed reasonable despite the fact that pro-nuclear broadcasts had been presented 34 times more frequently than anti-nuclear broadcasts. Other stations with close total time division[72] were held reasonable despite frequency variations of 25 to 1,[73] 16 to 1,[74] and 14 to 1.[75]

Focusing on total time comparison ignores the importance of broadcast repetition. Frequency of broadcast is important because a greater audience can be reached, because a more diverse audience can be tapped, since the broadcasts can be made at differing times of day, and because the larger number of broadcasts can be extended over a longer period of time thereby continuously stimulating dialogue in the community. The Commission itself has noted the capacity of frequently repeated spot announcements to have significant impact by reaching huge audiences. In assessing the impact of cigarette commercials, the Commission multiplied the frequency of each commercial times the estimated audience for each to determine the number of "exposures" of the cigarette message to the broadcast audience.[76] Is it fair to allow one side 34 times more broadcast opportunities than another, even if the total time each side is accorded is approximately the same? Obviously, licensees have been granted a very wide berth with respect to balancing the frequency of individual broadcasts. But the major articulated objective of the fairness doctrine is to inform the American public. Therefore, the audience reached—the number of Americans thus informed—theoretically should be a key measure for fairness comparisons. Such lopsided frequency ratios indicate that the FCC has not adequately considered the matter.[77]

The time of day when programming is aired is, of course, also critical to audience-reached considerations. In its sensitivity to broadcasts aired in prime time versus those shown in nonprime time, the Commission seemed concerned about audience-reached in *National Broadcasting.* However, in *Public Media Center* decisions were made about the activity of several licensees without considering prime time programming. Thus, station KVON broadcast 94 spot advertisements, 59 (over 60 percent) of which were aired in prime time.[78] Contrasting views were presented in a one-hour program and five newscasts, none of which was aired in prime time. The approximate 3 to 2 total time ratio and 16 to 1 frequency ratio were regarded as reasonable by the FCC, and it did not even mention the prime time to non-prime-time disparity.

When compared with *National Broadcasting* the total time ratios in *Public Media Center* appear inconsistent. Licensee total time ratios of approximately 3 to 1 were held to be unreasonable in *Public Media Center.* For example, KSRO[79] had a total time ratio of approximately 3 to 1, far below the 5 to 1 ratio held reasonable in *National Broadcasting,* and KSRO's frequency ratio of approximately 8 to 1 was similar to the frequency ratio in *National Broadcasting.* Despite these figures, KSRO's actions were held to be unreasonable.

Just what are the appropriate total time and frequency ratios? What combination of these figures makes a licensee's broadcasting unreasonable? How does prime time programming affect a licensee's judgment? These questions are not answered by *National Broadcasting* and *Public Media Center.* A confusing, and at times contradictory, set of indicators is all that can be extracted.

The 1970 *Committee for Fair Broadcasting* case further confused the situation. Among the complaints in that case were allegations that the commercial television networks had not adequately presented views on the Indochina war issue that contrasted with those expressed by President Nixon in five "prime-time uninterrupted addresses."[80] The networks had presented leading opposing spokesmen discussing views in prime time. ABC and CBS had presented the chairman of the Democratic National Committee, but he had addressed the war issue for only a few minutes. NBC, however, had presented a half-hour prime time presentation in which spokesmen opposed to the war expressed their views, uninterrupted by questions. In comparison with the "prime time" addresses of the

President, NBC's total time ratio on the war issue was approximately 4.4 to 1 (Nixon versus opposing views), and its frequency ratio was 5 to 1 (Nixon versus opposing views). If the other extensive programming on the war were included, such as newscasts, documentaries, and interview shows, which the Commission considered balanced, the total time and frequency ratios would be even smaller.

Despite these figures, the Commission considered all three networks' programming on the war issue unreasonable.[81] It ordered not only that the stations air more views on the war contrasting with those expressed by Nixon, but also that a leading spokesman be given time in an uninterrupted format.[82] Predictably, the Commission refused to specify the length of time to be given to the contrasting spokesman.

The Commission's format decision seems to contradict *Boalt Hall Student Association,* where an uninterrupted format was not deemed important. The total time ratios, at least for NBC, were lower than in *National Broadcasting,* yet the opposite result was reached. NBC's unreasonable frequency ratios were far lower than those considered reasonable in *Public Media Center,* and the concern for prime time programming was not consistently evidenced in prior cases. It should be noted that in subsequent cases the Commission has refused to order reply programming to presidential addresses, as it did in *Committee for Fair Broadcasting.*[83]

This is not to say that the result in *Committee for Fair Broadcasting* was bad for the country. On the contrary, conveying in prime time additional views about a vital public issue to tens of millions of Americans was an extremely valuable contribution to democratic debate. However, major questions remain concerning what is the precedent in this area to guide licensees as well as complainants, whether a government agency should engage in such inconsistent behavior, and whether the government should be involved in such a balancing exercise with broadcasters, who are afforded at least some protection under the First Amendment.

VII. BALANCE: THE ELAPSE TIME DYNAMIC

Another balancing factor that must be considered, and that further complicates the question of whether a licensee has been reasonable, is the length of time that may elapse between the airing of one side of an issue and the airing of the contrasting side. As in other fairness matters, the FCC has refused to set down precise guidelines on what is a reasonable length of elapse time. The Commission has asserted that there is a public interest in receiving "timely information on public issues" and that "[t]imeliness of the licensee's presentation of contrasting viewpoints" is a factor to be considered in "determining the reasonableness of the licensee's handling of an issue."[84] Despite the declared importance of elapse time considerations, the Commission has frequently failed to even mention elapse time, much less seriously consider it in its opinions.[85]

When it has focused on the elapse time question, the Commission has pointed out that the facts surrounding a particular controversy will bear on the licensee's reasonableness. Thus whether contrasting views are presented in "reasonably close proximity" may depend on whether the issue is a "continuing issue, issue of a seasonal nature, one that is to be resolved in a particular election, or a pending item of legislation."[86] The fairness doctrine goal of informing the public would be circumvented if contrasting views were not presented "before the issues become moot."[87] The Commission has gone so far as to recognize that when one viewpoint is broadcast closer to the day of an election, that view may have more impact on the public and is entitled to greater weight in any balancing judgment.[88]

However, when election days are not imminent and the issues are continuing, the FCC has allowed licensees vast discretion in the timing of contrasting view presentation. A six-month interval between broadcasts of contrasting views on sex education in public schools was reasonable,[89] as was a two-year interval between the airing of differing views on nuclear energy.[90]

The elapse time problem becomes even more acute when considered in light of the time it may take the FCC to decide a fairness matter. One detailed study of fairness cases considered by the Commission during the first six months of 1973 found that there was an "average delay of about eight months between broadcast and ruling," and there were a "number of cases in which several years elapsed."[91] Another study, charting six fairness cases ruled on in 1970, revealed an average of seven months between the date of a fairness complaint and the Commission ruling.[92]

In light of the wide elapse time parameters licensees are allowed and the other balancing problems discussed above, one is forced to question the value derived from the balancing part of the fairness doctrine. How many people who see the first presentation of views in an editorial during evening prime time are going to see the broadcast of contrasting views in an early morning interview show several months later? What portion of the original audience will see the second presentation even if it is made in a prime time interview show several months later? Surely only a small percentage. Suppose the opposing views are aired in a reply editorial on the same prime time program at the same time, but three months later? Viewer devotion to a particular show will certainly cause more of the original audience to see the reply editorial, but a sizable number will not. Even if all of the audience that saw the original broadcast see the reply broadcast, what effect would a three-month-old presentation have? Is there a fair basis for comparison? How does one account for the possibility that viewers may simply switch the dial if they do not want to hear particular views?[93]

From this perspective the fairness doctrine may be seen as actually causing unfairness. Its first component demands the airing of views on a controversial public issue. A spokesman may present biased views on a prime time show, say at 7:30 P.M. Viewers hear only that speaker's side of the issue. Three months later the part two component of the doctrine demands a contrasting presentation, which may be in prime time, although several hours later, say at 10:30 P.M. A different audience hears a biased view from the contrasting perspective. Even those persons who have heard the original broadcast may well have forgotten the arguments and facts presented. Where is the fairness? In a sense, the fairness doctrine becomes the unfairness doctrine, allowing biased presentations to different audiences.

Of course, many licensees include contrasting views within the contents of a single show, such as a panel discussion, a news story, or a documentary. If contrasting views are aired in a different show in prime time, as opposed to prime versus nonprime time, the audience carryover is greater. The smaller the elapse time between shows, the more recall viewers will have of the originally presented views.

The only way to ensure absolute fairness would be to require contrasting views to be presented in the same broadcast. Spokesmen of precisely equal vigor, with precisely equal time allotments, would have to be chosen. This would require a degree of interference with licensee freedom that the Commission wisely refuses to undertake. Even this could not assure complete equality, since the impact of spokesmen may differ and the viewers may temporarily leave their sets or turn the dial, missing parts of the arguments. The inherent limitations of any "fairness doctrine" in creating fairness must be realized.

VIII. BALANCE PROBLEMS: STOPWATCHES

Chairman Dean Burch, in a concurring opinion in *Wilderness Society,*[94] offered some insights into the problems of timing balance. In *Wilderness Society* the Commission, after using a stopwatch to find a 2 to 1 total time ratio of pro- to anti-Alaska-pipeline viewpoints,[95] and, without discussing in its decision prime time versus non-prime-time presentations, had concluded that the pipeline issue had been reasonably discussed. Burch, in concurring, stated:

> [T]his involves, first, an examination of the scripts to determine whether the material was pro-pipeline, anti-pipeline, or just neutral background. It then involves either counting lines in the scripts or pulling out the stop-watch to estimate the time afforded each side. (Which assumes, of course, that there are only two sides to the issue—and in this as in most such cases, there may in fact be a multiplicity of "sides" many of which may deserve an airing.) . . . All these figures must also be viewed against the fact that they are constantly changing, in view of NBC's continuing coverage of the issue.[96]

Looking to the previous cases the Chairman asked:

> [W]hat do past Commission precedents tell us about this specific matter? . . . I am forced to conclude that the answer, after twenty years of administration of the doctrine, is . . . "virtually nothing." . . . And I strongly suspect that the issue has not been resolved precisely because it is so thorny. I for one find it impossible to feel very confident or secure about a process that relies on the stopwatch approach —that is, making judgments, and then quantifying the category into

which each presentation falls. And this is only the beginning. There are such additional ramifications as the time and style of the various presentations (does a prime-time spot count two times more heavily than a mid-morning interview? three times? or ten times?), the size and make up of the audience, and (as NBC urges in this case) the relative weight that should be accorded an indirect commercial announcement as against the direct rebuttal that would be afforded under a remedial fairness doctrine ruling. And how do we take into account the fact that a broadcaster, like any good journalist, stays with a hot issue until it's resolved—do we simply adopt an arbitrary cut-off? It might even be argued that we have to consider the dial switching habits of the average viewer—which means that only rarely does he recall where he viewed which side of what controversial issue! The road here could lead to a series of decisions with enough variables and shadings to rival a medieval religious tract. . . . I fear that, under the present circumstances, both licensees and the public can only fall back on prayer to divine the Commission's intent. . . . I believe it markedly serves the public interest, and specifically, the purposes of the First Amendment, to face the issue head on: namely *is* there some workable middle course?[97]

John Eger, a former FCC staff member and later Acting Director of the Office of Telecommunications Policy, provided further perspective:

I was there when we used to take a stop-watch upon a complaint and we would watch a program or listen to it and we would say, "7 minutes pro, 6 minutes con, X minutes neutral." Now if that isn't getting into the broadcasters' knickers, I don't know what is. And it seems to me after 3 years of that . . . , that there was no way of really administering the fairness program on an ad hoc basis that was going to be satisfactory. Because as soon as we did that, someone would say, "Yes, but the fairness doctrine is balanced over a period of time." And they said, "Well get out the old programs." And we'd start counting them. And then we said, well what about the future? Well, we're going to write them and ask them. And there was never a satis-factory way. Furthermore, we used to argue about whether it was 7 minutes or 8 minutes, depending upon what someone thought. . . .[98]

Henry Geller, the noted fairness doctrine commentator, feels that a "middle course," at least in terms of balance ratio, would still be unsatisfactory. According to Geller it seems "inap-propriate for government to be engaged in a stop-watch process where it makes judgments as to positions taken in a presentation with regard to particular issues—for, against or neutral. This can be an editorial process of the most sensitive nature."[99]

The administrative problems in this area do indeed accentuate the very real First Amendment concerns of broadcasters. There is no objective way of determining precisely which format, program, frequency, and total time allocation is the most effective formula for reaching an audience. Advertising agencies and political candidates often have differing television and radio strategies. Any "second guessing" of a broadcaster's judgment in these matters cannot rest on an exact balancing science.[100]

IX. BALANCE DANGERS: A REPUBLICAN REPLY, *ZAPPLE*, AND A CBS NEWS COMPLAINT

The difficulties that may be generated by overzealous FCC involvement in licensees' balancing decisions is seen in an aspect of the *Committee for Fair Broadcasting* case not discussed above.[101] In that case the Commission also ruled on a complaint by the Republican National Committee (RNC) asserting that it was entitled to time to respond to an address by the Chairman of the Democratic National Committee (DNC). The DNC Chairman, Larry O'Brien, had been given time by CBS in a newly conceived "Loyal Opposition" series to respond to speeches of President Nixon and other Republican spokesmen[102] so that CBS could achieve "fairness and balance in the treatment of public issues."[103]

The Commission agreed with the RNC that it was entitled to reply time, relying on the well-known 1970 decision, *Nicholas Zapple*.[104] In *Zapple* the Commission had ruled that, if supporters or spokesmen for a candidate purchase broadcast time in which they discuss their candidate and/or the campaign issues and/or criticize another candidate, then comparable time must be offered spokesmen for the opposing candidate.[105] The *Cullman* free time requirement is not applicable.[106] The Commission saw the *Zapple* ruling as a means to implement the thrust of section 315's equal time rule, which could be thwarted if spokesmen were permitted to urge their candidate's election without a near equal time obligation for opposing spokesmen.[107] Indeed, the "*Zapple* doctrine" has been known as the "quasi-equal opportunities" corollary to the fairness doctrine.[108] It seemed inappropriate to require one campaign to subsidize another under a *Cullman* mandate. Thus *Zapple,* in the context of a political campaign, requires that almost equal balancing ratios be offered[109] to individuals, but comparable payment may be demanded for the reply opportunity.[110] In the Commission's words, *Zapple,* "because it does take into account the policies of Section 315, requires both more (comparable time) and less (no applicability of *Cullman*) than traditional fairness."[111]

According to the FCC[112] in *Committee for Fair Broadcasting,*[113] the Larry O'Brien broadcast on behalf of the Democratic National Committee fell four-square under the requirements of *Zapple,* providing a "political party" corollary to that doctrine.[114] O'Brien had spent only a few minutes addressing the Indochina war issue, which had been the focus of the President's five "prime-time" addresses. Thus the O'Brien talk could not be considered "responsive" to the presidential addresses under the general fairness doctrine.[115] CBS, said the Commission, should have taken steps to ensure that O'Brien concentrated on the war issue to balance out the presidential discussion. Instead, the bulk of O'Brien's remarks had roamed over a variety of issues, from the environment to crime. O'Brien had criticized the Nixon administration's policies, and his comments were "party oriented" not "issue oriented."[116]

In the Commission's view this was a statement by a political party spokesman hoping to benefit his party's candidates, and the RNC, as spokesman for the opposing candidates, would have to be offered comparable time.[117] CBS, which had broadcast the "Loyal Opposition" series to balance the Republican broadcasts with a Democratic viewpoint, ironically was ordered to air more Republican programming. Its plea that the Commission's decision required an unreasonable and unworkable "line-by-line" judgment of whether comments are party oriented or issue oriented was rejected.[118]

The Court of Appeals for the District of Columbia Circuit severely chastised the Commission for such circular reasoning. The court, speaking through Judge Skelly Wright, emphasized that CBS had offered O'Brien time in its "Loyal Opposition" series in an attempt to "achieve a balanced presentation of opposing opinions."[119] After noting that the Commission's decision was inconsistent with one of its recent precedents,[120] the court pointed out that the Commission had "shunned all reliance on the traditional balancing principles of the fairness doctrine," which afforded licensees "wide latitude."[121] In essence, the Commission was providing the Republican Party with "two bites of the apple"—with twice as much opportunity to influence public opinion as its critics had.[122] The "irrational and arbitrary" decision was reversed.[123]

By the time the Court of Appeals had reversed the Commission (over a year after the RNC had filed its first petition demanding reply time), CBS had long since discontinued its "Loyal Opposition" series. The network, faced with the prospect of continually offering the Republicans reply time as mandated by the FCC, and subject to intense political pressure,[124] put its dynamic program "in mothballs and hasn't been heard from since."[125] The FCC's excessive involvement in balancing contrasting viewpoints and its negation of the licensee's judgment contributed to the elimination of a valuable source of contrasting viewpoints on issues of public importance.

The potential for FCC abuse in attempting to determine a reasonable fairness balance is further exemplified in a fairness complaint filed by the American Security Council Education Foundation (ASCEF) against CBS-TV in September 1976.[126] The complaint had its genesis in a statistical analysis of CBS network news programming for 1972 and 1973. The analysis was sponsored and funded by the Institute for American Strategy (IAS), predecessor to ASCEF, and a staunchly anti-Communist organization. A principal mission of the IAS was "to train leaders for the battle against Communism."[127] The complaint, updated with an examination of news, special, and documentary programming in 1975 and May 1976, charges CBS with "virtually boycotting views suggesting that the U.S. is losing or has lost military superiority to the Soviet Union and that a greater effort should be made to strengthen American defenses."[128]

In THE GOOD GUYS, THE BAD GUYS, AND THE FIRST AMENDMENT, Fred Friendly perceptively analyzes the problems with the ASCEF complaint.[129] The IAS study itself was riddled with highly questionable methodological procedures, such as use of a floating center, which resulted in categorizing programming in a biased manner, and reliance on secondary sources for determination of program content.[130] Even assuming the study were valid, the prospect of the FCC grappling with such an extensive statistical study is frightening. This is not the typical fairness situation, where the FCC must examine alleged bias in a limited number of broadcasts, nor is it a situation where the Commission can find combined programming reasonably balanced on a licensee's prima facie showing that various broadcasts presented contrasting viewpoints. Confronted with a documented study challenging every relevant news item, the Commission may be forced into a massive examination of programming content. As Friendly points out, the Commission must first determine what the controversial issue of public importance is for each of the hundreds of items coded in the ASCEF study, and there will be many subjective judgments involved, such as whether space mission coverage is a defense issue. The Commission will then have to assess whether each news snippet is pro, anti, neutral, or some other view toward defense. Then, of course, there must be a judgment on total time ratios, frequency, and time of day for all of these items. Even this analysis can never determine the impact of "a single, two minute sequence of U.S. Marines using cigarette lighters to burn the huts in the villages of Cam Ne in 1965" in comparison with spoken editorials or secondhand news accounts.[131] To be truly fair, all of CBS's programming for the four-year period would have to be analyzed, not just that set forth by ASCEF.[132] The success of any such statistically based complaint would encourage other special interest groups, forever attempting to gain additional news coverage, to conduct their own studies and repeatedly involve the federal government, via the FCC, in second-guessing the news judgments of broadcast journalists who must make decisions based on the news demands of each day.

X. FAIRNESS DOCTRINE ENFORCEMENT PROBLEMS

Despite the wide range of sanctions available to the FCC,[133] fairness enforcement is less than vigorous.[134] Part of the reason is that a complainant has the burden of proof in making a case against a licensee and must outline the seven parts of the fairness complaint.[135] If the seven-pronged prima facie case is not made, a licensee will not even have to respond to a complaint, much less disprove it. As stated in *Allen C. Phelps,*[136] the Commission will not require a licensee to produce "recordings or transcripts of all news programs, editorials, commentaries, and discussion of public issues" based upon "vague and general charges of unfairness." It has held, "Absent detailed and specific evidence of failure to comply with the requirements of the fairness doctrine, it would be unreasonable to require licensees specifically to disprove allegations. . . ."[137] The *Phelps* burden" is a heavy load to carry.

Demonstrating that a licensee has not presented contrasting views in its overall programming is a particularly difficult aspect of a complaint to prove. Since a licensee need not show a complainant transcripts of its public issue programming, theoretically complainants have to spend their waking hours for months and months monitoring a licensee's broadcasts to substantiate that no other view has been presented. Time after time complaints have been rejected for failing to establish imbalance in total programming. In the 1974 *Fairness Report* the Commission, for the first time, stated that a complainant could make a valid claim about overall programming based solely on the "assertion that the complainant is a regular listener or viewer; that is, a person who consistently or as a matter of routine listens to the news, public affairs and other non-entertainment programs carried by the station involved."[138] However, the advantage to a complainant from this policy change was diminished when the Commission in April 1976 asserted that, if a licensee cites specific programming containing contrasting viewpoints, a complainant cannot rest on his or her bare statement of being a regular viewer.[139] Apparently what is required is a total monitoring of a licensee's programming by the complainant, which is nearly impossible, since commercial licensees need not keep transcripts of their public issue programming.[140] Even if a complainant succeeds in proving that a licensee has violated the general fairness doctrine or personal attack rules, the Commission's decisions on whether and how to sanction licensees have been unpredictable.[141]

Complainants may be further discouraged because the FCC has ruled that, even though public complaint is the only way the doctrine is to be enforced, successful complainants are not entitled to reimbursement for attorneys' fees.[142] If a complainant decides to proceed without legal help, he or she will find there are no easy complaint forms to fill out. Moreover, the Commission has not lived up to its promise to compile new fairness primers after its 1964 effort.[143] All the FCC will mail the complainant are copies of such items as the 1974 *Fairness Report* in FEDERAL REGISTER format and jargon. The complainant who goes to the case law for guidance will find an inconsistent and vague set of precedents in almost all aspects of fairness doctrine administration.

The key substantive barrier to the success of a fairness complaint is the FCC's deference to a licensee's judgment. If a licensee's judgment can be said to be reasonable and/or in good faith, it will be upheld. No matter how reasonable the complainant's position is on what issue has been raised in a broadcast, whether the issue is controversial or of public importance, or whether the balance in presentation is reasonable, if the licensee's judgment is contrary but also reasonable, it will be upheld.

The lack of vigorous fairness enforcement can best be seen by examining complaint and ruling figures for the past few years. As indicated in Charts 1 and 2, there has been an explosion of fairness doctrine complaints in the 1970s. In 1960 only 223 complaints or letters connected with fairness doctrine matters were received by the FCC.[144] By fiscal year 1969, the number of complaints had increased to 1,632. The complaint figures did not significantly change until FY 1973, when 2,406 complaints were received. By FY 1975, the figure 3,590 represented more than a 100 percent increase over the 1969 figure, and by FY 1976, the number had risen to 41,861 which represents over 2,500 percent more than the total 1969 complaints.

Particularly striking is the small number of complaints that result in station inquiries, much less rulings adverse to stations.[145] Thus, in FY 1976, just over one-twentieth of 1 percent (approximately .057) of all fairness complaints gave rise to station inquiries —a grand total of 24. There were only 16 adverse fairness rulings that year. In FY 1975 there were only 52 inquiries, or 1.4 percent of complaints, and only 10 (.28 percent of complaints) resulted in adverse rulings. If only general fairness doctrine rulings are considered, there was but 1 adverse ruling out of 3,590 complaints in FY 1975.[146] The situation was similar in FY 1974, with 1,874 complaints resulting in 6 (.32 percent) adverse rulings, including 1 general fairness doctrine adverse ruling.

If the fiscal years 1973 through 1976 are combined, a total of 49,801 fairness complaints received by the Commission resulted in 244 station inquiries (.406 percent of complaints), 54 adverse rulings (.108 percent of complaints), and 16 general fairness doctrine rulings (.0321 percent of complaints). Of every 1,000 complaints received between FY 1973 and FY 1976, approximately 4 resulted in station inquiries, 1 in an adverse ruling, and "⅓ of 1" in a general fairness adverse ruling. The average complainant truly had only about a one in a thousand chance.[147]

The enforcement perspective is brought further into focus when one considers that during these years over 8,900 stations were broadcasting, and all were obligated to obey the fairness doctrine. The majority of these stations broadcast for hundreds of hours each month, and tens of millions of people were reached each day. Surely one of the reasons that fewer than 50,000 complaints were received over a four-year period, and so few prima facie cases were made, was the public's lack of awareness of the fairness doctrine obligations and available remedies.[148]

Further, it should be emphasized that, in terms of enforcement, the doctrine existed only as the part two balancing requirement. Only a handful of complaints were filed concerning part one of the doctrine, and in only one case, *Representative Patsy Mink*,[149] did the Commission rule against a station on a part one complaint. Despite the fact that the part one requirement had been continually stressed in Commission pronouncements since the early 1940s,[150] two out of six FCC Commissioners interviewed in the summer of 1975 did not even include the part one obligation when asked to define the fairness doctrine.[151] Broadcasters have had their licenses renewed after having broadcast little or no public issue programming.[152]

XI. POTENTIAL FOR ABUSE—A DELICATE LINE

Traditionally, the First Amendment has kept government from interfering with the workings of the media. Thus, government restraints on a newspaper's publication plans,[153] government imposition of libel judgments on a major daily newspaper,[154] and a government licensing scheme for films,[155] have all been struck down as incompatible with First Amendment guarantees.

The First Amendment's relationship to the broadcast media, however, has been different. In the famous *Red Lion*

CHART 1

FD=Fairness Doctrine
PA=Personal Attack
PE=Political Editorial
ET=Equal Time

Fairness Doctrine, Equal Time Statistics, FY's 1973-1976

Fiscal Year	No. of FD† Inquiries[3]	No. of ET Inquiries	No. of Complaints FD†	No. of Complaints ET	Station Inquiries Resulting From Complaints FD	Station Inquiries Resulting From Complaints ET	Ratings Adverse to Station FD	PA	PE	ET	Letters of Admonition FD	PA	PE	ET	Forfeitures FD	PA	PE	ET	Other² FD	PA	PE	ET
Fiscal Year: 1976																						
Television[4]	663	201	41,178[5]	2,308																		
Radio: AM	334	127	583	515																		
Radio: FM	154	83	100	280																		
Total: 1976	1,151	411	41,861	3,113	24°	26	10	4	2	8	0	1	0	0	0	3	2	6	10	0	0	2
Fiscal Year: 1975																						
Television	1,307	205	3,016	916																		
Radio: AM	441	178	462	317																		
Radio: FM	197	92	112	122																		
Total: 1975	1,945	475	3,570	1,435	52		1	6	3	4	0	2	2	0	0	3	1	3	1	1	0	1
Fiscal Year: 1974																						
Television	1,150	194	1,304	525																		
Radio: AM	1,206	187	454	368																		
Radio: FM	543	94	111	91																		
Total: 1974	2,899	475	1,874	984	54°		1	5			1	4			1							
Fiscal Year: 1973																						
Television	1,460	583	1,824	2,505																		
Radio: AM	626	382	515	1,648																		
Radio: FM	207	145	67	81																		
Total: 1973	2,293	1,110	2,406	4,234	94°		4	2		7	4	2				7						

The above figures are based on interviews with Milton Gross, Chief, Fairness/Political Branch, Complaints and Compliance Division, Broadcast Bureau, FCC, by Steven J. Simmons, Sept. 3, 9, 1975, Dec. 8, 17, 1976, and a review of available statistics in the FCC ANNUAL REPORTS.

1. Only sanction totals were available. The Complaints and Compliance Division does not keep a separate count for television, radio-AM, radio-FM.

2. Ordinarily, this involves a staff request to the licensee on how it proposes to comply with the fairness doctrine or equal time obligation, or a staff directive to the station to give more time to a particular view or candidate.

3. Ordinarily, inquiries involve requests from the public for more information about the fairness doctrine or equal time obligations.

4. Includes VHF and UHF television figures. Although the vast number of figures concern VHF TV, the Complaints and Compliance Division does not keep a separate VHF-UHF count. There have been fewer than a dozen fairness complaints filed against cable system operators, and these are not included on the chart. Interview with James A. Hudgens and Barry D. Umansky, FCC Cable Television Bureau, by Steven J. Simmons, Sept. 11, 1975.

5. According to the Interview with Milton Gross, Dec. 8, 1976, approximately 36,000 of these complaints concerned the show "Guns of Autumn," requests for spokesmen to air views "combatting" sex and violence, and requests for spokesmen on behalf of decency and morality on TV. Not one prima facie fairness doctrine case was made out of the 36,000 complaints.

*Station inquiry figures for FD and ET are combined, since the Complaints and Compliance Division did not keep a separate count for these years. A large number of ET station inquiries were made and resolved by telephone and are not included, since these figures are not available.

†Includes PA and PE statistics. The Complaints and Compliance Division does not keep a separate count.

CHART 2

Fairness Doctrine, Equal Time Complaint Pattern Prior to FY 1973[1]

Fiscal Year: 1972	Number of Complaints	
	Fairness Doctrine	Equal Time
Television[2]	1,006	804
Radio: AM	506	462
Radio: FM	105	117
Total: 1972	1,617	1,383

Fiscal Year: 1971		
Television	714	585
Radio: AM	365	331
Radio: FM	45	25
Total: 1971	1,124	941

Fiscal Year: 1970		
Television	1,113	347
Radio: AM	562	204
Radio: FM	61	7
Total: 1970	1,736	558

Fiscal Year: 1969		
Television	911	221
Radio: AM	671	125
Radio: FM	50	20
Total: 1969	1,632	366
Calendar Year 1962 Total[3]	850	
Calendar Year 1961 Total[4]	409	
Calendar Year 1960 Total[5]	233	

Figures for Fiscal Years 1969–72 are based on interviews with Milton Gross, Chief, Fairness/Political Branch, Complaints and Compliance Division, Broadcast Bureau, FCC, by Steven J. Simmons, Sept. 3, 9, 1975, Dec. 8, 17, 1976, and a review of available statistics in the FCC ANNUAL REPORTS. Sources for figures in calendar years 1960–62 are indicated on the facing page.

case,[156] the Supreme Court placed the broadcast press in a special category. Broadcasters warranted special treatment due to the exclusive privilege they are accorded by the government to use a scarce airwave frequency that is "owned" by the public. In light of their powerful monopoly of this scarce public resource, the government was justified in imposing greater restrictions on the broadcast press in order to fulfill the First Amendment need of the American people for a diverse supply of information about important public issues. The fairness doctrine and the personal attack and political editorial rules, government policies that would not have been tolerated if imposed on the printed press,[157] were compatible with the First Amendment when applied to the broadcast press.

The scarcity rationale suggested by the Court is open to serious question.[158] If scarcity is viewed as a measure of excluding those who want to broadcast from use of a frequency, it must be noted that there are radio and television frequencies unused and available. FM radio and UHF television are fully subject to the fairness doctrine. According to Martin Levy, Chief of the FCC's Broadcast Facilities Division, "With respect to FM, there are currently 876 'vacant' channel assignments, 237 of which have been applied for. . . . In the top 25 markets . . . there are a total of 34 commercial and 12 educational UHF channels available."[159] Even VHF television and AM radio frequencies are available in some

---

1. The Complaints and Compliance Division does not have station inquiry and adverse ruling figures compiled for years prior to FY 1973, and they are not listed in the Commission's ANNUAL REPORTS.

2. Includes VHF and UHF television figures. Although the vast number of figures concern VHF TV, the Complaints and Compliance Division does not keep a separate VHF-UHF count. There have been fewer than a dozen fairness complaints filed against cable system operators, and these are not included on the chart. Interview with James A. Hudgens and Barry D. Umansky, FCC Cable Television Bureau, by Steven J. Simmons, Sept. 11, 1975.

3. Statement of Hon. E. William Henry, Chairman, FCC, *Hearings of the Subcommittee on Communications and Power of the House Committee on Interstate and Foreign Commerce, on Broadcast Editorializing Practices*, 88th Cong., 1st Sess. 88 (1964). An additional 2,200 complaints were received concerning the ABC Howard K. Smith program, "The Political Obituary of Richard M. Nixon." *Id.*

4. FCC ANNUAL REPORT 52 (1962). The Commission noted that the complaints "divided into these general categories: slanted news programs (biased, etc.), 47; slanted news documentaries, 16; fluoridation, 105; communism, 56; Medicare, 26; and miscellaneous controversial subjects, 159." *Id.*

5. Statement of Hon. E. William Henry, *supra* note 3, at 90.

areas of the country.[160] If scarcity is seen in terms of a comparison of the number of daily newspapers with the number of broadcast licensees the "scarce" licensees outnumber the newspapers by more than four to one.[161] If scarcity is considered on a local level, all large metropolitan areas have far more broadcast outlets than daily newspapers. Los Angeles, for example, has over fifty broadcasters but only three major daily newspapers.[162] With the growth of cable television, scarcity will truly be a thing of the past.[163]

Despite this weakness in a key underpinning of the doctrine,[164] recently the Supreme Court resoundingly affirmed its constitutionality.[165] However, in affirming the doctrine, the Court has been careful to recognize that broadcasters have First Amendment rights that merit protection.[166] The Court also reiterated that the public interest is best served by the maintenance of a delicate balance between the First Amendment interests of broadcasters in keeping some degree of editorial control over their public issue programming and the public's First Amendment need for diverse public affairs information. As expressed by the Court of Appeals for the District of Columbia:

> The essential task of the fairness doctrine is to harmonize the freedom of the broadcaster and the right of the public to be informed. . . . The salutary intent of the fairness doctrine must be reconciled with the tradition against inhibition of the journalists' freedom. That tradition, which exerts a powerful countervailing force, is rooted in the constitutional guarantee that has vitality for broadcast journalists, though not in exactly the same degree as for their brethren of the printed word. . . . In construing the fairness doctrine, both the Commission and the courts have proceeded carefully, mindful of the need for harmonizing these often conflicting considerations.[167]

Keeping in mind the need to respect broadcast journalists' rights as well as the public need to know, one must recognize the great potential for abuse and counterproductivity in fairness doctrine administration.[168] Under part two of the doctrine, presentation of one side of a controversial public issue requires presentation of a contrasting side. A spokesman for the contrasting side must be given free air time if he or she does not want to pay for it, inflicting financial loss on the broadcaster.[169] Any serious fairness doctrine complaint may cost a licensee dearly in litigation and other expenses, as well as in staff time. As noted in Chapter Six, one network recently paid well over $100,000 in legal expenses and thousands of hours in personnel time fighting a fairness complaint that it eventually won,[170] and a local licensee spent over $20,000 in legal expenses and 480 personnel hours to win another fairness attack.[171]

The unprofitable nature of most controversial issue programming is a disincentive to its airing. Licensees, especially less profitable ones, cannot help but be discouraged from presenting this type of broadcast when the potential fairness doctrine costs are considered. CBS's experience with the "Loyal Opposition" series and the *Committee for Fair Broadcasting* case has been previously noted. If one considers the implications of the ASCEF complaint, also mentioned above, the disincentive possibilities are vastly expanded.

Bill Monroe, veteran NBC broadcast journalist, pointedly summed up the disincentive effect of part two as follows:

> Every time a letter goes out from the FCC the manager of the station has a little chill go through him, he's gotten a letter from a government agency that could conceivably put him out of business. It doesn't make any difference that they don't often do it, because in broadcasting you know they can do it. And boy, you respond to these people. When the manager gets the letter, he has to cancel a number of appointments he's made for the next few days, talk to the producer of the possibly-offending program, make sure that all of the research of the program is gone through by him or the manager himself or some other assistant, so that he has a check on the producer. The producer's work has to be completely gone through all over again, by somebody operating for the manager to double check the producer, and they've got to go through a lot of things the producer left out of the program. They've got to talk to lawyers in their home town and in Washington, and put together a careful document to go to the FCC in the hopes that the program was fair, and usually it is.
>
> But when the manager gets through the process, he is likely to tell that producer to stay away from controversial subjects for the next three or six months so he doesn't have to go through this again. He winds up, even if the FCC sends him back a letter saying, "your program was okay, forget about it, you made a good answer," he winds up having been hassled by the government because he committed the sin of telling a producer to go ahead and tackle this tough subject. No newspaper publisher is answerable on this basis.[172]

The Supreme Court itself has explicitly recognized the inhibiting effect of government-imposed rights of reply. In striking down as unconstitutional a Florida law requiring a newspaper to grant equal space to political candidates whom the newspaper had editorially attacked, the Court noted that the law penalized print journalists because of the (1) additional printing costs, composing time, and materials necessary to print the reply, and (2) the required use for the reply of space that the newspaper may have preferred to use for another topic.[173] The Court concluded:

> Faced with [these] penalties that would accrue to any newspaper that published news or commentary arguably within the reach of the right-of-access statute, editors might well conclude that the safe course is to avoid controversy. Therefore, under the operation of the Florida statute, political and electoral coverage would be blunted or reduced.[174]

Compared to the newspaper situation, the "broadcast costs" are far greater for a licensee who must devote expensive programming seconds to fairness replies. The licensee also must suffer loss of composing time and materials in filming or taping reply spokesmen, and the licensee may well want to devote this programming time to other material. While the Florida reply statute was limited solely to political candidates seeking a nomination or election,[175] the fairness doctrine applies to all controversial public issues, whether or not they are the subject of an election. If the Florida statute in *Miami Herald* was inhibitory with respect to newspapers, the fairness doctrine part two requirement may be seen as even more inhibitory to broadcast licensees.

One might contend that the fairness doctrine part two requirement, as administered by the FCC, affords licensees so much discretion under the good faith reasonableness standard and is enforced with such lackluster that it cannot possibly be a disincentive to coverage of controversial public issues. Such an argument has a good deal of force. However, the part two requirement is certainly perceived by many broadcasters as inhibitory, which is likely to be an important factor in their programming decisions.[176] The requirement has undeniably imposed great costs on broadcasters when it has been enforced. The Supreme Court recognized the inhibitory effect of a similar, but even less strenuously enforced

Florida statute applicable to newspapers.[177] If the doctrine were enforced with any degree of vigor, as one would expect a congressionally mandated policy to be, the inhibitory effect would be greatly magnified. But at the bottom line, if the doctrine is so rarely enforced that licensees have virtually complete freedom under it, one must question why the doctrine, with its enormous abuse potential, should exist at all.

Fairness doctrine entanglement may take on an even more ominous aspect. By influencing the FCC's decision-making process, government itself may abuse the doctrine through imposition of its own interpretation of what issue has been raised in a particular broadcast, whether that issue is controversial and of public importance, and what is a reasonable opportunity to respond. Just such an activity was contemplated by the Nixon administration. To meet the concerns of President Nixon and his Chief of Staff, H. R. Haldeman, about "unfair coverage" over the broadcast media, White House Aide Jeb Stuart Magruder proposed "an official monitoring system through the Federal Communications Commission" to prove broadcaster bias as soon as Republican Dean Burch was "officially on board as chairman."[178] In at least one instance, the Nixon administration acted on its own, superseding the FCC, and deliberately misinformed the three commercial television networks of their fairness obligations in order to bias their coverage toward the President's point of view.[179]

The government may also abuse the fairness doctrine from the bottom of the enforcement ladder, *i.e.*, by complaining to local stations and to the Commission about local station programming. According to one author, this type of abuse is not mere fantasy. He alleges a massive fairness doctrine campaign on behalf of the Kennedy and Johnson administrations against conservative programming aired by local licensees.[180] Before the 1964 Johnson-Goldwater election, the Democrats "decided to use the fairness doctrine to harass the extreme right. . . ." Using a front group with secret Democratic funding, a national campaign was organized in which 1,035 letters were written to local stations, producing a total of 1,678 hours of free time to respond to right wing commentators. One key Democratic organizer declared, "Even more important than the free radio time was the effectiveness of this operation in inhibiting the political activity of these right wing broadcasts," and inhibiting the stations from broadcasting more "politically partisan programs." He concluded that most of these stations are "small rural stations . . . in desperate need of broadcast revenues. . . . Were our efforts continued . . . many of these stations . . . would start dropping the programs from their broadcast schedule."[181] Democratic liberals may applaud the silencing or inhibiting of right wing broadcasters, but they must remember that in another day and time such a doctrine may be used to silence their own viewpoints, as the Nixon episode suggests.

It is true that part one of the doctrine may be used to force broadcasters to cover controversial public issues, counteracting the inhibitory effect of the part two balancing requirements. Thus, in *Representative Patsy Mink*,[182] West Virginia Radio station WHAR was told that it had failed to cover the critical issue of strip mining adequately and was in violation of its part one obligation. But, as discussed in Chapter Six,[183] such governmental involvement in the broadcast press represents an even more severe First Amendment infringement than part two involvement and is inappropriate in a society attempting to maintain a free press. The Nixon, Johnson, and Kennedy abuses of part two of the doctrine pale in comparison to the potential abuse of part one by any administration inclined to do so. And the day-to-day administrative difficulties involved in active part one enforcement threaten severe First Amendment infringement.[184] Active part one enforcement would leave the public unduly influenced by government intervention in its daily information diet.

XII. THE UNFAIRNESS DOCTRINE

One is forced to conclude, after close scrutiny of the fairness doctrine, that in actuality it is an "unfairness doctrine." It is unfair to the public, because, although it promises to induce additional public issue coverage, including contrasting views, it does not do so. The doctrine has been so little enforced, the precedent is so inconsistent and vague, and licensees are afforded so much discretion, that fairness complainants are not likely to succeed in proving a case. The doctrine does not make any substantial contribution to increasing public issue debate over the airwaves, and, in fact, the part two requirement may actually discourage such debate. Any governmental use of the doctrine that limits broadcast journalists' freedom, in turn distorts the issue coverage received by the American people. The doctrine, theoretically geared to informing the American people fairly, may actually generate misinformation. When the doctrine is "legitimately" enforced, contrasting views may be presented long after the initial broadcast, and a substantially different audience may still hear viewpoints on only one side of an issue. There will be no "fairness" in the sense that each member of the public hears contrasting views on every issue.

The doctrine is also unfair to broadcast licensees. When the doctrine has been enforced, especially in the part one context, it has caused severe interference with the editorial judgments of the broadcast press, and it has been extremely expensive for licensees to react to fairness complaints. The money spent and personnel used to defend against fairness complaints could be better used to produce public issue programming. Such expenditures, occasional as they may be, act as a disincentive to airing such programming. If the doctrine were vigorously enforced with intensive FCC involvement, as some public interest groups suggest, the disincentive would be even greater. The potential for abuse of the doctrine by presidents, political parties, or any powerful interest group is enormous. Broadcast licensees see their print media brethren completely free of government interference and rightfully question why their own editorial judgments are so open to FCC interference. Even if a licensee wants to obey the doctrine, the guidelines are as difficult for it to follow as they are for a public complainant.

Groups seeking access to the broadcast media are also treated unfairly under the doctrine. They may be denied an opportunity to respond to a licensee editorial even though the contrasting view they want to air has been given far less coverage and in a comparatively unfavorable time slot. If they are granted an opportunity to respond to a licensee's views, they may be permitted to speak only many months after the relevant issue is moot, and the issues with which they are concerned may be given little attention by licensees. Yet fairness doctrine complaints do little to increase public issue coverage.

Finally, the FCC has put itself in an unfair position by its handling of the fairness doctrine. It quite rightly has been concerned about the freedom of broadcast licensees and has avoided a vigorous enforcement pattern, but such a policy has subjected the Commission to legitimate and severe criticism for failing to increase diverse public issue coverage over the nation's airwaves. However, when the Commission does get involved on a complaint-by-complaint basis, it often interferes with a broadcaster's editorial judgment, violating its own self-professed healthy concern for broadcasters' First Amendment rights.

The Commission's inconsistent and vague rulings have been in large part due to its own faulty decision making. But it has a hard road to travel, and in balancing competing interests it is, in a sense, damned if it does and damned if it does not enforce a fairness complaint. The doctrine also raises the possibility of the Commission being used as an instrument by political or private groups to harass broadcast spokesmen and impose their own points of view on the American people.

XIII. CONCLUSION: DROPPING PART TWO, ENFORCING PART ONE DIFFERENTLY

What should be done about the "unfairness doctrine"? The long-term answer to this question is to increase the number of electronic communications outlets available to the American people.[185] The FCC and Congress must do far more than they have to promote the growth of cable television, UHF television, additional VHF channels, and additional commercial networks. Public television must be given expanded and more permanent funding. The House Communications Subcommittee has begun an intensive review of the 1934 Communications Act,[186] and the study will provide an excellent chance for Congress to address these areas. With an abundance of communications outlets, especially with cable's huge channel capacity, there will be no scarcity of electronic media opportunities, even in major markets. Interest groups will have a variety of access options in presenting their views to the public. Diversity of opinion should develop inherently from the diversity of information sources, and public issues inevitably will be given coverage on a variety of channels. There will be no need or justification for government influence on the selection of issues to be covered and the way they should be covered.

But what about the immediate future? What should be done right now to cope with the problems generated by the "unfairness doctrine"? There is no easy answer. There is no perfect scheme. Competing arguments have a good deal of force, but one policy option that would at least be an improvement over the present structure is to drop the part two balancing requirements for all public issue programming except station editorials and to enforce the part one requirement only in terms of minimum percentages of time for public issue broadcasts and programming to meet ascertained community needs.

A great many broadcast licensees explicitly editorialize on a variety of issues[187] and are encouraged to do so by the FCC.[188] In such situations, the licensee is using its exclusive frequency to urge viewers to adopt its point of view. There is no pretense of journalistic fairness, as in a news story. The licensee's purpose is to bias the viewer to its viewpoint, and the issue is usually easier to identify in such editorials than in news documentaries. In editorials the licensee has chosen to cover an issue directly, and an enforced reply opportunity does not involve the part one infringement where issue coverage is mandated, nor even the kind of part two interference involved in editorial judgments on news, documentary, or panel shows. Replies to such editorials are an easily facilitated access opportunity for community groups, and there are indications that many broadcast journalists do not object to mandated reply opportunities to station editorials.[189]

For reasons such as these, a part two response requirement if it makes sense at all, is most appropriate in this broadcast editorial situation. But to be effective, the FCC must be much more consistent and rational in enforcing the reply obligation. Intensive licensee efforts, besides over-the-air announcements, should be required to find reply spokesmen to station editorials.[190] A reply broadcast should occur no later than 45 days after the original broadcast and in the same time period[191] so that it can make a more meaningful contribution to ongoing debate and so that more of the original audience will be likely to see the later reply. The same format should be offered the reply spokesman. If only one editorial is broadcast, the reply spokesman should be offered at least roughly the same amount of total time. If numerous editorials are involved, frequency of broadcast and time of broadcast must consistently be given proper attention.[192] With clear guidelines, FCC enforcement could be swift, consistent, effective, and limited to the more manageable explicit editorial area.

Most stations that editorialize would ordinarily provide such fair response opportunities for opposing spokesmen on their own initiative. But such guidelines would ensure fair treatment for reply speakers on all broadcast outlets, access opportunities to a variety of public interest groups, and a better opportunity for the public to receive diverse views on certain issues in timely fashion.[193] At the same time, broadcasters would be given better guidance about what is required of them in the editorial situation and would be freed from government interference in issue coverage in newscasts, news documentaries, interview shows, round table discussions, and other such public issue programming. Broadcasters' journalistic sense of fairness would be relied upon to ensure honest coverage in the latter situations. The quality of such coverage would, of course, vary as it does from newspaper to newspaper, or magazine to magazine, but the danger of government or interest group abuse would be greatly diminished. The ASCEF type of complaint and the Nixon and Kennedy variety of use of the doctrine would be undermined. The part two disincentive to air controversial news documentaries and other such programming would be eliminated.[194]

It must be recognized, however, that the disincentive to air such public issue programming involves much more than part two of the fairness doctrine. The fundamental reason is television's economic incentive to appeal to a mass audience, a common denominator, whose likes and dislikes are measured in Nielsen ratings, not in public issue information received. Despite the sizable minority of people who desire public affairs programming,[195] and the critical role that informational programming is supposed to play in the American broadcast structure,[196] game shows, situation comedies, and other entertainment programming draw higher Nielsen ratings and larger audiences than public issue programming. Higher rates can be charged to advertisers for supporting such programming. Commercial pressures thus act against the airing of public issue broadcasts.[197]

As noted above, the present part one fairness doctrine approach involves a severe infringement of broadcasters' First

Amendment rights, has great potential for abuse, lacks guiding criteria for what issues need coverage, and has not resulted in increased public issue coverage.[198] A far better way for the Commission to ensure public issue coverage is to require that a minimum percentage of public affairs programming be aired.[199] The FCC already requires licensees to report to it on the news and public affairs programming they have broadcast.[200] However, the Commission "has established no minimum amount of time which *must* be devoted to" news and public affairs to ensure the granting or renewal of a license.[201]

The Commission has delegated authority to its staff to automatically renew the licenses of network-affiliated television licensees who have proposed more than 5 percent "informational (news plus public affairs)" programming, assuming the renewal is otherwise uncontested and proper.[202] If a licensee has included less than 5 percent news and public affairs in its broadcast schedule, then the renewal must be referred to the full Commission for review.

Although these percentage requirements are an improvement over the ones previously used by the Commission,[203] they are still extremely low.[204] The Commission has emphatically declared that broadcasters have been allocated a portion of the frequency spectrum only in recognition of the "great contribution" they can make to the "development of an informal public opinion through the public dissemination of news and ideas concerning the vital public issues of the day." Indeed, it is the "right of the public to be informed" that is supposed to be the "foundation stone of the American system of broadcasting."[205] Yet a major VHF television station can be deemed to have acted in the public interest if it devoted 4.75 percent of its total programming to news, and .25 percent to other public affairs broadcasts.[206] That the renewal guidelines are too low is demonstrated by the results of a questionnaire of 86 VHF network affiliates in the top 50 markets, each with revenues of over $5 million. The median figure for news and public affairs aired was 15.5 percent, more than three times the Commission's delegated renewal standards.[207]

Perhaps even more striking than the FCC's low percentage figures is the Commission's failure to enforce a news and public affairs obligation. As the Commission itself acknowledges, the new delegation guidelines "do not identify a quantity—much less a quality—of programming below which no application will be granted. The amount and kind of programming is left largely to the reasonable, good-faith judgment of the individual licensee."[208] If a licensee's proposed programming falls below these low percentage figures, it is subjected to further review by the Commission. But as one FCC official stated: "To my knowledge the Commission has never failed to renew a license for falling below the percentage standard." The worst that has happened is that a license renewal "has been delayed" for a few months.[209] Indeed, as noted above, many television and radio stations have had their licenses renewed after airing little or no news or public affairs.[210]

The current guidelines also fail to require, or even emphasize, the need to broadcast local public affairs programming. The Commission has stressed the importance of broadcasters' airing programming that focuses on important local issues.[211] It promulgated the prime time access rule, reserving prime time evening viewing for local programming, in the hopes that stations subject to the rule would "devote a substantial proportion of prime time to programming of particular local significance."[212]

Unfortunately, as recently suggested in a proposal by the National Citizens Committee for Broadcasting (NCCB) "action by the FCC in the matter of television public affairs programming has been little more than words."[213] The local access periods have all too often been used not for local or even national public affairs programming but for syndicated situation comedies, game shows, and the like.[214] Many stations broadcast very little or no local public affairs programming.[215] The NCCB proposal that each television station be required to provide at least "one hour per week of regularly scheduled, prime time, *locally-originated,* public affairs programming" merits careful consideration.[216]

The Commission, in 1971, initiating proceedings to determine percentage guidelines for news and public affairs that would indicate "substantial service" giving television licensees a preference in any comparative renewal hearing.[217] However, the percentages suggested by the Commission, although a significant improvement over its delegation guidelines, were still far too low.[218] In March, 1977, the Commission brought its inquiry to a close, rejecting the percentage guideline formula.[219] However, the Commission had considered percentage guidelines only in the context of improving the comparative renewal process, and it rejected them because it concluded that guidelines would not make that process more efficient. It pointed out that they also would be an interference with licensee discretion. The Commission failed to consider the guidelines in conjunction with repealing the far more inhibitory fairness doctrine, and it failed to emphasize adequately the public interest benefit derived from increased public issue coverage.[220] The FCC and Congress should reconsider a guideline structure as part of a fairness doctrine revision package.[221]

Beyond this, the Commission must get tough in enforcing the ascertainment obligations it has imposed on broadcast licensees. As part of these obligations, licensees are required to conduct personal interviews with key community leaders[222] and a random sample survey of the general public[223] to determine the "problems, needs, and interests" in their community.[224] The objective of these ascertainment efforts is to make a licensee's programming more responsive to the local service area.

To determine if licensees are airing programming to reflect the issues discovered in their ascertainment efforts the FCC requires each licensee to place each year in its public inspection file "a list of *no more* than ten significant problems, needs and interests ascertained during the preceding months," and "typical and illustrative programs" that have been aired to meet these problems, needs, and interests must be documented.[225] These annual lists must be filed with a licensee's renewal application.[226] When a licensee's ascertainment procedures and programming have been woefully inadequate, the Commission has occasionally taken action against a broadcaster.[227] However, the Commission must become far more vigorous in seeing that licensees live up to their ascertainment programming obligations. With the present fairness doctrine responsibility eliminated, ascertainment would take on added significance. Enforcement of the ascertainment obligations, like requiring a minimum percentage of public affairs programming, would not produce an exact correlation with controversial issues of public importance. But the match would be close, and without the adverse fairness doctrine effects.[228]

The Commission must also change its listing requirements so that *at least* ten or even twelve significant problems, needs, and interests are enumerated with illustrative programming. The Commission's present wording suggests a maximum of ten, ironically discouraging additional broadcasting in these areas and seemingly

suggesting that six, five, or even three broadcasts reflecting community issues are satisfactory licensee service.

As previously noted, the short-term solutions discussed
above are not perfect. In this complex area, where so many competing interests must be resolved, any scheme will have its draw-
backs and will not afford every group all that it wants. But stripping
licensees of present fairness doctrine obligations, requiring a minimum percentage of public affairs programming, enforcing ascertainment requirements, and balancing of broadcast editorials are
steps forward. The development of a truly diverse electronic communications system is the ultimate solution to the "unfairness doctrine." Until that system exists, the plan suggested above is in the
public interest. The federal government would be out of the business of telling licensees what issues to cover and how to cover them.
Except in the limited area of editorials, where such questions may
be handled more easily, licensees would not have to worry about
what total time and frequency ratios are reasonable, what spokesmen should be presented, and what formats are acceptable to the
federal government. The danger of government abuse would be
greatly diminished, and licensees' obligations would be made more
clear. The Commission itself would not be placed in the awkward
position of constantly trying to second-guess broadcasters' editorial
judgments and possibly being used by powerful political or private
interests to further their own ends.[229]

At the same time, groups seeking access to the media would
benefit from much more vigorous and rational enforcement of editorial reply opportunities and public issue programming opportunities. The licensee would still act as editor, but would have many
more broadcast pages to fill. The ultimate winner would be the
American public which would receive an expanded supply of information about important public issues vital to the health of the
Republic.

Notes

1. As has been noted in previous chapters, key FCC fairness doctrine policy documents
include *Handling of Public Issues Under the Fairness Doctrine and the Public Interest
Standards of the Communications Act, Reconsideration of the Fairness Report,* 58 F.C.C.2d
691 (1976) [hereinafter cited as *Reconsideration Fairness Report*]; FCC, *Fairness Doctrine*

and *Public Interest Standards, Fairness Report Regarding Handling of Public Issues,* 39 FED. REG. 26372 (1974) [hereinafter cited as *Fairness Report*]; FCC, *Broadcast Procedure Manual,* 39 FED. REG. 32288, 32290 pars. 12–14 (rev. ed. 1974) [hereinafter cited as *Broadcast Procedure Manual*]; FCC, *Applicability of the Fairness Doctrine in the Handling of Controversial Issues of Public Importance,* 29 FED. REG. 10415 (1964) [hereinafter cited as *Fairness Primer*]; FCC, *Report on Editorializing by Broadcast Licensees,* 13 F.C.C. 1246 (1949) [hereinafter cited as *Report on Editorializing*].

2. *See* Chapter Six, pp. 147–54.

3. *See* Chapter Six, pp. 154–60.

4. *See* Chapter Six, pp. 166–73.

5. Only a handful of fairness doctrine cases decided by the FCC involve part one of the doctrine. Almost all cases focus on part two, the balancing part.

6. *See Editorializing Report, supra* note 1, at 1250 par. 8, 1255 par. 18; *Fairness Report, supra* note 1, at 26377 par. 36. However, if a licensee has not presented any prior programming on the issue involved and declares that it will not present any in the future, the FCC will judge the licensee on only the initial broadcast. *Reconsideration Fairness Report, supra* note 1, at 695 n.5. In this situation the initial broadcast constitutes the licensee's "overall programming" on the issue. It is possible to attain reasonable balance within the confines of a single show. For example, a panel discussion may present speakers who advocate different points of view; a news story may cover contrasting sides; a documentary may contain interviews with advocates from both ends of the spectrum.

7. *Broadcast Procedure Manual, supra* note 1, at 32270 par. 14.

8. *Report on Editorializing, supra* note 1, at 1248 par. 4. However, the licensee can rely on network programming to present contrasting viewpoints to those initially presented on a local-station- or network-originated show. If the network does not present such contrasting viewpoints, the licensee is responsible for seeing that they are aired. Capitol Broadcasting Co., 40 F.C.C. 615 (1964). Networks, through their ownership of up to five local stations, have also been considered subject to the fairness doctrine and "where a complaint is based on a network program and . . . addressed to a network organization . . . the Commission . . . has always accepted this approach as a basis for issuance of a ruling on the matter." Senator Eugene McCarthy, 11 F.C.C.2d 511 n.1 (1968).

9. *Fairness Report, supra* note 1, at 26377 par. 38. However, the Commission later diluted this declaration by stating that "[i]n many, or perhaps most, cases it may be possible to find that only two viewpoints are significant enough to warrant broadcast coverage." *Id.*

10. However, in its 1974 *Fairness Report,* the Commission did specifically indicate that a "particular issue may involve more than two opposing viewpoints." *Fairness Report, supra* note 1, at 26377 par. 38. The Commission then cited the following language from a law journal: "A principal purpose of the fairness doctrine is to educate the public on the major alternatives available to it in making social choices. . . . Acknowledging that there is a 'spectrum' of opinion on many issues, it is nonetheless true that there are often clearly definable 'colors' in the spectrum, even though the points at which they blend into one another may be unclear. The controversy concerning American policy in Indochina is illustrative. The alternatives [prior to America's withdrawal from the war] include[d] increasing military activity, maintaining the [then] present level of commitment, a phased withdrawal and immediate withdrawal. It might be argued that any licensee who does not present some coverage of at least these views has failed to educate the public about the major policy alternatives available." Howard Weinman, Note, *The F.C.C. Fairness Doctrine and Informed Social Choice.* 8 HARV. J. LEGIS. 333, 351–52 (1971), cited in *Fairness Report, supra* note 1, at 26377 n.15. However, the FCC has not enforced this multidimensional viewpoint concept.

11. *See, e.g.,* Democratic Nat'l Comm., 25 F.C.C.2d 437, 442 (1970) ("the licensee must afford reasonable opportunity for discussion of *both* sides" [emphasis added]).

12. And where licensees have presented various viewpoints, complainants who have attempted to get additional viewpoints aired have been met with the admonition that the "fairness doctrine does not require a licensee to provide an opportunity for the presentation of every viewpoint on an issue." Horace P. Rowley III, 39 F.C.C.2d 437, 442 (1973) (rejecting

complainant's claims that the "moderate viewpoint" on the Vietnam war and other "responsible viewpoints" on bias in television news should be broadcast). *See also* Sidney Willens, 33 F.C.C.2d 304 (1972) (rejecting complainant's claim that the "third point of view" on particular criminal cases and the roles of various public offices in fight against crime should be broadcast); Alfred M. Lilienthal, 24 F.C.C.2d 299 (1970) (rejecting complainant's claim that the Jewish-American viewpoint on the Arab-Israeli conflict should be broadcast). The courts have never reversed the FCC for failing to mandate the broadcast of more than two viewpoints, and they have reinforced the bipolar orientation by occasionally referring to the licensee's obligation to present "both" sides of an issue.

13. *Fairness Report, supra* note 1, at 26377 par. 37.

14. Mrs. J. R. Paul, 26 F.C.C.2d 591 (1969); *Report on Editorializing, supra* note 1, at 1249–50. Selecton of a reply spokesman is also not to be based on what a licensee believes to be the spokesman's personal motives. Columbia Broadcasting Sys., Inc., 34 F.C.C.2d 773, 777–78 (1972).

15. *Fairness Report, supra* note 1 at 26377 n.16. The Commission has also stated that licensees must only present *"representative* community views on controversial issues," Democratic Nat'l Comm., 25 F.C.C.2d 216, 224 (1970) (emphasis in original), and "responsible positions on matters of sufficient importance to be afforded radio time," *Report on Editorializing, supra* note 1, at 1250.

16. 40 F.C.C. 549 (1963).

17. And what of other candidates who had not mounted such an extensive campaign? *See* William Sheroff, 30 P & F RADIO REG. 2d 588 (1974); Anthony Bruno, 26 F.C.C.2d 656 (1970); Richard Kay, 24 F.C.C.2d 426, *aff'd* 433 F.2d 638 (D.C. Cir. 1970).

18. Dr. Benjamin Spock Peoples Party, 38 F.C.C.2d 316 (1972). The late complaint also suffered procedural defects. Commissioner Nicholas Johnson, in a forceful dissent, stated that it was "preposterous" not to consider Spock a serious candidate for the presidency, and claimed that CBS and NBC had not complied with their fairness obligations. *Id.* at 319, 321 (Commissioner Johnson, dissenting).

19. *Fairness Report, supra* note 1, at 26377 par. 37; *Report on Editorializing, supra* note 1, at 1251.

20. *Fairness Report, supra* note 1, at 26377 n.13.

21. In Cullman Broadcasting Co., 40 F.C.C. 576 (1963), the Commission articulated the doctrine as follows: "Where the licensee has chosen to broadcast a sponsored program which for the first time presents one side of a controversial issue, has not presented (or does not plan to present) contrasting viewpoints in other programming, and has been unable to obtain paid sponsorship for the appropriate presentation of the opposing viewpoint or viewpoints, he cannot reject a presentation otherwise suitable to the licensee—*and thus leave the public uninformed*—on the ground that he cannot obtain paid sponsorship for that presentation." *Id.* at 577 (emphasis in original). The licensee may first explore the possibility of obtaining paid sponsorship for the contrasting presentation, including inquiries about whether a particular reply spokesman will pay for air time. Such inquiries, however, cannot suggest that a contrasting view will not be presented unless paid sponsorship is forthcoming, nor can the licensee insist on a demonstration of financial inability to pay as a condition precedent to airing a reply spokesman. Letter to Rev. John H. Norris, 1 F.C.C.2d 1587 (1965); Station WGCB, 40 F.C.C. 656 (1965). Even if some contrasting views on an issue are presented, if there is a substantial imbalance in favor of one side, additional contrasting views have to be solicited without insisting that they be offered under paid sponsorship. Outlet Co. (WDBO-TV), 32 F.C.C.2d 33 (1971). However, when spokesmen for a candidate air views favorable to their candidate, then comparable time must be given to spokesmen for the opposing candidate, and *Cullman* does not apply, *i.e.,* free time need not be offered. Nicholas Zapple, 23 F.C.C.2d 707 (1970). See notes 104–12, *infra,* and accompanying text.

22. See notes 104–12, *infra,* and accompanying text.

23. CBS v. Democratic Nat'l Comm., 412 U.S. 94, 113 (1973); Hon. M. Gene Snyder, 49 F.C.C.2d 493, 494 (1974); Harry Britton, 40 F.C.C.2d 112, 113 (1973); *Availability of Network Programming Time to Members of Congress,* 40 F.C.C.2d 238, 246 (1973); Voters

Organized to Think Environment, 39 F.C.C.2d 571, 572 (1973); Boalt Hall Student Ass'n, 20 F.C.C.2d 612, 615 (1969).

24. Mid-Florida Television Corp., 40 F.C.C. 620 (1964). In the *Fairness Report, supra* note 1, at 26377 n.14, the Commission terminated a proceeding emanating from *Obligations of Broadcast Licensees Under the Fairness Doctrine (Notice of Inquiry and Proposed Rulemaking)* 23 F.C.C.2d 27 (1970) [hereinafter cited as *Obligations Inquiry*] in which adoption of specific procedures for seeking out opposition spokesmen under certain circumstances had been proposed.

25. Except in the personal attack, political editorial, and *Zapple* situations, broadcasters are not considered common carriers, 42 U.S.C. sec. 153(h) (1970). No party has a constitutional or statutory right of access to broadcast air time. CBS v. Democratic Nat'l Comm., 412 U.S. 94 (1973). "[T]he cornerstone of the fairness doctrine is not the right of any particular individual or group to speak but the public's right to be informed as to all significant points of view relating to an issue of public importance." Boalt Hall Student Ass'n, 20 F.C.C.2D 612, 615 (1969). See also authorities cited in note 23, *supra*.

26. *Obligations Inquiry, supra* n.24 at 30–31. The licensee cannot reply solely on happenstance, such as an unknown caller on a call-in program, or a general interview program not presenting selected guests with contrasting viewpoints. WIYN Radio, 52 F.C.C.2d 428, 436 (1975); Rudolph P. Arnold, 52 F.C.C.2d 405, 407 (1975).

27. *Fairness Report, supra* note 1, at 26377 par. 41.

28. *Report on Editorializing, supra* note 1, at 1253 par. 14; *accord,* CBS v. Democratic Nat'l Comm., 412 U.S. 94, 130–31 (1973); Red Lion Broadcasting Co. v. FCC, 395 U.S. 367, 392 n.18 (1969).

29. Albeit, to present a major, representative viewpoint.

30. Mid-Florida Television Corp., 40 F.C.C. 620, 621 (1964). In 1970 the FCC proposed that, where a series of one-sided broadcasts on a controversial issue of public importance was made over a period of nine months or less, the licensee could rely on over-the-air announcements to obtain reply speakers only for the first broadcast. If this fails, the licensee must directly contact specific individuals. The FCC also suggested that, whenever the licensee editorializes, over-the-air announcements by themselves may not be an adequate method of soliciting opposing spokesmen. *Obligations Inquiry, supra* note 24, at 29–30. The *Fairness Report, supra* note 1, at 26377 n.14, satisfied with the more flexible standard described below, terminated these proceedings.

31. *Fairness Report, supra* note 1, at 26377.

32. 40 F.C.C.2d 1147, 1149 (1973). The *Fairness Report* also quoted with approval Mid-Florida Television Corp., 40 F.C.C. 620 (1964), which had suggested that one way licensees could fulfill their fairness obligations was by over-the-air announcements. *Fairness Report, supra* note 1, at 26377, par. 37.

33. *Obligations Inquiry, supra* note 24, at 28–29. *See also* Ted Bullard, 23 F.C.C.2d 41 (1970) (after rejecting one reply spokesman as inappropriate, efforts by licensee to contact other spokesmen were necessary); Richard G. Ruff, 19 F.C.C.2d 838 (1969) (after rejecting one reply spokesman, additional efforts were necessary beyond offers specifically made to seven parties, which were refused).

34. Columbia Broadcasting Sys., Inc., 34 F.C.C.2d 773, *reconsideration denied sub nom.* Thomas M. Slaten, 39 F.C.C.2d 16 (1972). Commissioner Johnson dissented, stating that denying air time to Slaten, the one reply spokesman who came forward, made "a mockery of the fairness doctrine." *Id.* at 19 (Commissioner Johnson, dissenting). *See also* Sherwyn M. Heckt, 40 F.C.C.2d 1150 (1973), where, despite a gross imbalance in programming favoring Expo '74 (an international exposition) and a refusal to air the contrasting view of a reply spokesman, the licensee's over-the-air invitations, mailing of editorials to community leaders and others, and efforts to contact another key reply spokesman were deemed sufficient. If copies of editorials are used to solicit reply spokesmen, a specific offering of air time to present a contrasting viewpoint must also be included, at least to some individuals. Sending the editorial by itself is not enough. Capitol Broadcasting Co., 40 F.C.C. 615, 617 (1964).

35. *See* Columbia Broadcasting System, Inc., 40 F.C.C. 615 (1974).

36. Carol Los Mansmann, 40 F.C.C.2d 61, 63 (1973); Mrs. Lynne H. Heidt, 29 F.C.C.2d 328, 329 (1971).

37. Service Elec. Cable TV, 30 F.C.C.2d 831 (1971); Springfield Television Broadcasting Corp., 45 F.C.C. 2083, 2086 (1965); WSOC Broadcasting Co., 40 F.C.C. 468, 469 (1958).

38. Springfield Television Broadcasting Corp., 28 F.C.C.2d 339, 341 (1971).

39. *Reconsideration Fairness Report, supra* note 1, at 697 n.9; Public Communications Inc., 50 F.C.C.2d 395, 401 (1974).

40. WNCN Listener's Guild, 53 F.C.C.2d 149, 157 (1975). However, "[a] specific showing, not here given, that a licensee's personal financial self-interest did *in fact* influence the licensee in its fairness doctrine decisions [might] affect the Commission's review as to that licensee's reasonableness and/or good faith. However, the bare statement by a complainant that a licensee is or may be personally interested in some issue does not shift the burden of proof to the licensee to show that its decisions with regard to that issue were 'more' reasonable." *Id.* at 155 (emphasis added).

41. See notes 6–8, *supra,* and accompanying text. *See also* Horace P. Rowley III, 39 F.C.C.2d 437 (1973), *reconsideration denied,* 45 F.C.C.2d 1069 (1974); James Batal, 24 F.C.C.2d 301 (1970).

42. *Fairness Report, supra* note 1, at 26378 par. 42; *Report on Editorializing, supra* note 1, at 1251 par. 10, 1258 par. 21.

43. 20 F.C.C.2d 612 (1969).

44. *See* Phillip H. Schott, 25 F.C.C.2d 729 (1970), *review denied,* 29 F.C.C.2d 335 (1971) (uninterrupted presentation by Governor Ronald Reagan on the closing of California college campuses could be balanced by contrasting views presented in documentaries, public affairs programs, open mike programs, and newscasts). *See also* Democratic State Central Comm., 19 F.C.C.2d 833 (1968), where the Commission held that an uninterrupted 15 minute "Report to the People" containing Governor Reagan's views on state withholding taxes, a proposed tax increase, tuition fees, and other legislative proposals could be balanced by a "variety of formats including newscasts, public affairs and open mike programs." *Id.* at 835. However, one licensee, having refused complainant time and having aired only four brief news items, only two of which presented contrasting views, violated fairness obligations. *Id.*

45. Amedeo Greco, 22 F.C.C.2d 24 (1970).

46. Public Media Center, 59 F.C.C.2d (1976).

47. Happiness of Womanhood, Inc., 48 F.C.C.2d 1016 (1974). *See also* Judy Collins, 31 F.C.C.2d 847 (1970) (complainant's comments on the Chicago Seven Trial on the Dick Cavett show could be edited by ABC). The Commission has distinguished the personal attack situation from general fairness doctrine cases: "As to the format, while licensees have wide discretion in this area in generally meeting the requirements of the fairness doctrine . . . the matter stands on a different footing with respect to the response to a personal attack. In that situation, the licensee cannot properly insist upon a roundtable or panel discussion. The person attacked . . . might reasonably conclude that a panel or roundtable discussion does not afford a comparable opportunity to reply, in view of their different structure (*e.g.,* moderator; questions; debate). . . ." John Birch Soc'y, 11 F.C.C.2d 790, 791-92 (1968). See Chapter Four, pp. 78-80.

48. Butte Broadcasting Co., 22 F.C.C.2d 7 (1970). See note 28, *supra,* and accompanying text.

49. There is nothing wrong *per se* with a moderator engaging in harassing conduct. However, contrasting sides must be given "reasonably similar treatment in this respect." Brandywine-Main Line Radio, Inc., 24 F.C.C.2d 18 (1970), *petition for reconsideration denied,* 27 F.C.C.2d 565, 566 n.1 (1971), *aff'd on other grounds,* 473 F.2d 16 (D.C. Cir. 1972), *cert. denied,* 412 U.S. 922 (1973). "Fairness cannot be achieved when the expression of one view is deliberately treated in an antagonistic manner while the opposing view is given the opportunity for expression without any interference, harassment, or even opposing argument." *Id.,* 24 F.C.C.2d at 24.

50. *Id.* at 23.

51. Sidney Willens, 33 F.C.C.2d 304, 307–08 (1972), *petitions for reconsideration denied and dismissed,* 38 F.C.C.2d 443, 445–46 (1972). Such guidelines represent prior restraints

and are vague. *Id. See also* Shady Wall, 31 F.C.C.2d 484 (1971) (licensee cannot reasonably impose broad restrictions limiting reply spokesman's response to personal references originally made about him). On the other hand, the licensee cannot let a spokesman for one position veto the entire presentation of contrasting views on a controversial issue of public importance by refusing to appear in the format outlined by the licensee. Evening News Ass'n, 40 F.C.C. 441 (1950).

52. Ted Bullard, 23 F.C.C.2d 41 (1970). *See also* Brandywine-Main Line Radio, Inc., 27 F.C.C.2d 565, 569 (1971), in which the Commission stated that "[i]n the context of opposing views set forth at length by commentators, such complete reliance on ordinary newscasts is obviously inadequate. . . ."

53. Paul E. Fitzpatrick, 40 F.C.C. 443 (1950).

54. However, the FCC has refused to find fairness issues raised that require balancing in the entertainment and passing reference formats, despite its insistence that the label or type of format is irrelevant to fairness considerations. See Chapter Six, pp. 147–54.

55. For example, color films of an abortion operation, dramatically narrated by an anti-abortion speaker, may have far more impact than a pro-abortion spokesman airing views in the confines of a studio chair. Color footage of deer and other animals at play near an oil well may distort the "minimal" amount of environmental damage done by the well in comparison with a speaker who merely cites arguments substantiating more than "minimal" damage.

56. The length of time that may elapse between the broadcast of one viewpoint on a controversial issue of public importance and the broadcast of other viewpoints is another "timing" decision of importance. See pp. 200–03, *supra*.

57. *Fairness Report, supra* note 1, at 26378 par. 43.

58. Interview with Commissioner Benjamin Hooks by Steven J. Simmons, Sept. 4, 1975. FCC Commissioner Charlotte Reid stated, "Again, I think, I don't like to use the word, but it's kind of a gut reaction. . . . Each case is different." Interview with Commissioner Charlotte Reid by Steven J. Simmons, Sept. 16, 1975. Commissioner James Quello rejects any set time ratio and states, "The rule itself is not specific." Interview with Commissioner James H. Quello by Steven J. Simmons, Sept. 8, 1975. The other Commissioners interviewed also refused to state any personal formula for determining a set ratio of time that was so out of proportion that it violated the fairness doctrine. Each one said that his or her judgment varied with the situation and the factors discussed in the text *infra*.

59. Interviews with Milton Gross, Chief, Fairness/Political Branch, Complaints and Compliance Division, Broadcast Bureau, FCC, by Steven J. Simmons, Sept. 3, 9, 1975, Dec. 8, 17, 1976 [hereinafter cited as Interviews with Milton Gross].

60. *Fairness Report, supra* note 1, at 26378 par. 43. For examples of how the popular press confuses equal time and fairness, *see* Chairman Dean Burch's statement in Committee for Fair Broadcasting of Controversial Issues, 25 F.C.C.2d 283, 302 (1970) (separate statement of Chairman Burch). For more on the difference between equal time and fairness, *see* Chapter Two, p. 10.

61. *Fairness Report, supra* note 1, at 26378 par. 44. Various commissioners indicated personal reactions to the differing "signposts." Commissioner Wiley, stating that he did not have any set ratio for total time division, indicated that the overall context is important. He pointed to frequency and time of day as factors to consider. Interview with Commissioner Richard E. Wiley and Larry Secrest, Administrative Assistant, by Steven J. Simmons, Sept. 14, 1975. Commissioner Lee would not be "tied down to equal time" but a 10 to 1 total time division "would raise serious questions in my mind." Time of day, frequency of broadcast, and the reaching of approximately the same audience are factors he considers. Interview with Commissioner Robert E. Lee by Steven J. Simmons, Sept. 15, 1975. Commissioners Lee, Wiley, and Hooks specifically reject the "stopwatch" technique of precisely timing contrasting sides. Commissioner Quello stressed that the total time division among contrasting sides should be close to equal time, and that "if you are on record on one side, you should be on record with as much on the other if it's a real controversial issue." Interview with Commissioner James H. Quello by Steven J. Simmons, Sept. 8, 1975.

62. The Commission concludes its "timing" discussion by assuring licensees of protection by the key fairness doctrine decisional standard, *i.e.*, the FCC will not substitute its

judgment for the licensees' but will limit its inquiry to whether licensees have acted in an unreasonable fashion. *Fairness Report, supra* note 1, at 26378 par. 44.

63. 16 F.C.C.2d 956 (1969).

64. 59 F.C.C.2d 494 (1976).

65. 25 F.C.C.2d 283 (1970).

66. WCBS-TV, 8 F.C.C.2d 381, *petitions for reconsideration, rulemaking, and stay denied,* 9 F.C.C.2d 921 (1967), *aff'd sub nom.* Banzhaf v. FCC, 405 F.2d 1082 (D.C. Cir. 1968), *cert. denied,* 396 U.S. 842 (1969). In *National Broadcasting* a petition to revoke the New York station's license had been filed, based on alleged fairness violations. National Broadcasting Co., 16 F.C.C.2d 956 (1969).

67. Although the 5 to 1 time ratio is not specifically mentioned in the published decision, Dean Burch maintains the decision was based on a Commission study indicating that ratio. Wilderness Soc'y, 31 F.C.C.2d 729, 736 (1971) (Chairman Burch, concurring).

68. *See also* Wilderness Soc'y, 31 F.C.C.2d 729, 735, 739 (1971) (Chairman Burch, concurring) (appeal where a 2 to 1 ratio was held reasonable). Chairman Burch also indicated that an unpublished staff ruling on an urgent fairness matter once regarded a 3 to 1 time ratio as reasonable. *Id.* at 736. The full Commission, however, never reviewed the ruling. In terms of total time division between contrasting views, Tracy Weston, the noted communications law public interest attorney, has indicated that a ratio greater than 6 to 1 would be disproportionate enough to trigger the fairness doctrine in any instance, and that "the more important the issue, the closer the balance required." ACCESS, May 19, 1975, at 11. Andrew Shapiro states that the Commission has indicated "an imbalance in time exceeding ten-to-one is clearly unreasonable." ANDREW SHAPIRO, MEDIA ACCESS 158 (1976).

69. However, even this outside limit (one of the few times the FCC has illustrated a reasonable total time ratio) has little value as precedent, since the cigarette balancing decisions have been considered sui generis and were recently reversed in the *Fairness Report, supra* note 1, at 26382 par. 70.

70. 59 F.C.C.2d 494 (1970).

71. *Id.* at 499–500.

72. In no case was the total time ratio greater than 2 to 1. *Id.*

73. *Id.* at 503–04, 519 (KJOY).

74. *Id.* at 509, 523 (KVON).

75. *Id.* at 505–06, 520 (KPAY). *See also* Wilderness Soc'y, 31 F.C.C.2d 729, 735 (1971) (Chairman Burch, concurring) ("4 or 5" to 1); Leading Families of Am., 31 F.C.C.2d 594 (1971) (5 to 1); Letter to Marjorie Wood, 8330-E, C4-1644, C5-134 (FCC July 14, 1976) (mimeograph) (7 to 4). *But see* George E. Cooley, 10 F.C.C.2d 969 (1967), where, in the context of the political editorial rule, the Commission decided that a 4 to 1 frequency ratio of broadcasts of the same length did not constitute a reasonable presentation balance. The licensee had decided that "broadcast time could most effectively be used by frequent repetition of a brief statement rather than by less frequent broadcast of longer statements" and the complainant deserved a "comparable opportunity." *Id. See also* Citizens for Responsible Gov't, 25 F.C.C.2d 73 (1970) where, assuming editorials and editorial replies were about the same length, the total time ratio was roughly 4 to 1. The Commission emphasized the timing of the broadcasts before an election, and "the frequency of the broadcasts (which involve the factors of effective repetition and the reaching of possibly different audiences)" in determining that the licensee had acted unreasonably, where the frequency ratio was approximately 9 to 1. *Id.* at 74.

76. *Notice of Proposed Rulemaking, Advertisement of Cigarettes,* 16 F.C.C.2d 284 (1969).

77. With some licensees, however, the Commission professed concern about frequency and audience disparities. Thus with KSRO, the total time imbalance, "when coupled with gross disparities in frequency and audience" made KSRO's actions unreasonable. Public Media Center, 59 F.C.C.2d 494, 522 (1976) (KSRO). However, the frequency ratio of 8.6 to 1 for KSRO was far less than that for other stations that were found to have acted reasonably, and at least some of the contrasting views had been aired in prime time. *Id.* This

is not to say that the KSRO decision was wrong; however, it does raise questions about consistent decision making, and just what standard is to be followed.

78. *Id.* at 509 (KVON). KVON had also run 27 promotional announcements for its one-hour anti-nuclear show. *Id.* However, the FCC, and apparently the licensee, did not indicate what was said on these announcements. Without more, it is difficult to see how they can be weighed on the anti-nuclear side.

79. 59 F.C.C.2d 494, 507-08, 522 (1976).

80. 25 F.C.C.2d 283, 296 (1970). Actually, one of the addresses occurred between 6:00 P.M. and 6:14 P.M. The hours from 7:30 P.M. to 11:00 P.M. "usually encompass greater viewing." National Broadcasting Co., 16 F.C.C.2d 956, 957 asterisk note (1969).

81. However, despite the conclusion that NBC's activity had been unreasonable, in light of its half-hour prime time broadcast presenting contrasting views, NBC would have "the least requirement" for counterprogramming. Committee for Fair Broadcasting, 25 F.C.C.2d 283, 298 (1970). No specifics on the "requirement" were offered.

82. However, the Commission indicated that these responses were not required under the *Zapple* "political party" doctrine. See notes 104–12, *supra,* and accompanying text. Also, in Republican National Comm., 25 F.C.C.2d 739 (1970), the Commission stated: "Presidential appearances (other than as a candidate for re-election, when of course, 'equal opportunities' would be applicable, or, in the event of its repeal, fairness in the 'political party' sense) do not come within the 'political party' doctrine. . . ." *Id.* at 744.

83. The Democratic National Committee, litigating under the leadership of then noted Washington attorney Joseph Califano, was extremely active in seeking response time to President Nixon. Despite the Committee's vigorous efforts, the Commission refused to grant such requests. In a case where the Committee sought a reply to the President's economic message, the Commission stressed that prime time programming was an important balancing factor, in accord with Committee for Fair Broadcasting, 25 F.C.C.2d 283 (1970), but it found that two prime time radio-TV presidential addresses—for a 3.7 to 1 total prime time ratio—were distinguishable from five prime time addresses in an earlier opinion. Moreover, press conferences by the Treasury Secretary were not included in the calculation, and non-prime-time appearances by the President were deemphasized. Democratic Nat'l Comm., 33 F.C.C.2d 631 (1972), *aff'd,* 481 F.2d 543 (D.C. Cir. 1973).

In another decision the Commission seemingly ignored audience considerations, and refused the DNC's request to reply to two programs, one consisting of an interview of the President and the other of a presidential address on American Southeast Asia policy. The key fact that distinguished the case from *Committee for Fair Broadcasting* was that the interview programs ranged over a variety of issues and did not focus on the single issue of the Vietnam war. The Commission also refused to consider the presidential appearances as falling under the *Zapple* doctrine. Democratic National Comm. 31 F.C.C.2d 708 (1971), *aff'd,* 460 F.2d 891 (D.C. Cir. 1972). See also note 101, *infra,* and accompanying text.

In 1972 the Commission rejected the demand of the DNC and the American Civil Liberties Union that, whenever a President speaks, there be a mandated opportunity to reply by an opposition party spokesman. The Commission, aside from considering this a matter for Congress to resolve, suggested that such a regulation would infringe on licensee discretion and not be a sound policy. *Handling of Public Issues Under the Fairness Doctrine and the Public Interest Standards of the Communications Act (First Report—Handling of Political Broadcast),* 36 F.C.C.2d 40, 46–48 [hereinafter cited as *First Report*]. The ruling was later published as appendix A to the *Fairness Report, supra* note 1, at 23385, since it was the first part of the comprehensive report that resulted from the fairness inquiry. *See also* Richard B. Kay, 33 F.C.C.2d 1006 (1972) (Commission refused to order networks to make time available to presidential candidate of American Party to reply to State of the Union message); Senate of the Commonwealth of P. R., 37 F.C.C.2d 579 (1972) (Commission refused to order Puerto Rican television station to provide time for Senate to respond to State of the Commonwealth address by Governor of Puerto Rico).

84. Northern Plains Resource Council, 59 F.C.C.2d 482 (1976).

85. *See, e.g.,* Democratic Nat'l Comm., 33 F.C.C.2d 631 (1972): "I search the majority's

opinion in vain . . . for any evidence that it even *considered* the question of the time span within which the President's appearances took place. I cannot see how as a matter of rational common sense the majority can come to a decision without even considering this crucial factor." *Id.* at 641–42 (Commissioner Johnson, dissenting [emphasis in original]).

86. National Broadcasting Co., 22 F.C.C.2d 446, 448, *rev'd on other grounds*, 25 F.C.C.2d 735 (1970). *See also Fairness Report, supra* note 1, at 26378 par. 47 (the public's interest in "receiving timely information on public issues" must be safeguarded); James Batal, 24 F.C.C.2d 301 (1970) (opposing views must be presented "within a time reasonably approximate to the initial presentation").

87. Northern Plains Resource Council, 59 F.C.C.2d 482 (1976).

88. Citizens for Responsible Gov't, 25 F.C.C.2d 73 (1970). See note 74, *supra*, (additional importance given to broadcast made one day before the election); Timothy K. Ford, 57 F.C.C.2d 1208 (1976). "The purpose and goal of the fairness doctrine is 'the development of an informed public opinion through the public dissemination of news and ideas concerning the vital public issues of the day. . . . It is obvious that this goal could be frustrated if contrasting viewpoints on controversial issues of public importance were not presented in a timely fashion, before the issue involved becomes moot. Therefore, the fact that an issue may be a factor appropriately considered in determining the reasonableness of the licensee's handling of the issue." *Id.* at 1209.

89. Robert R. Soltis, 23 F.C.C.2d 62 (1970).

90. Public Media Center, 59 F.C.C.2d 494 (1976). But in this case the Commission failed to even mention that an election on the issues involved was imminent and to consider this in its balancing judgment. The decision appears inconsistent with National Broadcasting Co., 22 F.C.C.2d 446, *rev'd on other grounds*, 25 F.C.C.2d 735 (1970), in which the Commission stated, "The 2-year lapse between presentations of contrasting views on a particular issue clearly cannot be considered reasonable under the circumstances." 22 F.C.C.2d at 448. One distinguishing ground may be the Commission's assertion that the nuclear energy issue in *Public Media Center* was a continuing controversy and of public importance. But the Commission does not adequately deal with why the private pilot safety issue in *National Broadcasting* is not such a continuing issue. Indeed, in light of the NBC broadcast and the reaction it provoked, one would think that the issue was continuing and current. *See also* Northern Plains Resource Council, 59 F.C.C.2d 487 (1976) (alleged elapse time of approximately one year between contrasting view presentations on proposed power generating plants and transmission lines held not unreasonable; complaint that licensee neglected one viewpoint for significant period of time rejected, since controversy was continuing); John Cervase, 48 F.C.C.2d 335 (1974) (six-month interval between contrasting views on "Kawaida Towers" not unreasonable); William J. Strawbridge, 23 F.C.C.2d 286 (1970) (several-month interval between airing of contrasting views of Arab-Israeli situation not unreasonable).

91. HENRY GELLER, THE FAIRNESS DOCTRINE IN BROADCASTING 37 (1973).

92. John L. Swartz, *Fairness for Whom? Administration of the Fairness Doctrine, 1969–70,* 14 B.C. IND. & COM. L. REV. 457, 464 n.46 (1973). Two 1969 rulings were also charted in the study but were not included in calculating the average given in the text, which relates to 1970 decisions.

93. Indeed, how does one include the possibility that people may record a show and see it during a different time period, as is now possible with the Betamax (and similar home videotape machines)? *See Two Studios Sue Over Betamax,* BROADCASTING, Nov. 22, 1976, at 45.

94. 31 F.C.C.2d 729 (1971).

95. *Id.* at 740. The frequency ratio was "4 or 5 to 1." *Id.* at 735 (Chairman Burch, concurring). *See also* Miami Beach Betterment Ass'n, 27 F.C.C.2d 350, where the "stopwatch" technique was further complicated by counting lines on newscasts, getting a contrasting view ratio based on the line comparison, and combining this with time ratios for other programming to reach a judgment.

96. Wilderness Society, 31 F.C.C.2d 729, 735 (1971) (Chairman Burch, concurring).

97. *Id.* at 736–38. Commissioner Johnson in a separate opinion declared: "Of course, the fairness doctrine is subjective and difficult to enforce on a case by case basis. But that's what

the common law has been all about for centuries. And its creation is what commissioners and judges are paid to do. 'Fairness,' as it has been interpreted over the years, is no more difficult to apply—or to use in guiding men's behavior—than 'negligence,' 'false and misleading,' 'tend to create a monopoly' or the 'reasonable man.' Any of these concepts can be ridiculed and made to appear impossible of administration—especially by those who don't like their effect in the first place. But such is the stuff of which 'law and order' is made. It has worked pretty well. It should be improved where it can be. But the anarchy that remains when it's disposed of is a pretty poor substitute." *Id.* at 743 (Commissioner Johnson, concurring and dissenting).

98. Interview with John Eger, Acting Director, Office of Telecommunications Policy, by Steven J. Simmons, Sept. 2, 1975. Eger had worked as a legal assistant to Dean Burch and as an "attorney advisor" in the FCC General Counsel's office.

99. H. GELLER, *supra* note 91, at 33–34 (emphasis omitted).

100. If the FCC and Congress continue the fairness doctrine in its present form, the FCC should establish a consistent set of precedents, and explain how it reaches its decisions. A two-tiered approach should allow licensees far greater discretion in news broadcasts, documentaries, panel shows, and all other public issue programming than in explicit licensee editorials. With the former, only broad balancing parameters should be used to judge a licensee's reasonableness.

101. Committee for Fair Broadcasting, 25 F.C.C.2d 283, 299–301, *petition for reconsideration denied sub nom.*, Republican Nat'l Comm., 25 F.C.C.2d 739 (1970), *rev'd sub nom.* CBS v. FCC, 454 F.2d 1018 (D.C. Cir. 1971).

102. A few years later Lawrence O'Brien was personally subjected to a Republican communication offensive of a very different order, when his phone was wiretapped in the famous Watergate break-in.

103. Telegram from Frank Stanton, President of CBS, to Lawrence O'Brien, June 22, 1970, *cited in* CBS v. FCC, 454 F.2d 1018, 1021 n.3 (D.C. Cir. 1971).

104. 23 F.C.C.2d 707 (1970). The Commission acted in response to a letter from Nicholas Zapple, Communications Counsel, Committee on Commerce, U.S. Senate, requesting an interpretive ruling.

105. "[B]arring unusual circumstances, it would not be reasonable for a licensee to refuse to sell time to spokesmen for or supporters of candidate B comparable to that previously bought on behalf of candidate A." *Id.* at 708.

106. "When spokesmen or supporters of candidate A have purchased time, it is our view that it would be inappropriate to require licensees to in effect subsidize the campaign of an opposing candidate by providing candidate B's spokesmen or supporters with free time. . . ." *Id.* at 708. Even if criticism of a presidential candidate by an opponent's supporters is allegedly "false and misleading" and malicious, the criticized candidate's supporters are not entitled to free time under *Zapple.* Committee to Elect McGovern-Shriver, 38 F.C.C.2d 300 (1972).

107. 47 U.S.C. sec. 315 (1971). In fact, Commissioner Johnson declared: "I see no legal reason why the Commission could not rule that sec. 315(a) encompasses spokesmen for or supporters of political candidates as a logical extension of congressional intent. Instead, the majority has brought supporters and spokesmen in under the fairness doctrine, and then excluded them from its free time aspect established in *Cullman.* . . ." Nicholas Zapple, 23 F.C.C.2d 707, 710 n.2 (1970).

108. *First Report, supra* note 83, at 41, 48–49. However, the *Zapple* doctrine "does not overrule" the holding of Lawrence M.C. Smith, 40 F.C.C. 549 (1963). See note 16, *supra,* and accompanying text. Thus, "fringe party candidates" need not be given treatment comparable to major party candidates, and can still, in effect, be ignored. *First Report, supra* note 83, at 49–50.

109. The Commission has stated that treatment of competing supporters "while not mathematically rigid" must at least "take on the appearance of rough comparability. If the DNC were sold time for a number of spots, it is difficult to conceive on what basis the licensee could then refuse to sell comparable time to the RNC. Or, if during a campaign the latter were given a half hour of free time to advance its cause, could a licensee fairly reject the

subsequent request of the DNC that it be given a comparable opportunity? . . . No licensee would try to act in such an arbitrary fashion." *First Report, supra* note 83, at 49. Thus in the *Zapple* situation, frequency and total time ratios must be approximately equal, and the conditions offered for each individual broadcast must be comparable.

110. *See* Wyoming Broadcasting Co., 27 F.C.C.2d 752 (1971), in which the Commission ruled that charging one candidate's supporters $1.50 and another's $1.25 for a thirty-second announcement, and giving one candidate twice the amount of time as others for the same price, violated the *Zapple* doctrine.

111. *First Report, supra* note 83, at 50. Note also that, unlike the general fairness doctrine, *Zapple* is not applicable to bona fide "newscasts." *Id.* at 50 n.12. Although the FCC stops at "newscasts," it still discussed the nonapplicability of *Zapple* in the context of the equal time exemptions in 47 U.S.C. sec. 315, which include bona fide interviews, documentaries, and news events. Thus, presumably, *Zapple* is not applicable to these other news categories, despite the FCC's sloppy wording. This is the way the National Association of Broadcasters has interpreted *Zapple. See* NATIONAL ASSOCIATION OF BROADCASTERS, POLITICAL BROADCAST CATECHISM 36, Q.181 (7th ed. 1972). It also appears that *Zapple* is not applicable all year round but, "for all practical purposes," only during campaign periods. *First Report, supra* note 83, at 50. The FCC also has stated that, if free time is given to supporters of a candidate, the same amount of free time must be given to an opponent's supporters, presumably in the nonexempt, nonnews context. *Id.* at 49. Query as to the status of balancing free time in light of *Committee for Fair Broadcasting* and its litigation progeny. See notes 80–83, *supra,* and accompanying text. The Commission has not clarified whether, if opposing spokesmen or supporters refuse or are unable to pay for response time under *Zapple,* traditional fairness principles require the licensee to present the other candidate's views free of charge, or whether there is an affirmative obligation to seek out spokesmen to present those views. If candidates are not to "subsidize" each other's campaigns per the *Zapple* doctrine, the logical extension of that doctrine suggests that, once the offer to respond to the paid time has been turned down by the opposing candidate, the licensee's obligations end in terms of balancing the views presented by the first candidate's spokesmen in their broadcast. The licensee, nonetheless, would have a continuing obligation to cover the campaign and contrasting sides per general fairness doctrine principles. But if *Zapple* is to parallel the equal time obligation in section 315, there should be no "seek out" requirement, since in the equal time context opposing candidates must contact the licensee to initiate equal time programming. 47 C.F.R. secs. 73.657(e) (1976) (TV); 73.120(e) (1976) (AM); 73.290(e) (1976) (FM); 73.590(e) (1976) (noncommercial educational FM).

112. In the *Fairness Report* the Commission reaffirmed the *Zapple* doctrine, although it refused to extend it to ballot propositions. *Fairness Report, supra* note 1, at 26384 pars. 84–89. *See also First Report, supra* note 83, at 50 n.14. In the *First Report,* the Commission, aside from reaffirming the *Zapple* doctrine, refused to codify it. *Id.* at 48–50.

113. 25 F.C.C.2d 283, *petition for reconsideration denied sub nom.* Republican Nat'l Comm., 25 F.C.C.2d 739 (1970), *rev'd sub nom.* CBS v. FCC, 454 F.2d 1018 (D.C. Cir. 1971).

114. 25 F.C.C.2d at 743. Some cases indicate that the political party corollary actually began with the *Zapple* decision. *See, e.g.,* Democratic National Comm. v. FCC, 460 F.2d 891, 903 (D.C. Cir. 1972). Also see the suggestive language in *Zapple* itself: "(*e.g.,* the chairman of the national committee of a major party purchases time to urge the election of his candidate, and his counterpart then requests free time for a program on behalf of his candidate)," which is set forth as an example of where free time need not be given. Nicholas Zapple, 23 F.C.C.2d 707, 708 (1970).

115. CBS v. FCC, 454 F.2d 1018, 1032 (D.C. Cir. 1971). *See* Democratic Nat'l Comm., 31 F.C.C.2d 708, 713 (1971), for a later case where a reply broadcast on the Indochina war was considered "responsive" because of network supervision over the issues discussed on the program. "When appearances by party spokesmen in response to Presidential appearances are clearly limited to those issues discussed by the President, the licensee is exercising its discretion under the fairness doctrine to choose appropriate spokesmen to discuss contrasting views on controversial issues of public importance." *Id.* at 713.

116. 25 F.C.C.2d 739, 745 (1970).

117. *Id.* at 743. No matter that the O'Brien speech was on July 7, almost four months before the 1970 congressional elections; "electioneering," said the Commission, "is a continuing process." *Id.*

118. *Id.* at 741, 745.

119. 454 F.2d. 1018, 1020 (D.C. Cir. 1971).

120. Letter from FCC Chairman Rosel H. Hyde to Congressman Wayne L. Hays, Feb. 9, 1968, FCC Reference No. 8830–S, C2–105, *cited* in 454 F.2d 1018, 1024 n.35 (D.C. Cir. 1971). In the *Hays* situation, CBS had aired the Republican response to the Democratic President's State of the Union Address. CBS did not specify any issues that the Republicans had to cover, and a wide range was covered. The Commission rejected a Democratic request to reply to the Republican response, citing general fairness doctrine principles of licensee good faith and reasonableness. The Court, however, found unacceptable the Commission's failure to articulate its reasons for treating the similar *Committee for Fair Broadcasting* and *Hays* factual situations in different ways. This is not the only time the District of Columbia Court of Appeals has forced the Commission to abide by its own precedent in the fairness area. *See, e.g.,* Friends of the Earth v. FCC, 449 F.2d 1164 (D.C. Cir. 1971).

121. 454 F.2d 1018, 1028 (D.C. Cir. 1971). The Court stated that in the fairness doctrine area there is "*carte blanche* licensee discretion." *Id.* at 1029. Although the court did not outrightly reject the FCC's "political party corollary" to the *Zapple* doctrine, it declared that the Commission had applied it to a distorted and wholly unreasonable view of the facts. The O'Brien broadcast had been responsive to issues raised by the President and his spokesmen. In claiming that O'Brien's presentation had been "unresponsive" to the President's Indochina war speech (see note 115, *supra*), the Commission arbitrarily excluded other issues that the President had addressed in broadcasts, ranging from newscasts to press conferences, arbitrarily chose an eight-month period in which to analyze what issues had been presented, and arbitrarily ignored contrasting views aired by Republican spokesmen other than the President.

122. *Id.* at 1033.

123. *Id.* at 1034–35. The court also rejected a last-minute shift in rationale offered by the Commission, *i.e.,* that CBS failed to dictate to the DNC the precise issues to be discussed in the O'Brien broadcast. This switch from a "responsiveness" to a "specification of issues" rationale, *id.* at 1033–34, was an unacceptable post hoc rationalization by appellate counsel, was irrational, and raised serious First Amendment problems.

124. Fred Friendly, The Good Guys, the Bad Guys and the First Amendment 127–33 (1976).

125. Mickelson, *The First Amendment and Broadcast Journalism,* in The First Amendment and the News Media. Final Report, Annual Chief Justice Earl Warren Conference on Advocacy in the United States 57 (1973) (sponsored by the Roscoe Pound–American Trial Lawyers Foundation).

126. *CBS Charged With Undercovering Advocates of Military Power,* Broadcasting, Sept. 13, 1976, at 28.

127. Levine, *Anti-Communist Group Lobbies to Keep U.S. a Military Superpower,* Wall St. J., Aug. 1, 1972, at 1, col. 1.

128. Broadcasting, *supra* note 126, at 28.

129. F. Friendly, *supra* note 124, at 188–89.

130. *Id.* at 167–91.

131. *Id.* at 189.

132. Even before the ASCEF complaint was filed, CBS news was devoting an "enormous amount of time getting ready," with archivists, researchers, and producers reviewing past programming. According to Richard Salant, "we have to crawl through all our transcripts, all our broadcasts over two or three years, and you just stop dead with research." Interview with Richard Salant, president, CBS, by Steven J. Simmons, Aug. 15, 1975 [hereinafter cited as Interview with Richard Salant].

133. See Chapter Two, p. 12, for a discussion of FCC sanctions in the fairness area.

134. See Chapter Two, pp. 11-12, for a discussion of FCC fairness enforcement procedures.

135. See Chapter Two, pp. 11–12.
136. 21 F.C.C.2d 12 (1969). According to Milton Gross: "Under our fairness doctrine policy, the burden is on the complainant to prove his case. How he does it is up to him. We have set forth certain guidelines in the Fairness Report. . . ." Interviews with Milton Gross, *supra* note 59.
137. 21 F.C.C.2d 12, 13 (1969).
138. *Fairness Report, supra* note 1, at 26379 par. 52. The Commission continued: "This does not require that the complainant listen to or view the station 24 hours a day, seven days a week. One example of a 'regular' television viewer would be a person who routinely (but not necessarily every day) watches the evening news and a significant portion of the public affairs programs of a given station. In the case of radio, a regular listener would include a person, who, as a matter of routine, listens to major representative segments of the station's news and public affairs programming. Also, the assumption that a station has failed to present an opposing viewpoint would be strengthened if several regular viewers or listeners join together in a statement that they have not heard a presentation of that viewpoint. Complainants should specify the nature and extent of their viewing or listening habits, and should indicate the period of time during which they have been regular members of the station's audience." *Id.* Another factor that is particularly difficult for a complainant to substantiate is whether an issue is a controversial issue of public importance. Among the items a complainant may point to are: degree of media coverage, attention from government officials and other community leaders, and impact on the community. *Id.* at 26378. The precedents on this question are inconsistent and severely lacking in explanatory rationale. See Chapter Six, pp. 154–60.
139. W.C. Ponder, 58 F.C.C.2d 1222 (1976). In fact, the *Fairness Report*, whose guidelines were intended to clarify fairness obligations, thereby aiding complainants and licensees, may have hindered complainants. In explaining why the number of station inquiries decreased by more than half while the number of complainants increased more than tenfold in fiscal year 1976 as compared to FY 1975 and FY 1974, Milton Gross stated: "After the Fairness Report . . . the standards for proceeding on a complaint are fairly rigid. Unless a complaint makes a prima facie case, we do not go to the station. And the public has not come forward with prima facie complaints." Interviews with Milton Gross, *supra* note 59. Thus, although the *Fairness Report*'s guidelines may provide help to a conscientious complainant, they also provide a clearer standard by which the Commission can reject complaints.
140. *Fairness Report, supra* note 1, at 26379 par. 55. But the Commission does "expect that licensees will be cognizant of the programming which has been presented on their stations." *Id.*
141. *Compare* WIYN Radio, 35 F.C.C.2d 175 (1972), *with* Dr. John Gabler, 40 F.C.C.2d 579 (1973), Charlotte Observer, 38 F.C.C.2d 522 (1972), *and* Straus Communications, 51 F.C.C.2d 385 (1975), *vacated and remanded*, 530 F.2d 1001 (D.C. Cir. 1976).
142. Georgia Power Project, 53 F.C.C.2d 907 (1975).
143. *Fairness Primer, supra* note 1, at 10416.
144. In the 1950s there were but "a handful" of fairness complaints and rulings in any one year. Interviews with Milton Gross, *supra* note 59, and review of reported decisions (F.C.C. and P & F RADIO REG.), 1950 through 1960.
145. However, Bill Monroe of NBC News notes: "If 150 stations received a complaint, they had to answer. Over a period of two years, this means 150 stations have had to answer to the government during the period without a single newspaper publisher having to answer to the government. Station managers talk to each other. One station manager learns what the other station manager went through because he had the nerve to authorize a controversial editorial. So, the station manager that didn't even get a complaint from the FCC would like to avoid it, having heard the problem this fellow got into, because he had the nerve to try a controversial editorial. The whole industry is aware of the problem. If you're cited by the FCC for unfairness and asked to readjust the balance, and you've got the nerve to fight the FCC, the legal fees and the complexities of legal cases can build up. It might go to court, as in several noted cases, most recently the NBC "Pensions" program, which hasn't necessarily

run its course in the courts yet, but it's been through a number of courts and it's cost how many thousands of dollars? Even a network has to think twice about, are we going to get into another case like this, wouldn't it be easier to go along with the FCC, even though we disagree, and do something that we think journalistically is inhibiting to us . . . ?" Interview with Bill Monroe by Steven J. Simmons, Sept. 12, 1975 [hereinafter cited as Interview with Bill Monroe].

146. As discussed in Chapter Four, the personal attack and political editorial rules are considered subcategories of the fairness doctrine. The FCC does not keep complaint, station inquiry, or adverse ruling statistics beyond those shown on Chart 1.

147. However, there is no way of telling how many insufficient complaints returned by the Commission staff resulted in the complainants contacting the stations and working out the fairness matter to their mutual satisfaction. A follow-up study of returned complaints would provide a fertile area for further research.

148. According to Florence Kiser, Broadcast Analyst for the Fairness/Political Branch, Complaints and Compliance Division, Broadcast Bureau, who initially reviews all incoming fairness complaints, the "first and foremost" reason why complaints are returned to complainants as inadequate is the failure of complainants to indicate that they have contacted the involved station before complaining to the FCC. Another major problem is that the complainants are often "vague . . . in what they are complaining about. They will say there's too much broadcasting against gun ownership, but they don't give us any program or any reason—they just say it's too much, or there's too much sex on television, or there's too much anti-abortion, without giving us any specific program." Interview with Florence Kiser by Steven J. Simmons, Sept. 9, 1975. The FCC has never required broadcasters to air messages telling the public about the fairness obligation and how fairness complaints can be made.

149. 59 F.C.C.2d 987 (1976). See Chapter Six, pp. 169–71.

150. *See* Mayflower Broadcasting Corp., 8 F.C.C. 333 (1941); United Broadcasting Co., 10 F.C.C. 515 (1945); *Fairness Report. supra* note 1, at 26375 pars. 23–26.

151. The interviews were conducted at the Commission offices in Washington, D.C. between Sept. 3 and Sept. 16, 1975. An interview could not be arranged with Abbott Washburn, who had not yet been confirmed by the United States Senate.

152. *See, e.g., Renewal of Standard Broadcast Station Licenses,* 7. F.C.C.2d 122 (1967); *Renewal of Standard Broadcast and Television Licenses for Oklahoma, Kansas and Nebraska,* 14 F.C.C.2d 2 (1968); Herman C. Hall, 11 F.C.C.2d 344 (1968); *Broadcast Licenses for Arkansas, Louisiana, and Mississippi,* 42 F.C.C.2d 3 (1973).

153. New York Times Co. v. United States, 403 U.S. 713 (1971); Near v. Minnesota, 283 U.S. 697 (1931).

154. New York Times Co. v. Sullivan, 376 U.S. 254 (1964).

155. Joseph Burstyn, Inc. v. Wilson, 343 U.S. 495 (1952).

156. Red Lion Broadcasting Co. v. FCC, 395 U.S. 367 (1969).

157. Miami Herald Publishing Co. v. Tornillo, 418 U.S. 241 (1974).

158. Also questionable is the concept that, since the public "owns" the airwaves, this justifies content control. Does public ownership of forests from which trees are cut to make newsprint mean that the government can control the content of newspapers? Are speeches at outdoor rallies somehow subject to government direction because the "airwaves" are used? Indeed, are conversations on one's back porch subject to federal control due to vocal chord generation of a publicly owned resource? Drawn to its extreme, the ownership rationale raises fundamental and troubling questions.

159. Letter from Martin I. Levy, Chief, Broadcast Facilities Division, FCC Broadcast Bureau to Steven J. Simmons, Dec. 8, 1976 (material relating to channel scarcity prepared under Levy's supervision, material relating to renewal process prepared under supervision of Richard J. Shiben, Chief, Renewal and Transfer Division) [hereinafter cited as Levy Letter]. However, Levy did not comment on the continued viability of the fairness doctrine, and the frequency figures he supplied should not be construed as a reflection of his views on the doctrine.

160. However, in both major and intermediate markets available "vacant" frequencies for AM radio and VHF television are hard to come by. "The only VHF channel in the top 25 markets which can presently be applied for is an educational allocation in the Dallas-Fort Worth market. . . . There is no easy way to estimate the number of additional stations that can ultimately be accommodated in the AM band . . . it is apparent that little, if any, further expansion is possible in major and intermediate markets." *Id.* It should be noted that frequencies that are not "vacant" but are used by a licensee may be obtained in connection with the sale of a station's facilities. In 1975, 363 radio stations and 22 TV stations changed hands, 1976 BROADCASTING YEARBOOK A-52.

161. According to FCC tabulations, as of Sept. 30, 1976, there were a total of 8,077 licensed radio stations and 932 licensed TV stations, or a total of 9,009 broadcast licensees. BROADCASTING, Dec. 13, 1976, at 77. As of Jan. 1, 1971, there were 1,749 daily newspapers in the United States.

162. 1976 BROADCASTING YEARBOOK B-41, C-19, 20.

163. *See* Steven J. Simmons, *The Fairness Doctrine and Cable TV*, 11 HARV. J. LEGIS. 629 (1974).

164. The Supreme Court has not yet fully worked out another constitutional rationale. Factors that might be considered in developing such a rationale include the intrusive and "captive" nature of television, the power of a network to reach a vast audience, the obligation to provide time to others as a condition of receiving a valuable license relatively free of charge, the ability of the government to cause citizens of all ages to be exposed to vital public educational information just as it causes young citizens to attend school and be exposed to a school curriculum, and the economic monopoly generated from government action.

165. CBS v. Democratic Nat'l Comm., 412 U.S. 94 (1973).

166. *Id.* at 116-18.

167. National Broadcasting Co. v. FCC, 516 F.2d 1101, 1110-11 (D.C. Cir. 1974). Judge Tamm stated: "Properly understood, the fairness doctrine is a balancing influence between the public's right of access to the broadcast media and the right of licensees to transmit their own message." *Id.* at 1192 (Tamm, J., concurring in support of the order). According to Chief Justice Burger, the "role of the Government as an 'over-seer' and ultimate arbiter and guardian of the public interest and the role of the licensee as a journalistic 'free agent' call for a delicate balancing of competing interests. The maintenance of this balance for more than 40 years has called on both the regulators and the licensees to walk a 'tightrope' to preserve the First Amendment values written into the Radio Act and its successor, the Communications Act." CBS v. Democratic National Comm., 412 U.S. 94, 117 (1973) (Burger, C.J., concurring).

168. This potential is acknowledged by the FCC: "We recognize, however, that there exists within the framework of fairness doctrine administration and enforcement the potential for undue governmental interference in the processes of broadcast journalism, and the concomitant diminution of the broadcaster's and the public's legitimate First Amendment interest." *Fairness Report, supra* note 1, at 26374.

169. See note 21, *supra*.

170. Accuracy in Media, Inc., 40 F.C.C.2d 958, *application for review denied,* 44 F.C.C.2d 1027 (1973), *rev'd, but then reversal vacated and case remanded with direction to vacate order and dismiss complaint sub nom.* National Broadcasting Co. v. FCC, 516 F.2d 1101 (D.C. Cir. 1974), *cert. denied,* 424 U.S. 910 (1976). NBC personnel and legal expense estimates were supplied in interview with Marshall Wellborn, NBC Assistant General Attorney, and Russell Tornabene, NBC Public Relations, by Steven J. Simmons, Aug. 26, 1975. See the discussion of the "Pensions" case in Chapter Six, pp. 160-66.

171. H. GELLER, *supra* note 91, at 40-43 app. E.

172. Interview with Bill Monroe, *supra* note 145.

173. Miami Herald Publishing Co. v. Tornillo, 418 U.S. 241, 256 (1974).

174. *Id.* at 257. The Court continues, "Government-enforced right of access inescapably 'dampens the vigor and limits the variety of public debate.' " *Id.*

175. FLA. STAT. sec. 104.38 (1973). The statute reads as follows: "Sec. 104.38. *News-*

paper assailing candidate in an election; space for reply—If any newspaper in its column assails the personal character of any candidate for nomination or for election in any election, or charges said candidate with malfeasance or misfeasance in office, or otherwise attacks his official record, or gives to another free space for such purpose, such newspaper shall upon request of such candidate immediately publish free of cost any reply he may make thereto in as conspicuous a place and in the same kind of type as the matter that calls for such reply, provided such reply does not take up more space than the matter replied to. Any person or firm failing to comply with the provision of this section shall be guilty of a misdemeanor of the first degree, punishable as provided in sec. 775.082 or sec. 775.083."

176. *See* F. WOLF, TELEVISION PROGRAMMING FOR NEWS AND PUBLIC AFFAIRS 77 (1972); *ABC Took Strict View of Fairness Doctrine in Its Cavett Ruling,"* Wall St. J., Mar. 11, 1974, at 14, cols. 4–5. In any month there may well be a BROADCASTING editorial lambasting the fairness doctrine. In personal interviews broadcast journalists have stressed the First Amendment chill generated by the fairness doctrine. *See, e.g.,* Interview with Bill Monroe, *supra* note 145; Interview with Richard Salant, *supra* note 132.

177. The Florida statute in *Miami Herald* was enacted in 1913, and the 1974 Supreme Court decision was only the second ever decided under its provisions. Miami Herald Publishing Co. v. Tornillo, 418 U.S. 241 (1974).

178. Memorandum For: H. R. Haldeman, From J. S. Magruder, Re: The Shot-gun versus the Rifle, Oct. 17, 1969, reprinted in David Bazelon, *FCC Regulation of the Telecommunications Press,* 1975 DUKE L.J. 213, 247–48 app. B. In the memorandum, Magruder also lists seven specific requests that the President made in less than a 30-day period for staff action to counter broadcast coverage, such as, "President's request that you take appropriate action to counter biased TV coverage of the Adm. over the summer. (Log 1644) CONFIDENTIAL." *Id.* at 249. It should be stressed that no evidence has been revealed to indicate that Chairman Burch participated in such a "monitoring" scheme. For a decision that was subject to at least charges of political motivation, see Committee for Fair Broadcasting, 25 F.C.C.2d 283 (1970), Letter to Wayne Hays, Feb. 9, 1968, FCC Reference No. 8830–5, C2–105, cited in 454 F.2d 1108, 1024. See note 120, *supra.* See also CBS v. FCC, 454 F.2d 1018, 1035–36 (D.C. Cir. 1971) (Tamm, J., concurring). NBC broadcast journalist Bill Monroe has stated: "Our impression was that the Nixon administration . . . would, in some cases, withhold spokesmen from their side in order to play the issue down in the hopes that this would result in the broadcaster feeling that rather than present an unbalanced program, he would have to go away from the subject altogether." Interview with Bill Monroe, *supra* note 145.

179. Memorandum for H. R. Haldeman, from Chuck Colson, reprinted in Bazelon, *supra* note 178, at 244 app. A.

180. *See* F. FRIENDLY, *supra* note 124, at 32–42. Friendly alleges that even the *Red Lion* litigation may have been begun as part of this Democratic fairness campaign. According to Friendly, Fred Cook, the complainant in the case, worked closely with the Democratic National Committee and "may have been unwittingly manipulated." *Id.* at 42.

181. *Id.* at 41–42. Friendly also alleges that the Kennedy administration was involved in a 1963 national fairness doctrine campaign to aid passage of the nuclear test ban treaty by providing pro-treaty viewpoints over the air to counteract broadcasters with contrasting views. *Id.* at 34.

182. 59 F.C.C.2d 987 (1976).

183. See Chapter Six, p. 172.

184. See Chapter Six, pp. 171–73.

185. Indeed, in light of the availability of FM radio and UHF television frequencies in many markets, and the abundance of existing AM and FM radio stations in major market areas, an argument can be made for eliminating fairness doctrine obligations for these UHF and radio media outlets. See Chairman Wiley's proposal to deregulate radio in certain major markets in *A Determined FCC Is Setting New Course for Industry on Fairness and Equal Time,* BROADCASTING, Sept. 22, 1975, at 22–34. The Commission has decided not to proceed with the proposal "at this time." *Reconsideration Fairness Report, supra* note 1, at 699 n.1. A major reason for the FCC's decision was concern with the legal authority of the

Commission to take such a step in light of the 1959 amendment to the Communications Act of 1934, which incorporated the fairness doctrine as applicable to each licensee. *Id.* at 702 (Commissioner Hooks, concurring). *See* Chapter Two, pp. 52-53.

186. *Thoughts of the Chairman on Rewrite of 1934 Act,* BROADCASTING, Nov. 22, 1976, at 20. The House study also provides a good opportunity to consider short-term improvements on the "unfairness doctrine," such as those discussed below. Indeed, the fairness doctrine will be carefully considered by the subcommittee. Interview with Chip Shooshan, Counsel, House Communications Subcommittee, by Steven J. Simmons, Oct. 25, 1976.

187. "65% of AM stations, 54% of FM stations, and 58% of TV stations are now editorializing at least occasionally." 1976 BROADCASTING YEARBOOK C-300.

188. *Report on Editorializing, supra* note 1, at 1254 par. 16; *Report and Statement of Policy Re: Commission en Banc Programming Inquiry,* 44 F.C.C. 2303, 2314 (1960) [hereinafter cited as *Programming Report*].

189. Interview with Richard N. Hughes, President, National Broadcasting Editorial Association, by Steven J. Simmons, Aug. 27, 1975. Letter from Richard N. Hughes to Chairman Richard Wiley, Aug. 20, 1975. The disincentive to air editorials resulting from the balancing obligations would be mitigated by the requirement to air a minimum percentage of public issue programming, including local public issues, and programming responsive to ascertained needs, as discussed below. Editorials could be offered in fulfillment of these requirements. See note 221, *infra.* Licensees' desires to air their views directly would also act as a mitigating factor.

190. Licensees should be familiar with community leaders as a result of their ascertainment efforts. If over-the-air announcements do not produce reply speakers acceptable to the licensee, these leaders or other parties concerned with the issue may be contacted. Letters may be written to appropriate institutions or organizations. Licensees should undertake response recruitment efforts at the very least similar to those required if a reply spokesman is rejected by a licensee. See notes 33-34, *supra,* and accompanying text.

191. Perhaps within an hour before or after the original broadcast. Thus, if an editorial were broadcast at 6:00 P.M., a reply could be aired anywhere between 5:00 and 7:00 P.M. on another evening. Another, possibly more manageable, alternative is to require that prime time editorials be balanced with prime time replies.

192. The FCC might regard certain balance ratios as inherently suspect. A frequency ratio of greater than 3 to 1 might be so regarded. This would require the licensee to rebut the presumption that its balance is unreasonable by demonstrating that the total time balance is significantly skewed the other way (*i.e.,* at least 2 to 1 the other way). As noted, the issue addressed should be easier to identify with explicit editorials. Nonetheless, licensees should be given wide discretion in determining which issue or subissues were raised that require rejoinder, avoiding potential government intervention on so delicate an editorial matter.

193. Licensees should also do much more on their own initiative to provide time for various community and public interest groups to speak their minds in short spot advertisements or messages. For an example of a successful licensee effort in this regard, *see* W. Hanks & P. Longini, *Television Access: A Pittsburgh Experiment,* 18 J. BROADCASTING 289 (1974). Also, the traditional policy of the commercial networks and most licensees to refuse airing of independently produced documentaries deprives the public of potentially interesting investigative journalism and deprives documentary makers of an outlet for their work. Broadcasters can adequately relieve their concern about the integrity of such independent work by carefully screening out what appears unreliable, and airing a disclaimer before the documentary.

194. Licensees would still be subject to sanction anytime during the license period if "substantial extrinsic evidence or documents" that "on their face" reflect "deliberate distortion" of news reporting are submitted to the FCC. *Fairness Report, supra* note 1, 26380 par. 58. *See* Selling of the Pentagon, 30 F.C.C.2d 150, 152 (1971) ("lacking extrinsic evidence or documents that on their face reflect deliberate distortion, we believe that this government licensing agency cannot properly intervene"); Hunger in America, 20 F.C.C.2d 143, 151 par. 22 (1969) ("Rigging or slanting the news is a most heinous act against the public interest— indeed, there is no act more harmful to the public's ability to handle its affairs"); Mrs. J.R.

Paul, 26 F.C.C.2d 591, 591–92 (1969) ("the Commission does act appropriately to protect the public interest . . . where we have received extrinsic evidence of such rigging or slanting (for example, testimony, in writing or otherwise, from 'insiders' or persons who have direct personal knowledge of an intentional attempt to falsify the news). We would be particularly concerned were the extrinsic evidence to reveal orders to falsify the news from the licensee, its top management, or its news management"). *See also* Shady Wall, 31 F.C.C.2d 484, 485 (1971); *Inquiry Into WBBM-TV's Report on a Marihuana Party*, 18 F.C.C.2d 124, 131–40 (1969); *Network Coverage of the Democratic Nat'l Convention*, 16 F.C.C.2d 650, 656–60 (1969).

Another idea worth considering is Henry Geller's suggestion that, although licensees should not be subject to the Commission's judgment or formal complaint proceeding during the term of the license, at license renewal time the licensee should be subject to sanction on a successful challenge by public interest groups or other parties who present evidence of a flagrant pattern of abuse of fairness principles. Thus, a licensee who continually spewed forth one-sided "propaganda" in public affairs programming, violating even a *New York Times v. Sullivan* malice-type protective standard, would be subject to sanction at renewal time. But "[n]o conscientious broadcaster need fear review with a standard so heavily weighted in his favor." H. GELLER, *supra* note 91, at 51. *But see* the note at the end of Chapter Five on *National Citizens Comm. for Broadcasting, et al. v. FCC*, 46 U.S.L.W. 2264 (1977). Another factor working against a licensee presenting one-sided, biased public issue programming is the economic incentive not to offend an audience. Even parts of audiences opposed to views aired over a station may accept a licensee's broadcasting of those views if the licensee also presents other sides fairly. People are likely to respect a licensee who approaches public issues with integrity and fairness. Continuously one-sided presentations, however, may well result in loss of a significant part of an audience.

195. One survey conducted at the end of 1974 by the Roper Organization indicated that fully 39 percent of the American people felt television was devoting "too little time" to "having people express their opinion on the air." ROPER ORGANIZATION, TRENDS IN PUBLIC ATTITUDES TOWARD TELEVISION AND OTHER MASS MEDIA, 1959–1974 at 13 (1975). Although perhaps biased by the question's wording and reference to the different roles of television and magazines, only 22 percent of those surveyed (still a sizable minority) indicated that they wanted television to air "more news and public affairs." *Id.* at 19.

196. In its definitive 1949 *Report on Editorializing, supra* note 1, at 1249 par. 6, the Commission declared: "It is axiomatic that one of the most vital questions of mass communication in a democracy is the development of an informed public opinion through the public dissemination of news and ideas concerning the vital public issues of the day. Basically, it is in recognition of the great contribution which radio can make in the advancement of this purpose that portions of the radio spectrum are allocated to that form of radio communication known as radiobroadcasting. Unquestionably, then, the standard of public interest, convenience and necessity as applied to radiobroadcasting must be interpreted in the light of this basic purpose. It is this right of the public to be informed rather than any right on the part of the Government, any broadcast licensee or any individual member of the public to broadcast his own particular views on any matter, which is the foundation stone of the American system of broadcasting."

197. For a discussion of the Nielsen rating system, *see* L. BROWN, TELEVISION: THE BUSINESS BEHIND THE BOX 31–35, 177–78, 196–98 (1971). Controversial issue programming may also make audiences hostile to a particular sponsor, causing advertisers to shy away from such programming. *See* the adverse advertiser reacton to "Guns of Autumn," a CBS documentary, in BROADCASTING, Sept. 15, 1975, at 50. *See also* the discussion of "Migrant," an NBC documentary, in L. BROWN, TELEVISION; THE BUSINESS BEHIND THE BOX 267 (1971). Controversial programming may also interrupt "audience flow," diminishing viewer levels for adjacent entertainment programs. *See id.* at 115–16 for a discussion of audience flow. It should be noted that good public issue programming has occasionally done well in the Nielsen ratings, as the success of CBS's "60 Minutes" indicates.

198. In fact, under the double standard for part one issue coverage, FCC intervention comes when least needed. See Chapter Six, pp. 172–73.

199. Public affairs programs are defined by the Commission as follows: "(d) Public affairs programs (PA) are programs dealing with local, state, regional, national or international issues or problems, including, but not limited to, talks, commentaries, discussions, speeches, editorials, political programs, documentaries, mini-documentaries, panels, round-tables, vignettes, and extended coverage (whether live or recorded) of public events or proceedings,such as local council meetings, Congressional hearings, and the like." *Radio Broadcast Services,* 47 C.F.R. sec. 73.112 (note 1: *Program definitions* (d)).

News programs are defined as: "(c) News programs (N) include reports dealing with current local, national and international events, including weather and stock market reports; and when an integral part of a news program, commentary, analysis, and sports news." *Id.* at (c).

200. "Each commercial television licensee is required to file by February 1 of each year an Annual Programming Report (F.C.C. Form 303-A . . .) covering a selected composite week during the preceding calendar year and showing the amount of time and percentage of total operating time devoted to various types of local and informational programming during certain peak time periods. For each program included in the categories of 'public affairs' and 'all others,' the date and time of broadcast, duration and source is submitted. Each year the Commission compiles the statistics submitted by the stations on Form 303-A into an 'Annual Programming Report for Commercial Television Stations' which shows the relative amounts of broadcast time each station devotes to news, public affairs, and other non-entertainment/ non-sports programs, along with summaries for each television market and for the nation." Levy letter, *supra* note 159. At renewal time, if a television applicant's programming, as reflected in the current Annual Programming Report, varies "substantially" from programming representations made at the previous renewal, the applicant must explain the discrepancy. *See Broadcast Station License Renewal Application Form, Revision of Form 303,* 41 FED REG. 19536, 19571 app. D (1976). (FCC Form 303 1976, sec. IV, 8c. [hereinafter cited as *License Renewal*). The television applicant must also indicate the minimum amount of time it normally plans to devote to news and public affairs each week. *Id.* at 19572 (Q.9). Although radio stations are not required to submit Annual Programming Reports, at renewal time they are required to report on past and proposed news and public affairs programming percentages. *See id.* at 19559 app. C (Q.14) (FCC Form 303-R 1976). *See also id.* at 19556 app. B, pt. IV (Renewal Checklist, Programming).

201. Levy letter, *supra* note 159.

202. *Amendment to Section 0.281 of the Commission's Rules: Delegations of Authority to the Chief, Broadcast Bureau,* 59 F.C.C.2d 491, 493 (1976) [hereinafter cited as *Amendment, 0.281*]. Under the rule, renewal authority is not delegated for AM and FM licensee proposals for "less than eight and six percent, respectively, of total non-entertainment programming" and for TV proposals excluding unaffiliated UHF stations for less than "five percent total local programming." *Id.* at 493.

203. Under the previous rule, AM, FM, and television proposals had to be referred to the Commission for review if they contained less than 6, 8, and 10 percent, respectively, nonentertainment material. There was no percentage for local or informational (*i.e.,* news and public affairs) programming. Nonentertainment broadcasts included everything from agricultural to religious programming. *Id.* at 492.

204. The percentage guidelines also suffer from a failure to distinguish news from public affairs. News, especially local news, has often become a profitable endeavor in recent years. *See* F. WOLF, *supra* note 176, at 133. But presentations such as documentaries, round-table discussions, interview shows, and live coverage of legislative hearings are often unprofitable. By lumping public affairs programming with news in the 5 percent category, the Commission further discourages airing of these educational shows.

205. *Report on Editorializing, supra* note 1, at 1249 par. 6.

206. In fact, the automatic renewal percentages are based on prospective programming. The Commission has also ruled that the staff, after a retrospective look at what was programmed over the preceding three years, need not regard a variation of under 15 or 20 percent as "substantial" requiring further examination of the licensee's variance explana-

tion. Thus a variation of 15 percent less than the promised 5 percent informational programming would seemingly not be a cause for concern. *Amendment, 0.281, supra* note 202, at 492–93.

207. *Formulation of Policies Relating to the Broadcast Renewal Applicant, Stemming From the Comparative Hearing Process, Docket No. 19154, Third Further Notice of Inquiry,* 43 F.C.C.2d 1043, 1047 (1973) [hereinafter cited as *Third Further Notice of Inquiry*]. In the FCC survey these VHF affiliates aired a median of 15.5 percent news and public affairs from sign-on to sign-off. The 50 next largest (38 stations with revenues under $5 million) aired a median of 13.9 percent. UHF affiliates aired medians of 11 percent (38 stations with revenues over $1 million) and 10.7 percent (57 stations with revenues under $1 million). *Id.* at 1047. In the two-year-average percentages based on Annual Programming Reports filed with the FCC for 1975 and 1974, 686 commercial television stations reported an average of 9.3 percent news and 4.5 percent public affairs programming or a total of 13.8 percent informational programming. *Programming by Commercial Television Stations,* TELEVISION BROADCAST PROGRAMMING DATA, 1975, FEDERAL COMMUNICATIONS NEWS, ATTACHMENT, 66002 (June 18, 1976).

208. *Amendment, 0.281, supra* note 202, at 491.

209. Interview with James J. Brown, Assistant Chief, Renewal and Transfer Division, Broadcast Bureau, by Steven J. Simmons, Dec. 24, 1976.

210. See note 102, *supra.* See also the range of public affairs median percentages, especially in the prime time periods, in the FCC surveys charted in *Third Further Notice of Inquiry, supra* note 207, at 1045.

211. *Report on Editorializing, supra* note 1, at 1247–48 par. 4; *Programming Report, supra* note 188, at 2314; *Fairness Report, supra* note 1, at 26376 pars. 29–34.

212. *Consideration of the Operation of, and Possible Changes in, the Prime Time Access Rule, sec. 73.658(k) of the Commission's Rules (Second Report and Order),* 50 F.C.C.2d 829 (1975) [hereinafter cited as *Prime Time, Second Report*].

213. F. Lloyd & D. Glazer, Public Affairs Programming Proposal 5, Mar. 1976 (National Citizens Committee for Broadcasting) (mimeograph) [hereinafter cited as NCCB Proposal].

214. *See Prime Time, Second Report, supra* note 212, at 886 app. D; *Status Report on Access Entries,* BROADCASTING, Dec. 20, 1976, at 43–44 ("The Lawrence Welk Show" and "Hee Haw" are the "two biggest hits in prime-access time periods"; "Hollywood Squares" is the winner for "pure access shows," based on Nielsen 22–23 market survey).

215. *See Third Further Notice of Inquiry, supra* note 207, at 1048.

216. The NCCB Proposal includes two other points. In its entirety it reads:

"1) Each television station must provide at least one hour per week of regularly scheduled, prime time, *locally-originated,* public affairs programming.

"2) Each of the three major network affiliates must provide one hour per week of regularly scheduled, prime time, national public affairs programming. This hour may be supplied by the network; and

"3) Each network affiliate not wishing to carry the network offering must provide a second hour of prime time, locally-originated or syndicated, public affairs programming." NCCB Proposal, *supra* note 213, at 3 (footnote omitted).

217. *Formulation of Policies Relating to the Broadcast Renewal Applicant, Stemming From the Comparative Hearing Process (Notice of Inquiry),* 27 F.C.C.2d 580 (1971) [hereinafter cited as *Notice of Inquiry*]; *Formulation of Policies Relating to the Broadcast Renewal Applicant; Stemming From the Comparative Hearing Process (Further Notice of Inquiry),* 31 F.C.C.2d 443 (1971) [hereinafter cited as *Further Notice of Inquiry*]; *Third Further Notice of Inquiry, supra* note 207. *See also Bills to Amend the Communications Act of 1934 With Regard to Renewal of Broadcast Licensees: Hearings Before the Subcommittee on Communications and Power of the House Committee on Interstate and Foreign Commerce,* 93 Cong., 1st Sess. 1121–24 (1973) (statement of Chairman Dean Burch). The percentage guidelines also include specific percentages for prime time programming. See note 218, *infra.* In its percentage guidelines, the Commission wisely separated news and public affairs, providing the latter with a needed special emphasis. See note 218, *infra.* It also issued

specific figures for the all-important prime time periods, something totally lacking in the Commission's delegation authority percentage instructions.

218. The tentative percentages proposed to reflect "substantial service" were as follows:

"(i) With respect to local programming, a range of 10–15% of the broadcast effort (including 10–15% in the prime time period, 6–11 P.M., when the largest audience is available to watch).

"(ii) The proposed figure for news is 8–10% for the network affiliate, 5% for the independent VHF station (including a figure of 8–10% and 5%, respectively in the prime time period).

"(iii) In the public affairs area, the tentative figure is 3–5%, with as stated, a 3% figure for the 6–11 P.M. time period." *Notice of Inquiry, supra* note 217, at 582. The median news figures for VHF affiliates in the top 50 markets according to an FCC poll were 10.3 percent (86 stations each grossing over $5 million) and 9.2 percent (38 stations each grossing under $5 million). The median news figures during prime time (6 P.M. to 11 P.M.) were 15 percent (86 stations grossing over $5 million) and 12.2 percent (38 stations grossing under $5 million), far in excess of the FCC's "substantial service" figures. The public affairs median figures for the top 50 VHF affiliates were 5.3 percent (over $5 million) and 4.7 percent (under $5 million), again far in excess of the Commission's figure. *See Third Further Notice of Inquiry, supra* note 207, at 1045. *See also* Citizens Communication Center v. FCC, 447 F.2d 1201 (D.C. Cir. 1971). In that case the court held violative of the Communications Act the Commission's policy statement that suggested that a licensee with a record of "substantial" community service would be entitled to renewal despite promises of better performance by a challenger. The stricter policy statement also had provided that a full comparative hearing would be granted a challenger only after the Commission refused to renew an incumbent's license for failure to provide substantial service. The court stated: "Insubstantial past performance should preclude renewal of a license. . . . At the same time *superior* performance should be a plus of major significance. . . ." *Id.* at 1213 (footnote omitted) (emphasis in original). The court urged that the Commission in its Docket No. 19154 proceeding clarify what constitutes "superior performance." *Id.* at 1213 n.35. In its *Further Notice of Inquiry, supra* note 217, the FCC reacted to the court's decision. The Commission stated that the percentage guidelines it had originally proposed were indeed suggested as standards to judge superior service, and were not meant to illustrate "minimal service meeting the public interest standard." Rather, meeting of the guideline percentages would "*prima facie* indicate the type of service warranting a 'plus of major significance' in the comparative hearing . . . the type of service which, if achieved, is of such nature that one can '. . . reasonably expect renewal.' " *Further Notice of Inquiry, supra* note 217, at 444. If the percentage guidelines discussed above are indeed to represent "superior service," then they are far too low. As indicated, the upper limit of many of the guideline ranges falls below present median performances of broadcasters. How can a broadcaster who falls far below the median performance of his fellow licensees be considered a "superior" performer?

219. Formulation of Policies Relating to the Broadcast Renewal Applicant, Stemming from the Comparative Hearing Process, Docket No. 19154, Report and Order, FCC 77-204, Apr. 7, 1977 (mimeograph).

220. Also, given that some standards must be applied in comparative renewal hearings, the FCC should not throw up its hands and say that the public interest determinations it will make in such hearings "cannot be foreshadowed today. . . ." *Id.* at 17, par. 23. The lack of adequate guidelines leaves licensees uncertain about what is expected of them, provides no indication to potential challengers of how they might fare in a comparative renewal proceeding, and provides no answer for the public about whether a licensee is performing its duties adequately. Such guidelines should not be the sole determining factors in a comparative renewal, but they could play an extremely useful role along with other indicators, if, indeed, there is to be a comparative renewal process.

It should be noted that the Commission admitted that the guidelines would "result in increased levels of local, news, and public affairs programming. . . ." *Id.* at 13 par. 15. Broadcasters, wanting to secure some advantage in any possible license challenge, would strive to surpass the guidelines. But the Commission questioned whether the quality of such programming would be improved. One would think that, with significantly more news and public affairs programming being produced, there is much public benefit to be gained from increasing the opportunity for the public to be exposed to informational programming at more convenient hours, and in greater quantity and range.

221. To encourage editorials, and the replies to editorials through the structure discussed in the text, the FCC might slightly inflate the value of editorial and editorial reply time, or time devoted to a similar public access scheme, in calculating a station's compliance with minimum percentage guidelines. Such access time is particularly important in allowing local groups to air their views. The Commission's taking "into account the different revenue posture of stations" in complying with percentage guidelines seems sound. Those stations that make more money from the use of their exclusive frequency should be expected to contribute more. See *Notice of Inquiry, supra* note 217, at 581–82. It should be noted that, in light of the far greater number and diversity of radio than TV stations in most markets, the greater availability of radio frequencies for new applicants, the presence of radio stations devoted wholly to news and public affairs and phone-in programming in many markets, the unique role that radio stations may play in supplying seldom interrupted background or listening music, and the lower revenue intake of most radio as opposed to TV stations, it seems appropriate to require far different standards in the AM-FM radio market than in the VHF TV market.

222. See *Ascertainment of Community Problems by Broadcast Applicants, Primer (First Report and Order),* 41 FED REG. 1371, 1381 app. B (1976) [hereinafter cited as *Ascertainment Primer*]. See also *Ascertainment of Community Problems by Nomcommercial Educational Broadcast Applicants,* 41 FED. REG. 12423 (1976); *Primer on Ascertainment of Community Problems by Broadcast Applicants (Report and Order),* 27 F.C.C.2d 650 (1971).

223. See *Ascertainment Primer, supra* note 222, at 1382.

224. *Id.* at 1381 (Q.3).

225. *Id.* at 1383 (Q.33) (emphasis added). However, programs listed should "not include announcements (such as PSA's) or news inserts of breaking events (the daily or ordinary news coverage of breaking newsworthy events)." *Id.*

226. *License Renewal, supra* note 200, at 19570 (FCC Form 303 1976, sec. IV, 3); 19559 (FCC Form 303-R 1976, pt. IV, 13).

227. See, *e.g.,* Vogel-Hendrix Corp., 60 F.C.C.2d 821 (1976); Alabama Educ. Television Comm'n, 50 F.C.C.2d 461 (1975). It should be stressed that public interest groups should continue to play their important role in improving programming during renewal procedures, especially with respect to whether a licensee has aired a minimum percentage of news and public affairs programming as well as programming relating to ascertained needs.

228. The former General Counsel of the National Association of Broadcasters (NAB) has stated: "I think, to a great extent, the ascertainment process requirement fulfills this aspect [part one] of the Doctrine. . . . [T]he broadcaster, in meeting the ascertainment requirements, has to connect issues with programming that he proposes to do." Interview with John B. Summers by Steven J. Simmons, Sept. 11, 1975. However, the Commission has indicated that the "matters cited by a licensee in its ascertainment survey as the problems, needs and interests of the residents of the community which it serves do not necessarily correspond to local, state-wide or nationwide controversial issues of public importance. Moreover, not even the most thorough of ascertainment methods would guarantee that the licensee would identify all those issues which are matters of controversy and public importance." Public Media Center, 59 F.C.C.2d 494, 515–16 (1976).

The Commission is undoubtedly correct. If the procedural requirements of ascertainment, as set forth in the *Ascertainment Primer, supra* note 222, are effectively followed and enforced, however, the survey will inevitably uncover a substantial number of important and controversial issues. The requirement to air a minimum percentage of news and public affairs will cause licensees to focus on issues even more. By emphasizing procedural reporting and quantitative standards, the FCC removes itself from the difficult and delicate involvement in determining the problem of issue. Licensees are given greater journalistic freedom, yet the public receives more public affairs information.

229. The FCC's role should be principally confined to renewal time review, except where a

station violates editorial reply obligations. It should not have to be engulfed constantly in fairness adjudications. When it does become involved, the guidelines should be clearer and easier to apply. There would, of course, be a certain degree of subjectivity in renewal time review of whether particular programs were public affairs oriented, and whether programming was related to ascertained needs. Licensees should be afforded the discretion to exercise good faith and reason on these questions. However, licensees who substantially vary from percentage guidelines should be easy to pinpoint.

BIBLIOGRAPHY
of Cited Publications

Archer, Gleason L. HISTORY OF RADIO TO 1926. New York: American Historical Society, 1938. (Reprinted, New York: Arno Press, 1971.)

Bagdikian, Ben H. *Pensions: The FCC's Dangerous Decision Against NBC.* COLUMBIA JOURNALISM REVIEW, March/April 1974, at 16.

Barnouw, Erik. A TOWER IN BABEL—A HISTORY OF BROADCASTING IN THE UNITED STATES (vol. I, to 1933). New York: Oxford University Press, 1966.

Barron, Jerome A. *The Federal Communications Commission's Fairness Doctrine: An Evaluation.* 30 GEORGE WASHINGTON LAW REVIEW 1 (1969).

Barrow, Roscoe L. *The Equal Opportunities and Fairness Doctrines in Broadcasting: Pillars in the Forum of Democracy.* 37 UNIVERSITY OF CINCINNATI LAW REVIEW 447 (1968).

Bazelon, David L. *FCC Regulation of the Telecommunications Press.* 1975 DUKE LAW JOURNAL 213.

Blake, Jonathan D. Red Lion Broadcasting Co. v. FCC: *Fairness and the Emperor's New Clothes.* 23 FEDERAL COMMUNICATIONS BAR JOURNAL 75 (1969).

Brown, Lester L. TELEVISION: THE BUSINESS BEHIND THE BOX. New York: Harcourt Brace Jovanovich, 1971.

Chase, Francis S., Jr. SOUND AND FURY: AN INFORMED HISTORY OF BROADCASTING. New York: Harper & Bros., 1942.

Collins, Tom A. *Counter Advertising in the Broadcast Media: Bringing the Administrative Process to Bear on a Theoretical Imperative.* 15 WILLIAM AND MARY LAW REVIEW 799 (1974).

Comment, *The Fairness Doctrine and Entertainment Programming: All in the Family.* 7 GEORGIA LAW REVIEW 554 (1973).

Comment, *The FCC's Fairness Doctrine in Operation.* 20 BUFFALO LAW REVIEW 663 (1971).

Comment, *FCC's Formal Rules Concerning Personal Attacks and Political Editorials Contravene the First Amendment.* 44 NOTRE DAME LAWYER 447 (1969).

Comment, *Mayflower Rule—Gone But Not Forgotten.* 35 CORNELL LAW REVIEW 574 (1950).

Comment, *And Now a Word Against Our Sponsor: Extending the FCC's Fairness Doctrine to Advertising.* 60 CALIFORNIA LAW REVIEW 1416 (1972).

Comment, *Power in the Marketplace of Ideas: The Fairness Doctrine and the First Amendment.* 52 TEXAS LAW REVIEW 727 (1974).

Comment, *A Proposed Statutory Right to Respond to Environmental Advertisements: Access to the Airways After* CBS v. Democratic National Committee. 69 NORTHWESTERN UNIVERSITY LAW REVIEW 234 (1974).

Comment, *The Regulation of Competing First Amendment Rights: A New Fairness Doctrine Balance After* CBS? 122 UNIVERSITY OF PENNSYLVANIA LAW REVIEW 1283 (1974).

Cox, Edward F., Robert C. Fellmeth, and John E. Schulz. THE NADER REPORT ON THE FEDERAL TRADE COMMISSION. New York: R.W. Baron, 1969.

Dean, John W., III. *Political Broadcasting: The Communications Act of 1934 Reviewed.* 20 FEDERAL COMMUNICATIONS BAR JOURNAL 16 (1966).

Department of Commerce, Bureau of Navigation, RADIO SERVICE BULLETIN. April 2, 1923.

Derby, E. Stephen, *Section 315: Analysis and Proposal,* 3 HARVARD JOURNAL OF LEGISLATION 257 (1965-66).

Emery, Walter B. BROADCASTING AND GOVERMENT: RESPONSIBILITIES AND REGULATIONS. Revised edition. East Lansing: Michigan State University Press, 1971.

Erbst, Laurence A. *Equal Time for Candidates: Fairness or Frustration?* 34 SOUTHERN CALIFORNIA LAW REVIEW 190 (1961).

Federal Communications Commission. *Adoption of Standards Designed to Eliminate Deceptive Advertising From Television (Petition of TUBE [Termination of Unfair Broadcasting Excesses]).* 32 F.C.C.2d 360 (1971).

_____. *Applicability of the Fairness Doctrine in the Handling of Controversial Issues of Public Importance* (Fairness Primer). 29 Fed. Reg. 10415 (1964).

_____. *Ascertainment of Community Problems by Broadcast Applicants, Primer* (First Report and Order) (Ascertainment Primer). 41 Fed. Reg. 1371 (1976).

_____. *Ascertainment of Community Problems by Non-commercial Educational Broadcast Applicants.* 41 Fed. Reg. 12423 (1976).

_____. *Availability of Locally Maintained Records for Inspection by Members of the Public.* 28 F.C.C.2d 71 (1971).

_____. *Availability of Network Programming Time to Members of Congress.* 40 F.C.C.2d 238 (1973).

_____. *Broadcast Procedure Manual.* 37 Fed. Reg. 20510, 37 F.C.C.2d 286 (1972).

_____. *Broadcast Procedure Manual.* 39 Fed. Reg. 32288 (rev. ed. 1974).

_____. *Consideration of the Operation of, and Possible Changes in, the Prime Time Access Rule, sec. 73.658(k) of the Commission's Rules* (Second Report and Order). 50 F.C.C.2d 829 (1975).

_____. *Fairness Doctrine and Public Interest Standards, Fairness Report Regarding Handling of Public Issues* (Fairness Report). 39 Fed. Reg. 26372, 48 F.C.C.2d 1 (1974).

_____. *Fairness Doctrine and Public Interest Standards, Reconsideration of the Fairness Report Regarding Handling of Public Issues* (Reconsideration, Fairness Report). 58 F.C.C.2d 691 (1976).

_____. *Formulation of Appropriate Further Regulatory Policies Concerning Cigarette Advertising and Antismoking Presentations.* 27 F.C.C.2d 453 (1970).

_____. *Formulation of Policies Relating to the Broadcast Renewal Applicant, Stemming From the Comparative Hearing Process*: Notice of Inquiry, 27 F.C.C.2d 580 (1971); Further Notice of Inquiry, 31 F.C.C.2d 443 (1971); Third Further Notice of Inquiry, 43 F.C.C.2d

1043 (1973); Docket No. 19154, F.C.C. 77–204, Apr. 7, 1977 (mimeograph).

_____. *Formulation of Rules and Policies Relating to the Renewal of Broadcast Licenses, Final Report and Order.* 43 F.C.C.2d 1 (1973).

_____. *Handling of Public Issues Under the Fairness Doctrine and the Public Interest Standards of the Communications Act* (First Report—Handling of Political Broadcast). 36 F.C.C.2d 40 (1972).

_____. *Handling of Public Issues Under the Fairness Doctrine and the Public Interest Standards of the Communications Act* (Notice of Inquiry). 30 F.C.C.2d 26 (1971).

_____. 1962 ANNUAL REPORT.

_____. *Notice of Proposed Rulemaking, Advertisement of Cigarettes.* 16 F.C.C.2d 284 (1969).

_____. *Obligations of Broadcast Licensees Under the Fairness Doctrine* (Obligations Inquiry). 23 F.C.C.2d 27 (1970).

_____. *Primer on Ascertainment of Community Problems by Broadcast Applicants,* Part I, sections IV–A and IV–B of FCC Forms. 27 F.C.C.2d 650 (1971).

_____. *Procedures in Event of Personal Attack or Where Station Editorializes as to Political Candidates.* 32 FED. REG. 11531 (1967).

_____. PUBLIC SERVICE RESPONSIBILITY OF BROADCAST LICENSEES. Washington: Government Printing Office, 1946.

_____. *Report and Statement of Policy re: Commission en Banc Programming Inquiry.* 44 F.C.C. 2303 (1960).

_____. *Report on Editorializing by Broadcast Licensees.* 13 F.C.C. 1246 (1949).

_____. SIXTH ANNUAL REPORT. 1940.

Federal Radio Commission. SECOND ANNUAL REPORT. 1928.

_____. THIRD ANNUAL REPORT. 1929.

Firestein, Charles L. *Red Lion and the Fairness Doctrine: Regulation of Broadcasting "in the Public Interest."* 11 ARIZONA LAW REVIEW 807 (1969).

THE FIRST AMENDMENT AND THE NEWS MEDIA. Final Report, Chief Justice Earl Warren Conference on Advocacy in the United States.

Cambridge, Mass.: Roscoe Pound–American Trial Lawyers Foundation, 1973.

First National Radio Conference. Minutes of Department of Commerce Conference on Radio Telephony. 1922 (mimeograph).

Fly, James L. *Regulation of Radio Broadcasting in the Public Interest.* 213 ANNALS OF THE AMERICAN ACADEMY OF POLITICAL AND SOCIAL SCIENCE 102 (1941).

Fourth National Radio Conference. PROCEEDINGS AND RECOMMENDATIONS FOR REGULATION OF RADIO. Washington, November 9–11, 1925.

Friendly, Fred W. THE GOOD GUYS, THE BAD GUYS AND THE FIRST AMENDMENT. New York: Random House, 1976.

Geller, Henry. THE FAIRNESS DOCTRINE IN BROADCASTING. Santa Monica, Calif.: Rand, 1973.

Hanks, W., and P. Longini. *Television Access: A Pittsburgh Experiment.* 18 JOURNAL OF BROADCASTING 289 (1974).

Hauser, Thomas J. *The Fairness Doctrine—an Historical Perspective.* 47 NOTRE DAME LAWYER 550 (1972).

Heffron, Edward J. *Should Radio be as Free as the Press?* 47 COMMONWEAL 466 (1948).

Hentoff, Nat. *How Fair? The Fairness Doctrine. Civil Liberties,* May 1973, at 4.

Herron, Edward A. MIRACLE OF THE AIR WAVES: A HISTORY OF RADIO. New York: Julian Messner, 1969.

Jacklin, Phil. *A New Fairness Doctrine—Access to the Media.* THE CENTER MAGAZINE, May/June 1975, at 46.

Jaffe, Louis L. *The Editorial Responsibility of the Broadcaster: Reflections on Fairness and Access.* 85 HARVARD LAW REVIEW 768 (1972).

Kahn, Frank J., ed. DOCUMENTS OF AMERICAN BROADCASTING. 2d edition. New York: Appleton-Century-Crofts, 1973.

Kurnit, Richard. Note, *Enforcing the Obligation to Present Controversial Public Issues: The Forgotten Half of the Fairness Doctrine.* 10 HARVARD CIVIL LIBERTIES-CIVIL RIGHTS LAW REVIEW 137 (1975).

Lloyd, F., and D. Glazer. PUBLIC AFFAIRS PROGRAMMING PROPOSAL. National Citizens Committee for Broadcasting, March 1976 (mimeograph).

Loevinger, Lee. *The Politics of Advertising.* 15 WILLIAM AND MARY LAW REVIEW 1 (1973).

National Association of Broadcasters. CODE OF STANDARDS OF BROADCASTING PRACTICE. Washington: NAB, 1939.

———. THE CODE OF THE NATIONAL ASSOCIATION OF BROADCASTERS. Washington: NAB, 1939 (amended 1941).

———. THE RADIO CODE OF THE NATIONAL ASSOCIATION OF BROADCASTERS. 14th edition. Washington: NAB, 1968.

———. STANDARDS OF PRACTICE OF THE NATIONAL ASSOCIATION OF BROADCASTERS. Washington: NAB, 1945 (amended 1946).

———. THE TELEVISION CODE OF THE NATIONAL ASSOCIATION OF BROADCASTERS. 17th edition. Washington: NAB, 1974.

———, Legal Department. POLITICAL BROADCAST CATECHISM AND THE FAIRNESS DOCTRINE. 7th edition. Washington: NAB, 1972.

National Broadcasting Company, Inc. BROADCASTING IN THE PUBLIC INTEREST. New York: NBC, 1939.

1974 BROADCASTING YEARBOOK. Washington: Broadcasting Publications, Inc., 1974.

1976 BROADCASTING YEARBOOK. Washington: Broadcasting Publications, Inc., 1976.

Noll, Roger G., Merton J. Peck, and John J. Gowan. ECONOMIC ASPECTS OF TELEVISION REGULATION. Washington: Brookings Institution, 1973.

Note, *Advertising, Product Safety, and a Private Right of Action Under the Federal Trade Commission Act.* 2 HOFSTRA LAW REVIEW 669 (1974).

Note, *Constitutional Law—Freedom of Expression—Violation of First Amendment for Radio and Television Stations to Deny Complete Broadcasting Time to Editorial Advertisers When Time Is Sold to Commercial Advertisers.* 85 HARVARD LAW REVIEW 689 (1972).

Note, *The Fairness Doctrine and Access to Reply to Product Commercials.* 51 INDIANA LAW JOURNAL 756 (1976).

Note, *The F.C.C. Fairness Doctrine and Informed Social Choice.* 8 HARVARD JOURNAL ON LEGISLATION 333 (1971).

Note, *The F.T.C. Ad Substantiation Program.* 61 GEORGETOWN LAW JOURNAL 1427 (1973).

Note, *The Mayflower Doctrine Scuttled.* 59 YALE LAW JOURNAL 759 (1950).

Note, *Private Judicial Remedies for False and Misleading Advertising.* 25 SYRACUSE LAW REVIEW 747 (1974).

Note, *Radio Regulation and Freedom of the Air.* 54 HARVARD LAW REVIEW 1220 (1941).

Note, *Radio and Television—Fairness Doctrine—Network Documentary Presenting Only One Side of a Controversial Issue of Public Importance Violates the Fairness Doctrine.* 52 TEXAS LAW REVIEW 797 (1974).

Paley, William S. Broadcast Journalism: At the Crossroads of Freedom. Dedication of Newhouse Communications Center, Syracuse University, May 31, 1974 (mimeograph).

Pennybacker, John H., and Waldo W. Braden, eds. BROADCASTING AND THE PUBLIC INTEREST. New York: Random House, 1969.

Phillips, Wayne. *Snow from the Networks.* 220 NATION 532 (1975).

The Press: Who Decides Fairness? TIME, February 4, 1974, at 59.

Putz, C. Delos, Jr. *Fairness and Commercial Advertising: A Review and a Proposal.* 6 UNIVERSITY OF SAN FRANCISCO LAW REVIEW 215 (1972).

The Right of Reply. Fairness in the News. NEW REPUBLIC, March 23, 1974, at 11.

Robinson, Glen O. *The FCC and the First Amendment: Observations on 40 Years of Radio and Television Regulation.* 52 MINNESOTA LAW REVIEW 67 (1967).

Roper Organization, Inc. TRENDS IN PUBLIC ATTITUDES TOWARD TELEVISION AND OTHER MASS MEDIA, 1959–1974. N.p.: Roper, 1975.

Rosenfeld, Michel. *The Jurisprudence of Fairness: Freedom Through Regulation in the Marketplace of Ideas.* 44 FORDHAM LAW REVIEW 877 (1976).

Sandman, Peter M., et al. MEDIA—AN INTRODUCTORY ANALYSIS OF AMERICAN MASS COMMUNICATIONS. Englewood Cliffs, N.J.: Prentice-Hall, 1972.

Sarno, Edward F., Jr. *The National Radio Conferences.* 13 JOURNAL OF BROADCASTING 189 (1969).

Schiller, Herbert I. MASS COMMUNICATIONS AND AMERICAN EMPIRE. New York: Augustus M. Kelley, 1969.

Schmidt, Benno C., Jr. FREEDOM OF THE PRESS VS. PUBLIC ACCESS. New York: Praeger, 1976.

Shapiro, Andrew O. MEDIA ACCESS: YOUR RIGHTS TO EXPRESS YOUR VIEWS ON RADIO AND TELEVISION. Boston: Little, Brown, 1976.

Sheehan, William, and Julian Goodman. *Guest Debate, The Fairness Doctrine: Fair or Foul?* DEADLINER, July 1975.

Simmons, Steven J. *Commercial Advertising and the Fairness Doctrine: The New FCC Policy in Perspective.* 75 COLUMBIA LAW REVIEW 1083 (1975).

_____. *Fairness Doctrine: The Early History.* 29 FEDERAL COMMUNICATIONS BAR JOURNAL 107 (1976).

_____. *The Fairness Doctrine and Cable TV.* 11 HARVARD JOURNAL ON LEGISLATION 629 (1974).

_____. *The FCC's Personal Attack and Political Editorial Rules Reconsidered.* 125 UNIVERSITY OF PENNSYLVANIA LAW REVIEW 990 (1977).

_____. *The Problem of "Issue" in the Administration of the Fairness Doctrine.* 65 CALIFORNIA LAW REVIEW 546 (1977).

_____. *The "Unfairness Doctrine"—Balance and Response Over the Airwaves.* 1 COMM/ENT 1 (1977).

Smead, Elmer E. FREEDOM OF SPEECH BY RADIO AND TELEVISION. Washington: Public Affairs Press, 1959.

Socolow, Abraham W. THE LAW OF RADIO BROADCASTING. New York: Baker, Voorhis, 1939.

Sullivan, John P. *Editorials and Controversy: The Broadcaster's Dilemma.* 32 GEORGE WASHINGTON LAW REVIEW 719 (1964).

Summers, Robert E., and Harrison B. Summers. BROADCASTING AND THE PUBLIC. Belmont, Calif.: Wadsworth, 1966.

Swartz, John L. *Fairness for Whom? Administration of the Fairness Doctrine, 1969–70.* 14 BOSTON COLLEGE INDUSTRIAL AND COMMERCIAL LAW REVIEW 457 (1973).

U.S. Congress, House, Committee on Interstate and Foreign Commerce. *Broadcast Editorializing Practices, Hearings Before the Subcommittee on Communications,* 88th Congress, 1st Session. Washington: Government Printing Office, 1963.

_____. *Communications Act Amendments, Hearings Before the Subcommittee on Communications,* 84th Congress, 2d Session. Washington: Government Printing Office, 1956.

_____. LEGISLATIVE HISTORY OF THE FAIRNESS DOCTRINE. Study for the Committee on Interstate and Foreign Commerce, 90th Congress, 2d Session. Washington: Government Printing Office, 1968.

_____. Paper No. 3, Glen O. Robinson: *The Fairness Doctrine, the Law and Policy in its Present Application. Hearings before the Special Subcommittee on Investigations,* 90th Congress, 2d Session. Washington: Government Printing Office, 1968.

_____. *Political Broadcasting, Hearings before the Subcommittee on Communications,* 86th Congress, 1st Session. Washington: Government Printing Office, 1959.

_____. REGULATION OF BROADCASTING; HALF A CENTURY OF GOVERNMENT REGULATION OF BROADCASTING AND THE NEED FOR FURTHER LEGISLATIVE ACTION. Study on H.R. Res. No. 99 (85th Congress, 1st Session) for the Committee on Interstate and Foreign Commerce, 85th Congress, 2d Session. Washington: Government Printing Office, 1958.

U.S. Congress, Senate, Committee on Commerce. *Fairness Doctrine, Hearings on S. 2, S. 608, and S. 1178 Before the Subcommittee on Communications,* 94th Congress, 1st Session. Washington: Government Printing Office, 1975.

_____. *Hearings on S. 251, S. 252, S. 1696, and H.R. J. Res. 247 Before the Subcommittee on Communications,* 88th Congress, 1st Session. Washington: Government Printing Office, 1963.

Weston, Glen E. *Deceptive Advertising and the Federal Trade Commission: Decline of Caveat Emptor.* 24 FEDERAL BAR JOURNAL 548 (1964).

White, Llewellyn, THE AMERICAN RADIO. Chicago: University of Chicago Press, 1947. (Reprinted, New York: Arno Press, 1971.)

Wolf, Frank. TELEVISION PROGRAMMING FOR NEWS AND PUBLIC AFFAIRS: A QUANTITATIVE ANALYSIS OF NETWORKS AND STATIONS. New York: Praeger, 1972.

Case and Document
INDEX

TABLE OF CASES

Cases significantly discussed are in *italic* type. Other cases are in roman type.

FCC REPORTS AND MISCELLANEOUS DOCUMENTS

STATUTES

THE FAIRNESS DOCTRINE
AND THE MEDIA
Steven J. Simmons

Television and radio have an enormous impact on the American consciousness. The
"fairness doctrine" which regulates them
requires that broadcasters must air programming on important controversial issues, and
do so fairly. Many attack this federal regulation as an infringement of the First Amendment and the freedom of the telecommunications press. Others praise the regulation as
vital to the health of a democracy.

In this book Steven J. Simmons, a brilliant
young author and legal scholar, sets forth the
most comprehensive analysis of the fairness
doctrine ever published. He describes the
doctrine and how it is enforced, outlines its
early history, and examines the Federal Communications Commission's rules requiring
air time being given to persons who have
been personally attacked over the air, or to
political candidates opposed in station editorials. He also discusses how the doctrine
applies to newscasts and to commercial advertising, how "important controversial
public issues" are defined, and what balance
of contrasting views amounts to "fairness."

Throughout the book Simmons severely
criticizes the administration of the fairness
doctrine by the FCC and the courts—
pointing to inconsistent rulings, lack of
explanatory rationale, weak enforcement,
and other failings. His critical diagnosis,
based on a sound history of the doctrine in